HOW TO DRAW
THE HUMAN FIGURE

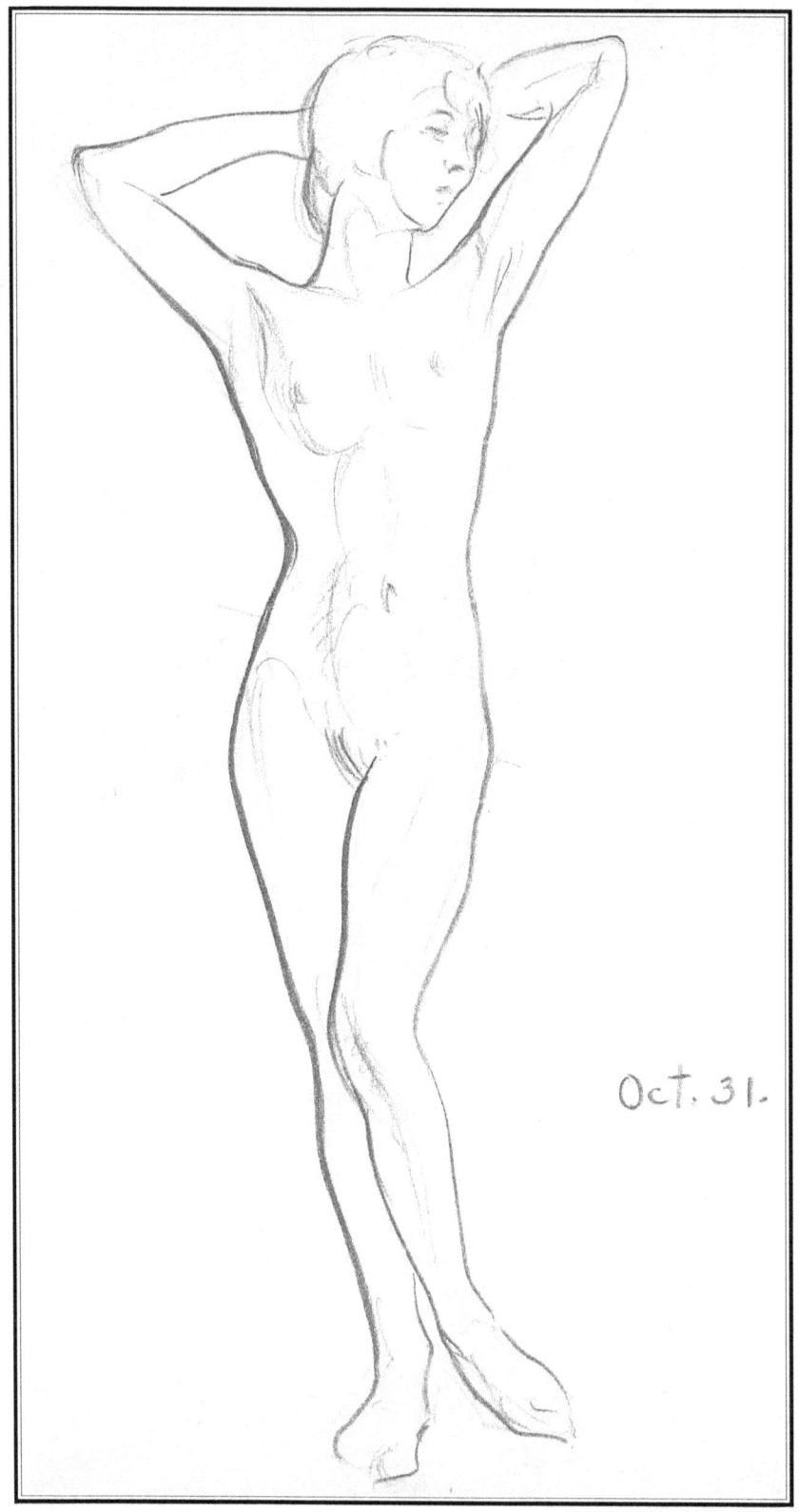

HOW TO DRAW THE HUMAN FIGURE

The Figure Drawings
of Grace Young
and
Contemporary Methods
of Instruction

By Tom Richardson

Published by Tom Richardson Design.
ISBN 978-0-9821678-1-6

TABLE OF CONTENTS

GRACE YOUNG

The inspiration of this book is a journal of drawings by Grace A. Young who graduated in 1928 from the Philadelphia Art School, which she notes on the cover of her journal. Based on a small notice in The New York Times of September 14, 1884 in which Mr. Charles G.Leland recalls a lecture he gave in Shropshire "at which he was asked to describe the system of design pursued at the Philadelphia Art School. ' *There are as yet no industrials schools in England organized on the plan pursued in Philadelphia...*'" I believe this refers to the Philadelphia School of Design for Women, founded in 1848 to train "needy and deserving" young women in practical artistic skills such as textile design, wallpaper design, and wood engraving.

There was a general movement to establish similar institutions in Boston, New York, Pittsburg and Cincinnati during the 1850s and 1860s. The institutions grew out of a charitable concern that many thousands of women worked at home, and were the support of their families.

Another concern was the imbalance between men and women as a result of both the Civil War and the Western Migration.[1] Theodore Christian Knauff describes the situation in his book "An Experiment in

---

1 Art and Industry in Philadelphia: Origins of the Philadelphia Shool of Design for Women by Nina de Angeli Walls, Resouces Library Magazine, January 24, 2003.

Training for the Useful and the Beautiful:" "Anyone familiar with the education of girls and women to-day can hardly realize what kind of instruction was given them only a short a time ago as eighty years. Girls with conscientious mothers were taught to be housekeepers in expectation of marraige. People with some means, whose children it was thought would not ordinarily be thrown on their own resources, gave their daughters what was called a fashionable education. This generally included fair penmanship, a limited knowledge of their mother tongue, a very little arithmetic, a few words or phrase of French which could be interpolated in English letters or conversation, and some drawing or painting which was copied from the flat...

"If a girl so educated happened to be thrown on her own resources and did not care to marry or had not the opportunity, she had nothing to fall back upon which she could fall back for support."[2]

The school was founded by Sarah Peters who wrote, "Having for a number of years observed with deep concern the privation and suffering to which a large and increasing number of deserving women are exposed in this city and elsewhere for want of a wider scope in which to earn their living;...I resolve to attempt the instruction of a class of young girls in the practice of such arts of design as were within my reach; but also because these arts can be practiced at home, without materially interfering with the routine of domestic duty, which is the peculiar province of women."[3]

The School opened by Sarah Peters was the pioneering school for teraching industrial art in the United States, and was among a long list of other Philadelphia Institutional firsts which included the first trust company, the first savings fund, the first building association, the first circulating library, the first fire insurance company, the first stock

---

2 Knauff, Theodore Christian. An Experiment in Training for the Useful and the Beautiful; A History. Philadelphia, Philadelphia School of Design for Women, 1922
3 Franklin Institute, Proceedings...Relative to the Establishment of a School of Design for Women (Philadelphia, 1850)

exchange, the first hospital in America, founded by Dr. Rush, the first Academy of Natural Sciences, and:

"The Academy of Fine Arts, the first in its line, was founded here in 1805, notwithstanding the opposition of Gilbert Stuart, who thought is would enlarge the profession to such an extant as to affect a painter's income adversely. From that date the Academy's permanent collection and exhibitions began, which became a feature in the city. It is true that Philadelphia Quakers thought its reproductions from the Antique and Classic, in the nude, though in white plaster or marble, were objectionable when viewed by both men and women at one and the same time, but Ladies Days were invented, on which occasions all such models were carefully covered."[4]

By the early 1920s thousands had already graduated. And when Grace Young attended the school had undergone some changes.

One of the most influential and longest serving Directors was John Sartrain who became a member of the Board in 1868 and served as a Director for 28 years. He was an engraver and and artist, an editor and owner of a magazine.

His daughter Emily Sartrain, an artist trained both in the United States and Europe took charge as Principal in 1886, and made changes to the management of the school. Miss Sartrain was close to Thomas Eakins. Eakins went to school with her brother William.

She studied at the Pennsylvania Academy from 1872-1876 and studied in Paris from 1868-1870. She was a close friend of Mary Cassatt while in Paris. When she began as Principal the school had a foundation in drawing from the flat, mechanics, mathematics and perspective and geometry. Emily Sartrain found students regarded the study of perspective to be an abstract mathematical concept and made a change that put the emphasis on daily drawing of objects. The intent

---

4   Knauff, Theodore Christian. An Experiment in Training for the Useful and the Beautiful; A History. Philadelphia, Philadelphia School of Design for Women, 1922

was to strengthen the powers of observation and perception.

Miss Sartrain, "French methods and French comprehension of art and nature are being introduced into the school work as fast as possible. The point of view is changed. Instead of flattening the model to a plane surface, and only mathematically squaring circles and comparing lines – a process which results in a species of lifeless chart – the emphasis is laid upon the construction, the solidity and the values. The effort is to convert the flat paper into a plastic reality, which in its planes, facing, retiring and turning away from the source of lide, becomes and entity which can be grasped, which could be translated into clay. Life and nature are urged for study, not only in studio work from the portrait and full length models, but, when weather permits, in outdoor work form landscape and animals...

STUDYING FROM THE HUMAN FORM

"An eye trained to accuracy and to delicate discernment of *subtlety* of line, and form and color – trained by study of the swaying, melting, yet strong and meaningful curves of the human body – can quickly seize and express the characteristic of simpler forms. Even if the designer never needs to reproduce the human form, constantly as it occurs in decoration, yet if he has neglected to study it, his combinations will be hackneyed, his curves poorly drawn. This is sufficient answer to the question of why we have establised a life class. Not only is it a recognized necessity for the illustrator – a career chosen by many of our students – but it is equally a necessity for the designer, although not so generally recognized; and it is the source of all true art knowledge. So important does the French government consider the study of the human form to art applied to manufacture, that at the Sevres China Factory and at the Gobelin Tapestry Works, it maintains free life classes for the workmen."[5]

Grace Young attended the School in the late 1920s and must have been a contemporary of Alice Neel, who was born in a suburb of Philadelphia and attended the school in the mid 1920s. Although Grace Young did not develop the reputation of Alice Neel or of The Philadelphia Ten, a group of Philadelphia female artists who exhibited together from 1917 to 1945 and nine of whom attended the Philadelphia School of Design for Women, she demonstrates in these drawings the success of the course of study developed by Emily Sartrain.

In 1932 the school merged with the Moore Institute of Art, Science and Industy. It continues to flourish as the Moore College of Art and Design.

THE ANATOMY OF THE HUMAN FIGURE

The study of anatomy as we know it dates as far back as ancient Egypt and artists contributed their talents to published works thoughout history. The Medieval Islamic world provided most of the advances during that time period, followed by a renaissance of all sciences including anatomy during that period in the west.

In the sixteenth, seventeenth and eighteenth centuries the printing press enabled the spread of knowledge. There were significant works by Vesalius and Juan Valverde de Amusco. Later Michelangelo and Rembrant made their own studies of anatomy.

The nineteenth century saw descriptive anatomy systematised. In the nineteeth and early twentieth further advances in printing techniques enabled books to be published with more detail than ever before.

-----

5   ibid.

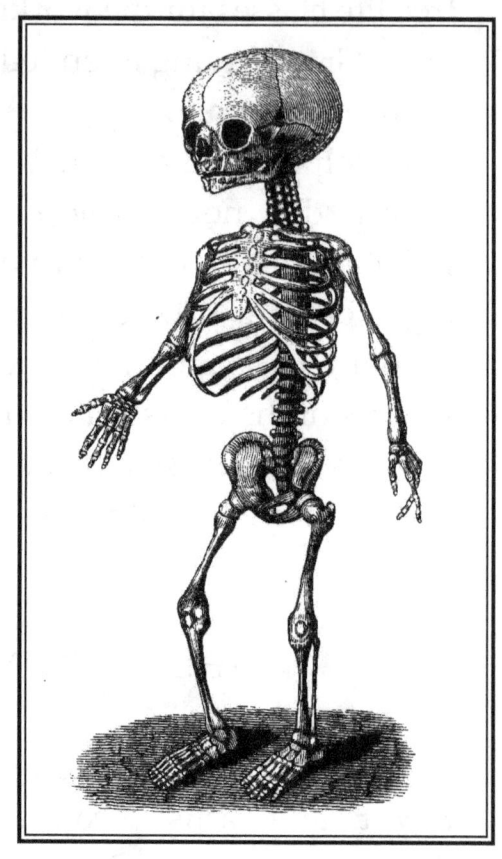

A SIDE VIEW OF THE FOETAL SKELETON, SHOWING THE
GREAT EXPANSION OF THE CHEST AND THE IMPERFECT
DEVELOPEMENT OF THE BONES[6]

---

6   Anatomical Plates, Henry H. Smith, Philadelphia 1867

A FRONT VIEW OF THE ADULT SKELETON[7]

1. Frontal Bone.
2. Parietal Bone.
3. Nasal Bones.
4. Occipital Bone.
5. Orbits of Eyes.
6. Malar Bone.
7. Upper and Lower Maxilla.
8. Nasal Cavity.
9. Cervical Vertebrae.
10. Clavicle
11. Scapula.
12. Sternum
13. Ribs.
14. Dorsal and Lumbar Vertebrae.
15. Innominata.
16. Sacrum.
17. Humerus.
18. Radius.
19. Ulna
20. Carpus.
21. Metacarpus
22. Phalanges of Hand.
23. Femur.
24. Patella.
25. Fibula.
26. Tibia.
27. Calcis & Astragalus.
28. Cuneiform & Cuboid.
29. Metatarsus.
30. Phalanges of Toes.

----

7   Anatomical Atlas, Henry H. Smith, M.D., Philadelphia. 1867

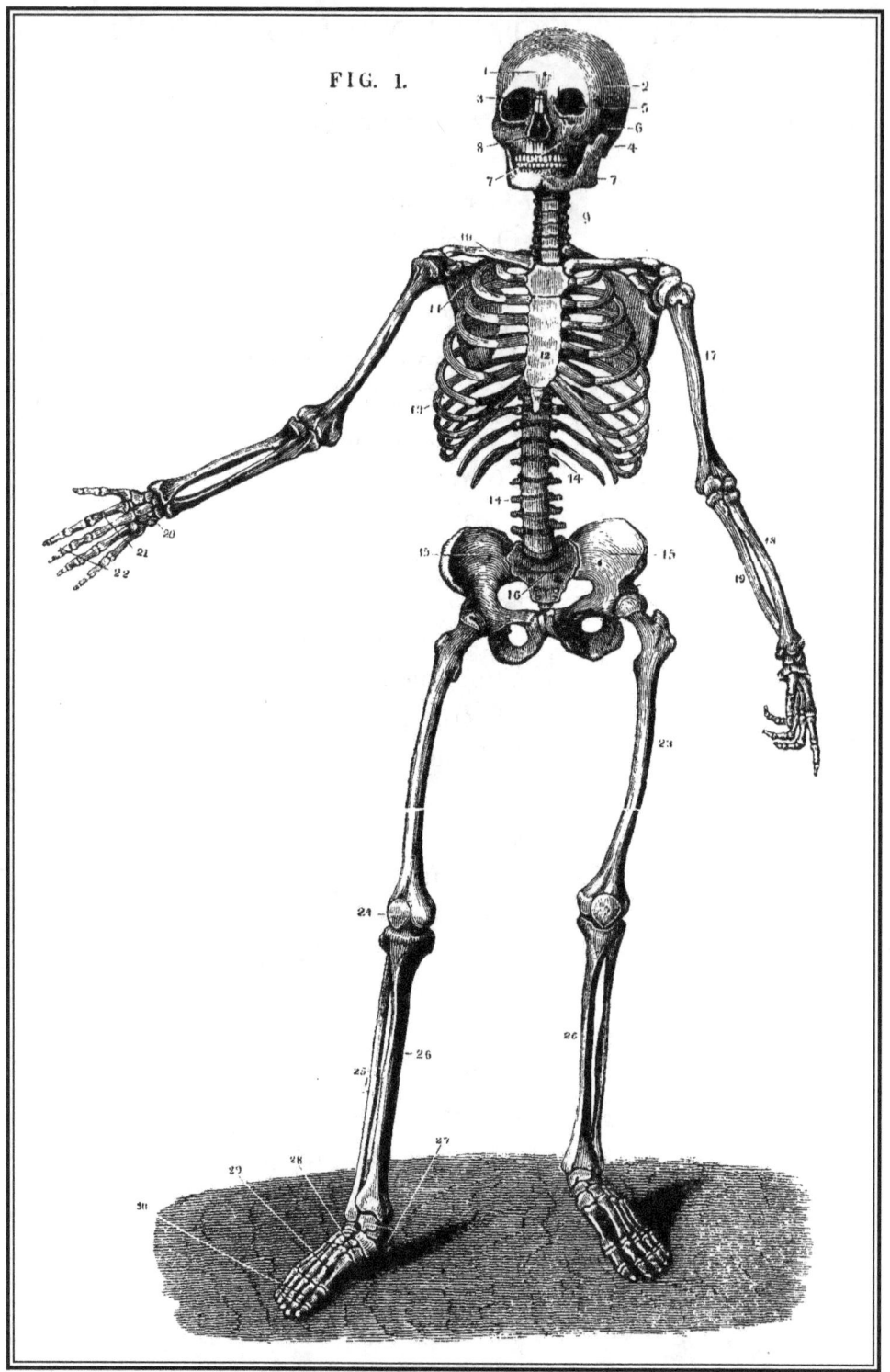

A FRONT VIEW OF THE ADULT SKELETON[8]

A BACK VIEW OF THE ADULT SKELETON[9]

1. Occipital Bone.
2. Cervical Vertebrae.
3. Scapula.
4. Dorsal Vertebrae.
5. Lumbar Vertebrae.
6. Ilia.
7. Ischia.
8. Trochanter Major.
9. Trochanter Minor.
10. Condyles of Femur.

_____

8   Ibid
9   Ibid.

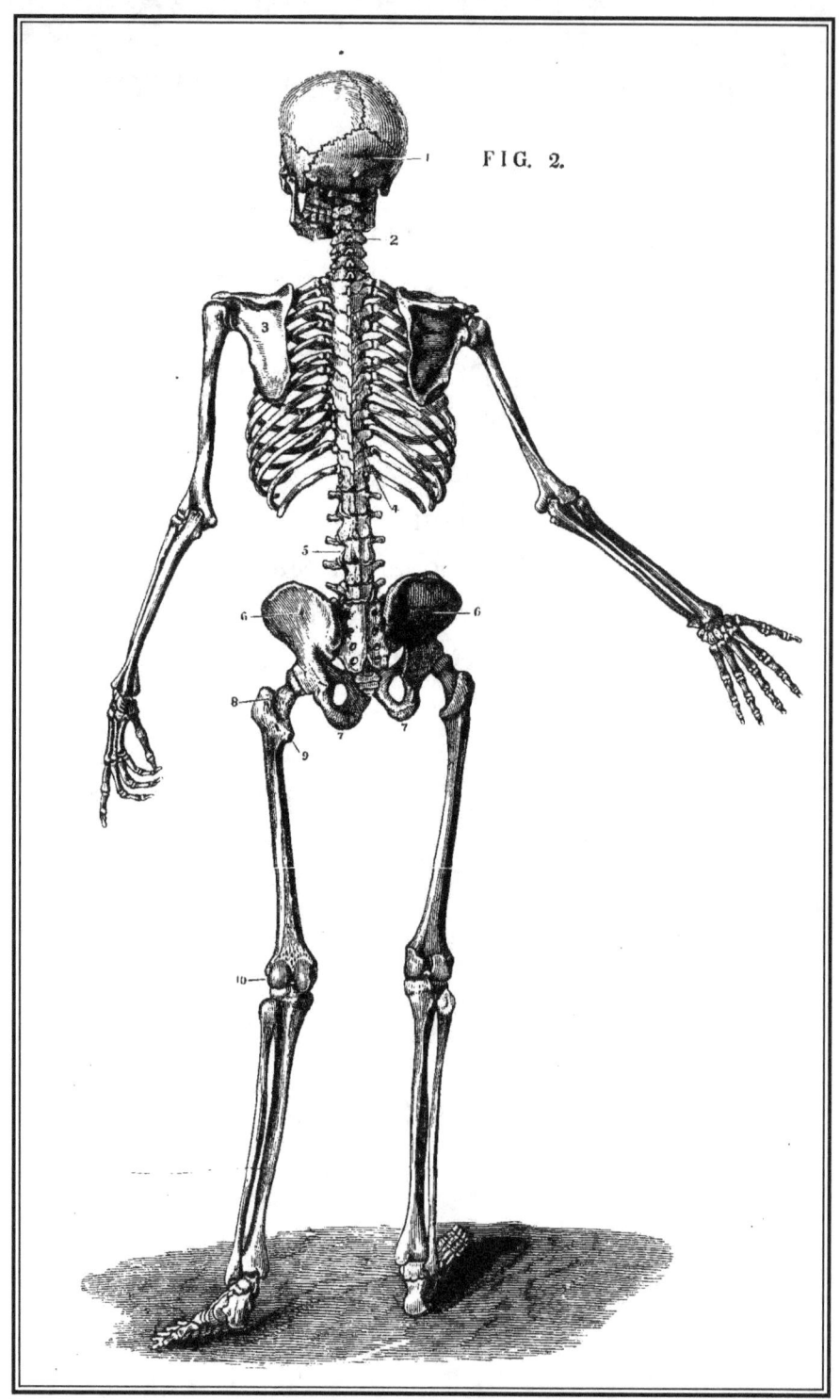

FIG. 2.

A BACK VIEW OF THE ADULT SKELETON[10]

A SIDE VIEW OF THE HUMAN SKELTON[11]

1. Frontal.
2. Parietal.
3. Temporal.
4. Occipital.
5. Males.
6. Nasal.
7. Maxillary.
8. Mandible.
9. First cervical vertebra.
10. Seventh vertebra.
11. Ilium.
12. Sacrum.
13. Coccyx.
14. Clavicle.
15. Sternum.
16. Scapula.
17. First rib.
18. Last rib.
19. Humerus.
20. Ulna.
21. Radius.
22. Carpus.
23. Metacarpus.
24. Phalanges.
25. Femur.
26. Patella.

---

10 Ibid.
11 Anatomy in Art – A Practical Text Book for the Stgudent in the Study of the Human Form, Jonathon Scott Hartley, New York, 1891.

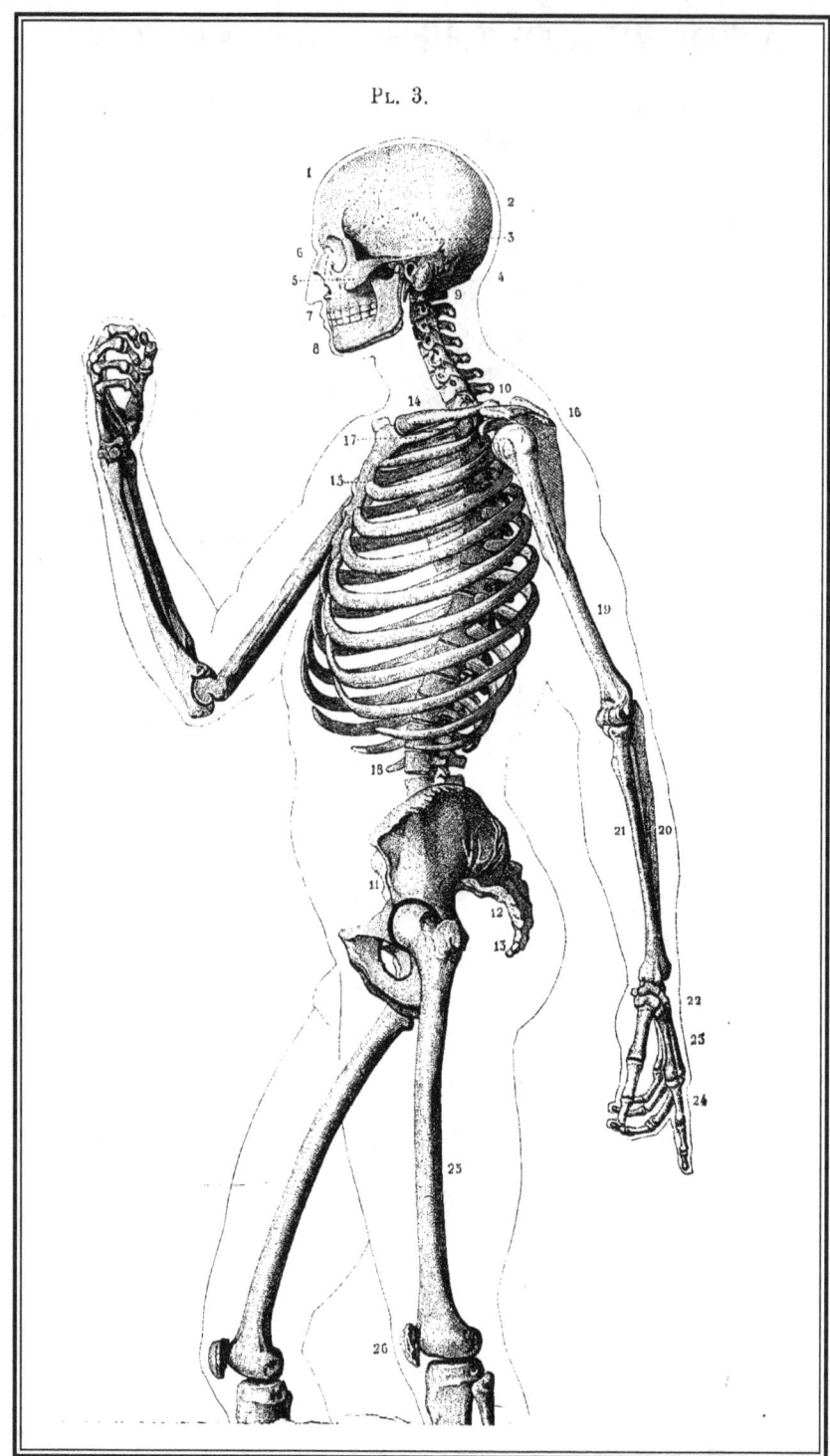

Pl. 3.

A SIDE VIEW OF THE HUMAN SKELETON[12]

12 Ibid.

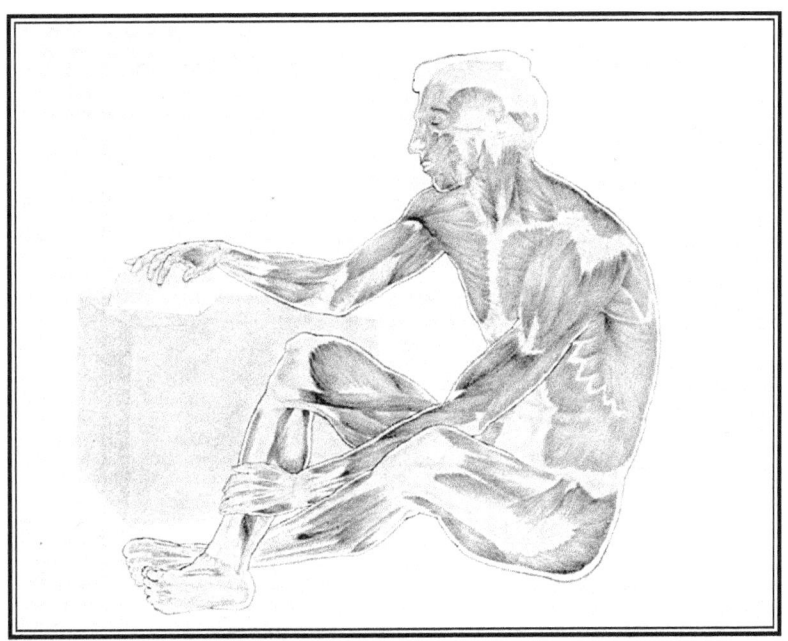

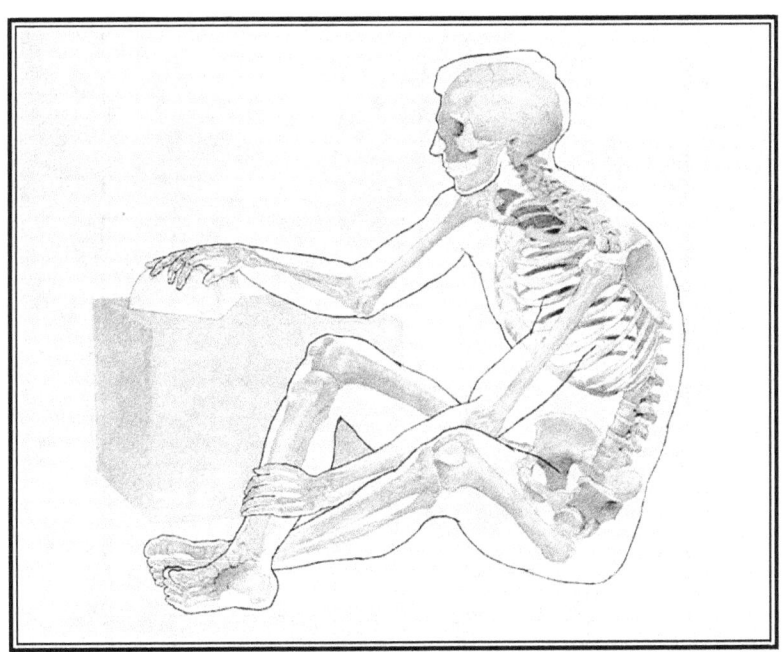

Studies of Muscles and Skeleton
By R. F. Wilson, Nottingham School of Art[13]

_____

13 Studies of the Human Figure, G.M.Ellwood and F.R. Yerbury, London, 1918

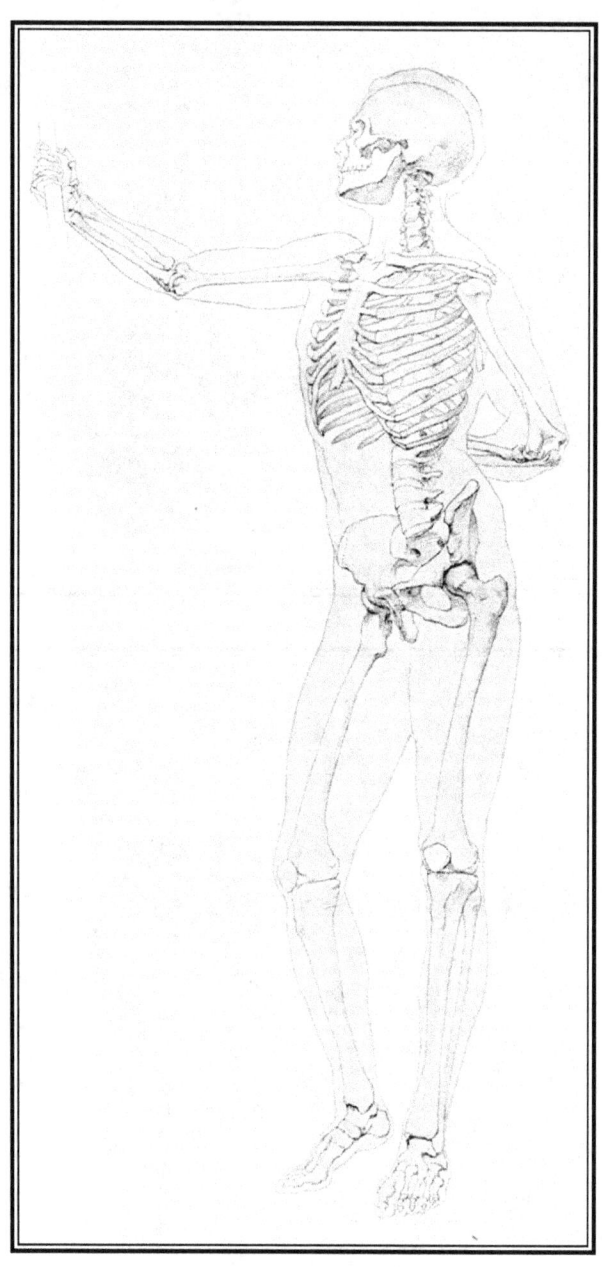

Study of the Skeleton
by Ethel Marsh, Nottingham School of Art[14]

---

14 Ibid.

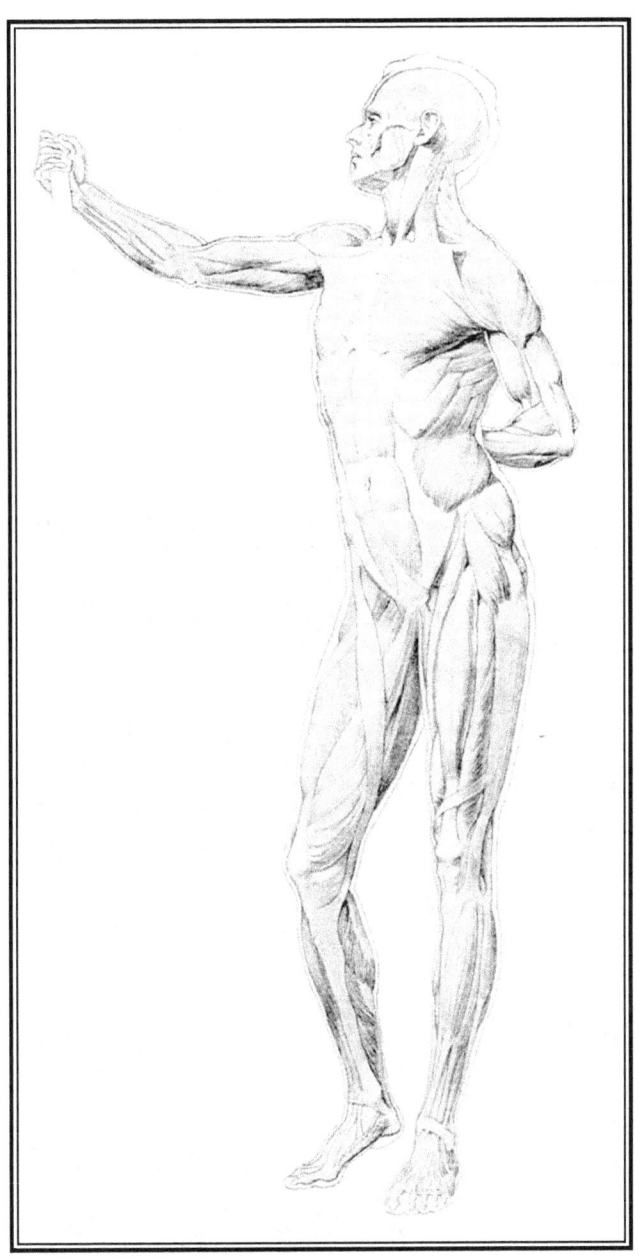

Study of the Muscles of the Body
by Ethel Marsh, Nottingham School of Art[15]

---

15 Ibid.

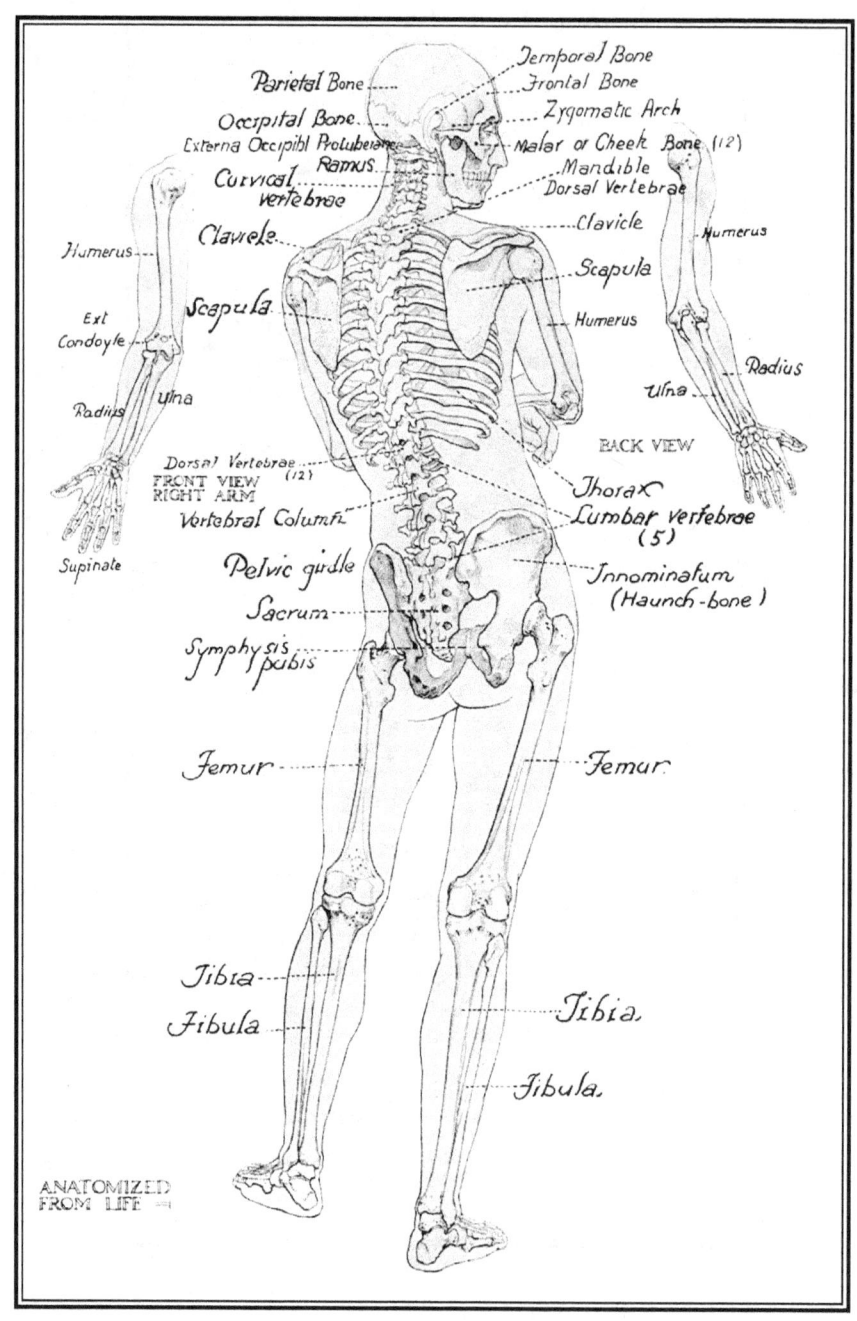

A Study of Back View of the Skeleton
by Eugenie Richards, Nottingham School of Art[16]

16 Ibid

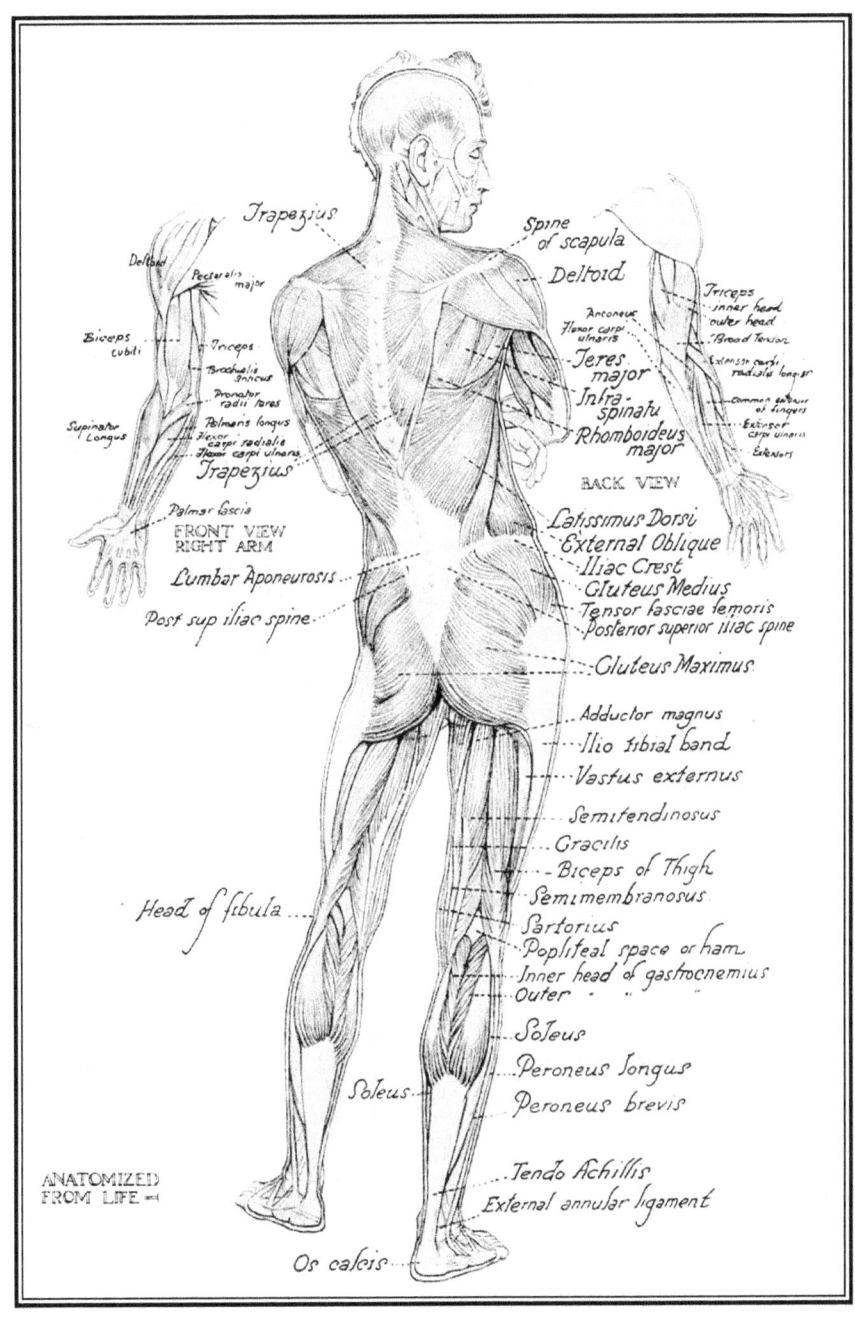

A Study of Back View of the Muscles
by Eugenie Richards, Nottingham School of Art[17]

---

17 Ibid.

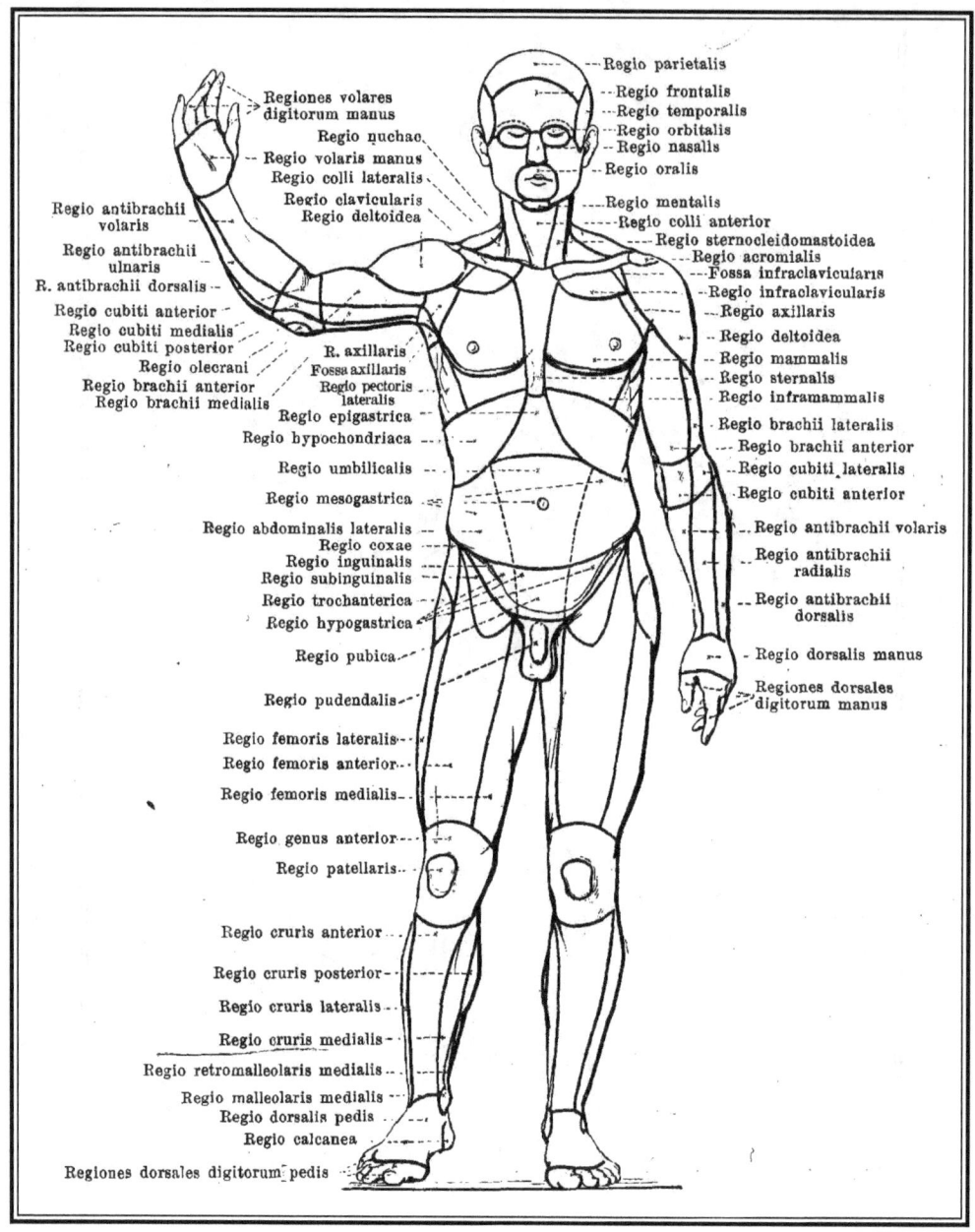

Areas of the Body from the Front[18]

---

18 Handatlas der Anatomire des Menschen, Werner Spalteholz, Leipzig 1920

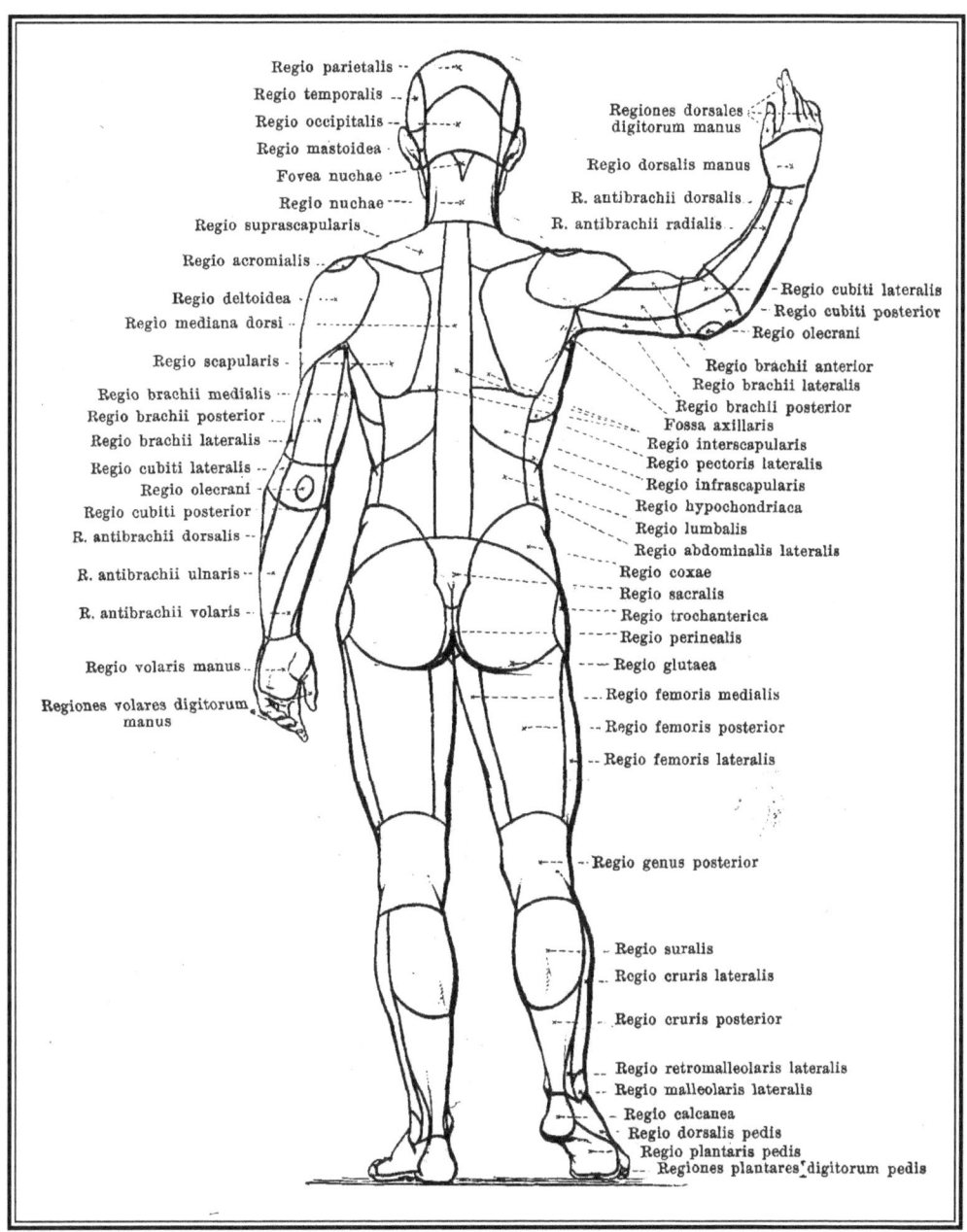

Areas of the Body from Behind[19]

___

19 Ibid.

PROPORTIONS OF THE HUMAN FIGURE

In 1883 Dr. Johann Gottfried Schadow, the famous German sculptor of the Brandenburg Gate, published a treatise on the proportions of the human form for the benefit of art students. He based the work on the classical proportions of Polycletus who was one of the sculptors who created the classical Greek style and created a new naturalistic approach to sculpture which showed a relaxed pose and an illustration of the effect of shifting the balance and weight of the body which is now known as contrapposto.

Dr. Schadow's book was called *Atlas Zu Polyclet Oder Von Des Menschen Nach Dem Geshlecte Und Alter.* It consisted of oversized plates showing both the proportions of natural figures drawn from life and the proportions of heroic Greek and Roman statuary. It was the first attempt to assign proportions to the human form on the basis of natural forms rather than ideal proportions of the Golden Section.

An English translation was published by John Sutcliffe called *The Sculptor and Art Student's Guide to the Proportions of the Human Form – With Measurements in Feet and Inches of Full Grown Figures of Both Sexes & of Various Ages.*

Because of the detail of providing measurements the book gained currency not only among artists but manufacturers of clothing. The information contained helped enable an industry to make mass production of standard sizes as opposed to custom fabrication of clothing.

Other authors advanced the art of figure drawing through their books.   E. G. Lutz wrote *Practical Drawing* in 1915 and R. G. Hatton wrote *Figure Drawing and Composition* in 1902. The Hatton book, in particular, became very popular going into several editions and influencing authors of the future including Andrew Loomis.

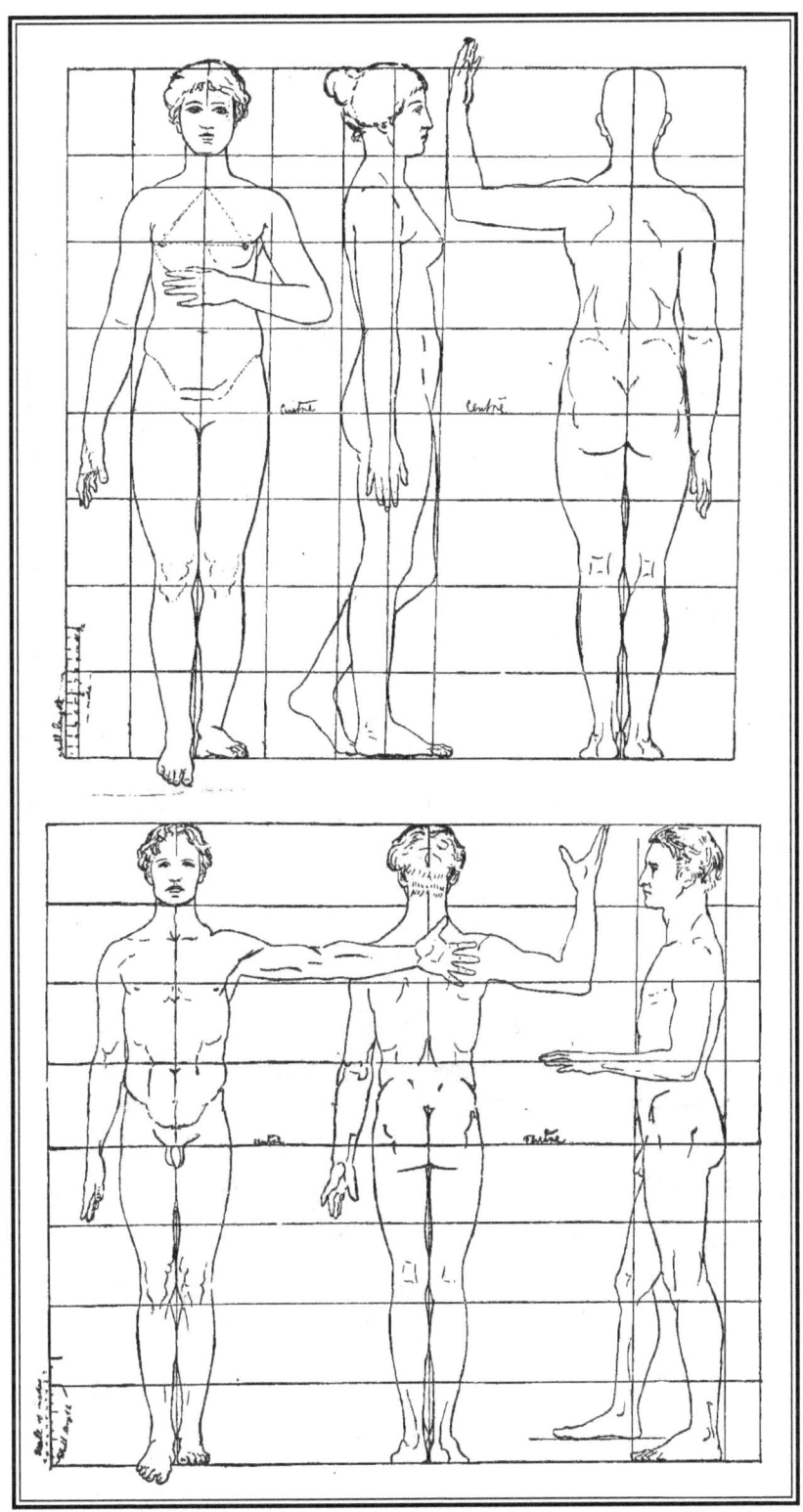

Greek Standard of Proportions[20]

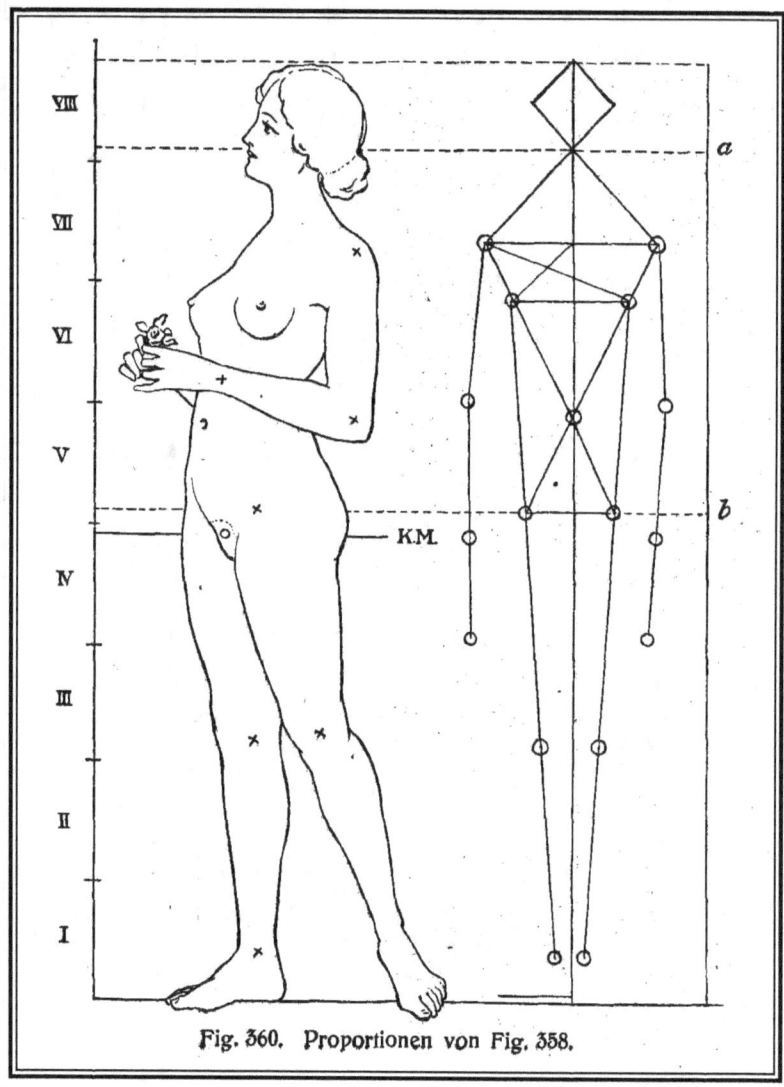

Fig. 360. Proportionen von Fig. 358.

Another study of proportion was made by Prof. Dr. C. H. Stratz titled *Die Rassenshoenheit des Weibes*.[21] This was a work on the comparative proportions of the female figure of all races. The advent of photography and advances in photographic lithography enabled the publication of such works. Their availability to artists as well as

---

20 Ibid. After Atlas Zu Polyclet Oder Von Den Maassen Des Menschen, Dr. Johann Gottfired Schadow, Berlin, 1883
21 Die Rassenshoenheit des Weibes, Prof. Dr. C. H. Stratz, Stuttgart, 1921

everyone else undoubtedly influenced the trend toward naturalism in the depiction of the human form.

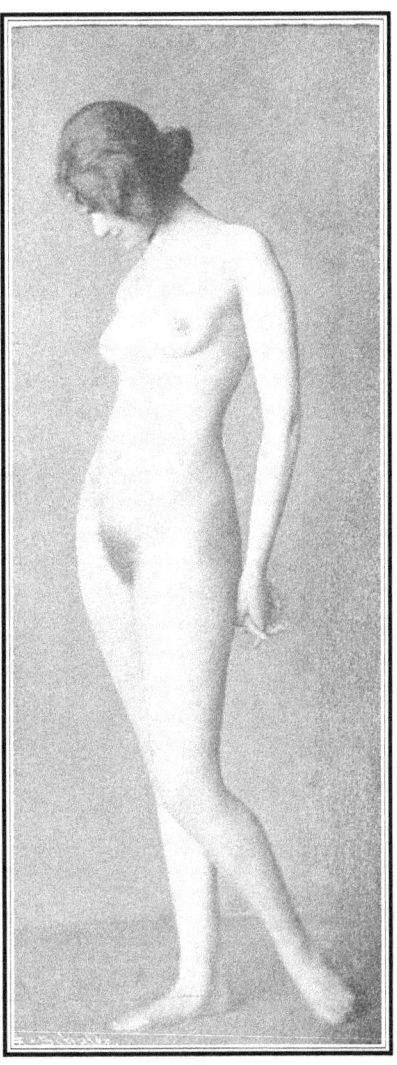

Hardanger Mädchen[22]

---

22 Ibid.

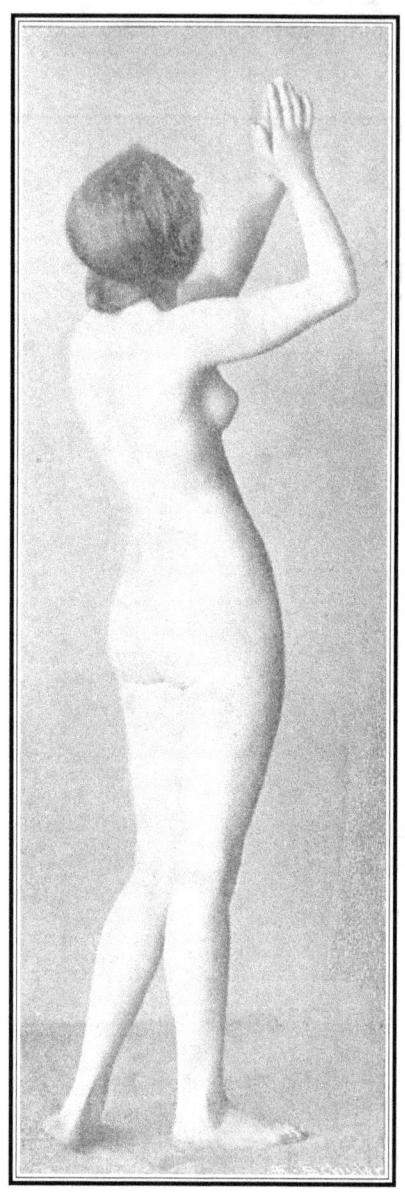

Rückansicht[23]

---

23 Ibid.

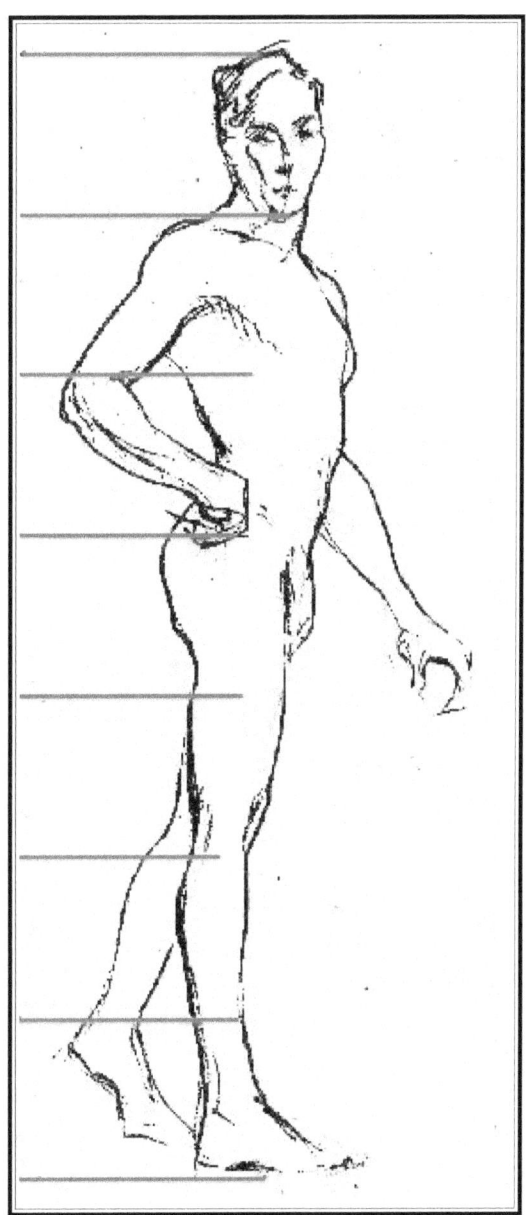

Grace Young, showing how her figures divide into 7 parts.

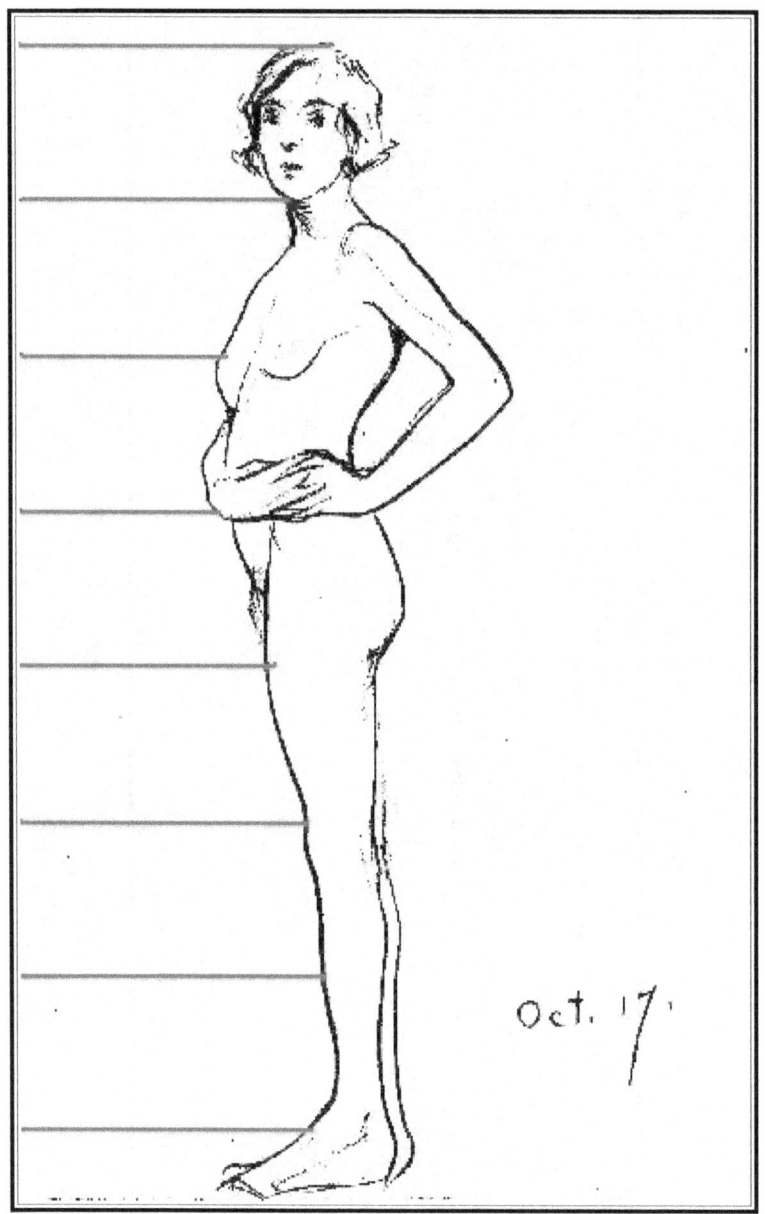

Grace Young, showing how her figures divide into 7 parts.

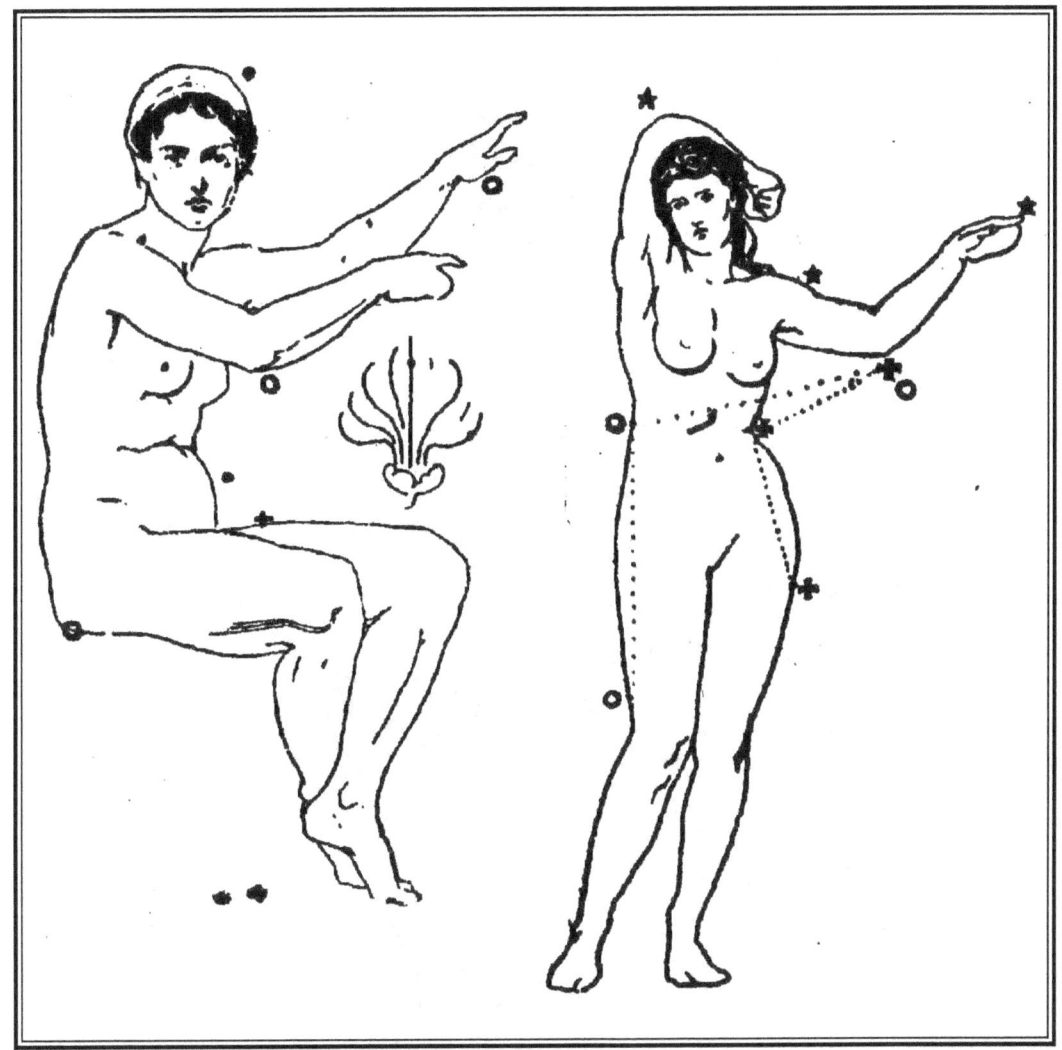

Another method artists use to help define the proportions of the figure and the accurate depiction of the form is to use some straight lines in the initial drwing to help define the placement of a figure. This is particularly true if the figure is in a posture other than a simple standing posture, although the use of lines and divisions to make an accurate depiction is useful even then.

This illustration and the next are from *Figure Drawing andComposition.*[24]

24 Figure Drawing and Composition, R. G. Hatton, London, 1902

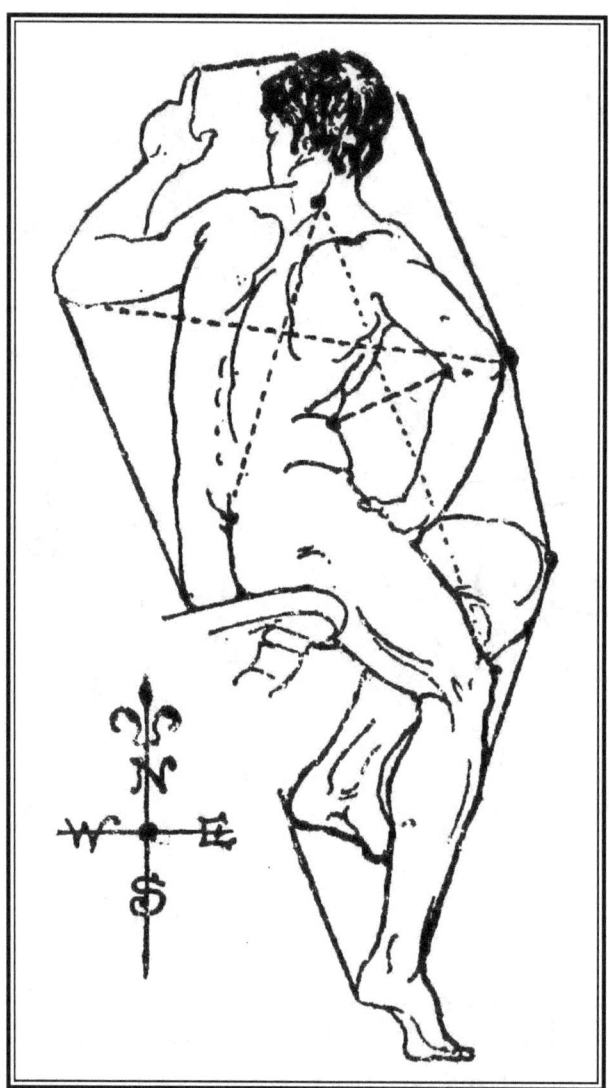

Slanting Lines[25]

---

25 Ibid.

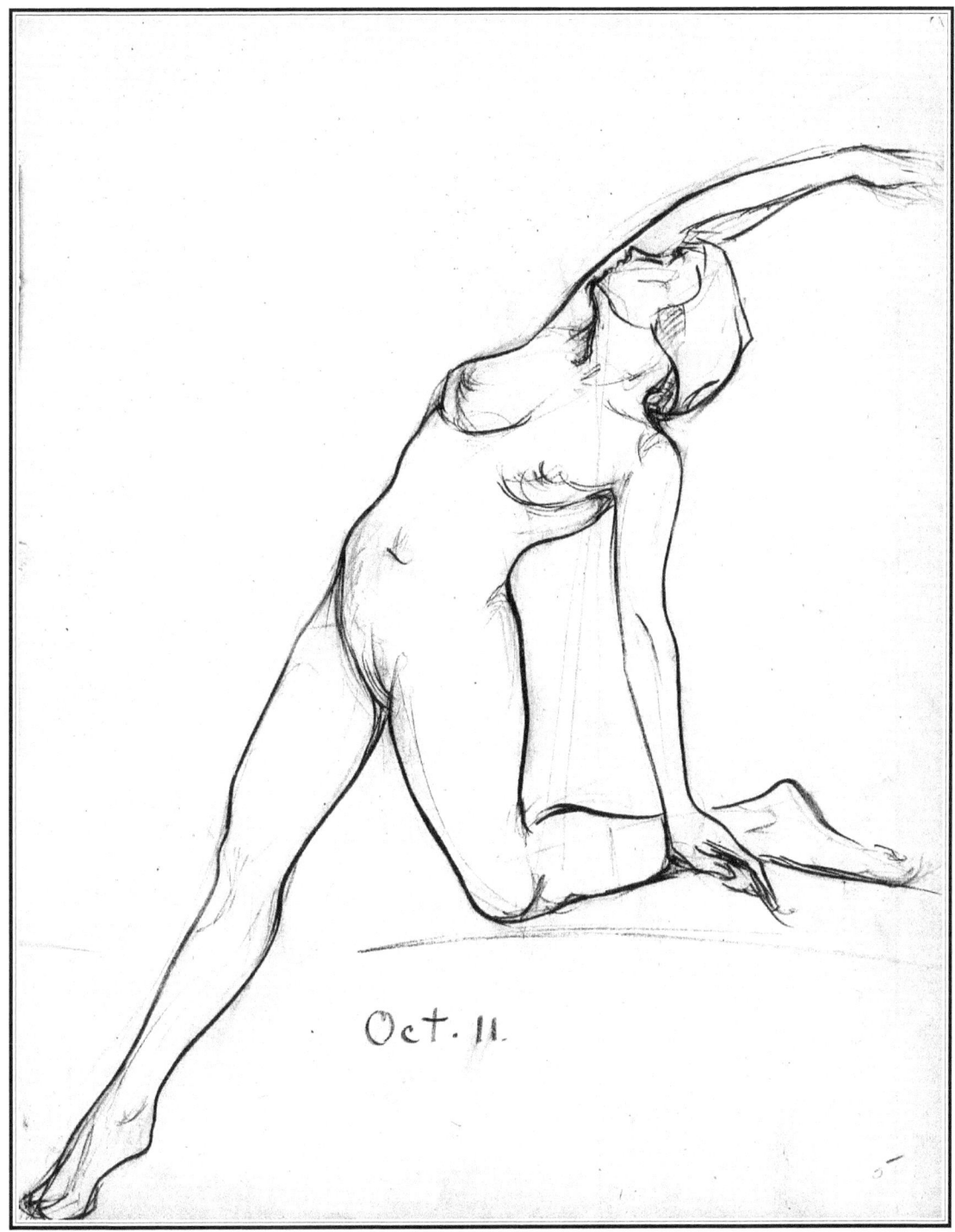

Grace Young, notice the use of slanting lines to determine the form.

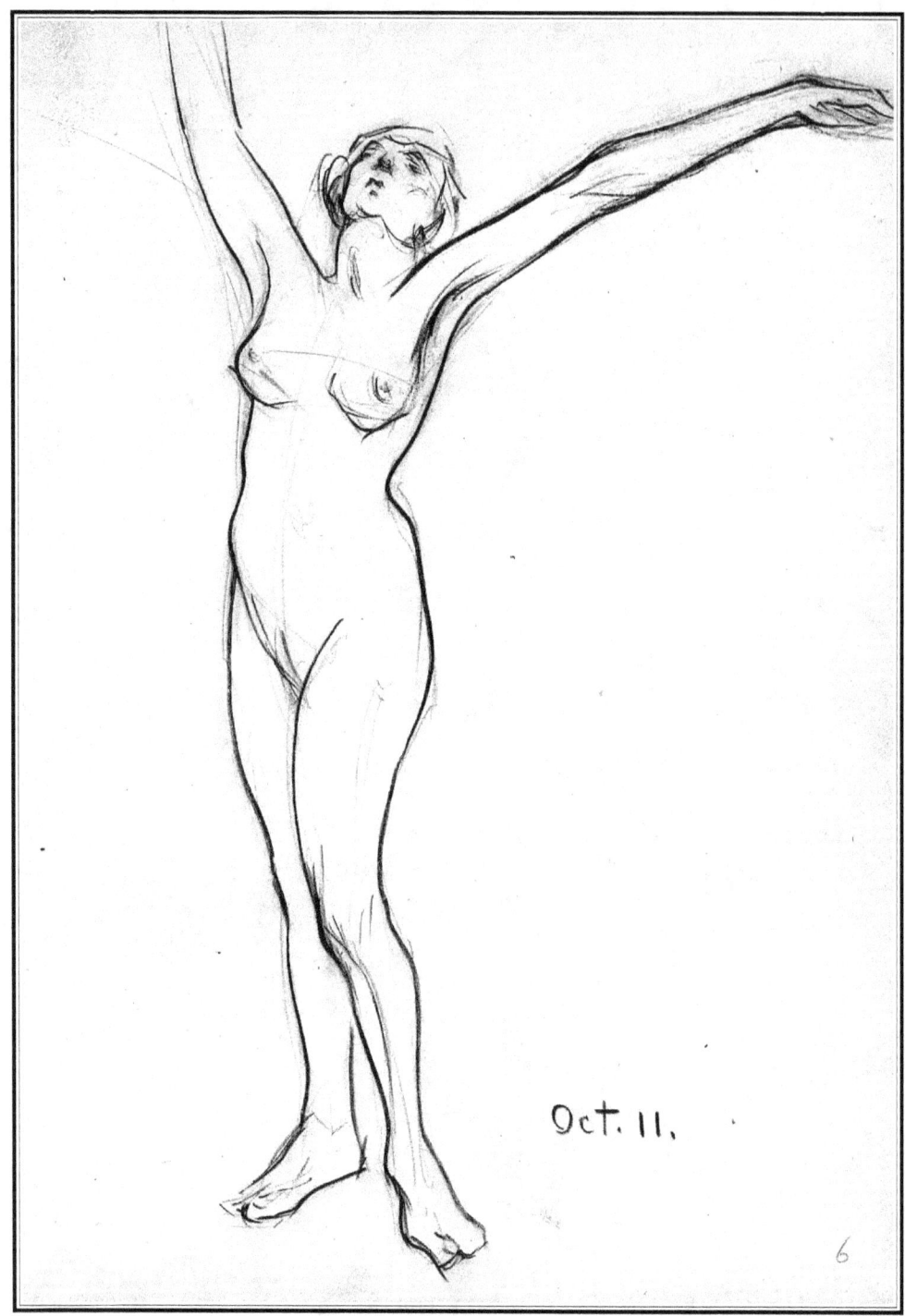

Grace Young, notice the use of lines to determine proportions.

POSTURE

The accurate depiction of posture is a key to making figure drawings believable. Here is an example of positioning the figure using cubist forms to help find the placement of the parts of the body.

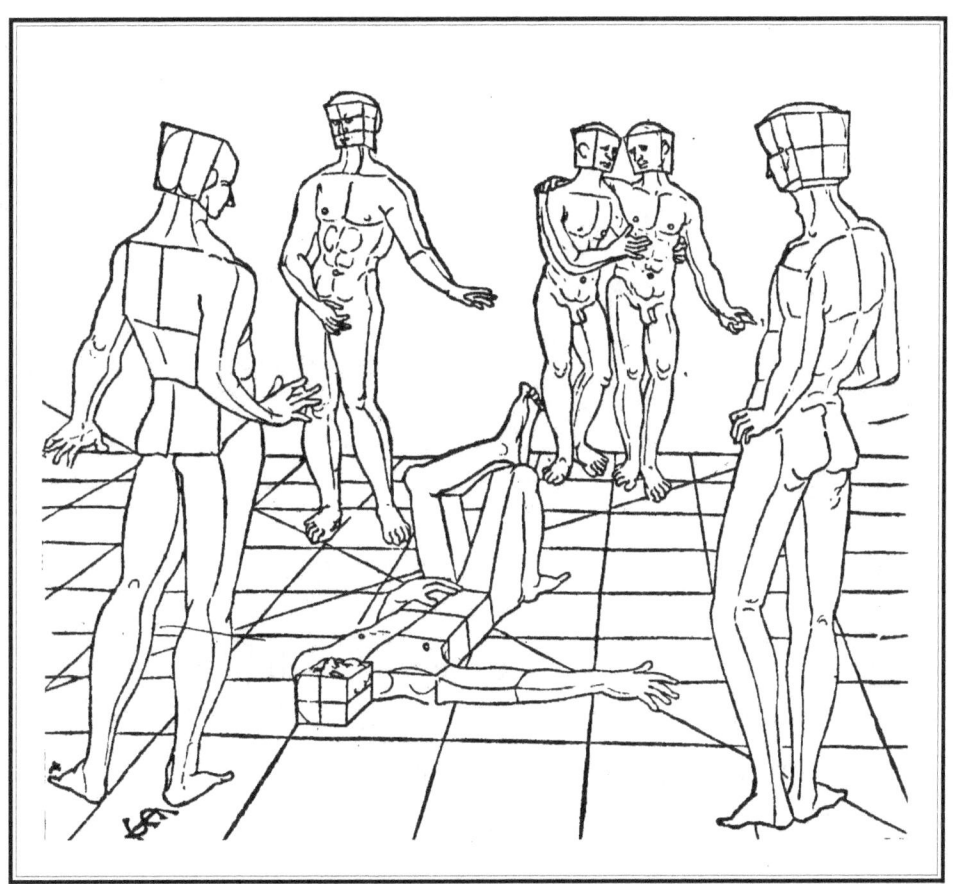

Erhard Schon, 1491-1542, Konstruction mit kubischen figuren.[26]

---

26 Die Handzeichnung Ihre Technik und Entwicklung, Joseph Meder, Wien 1922

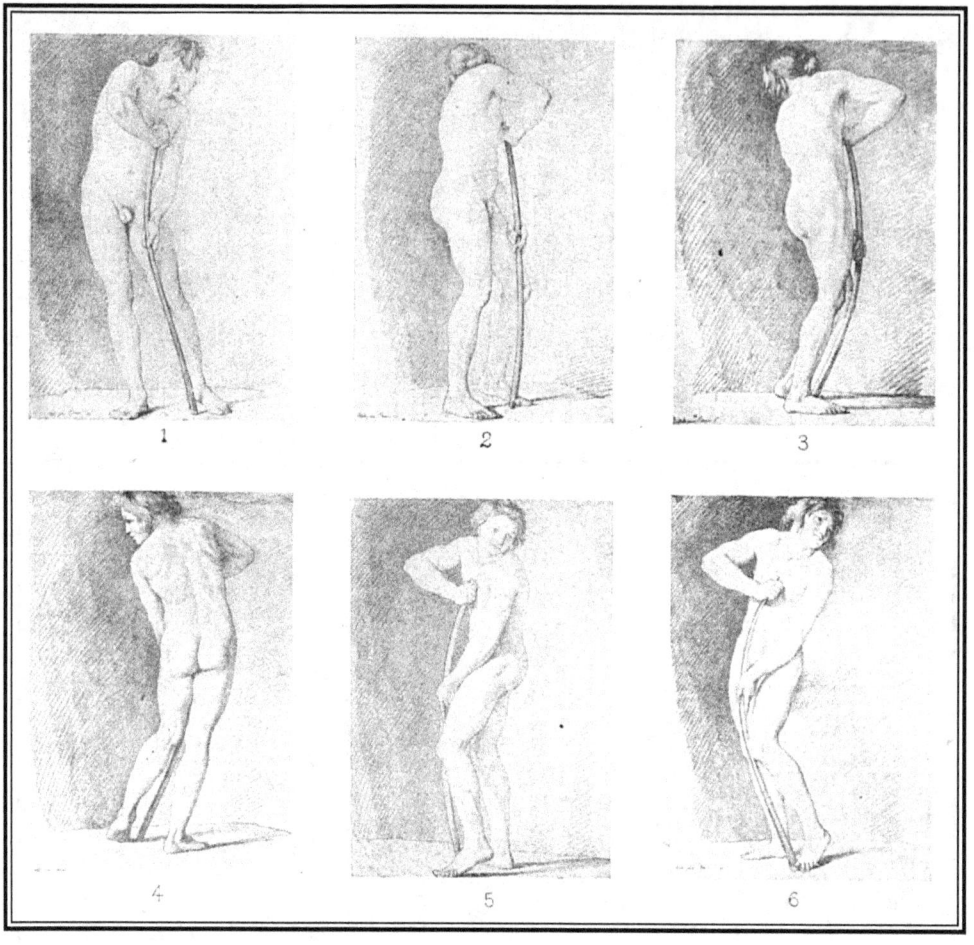

Edme Bouchardon (1698-1762) Six Figure Drawings.[27]

An artist may make several drawings of the figure from different points of view in order to arrive at the final form to paint or sculpt from. Shown are six figure studies by Edme Bouchardon, the French sculptor, which were used as the basis for his sculpture Amor now in the Louvre.

27 Ibid.

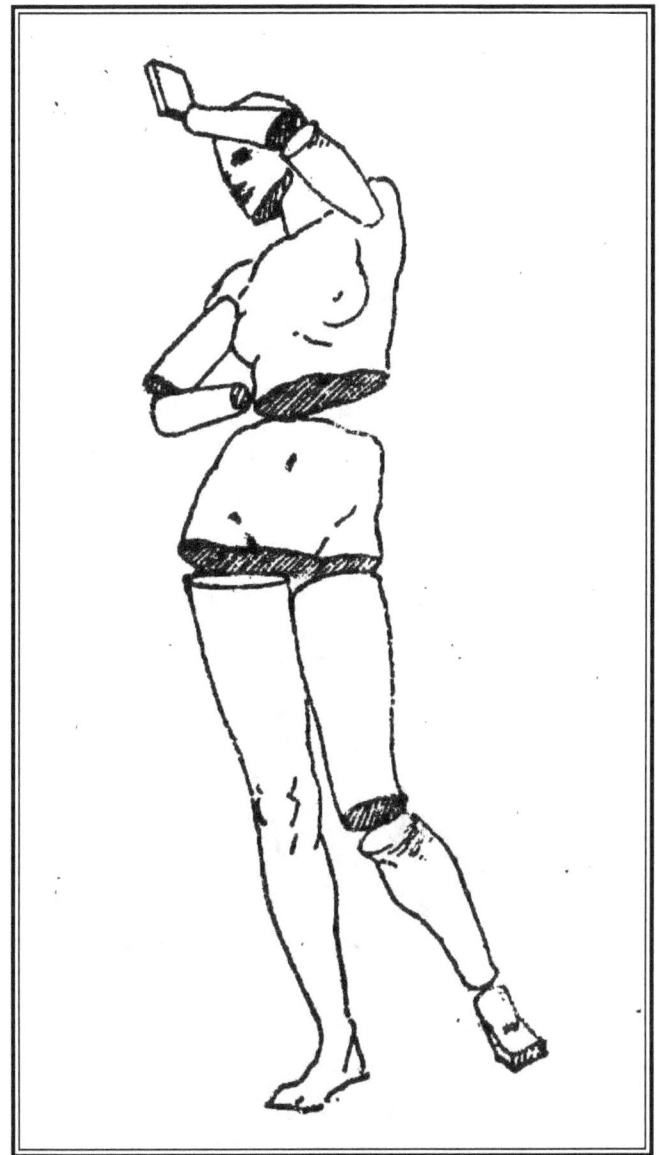

Angles and perspective of different parts of the body.[28]

To make a convincing drawing the artist must take into account the center of gravity of the figure. This point is approximately in the belly of a figure. About half of the weight of the body is in the legs. When drawing a figure a perpendicular line drawn from the head will

---

28 Figure Drawing and Composition, R. G. Hatton, London, 1902.

intersect the balance point of the figure whether the figure is standing or in some other pose.

The drawings and photographs that follow illustrate this.

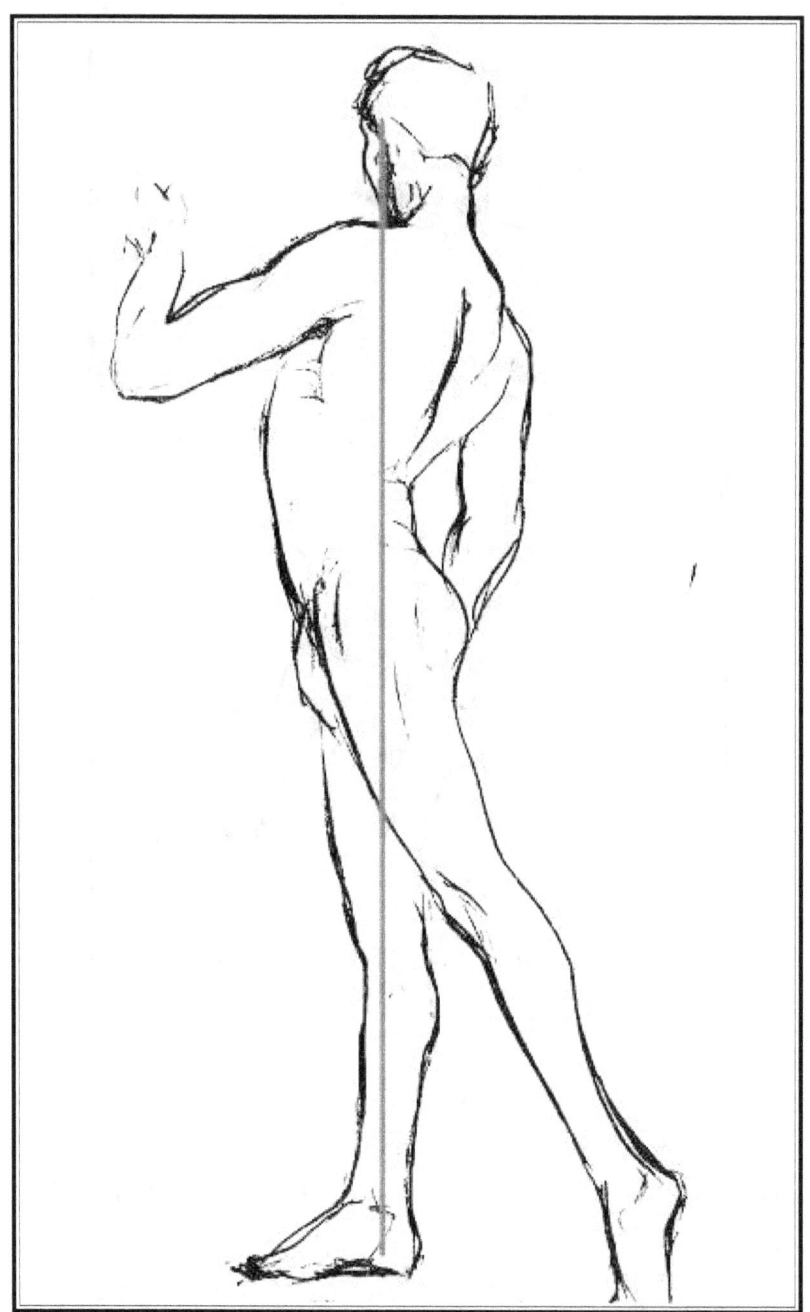

Grace Young

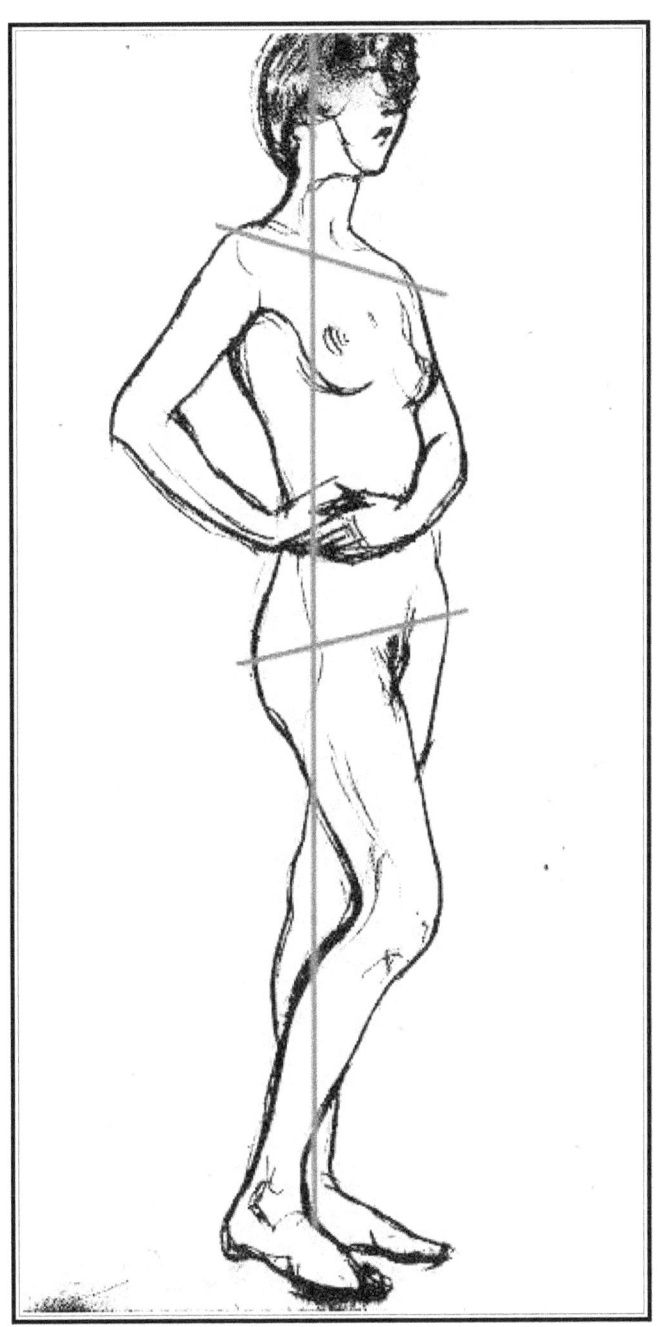

Grace Young

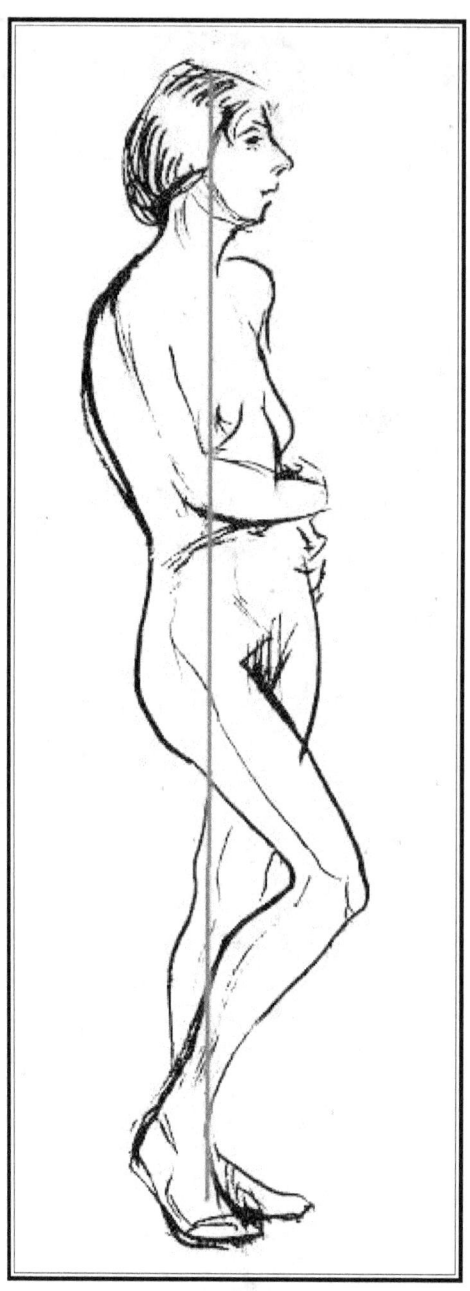

Grace Young

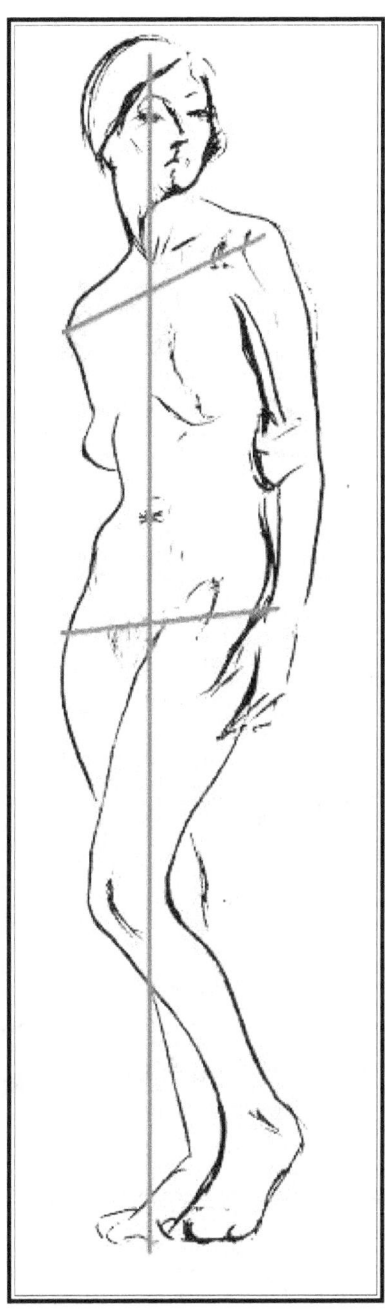

Grace Young

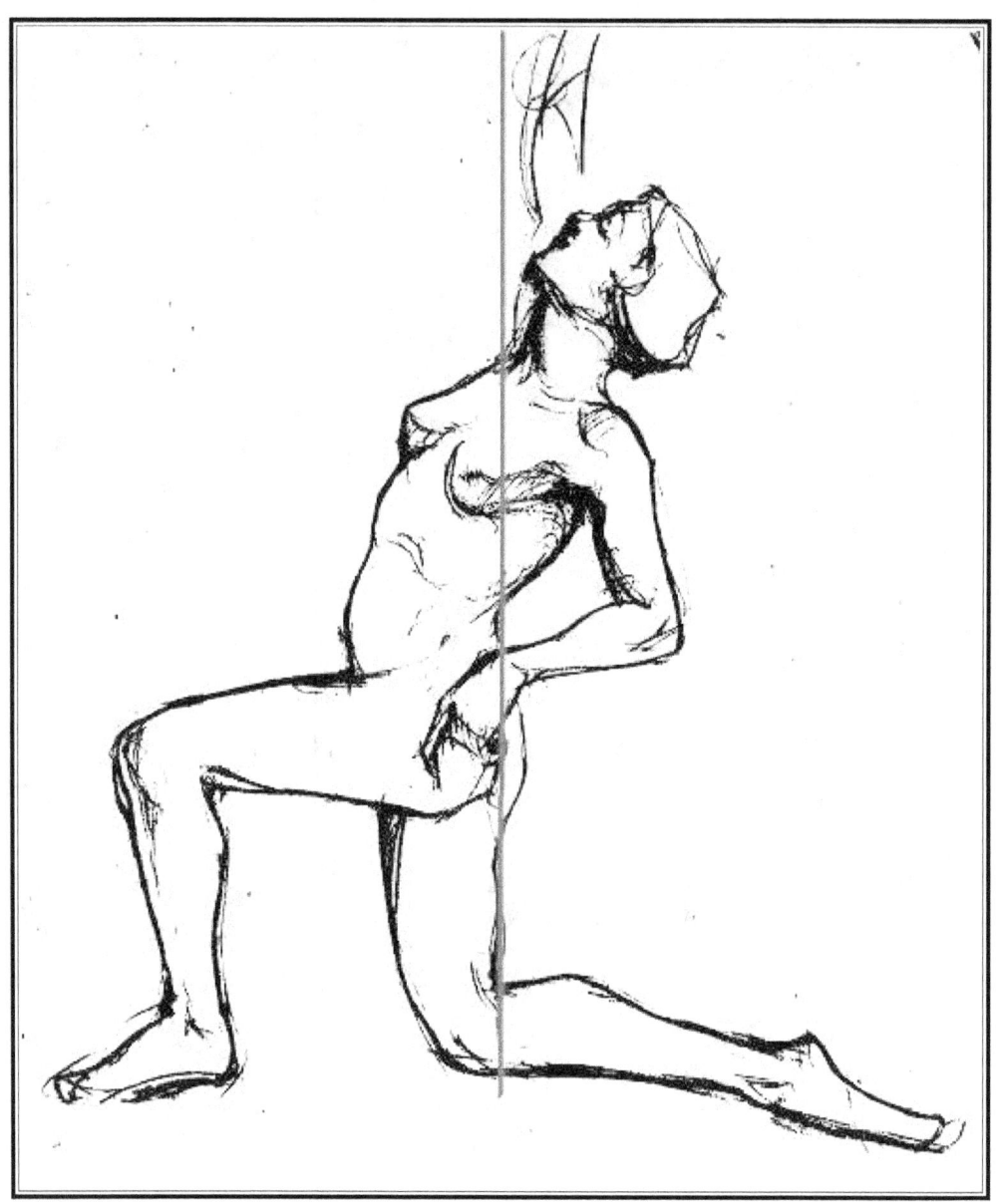

Grace Young

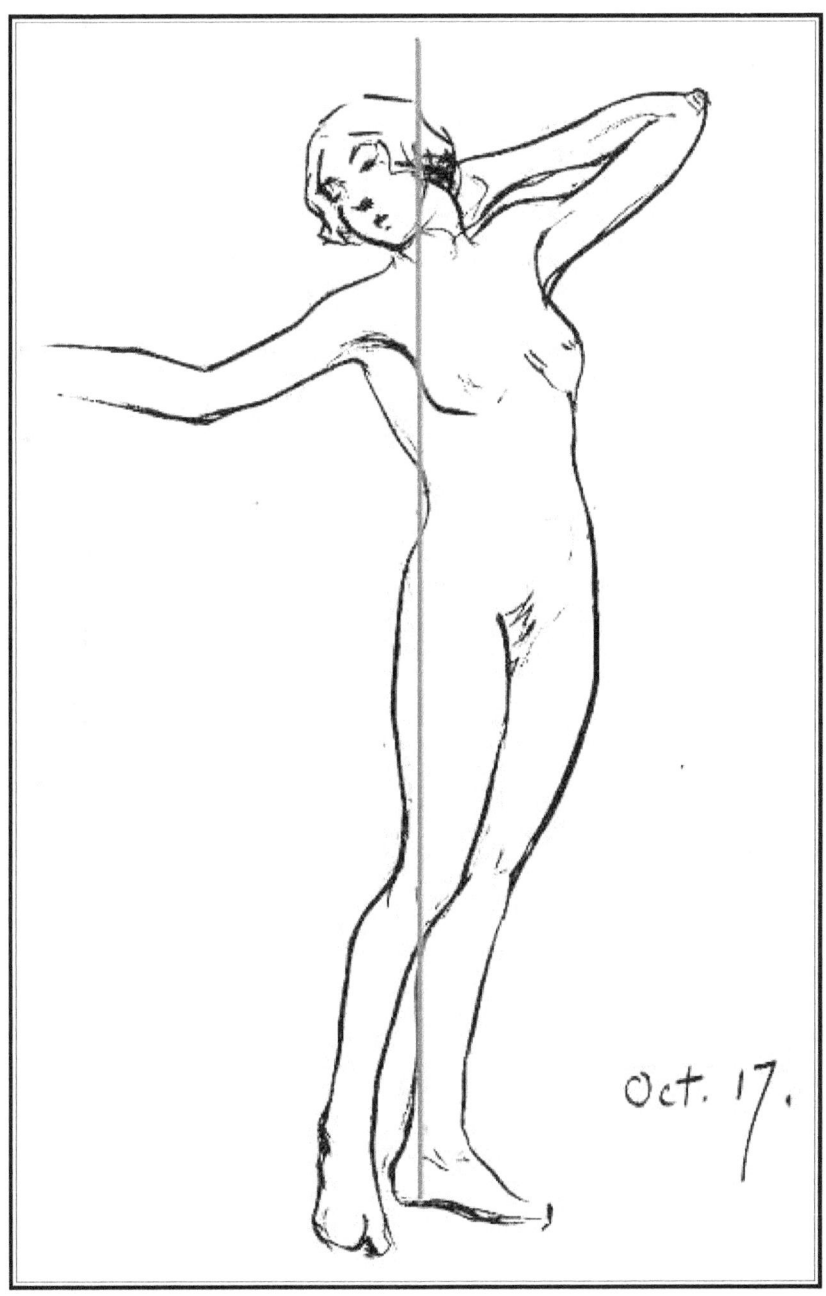

Grace Young

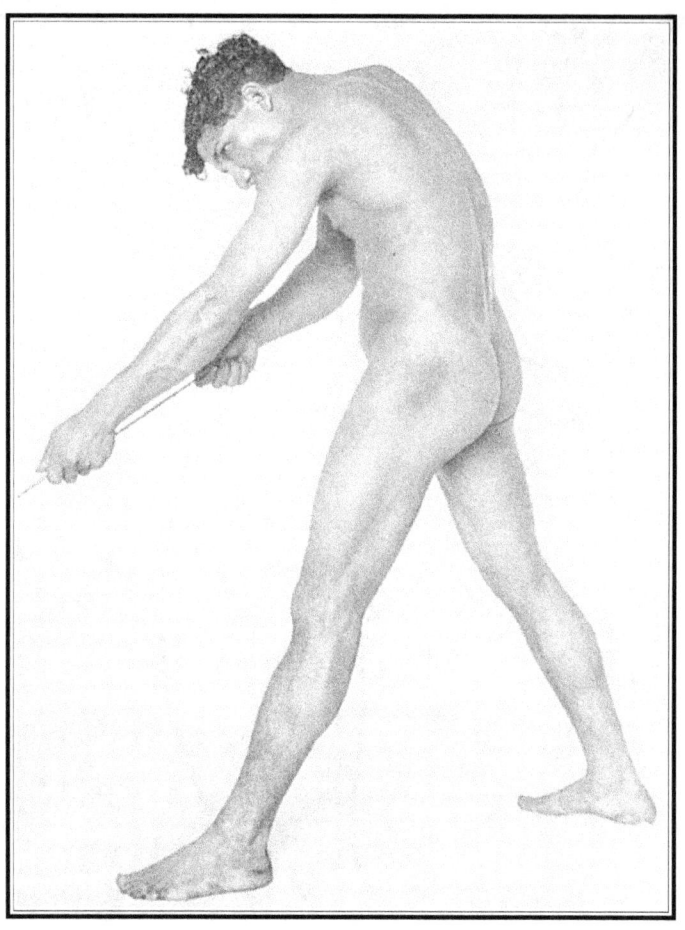

Pulling pose.[29]

---

29 The Human Form and Its Use in Art, F. R. Yerbury and G. M. Ellwood, London 1924.

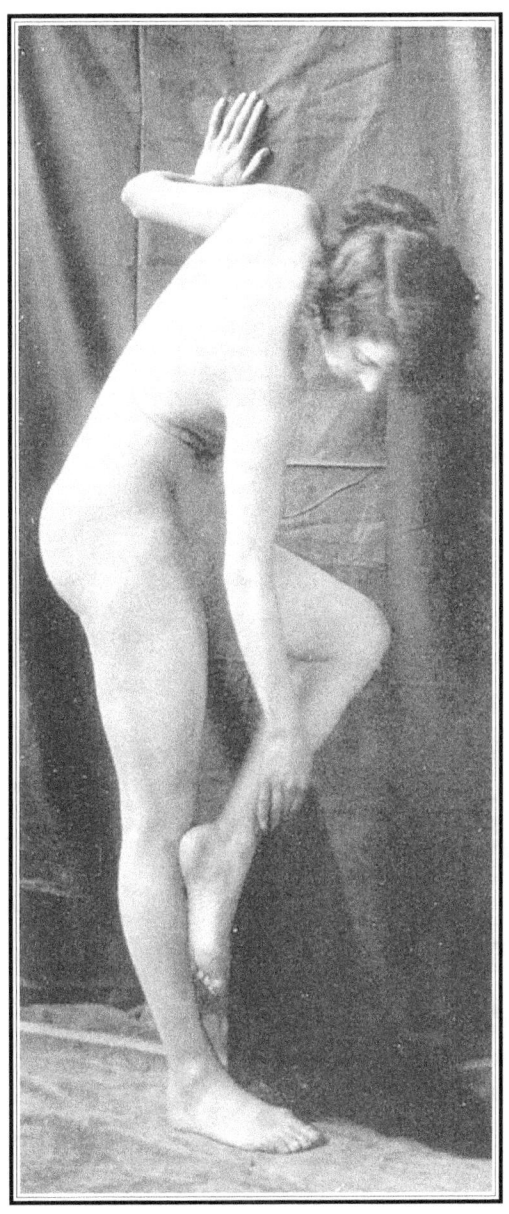

A pose showing parallel lines and a foreshortened arm.[30]

---

30 Ibid.

DRAWING THE HAND

The traditional drawing lessons that Emily Sartrain replaced involved drawing either from casts or from paintings or reproductions of paintings and prints. The following are several engravings representing drawings from such sources.[31]

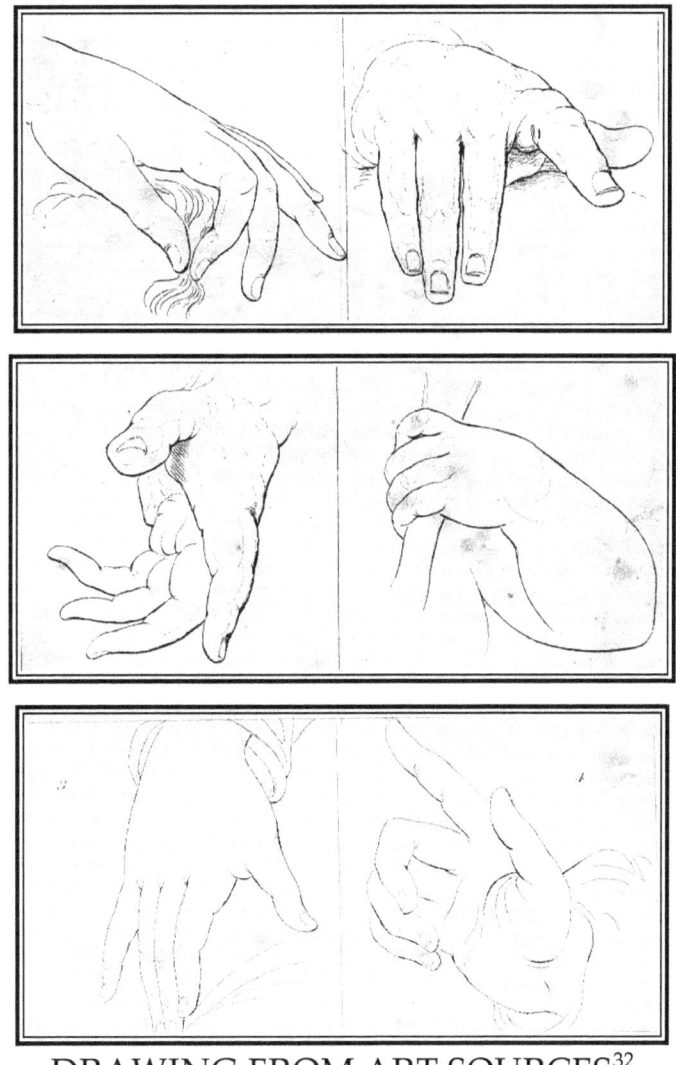

DRAWING FROM ART SOURCES[32]

31 Buchanan's Initiatory Drawing Lessons, Edinburgh, 1828
32 Buchanan's Initiatory Drawing Lessons, Edinburgh, 1828

Here are some details of the work of Grace Young as drawn from life. Note the animation and liveliness of the sketches. Despite their simplicity they convey the essential form of the hand.

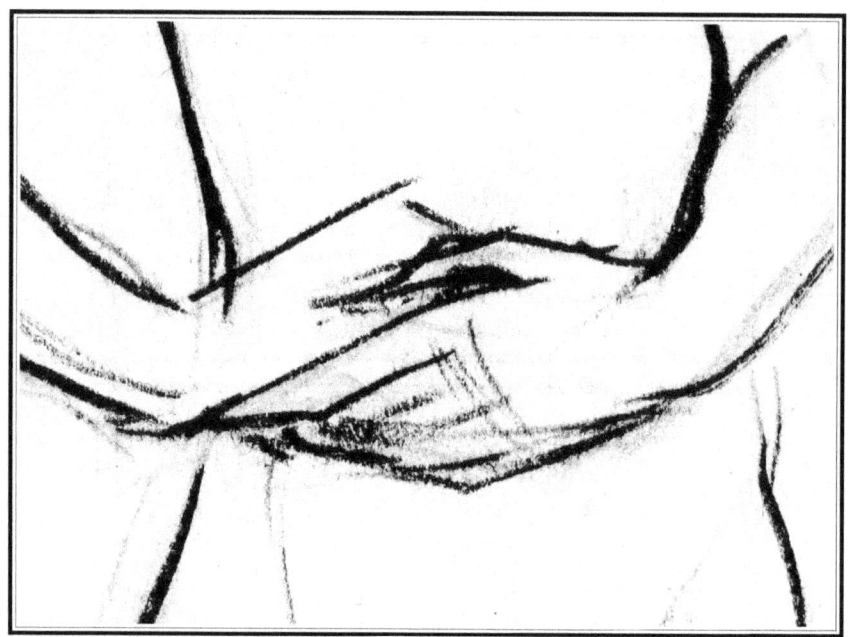

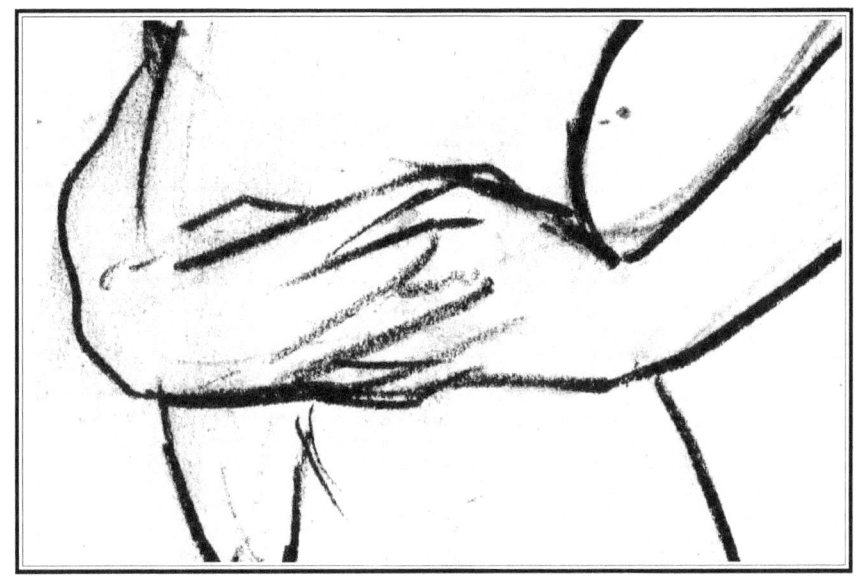

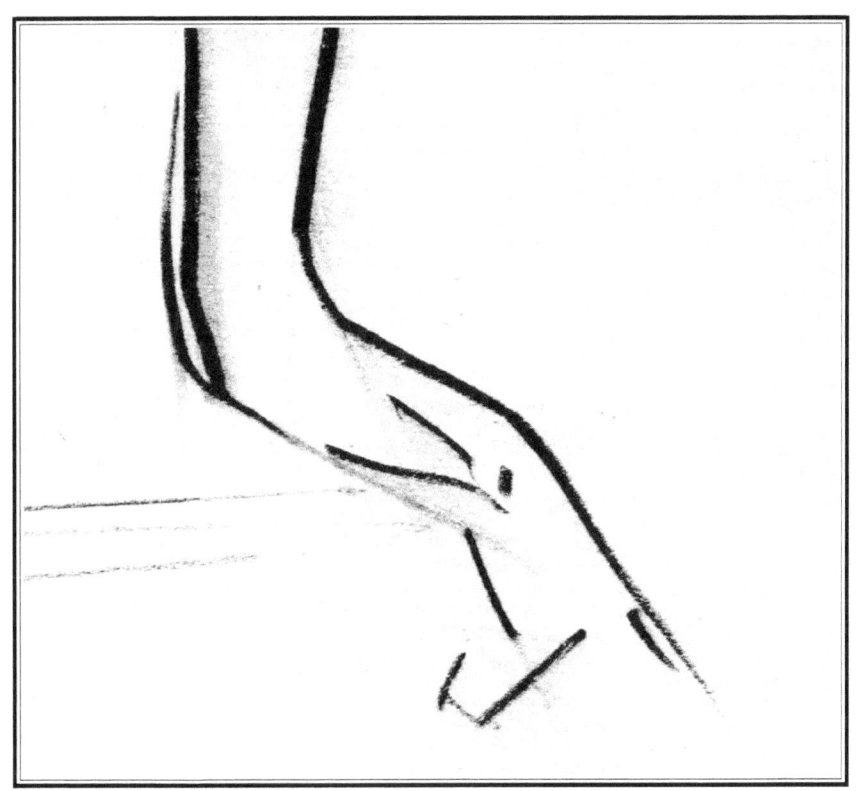

Fig. 1.

A. Scapula.

B. Collar bone.

C. Humerus.

D. Ulna.

B. Radius.

F. Carpus.

G. Metacarpus.

H. First phalanges.

I.Second phalanges.

J, Third phalanges.

Fig. 2.

A. Scapula.

B. Collar bone.

C. Olecranon process.

D. Radius.

1. Trapezius muscles.

2. Great pectoral.

3. Deltoid.

4. Muscles of the scapula.

5. Biceps.

6. Brachialis flexor.

7. Triceps.

8. Long supioator

Fig. 3.

A. Humerus.

B. Olecranon process of the nba.

C. The radius.

D. The carpus.

E. The metacarpus.

Fig. 4.

A. The olecranon.

B. Lower end of the nina.

1. Deltoid muscle.

2. Biceps.

3. Brachialis flexor.

4. External portion of the triceps.

5. Long supinator.

6. First radial extensor.

7. Second radial extensor.

8. Long common extensor of the fingers.

9. Proper extensor of the little finger.

10. Posterior or cnbital extensor.

11. Anconens muscle.

12. Anterior or flexor cubital muscle.

13. Long abductor and short extensor of the thumb.

14. Abductor of the little finger.

15. Cntaneons or short palmar muscle, cut across.

16. Annular ligament of the carpus.

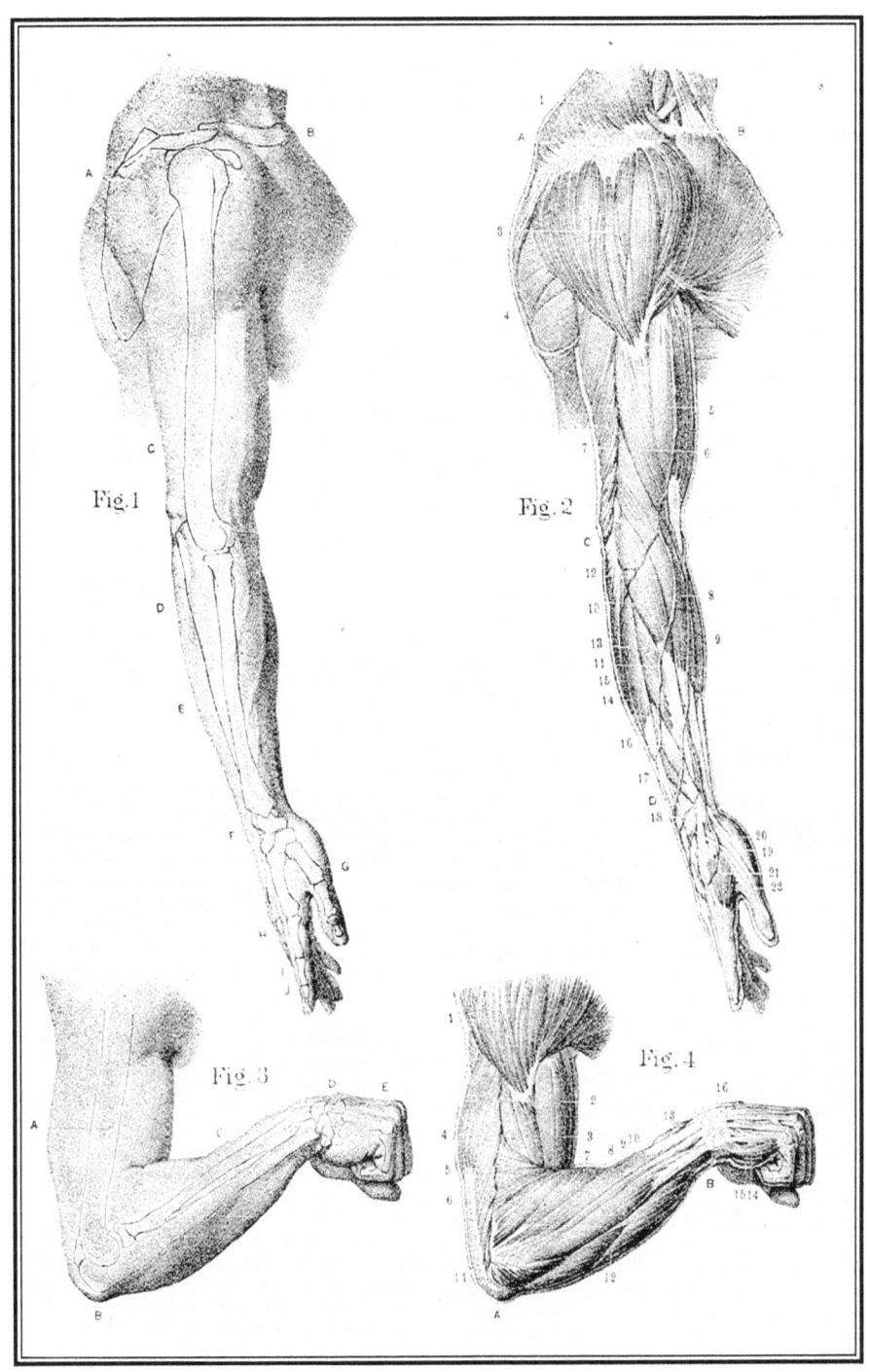

THE ARM[33]

33 Anatomy in Art, Jonathon Scott Hartley, New York, 1891

Fig. 1.

1. Portion of the trapezius.
2. Pectoralis magnus.
3. Deltoid.
4. Infraspinatus.
5. Teres minimus.
6. Teres magnus.
7. Dorsalis longus.
8. Biceps.
9. Brachialis anticus.
10. Triceps.
11. iong supinator.
12. Palmaris grandis.
13. Anconeus.
14. First external radial.
15. Second external radial.
16. Extensor longuscommunis digitorum.
17. Extensor proprii minimi digiti and ulnaris posticus.
10. Palmaris minimus.
11. Superficial flexor of the toes.
12. Ulnaris anticus.
13. Carpal ligament.
18. Long adductor of the thumb.
19. Short extensor of the thumb.
20. Carpal ligament.

Fig. 2.

1. Tendon of the long extensor of the thumb.
2. Opponens pollicis.
3. First dorsal interosseous.
4. Adductor pollicis.

Fig. 3.

1. Deltoid.
5. Pectoralis grandis.
3. Biceps.
4. Brachialis anticus.
5. Coraco-brachialis.
6. External portion of the triceps.
7. Round pronator.
8. Long supinator.
9. Palmaris grandis.
10. Palmaris minimus.
11. Ulnaris anticus.
12. Carpal ligament.

Fig. 4.

1. Adductor of the little finger.
2. Section of the cutaneous palmar muscle.
3. Short abductor of the thumb.

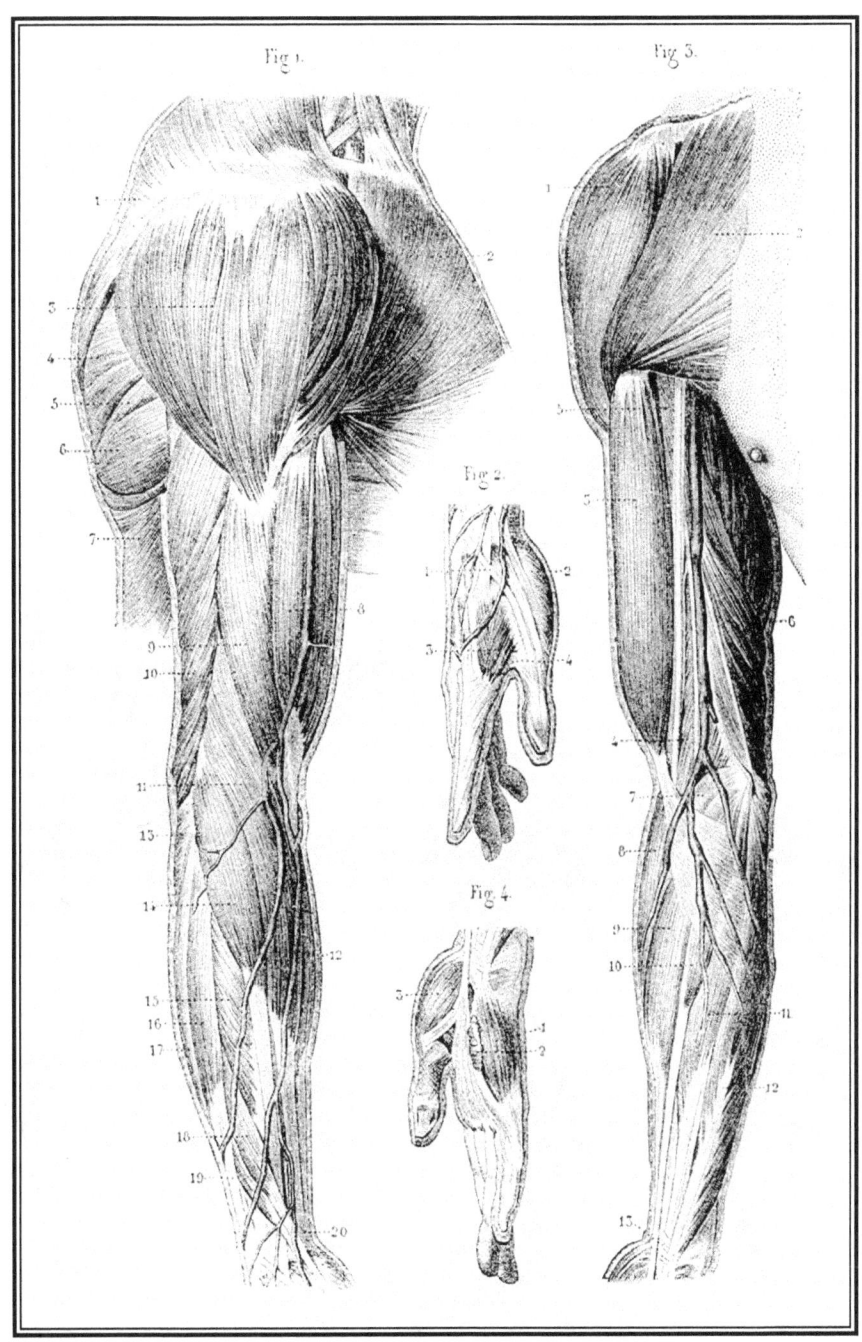

UPPER LIMB – SIDE VIEW[34]

34 Ibid

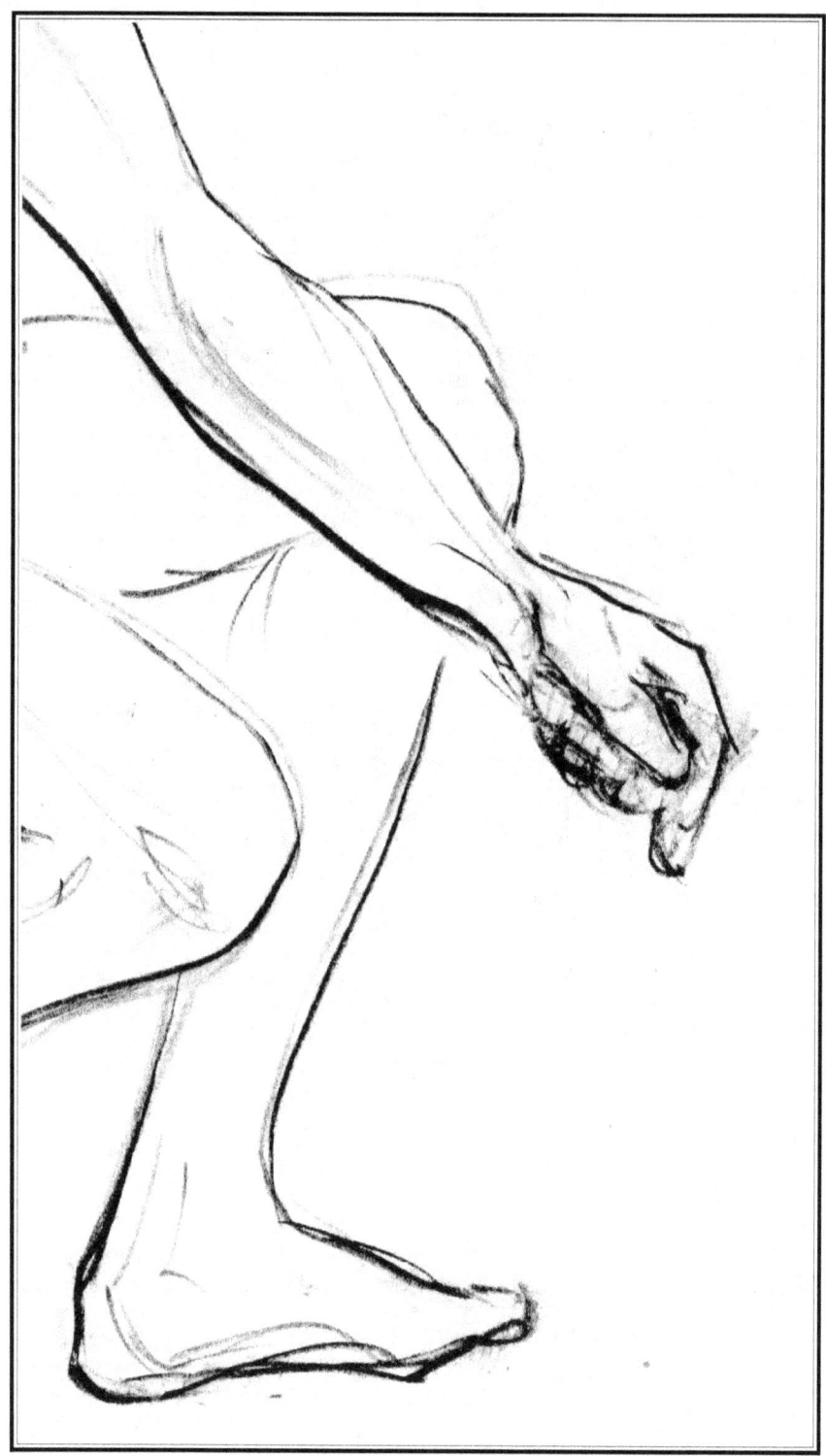

Grace Young

DRAWING THE HEAD

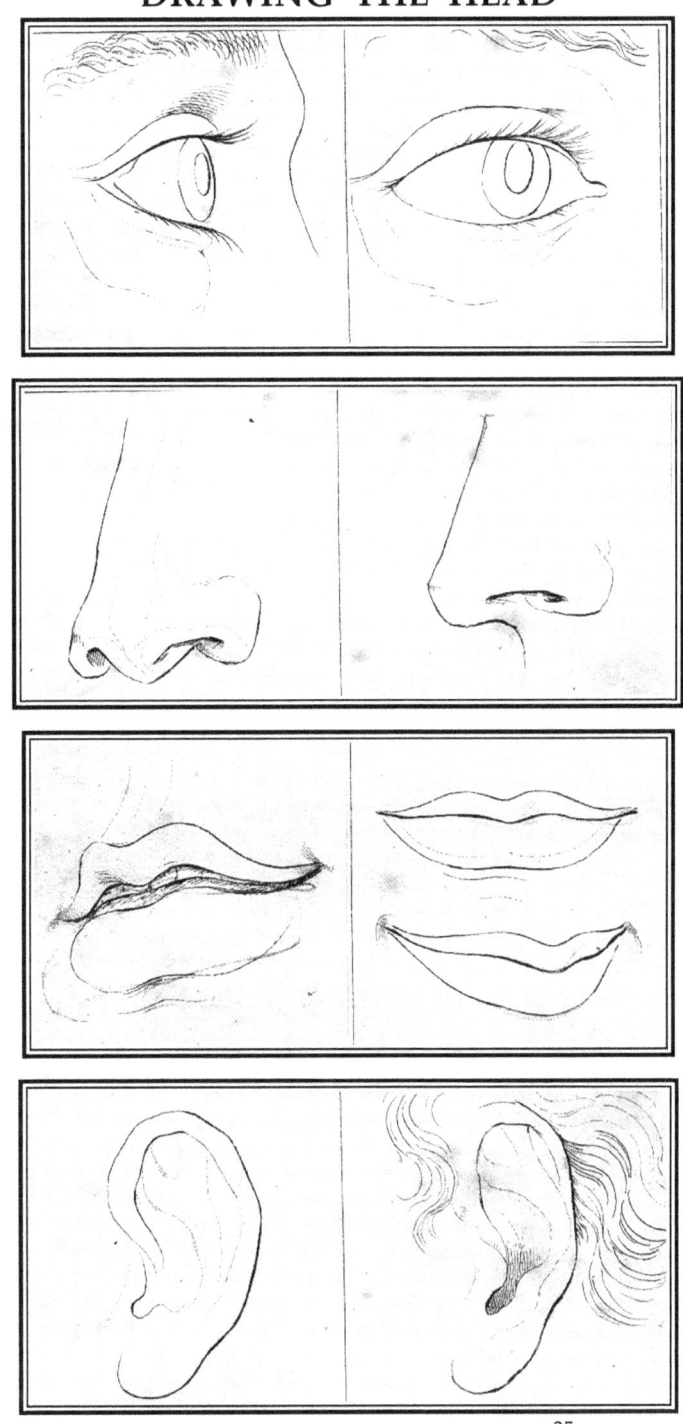

DRAWING FROM CASTS[35]

---

35 Buchanan's Initiatory Drawing Lessons, Edinburgh, 1828

59

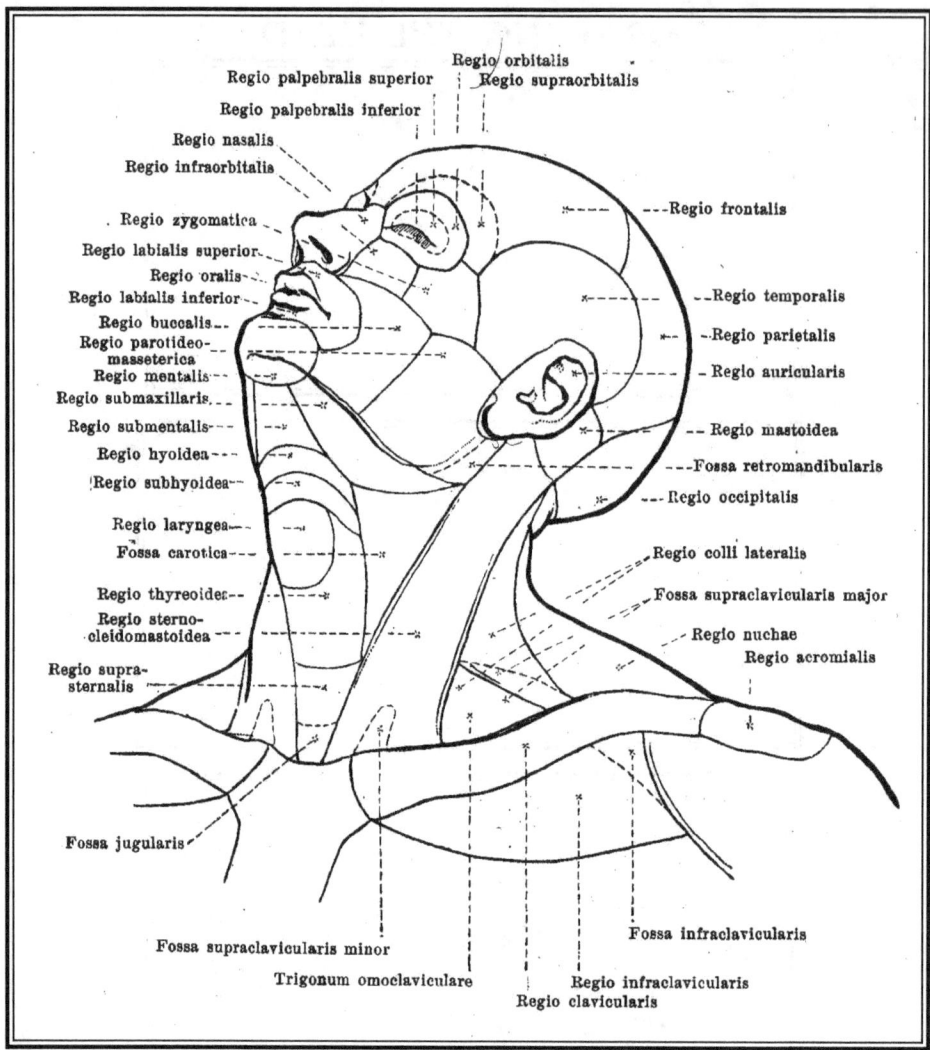

AREAS OF THE HEAD AND NECK[36]

THE UPPER BODY

36 Handatlas der Anatomire des Menschen, Werner Spalteholz, Leipzig 1920

Fig. 1.
A. The ulna.
B. The radius.
C. The humerus.
D. The scapula.
E. The collar boue.

Fig. 2.
A. The ulna.
B. The radius.
C. The humerus.
1. Flexor ulnaris.
2. Superficial common flexor.
3. Long palmar.
4. Great palmar, flexor radialis
5. Long supinator.
6. Biceps.
6'. Its aponeurotic expansion.
7. Brachialis flexor.
8. Tricep.
8'. Its inferior tendon.
9. Ceraco-brachialis.
10. Great pectoral.
11, and 11*. Deltoid.
12. Teres major.
13. Sub-scapular.
14. Latissimus dorsi.
15. Serratus magnus.

Fig. 3.

A. Cubit.

B. Radius.

C. Humerus.

D. Scapula.

E. Collar bone.

Fig. 4.

D. Spine of the scapula.

1. Anconeus muscle.

2. Anterior cubital.

3. Posterior cubital.

4. Proper extensor of the little finger.

5. Common extensor of the fingers.

6. Short extensor of the thumb.

7. Long abductor of the thumb.

8. 2° Radialis externus.

9. 1° Radialis externus.

10. The long supinator.

11. Brachialis flexor.

12. Biceps.

13. Triceps.

13'. Its inferior tendon.

14. Deltoid.

15. Latissimus dorsi.

16. Teres major.

17. Teres minor.

18. Infra spinatus.

19. Rhomboidens.

20. Trapezius, of which a portion has been removed to show the position and action of the supra-spinatus muscle.

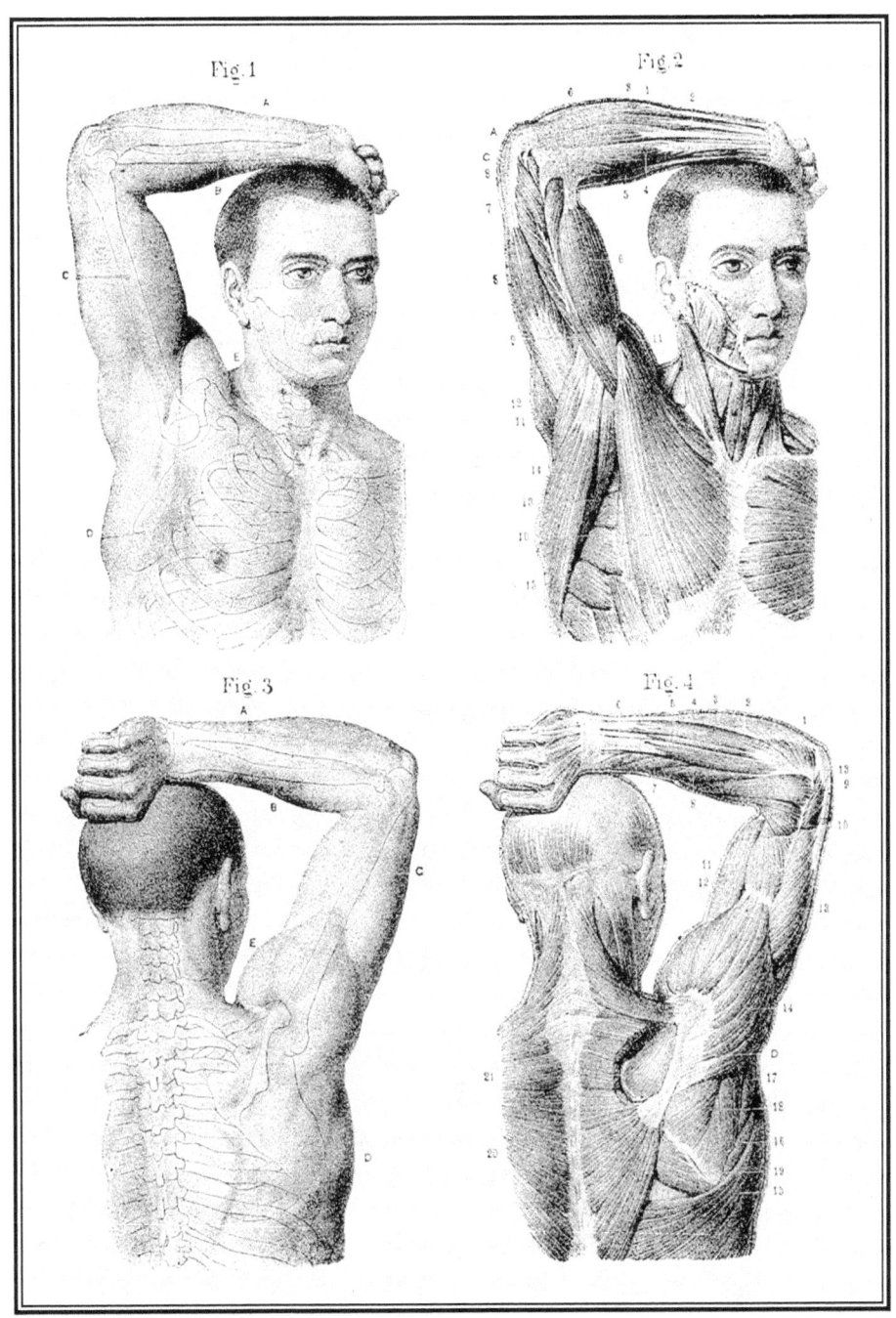

THE UPPER BODY[37]

---

37 Anatomy in Art, Jonathon Scott Hartley, New York, 1891

THE HEAD – FACE AND PROFILE

Fig. 1.

1. Frontal portion of the occipitofrontalis muscle. (a.)
2. Orbicular muscle of the eye-lids.
3. Common elevator of the nose and upper lip.
4. Triangular of the nose; the pyramidal is above it.
5. Proper elevator of the upper lip.
6. Smaller zygomatic.
7. Larger zygomatic.
8. Orbicular of the lips.
9. Triangular of the chin.
10. Square muscle of the chin.
11. Elevator of the chin.
12. Masseter muscle. (See fig. 3.)
13. Latissimus colli muscle. (See fig. 2.)
14. Sterno-cleido mastoideus. (b.)
15. Sterno-thyroideus. (c.)
16. Sterno-hyoideus. (d.)
17. Trapezius. (See fig. 8.)

Fig. 2.

1. Anterior auricular.
2. Superior auricular.
3. Posterior auricular.
4. Parotid gland.
5. Risorius muscle of Santorini.
6. Latissimus colli. (e.)

Fig. 3.

1. Frontal portion of the occipitofrontal muscle. (See fig. 1.)

1. Occipital portion of the same muscle. (J.)

2. Temporal. (g.)

3. Orhicular of the eyelids.

4. Common elevator of the wing of the nose and of the upper lip.

4′. Proper elevator of the upper lip.

5. Triangular of the nose.

6. Small zygomatic.

7. Great zygomatic.

8. Orbicular muscle of the lips.

9. Buccinator.

to. Triangular muscle of the chin.

11. Square muscle of the chin.

12. Masseter. (In)

13. Sterno-cleido mastoid. (See fig. 1.)

14. Digastric. (1.)

15. Mylo-hyoid. (j.)

16. Steruo-hyoid. (See fig. 1.)

17. Omo-hyoid. (See fig. 1.)

18. Thyro-hyoid. (k.)

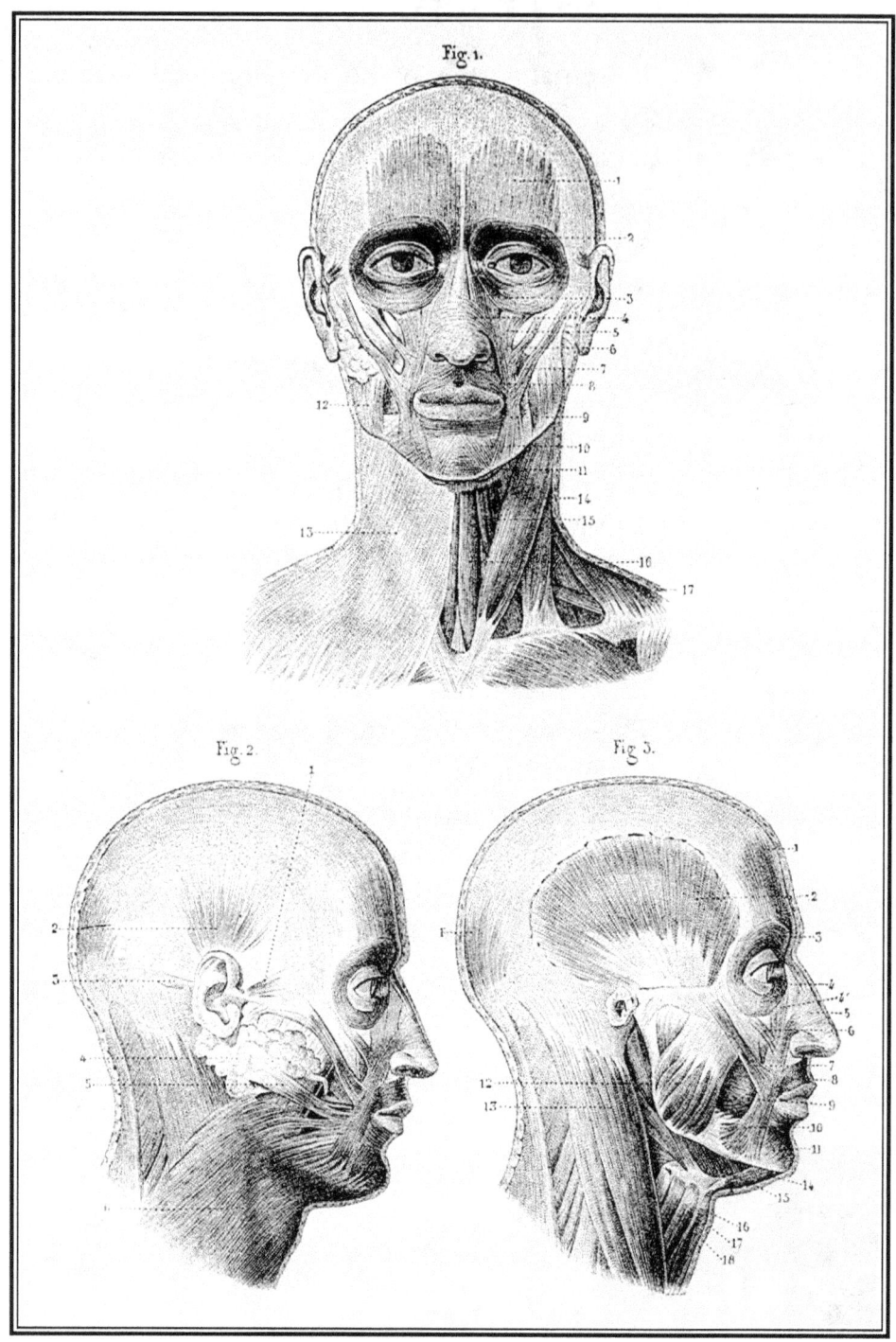

THE HEAD – FACE AND PROFILE[38]

38 Ibid.

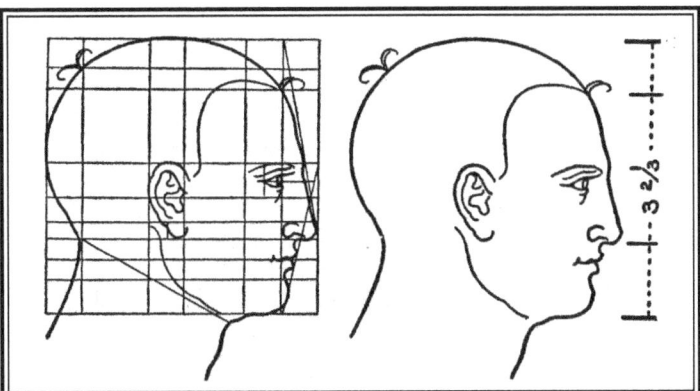

IDEAL MALE HEAD AS PROPORTIONED BY DÜRER AND THE SAME HEAD WITHOUT THE NETWORK OF LINES[39]

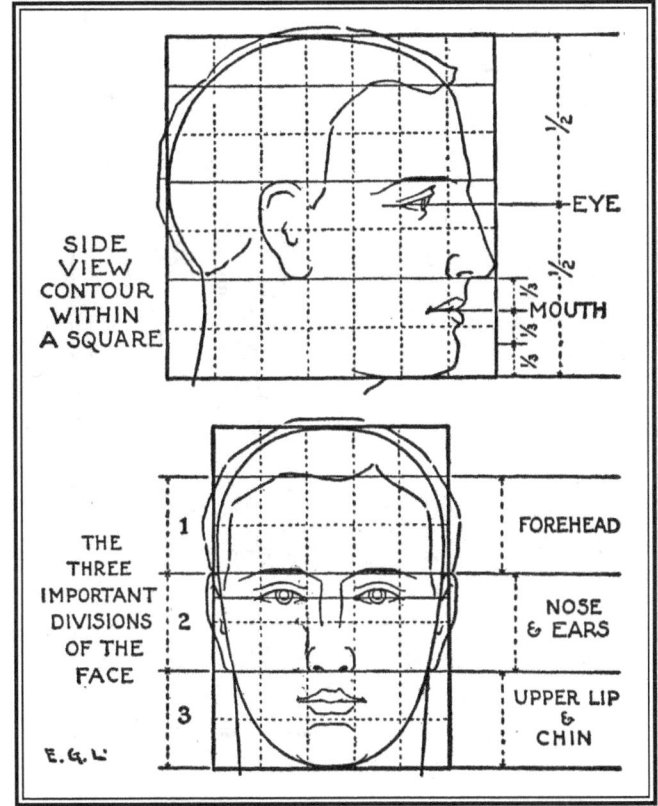

PROPORTIONS OF THE HEAD AND FACE[40]

---

39 Practical Drawing, E. G. Lutz, Philadelphia, 1915
40 Ibid.

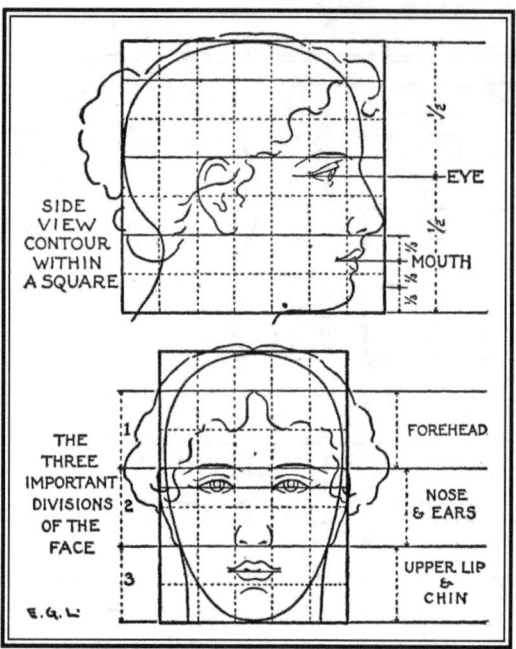

PROPORTIONS OF THE HEAD AND FACE[41]

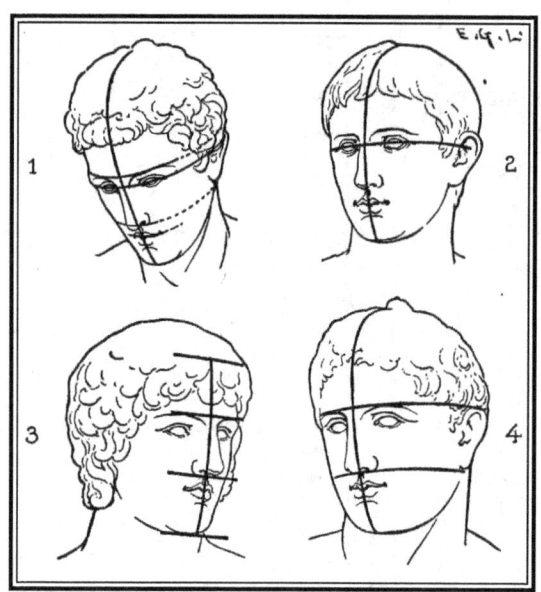

THREE QUARTER VIEW FACES AND THE CONSTRUCTION LINES[42]

---

41 Ibid.
42 Ibid.

After looking at the classical methods of drawing the head, and the anatomy of the head and neck that was available to students of the time let's look at how Grace Young handles her sketches.

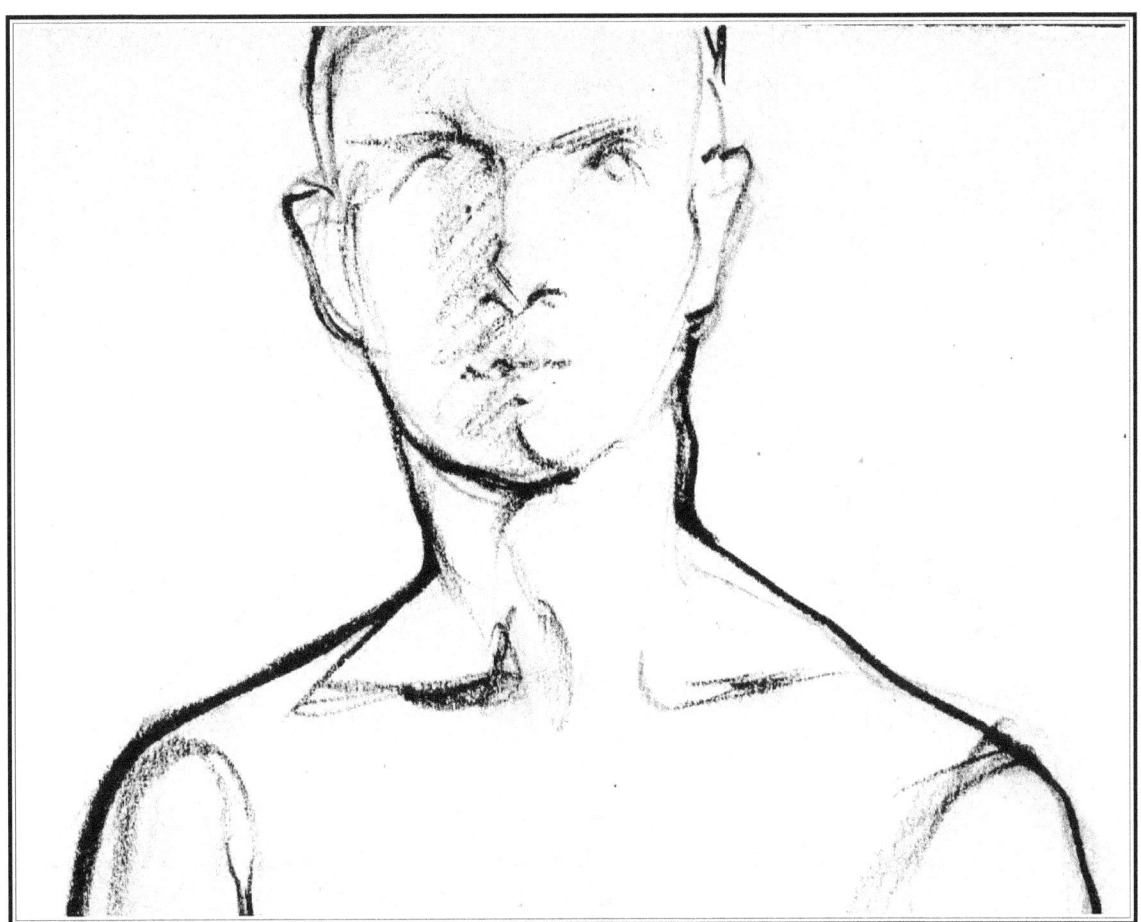

Grace Young – Male Figure

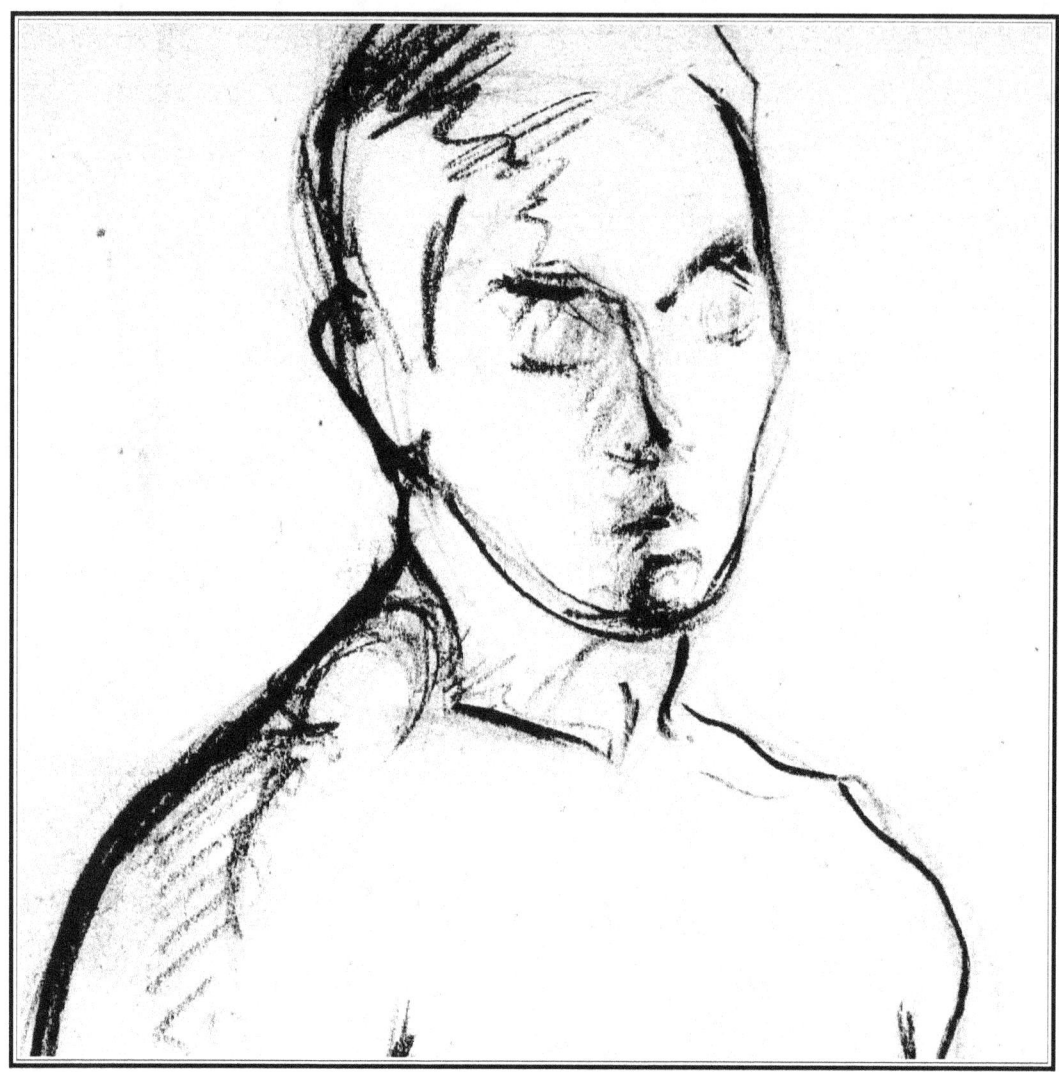

Grace Young – Male Figure

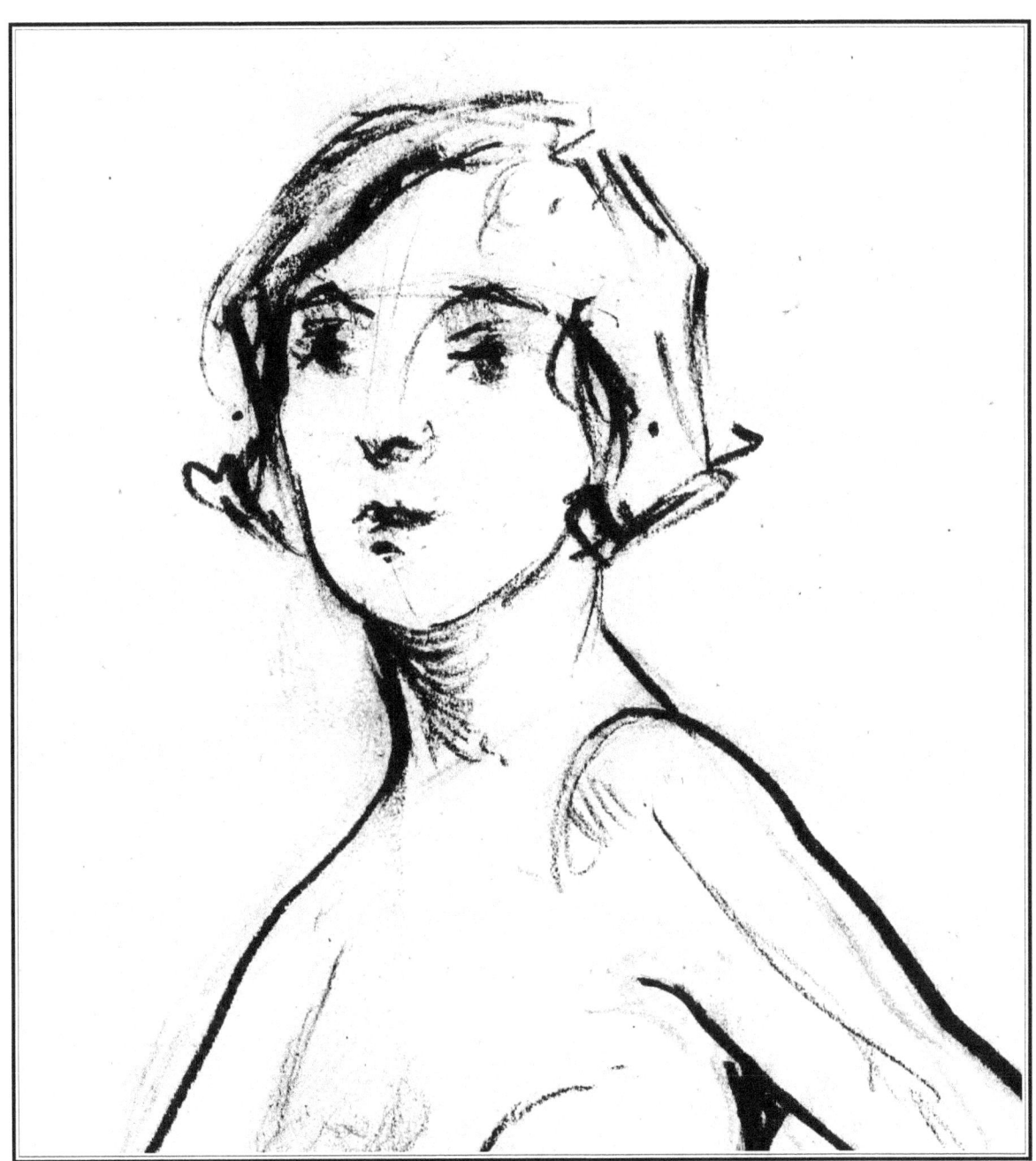

Grace Young – Female Figure

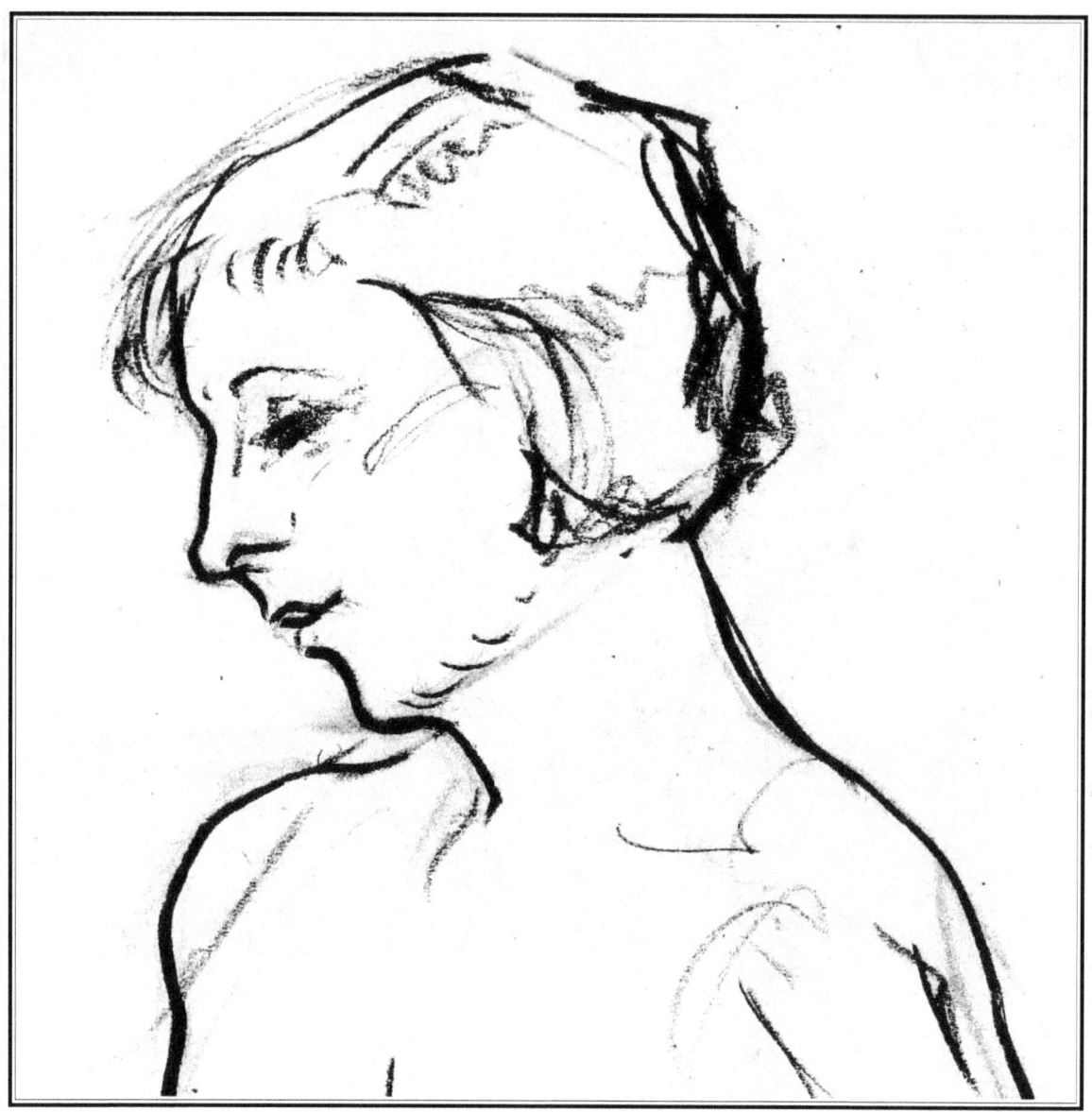

Grace Young – Female Figure

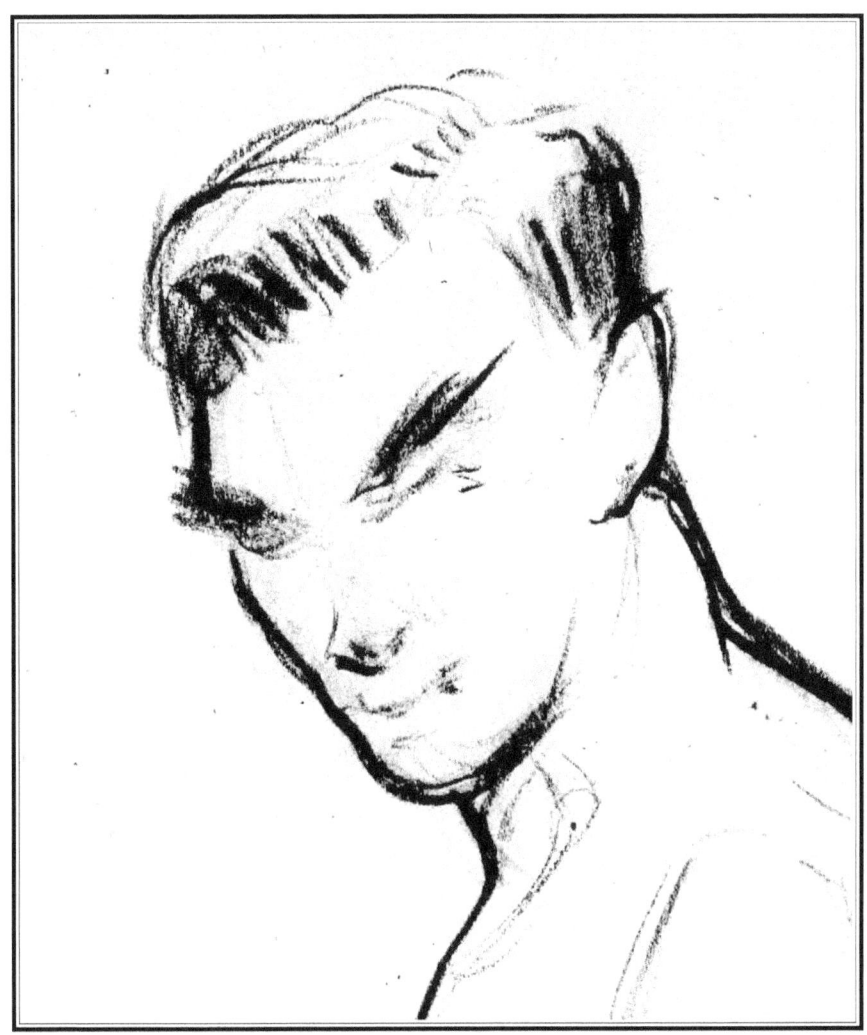

Grace Young – Male Figure

DRAWING THE FEET

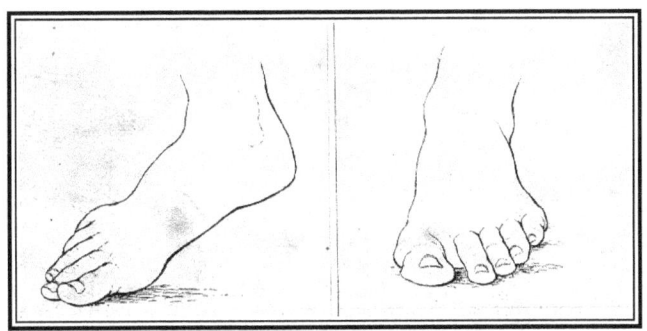

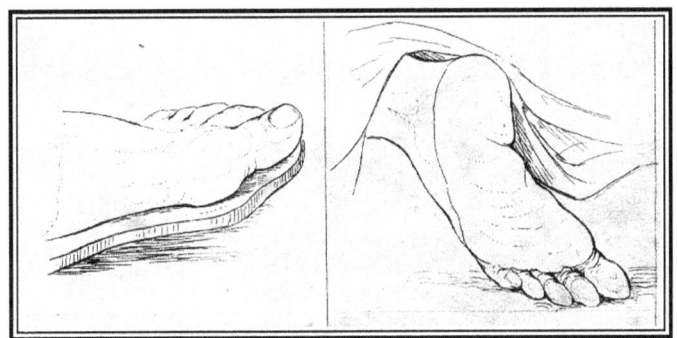

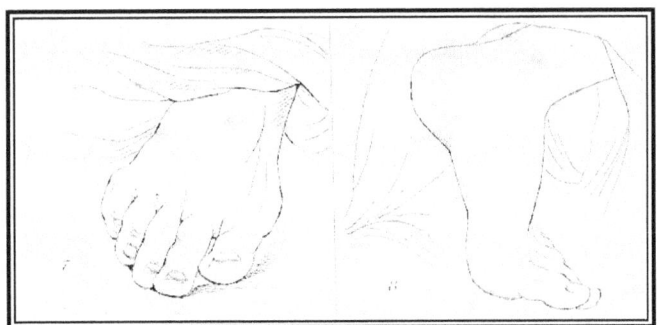

DRAWING FROM CASTS[43]

---

43 Buchanan's Initiatory Drawing Lessons, Edinburgh, 1828

THE LEG AND FOOT

Fig. 1.

A. Coxal Bone.

B. Sacrum and coccyx.

C. Femur.

D. Rotula.

E. Tibia.

F. Fibula.

0. Tarsus.

H. Metatarsus.

I. Phalanges.

Fig. 2.

A. Iliac crest.

C. Great trochanter.

D. Rotula.

E. External tuberosity of the tibia.

F. Head of the fibula.

1. Tensor of the aponeurosis of the thigh.

1'. Aponeurotic band.

2. Gluteus medius.

8. Gluteus maximus.

4. Triceps.

5. Biceps.

6. Sem-tendinosus.

7. Gastro-cnemii.

8. Soleus muscle.

9. Peroneus longus.

10. Peroneus brevis.

11. Long common extensor of the toes.

11'. Tendons of this muscle.

12. Anterior, or third peroneal muscle.

18. Long extensor of the great toe.

14. Tibialis anticus.

15. Short common extensor of the toes.

16. Abductor of the little toe.

17. Annular ligament of the tarsus.

Fig. 3.

A. Calcaneum.

B. Astragalus.

C. Scaphoid.

D. First cuneiform bone.

E. Second cuneiform.

F. Third cuneiform.

G. Cuboid.

H. Metatarsus.

I. Phalanges.

Fig. 4.

A. Calcaneum.

1. Short common flexor of the toes.

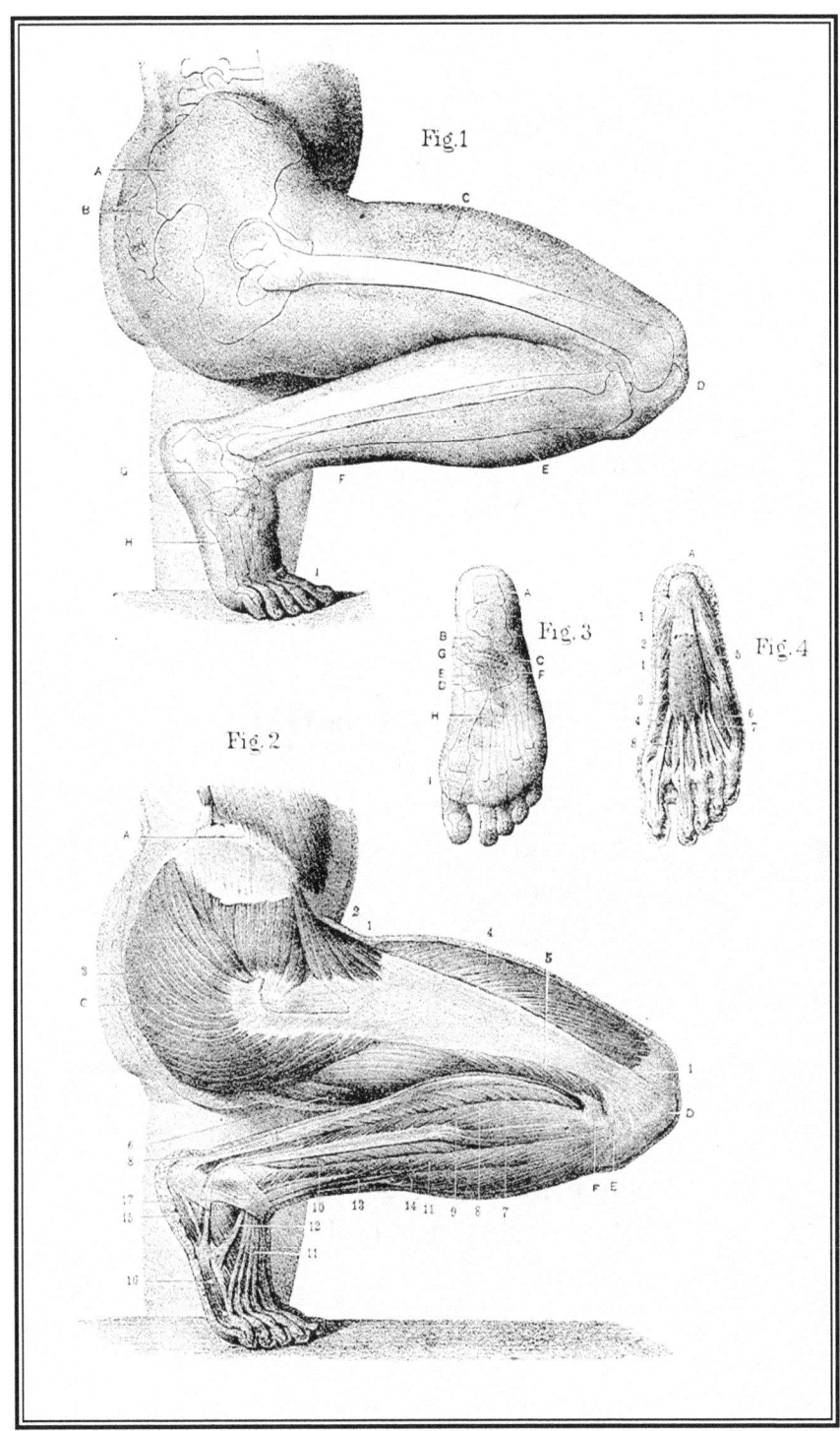

THE LEG AND FOOT[44]

44 Anatomy in Art, Jonathon Scott Hartley, New York, 1891

LOWER LIMB

Fig1.

A. Iliac crest.

B. Great trochanter.

C. Patella.

D. External condyle of the tibia.

1'. Tensor muscle of the aponeurosis of the fascia lata. (a.)

1. Large band of this aponeurosis.

2. Gluteus medius. (6.)

3. Gluteüs maximus.

4. Sartorius.

5. Rectus anticus.

6. Triceps.

7. Biceps.

Fig. 2.

A. External condyle of the tibia.

B. Head of the fibula.

C. Malleolus externus.

1. Tibialis anticus muscle.

2. Gastrocnemii.

3. Soleus and tendon of Achilles.

4. Peroneus longus lateralis. (c.)

5. Peroneus brevis lateralis. (d.)

6, 6'. Long common extensor of the toes and its tendons.

7. Peroneus anticus. (e.)

8. Pediosus. (f)

9. Adductor minimi digitis. (g.)

10. Annular ligament of the tarsus.

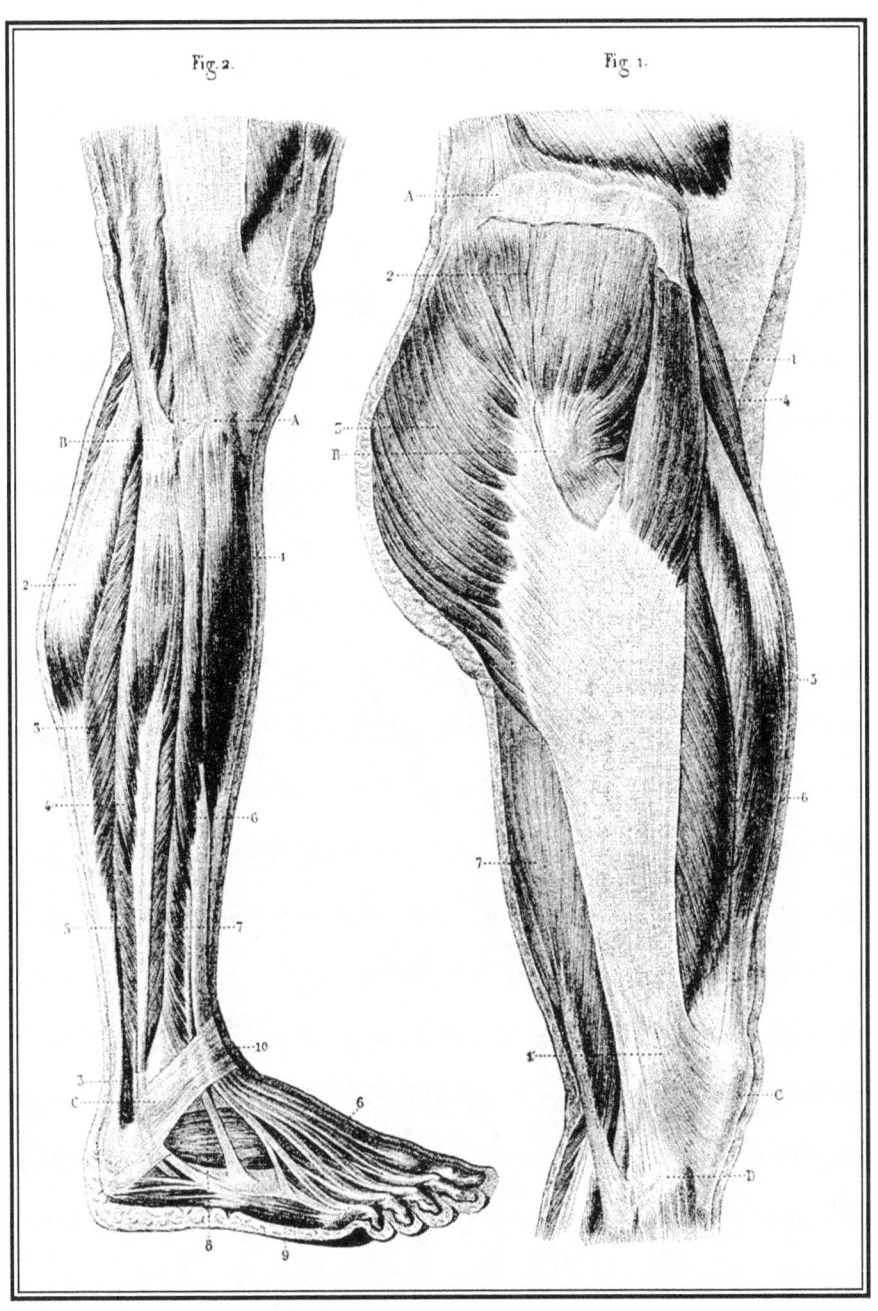

LOWER LIMB[45]

---

45 Ibid.

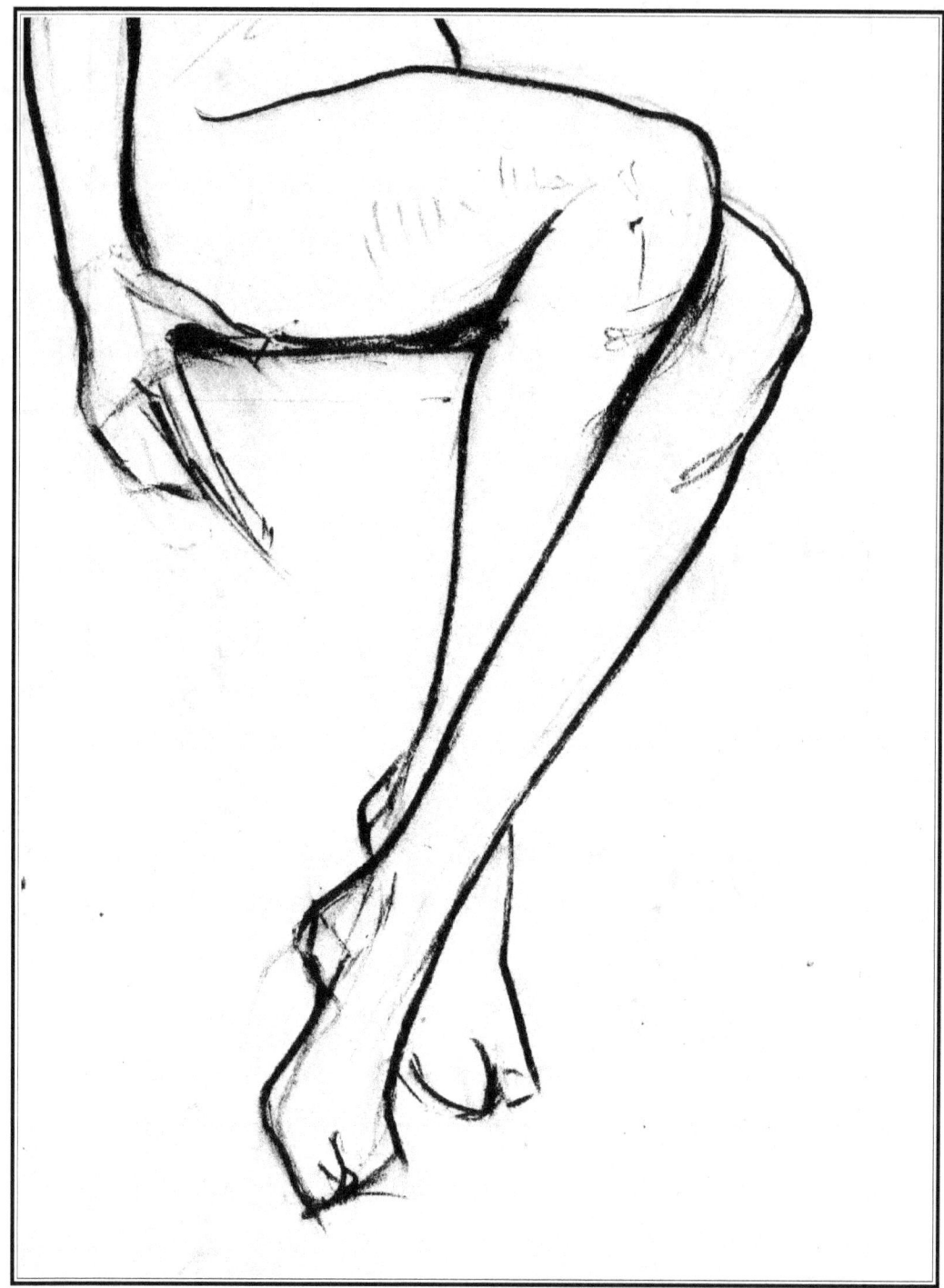

Grace Young

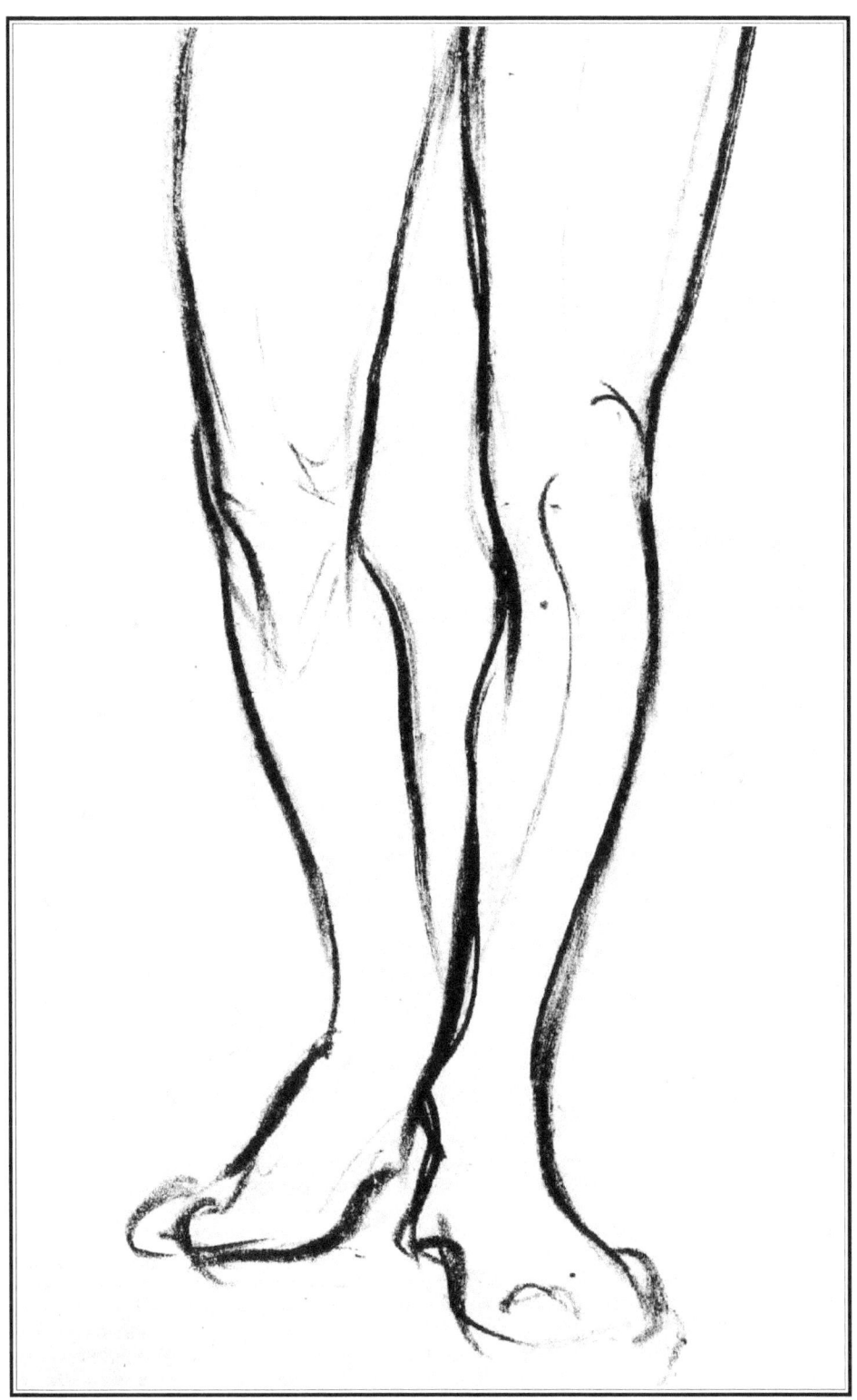

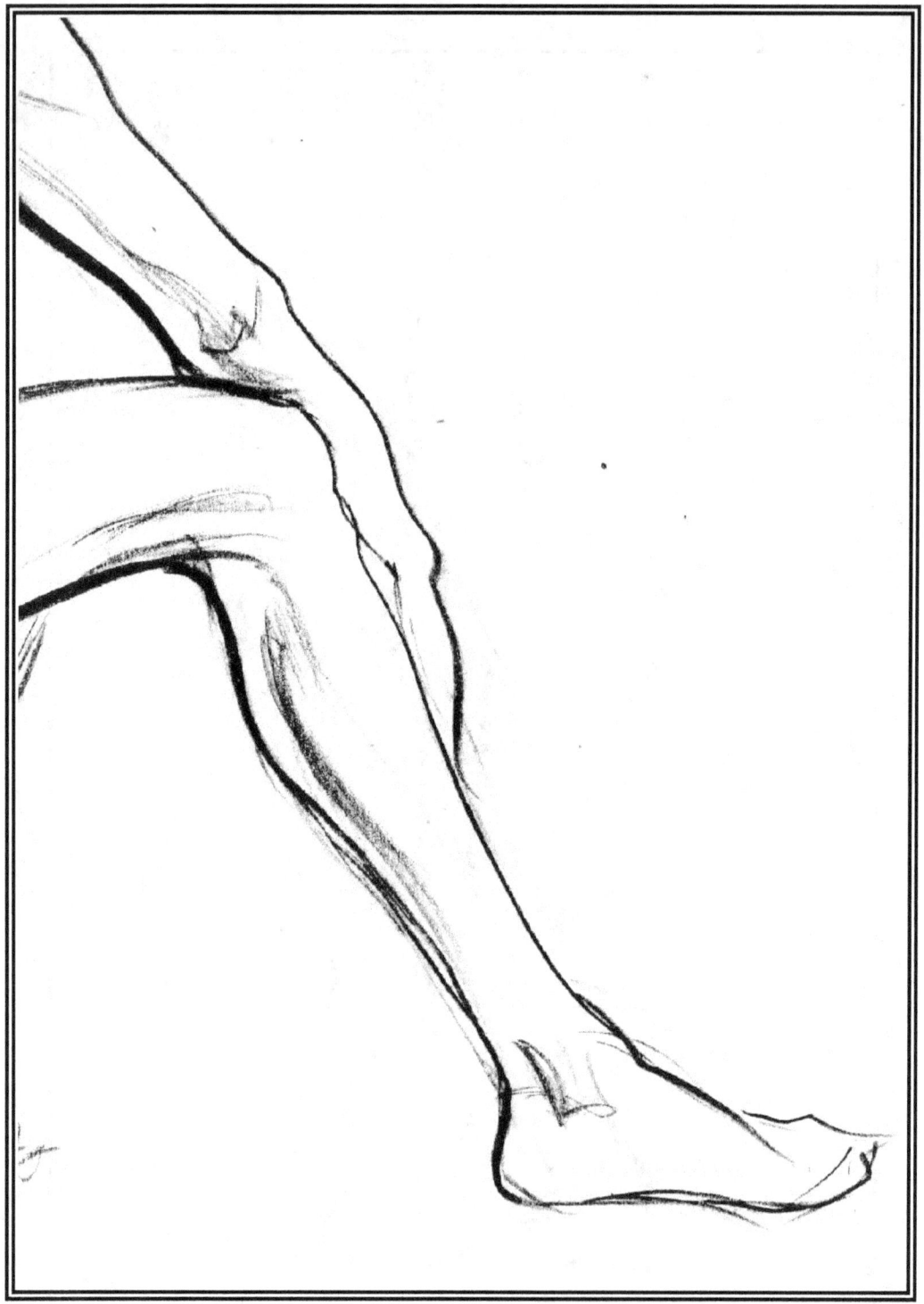

Grace Young

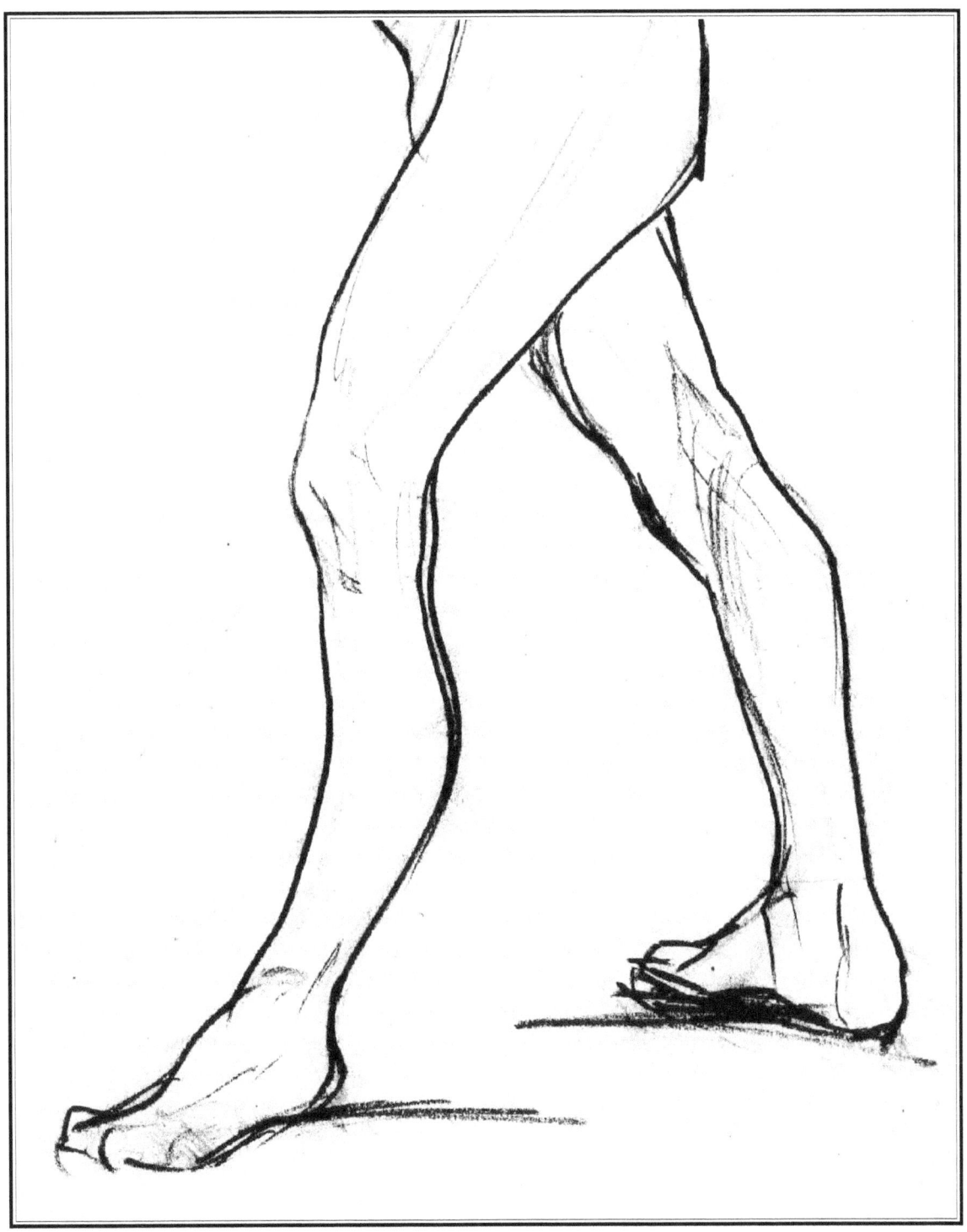

DRAWING THE BODY

TRUNK

Front View

A. Lower jaw.
B. Clavicle.
C. Sternum.
D. Anterior and superior iliac spine.
E. Pubis.
1. Latissimus colli. (a.)
2. Digastric.
3. Sterno-cleido mastoid.
4. Sterno-hyoid.
5. Omo-hyoid.
6. Trapezius.
7. Deltoid.
8. Great pectoral. (b.)
9. Serratus magnus.
10. Latissmus dorsi.
11. Great obliquemuscle.
12. Rectus abdominis. (c.)
13. Pyramidalis. (d.)
14. Tensor of the fascia lata.
15. Sartorius. The corresponding muscle is covered by the aponeurosis. 15.
16. Pectineus.
17. Testicular cord.

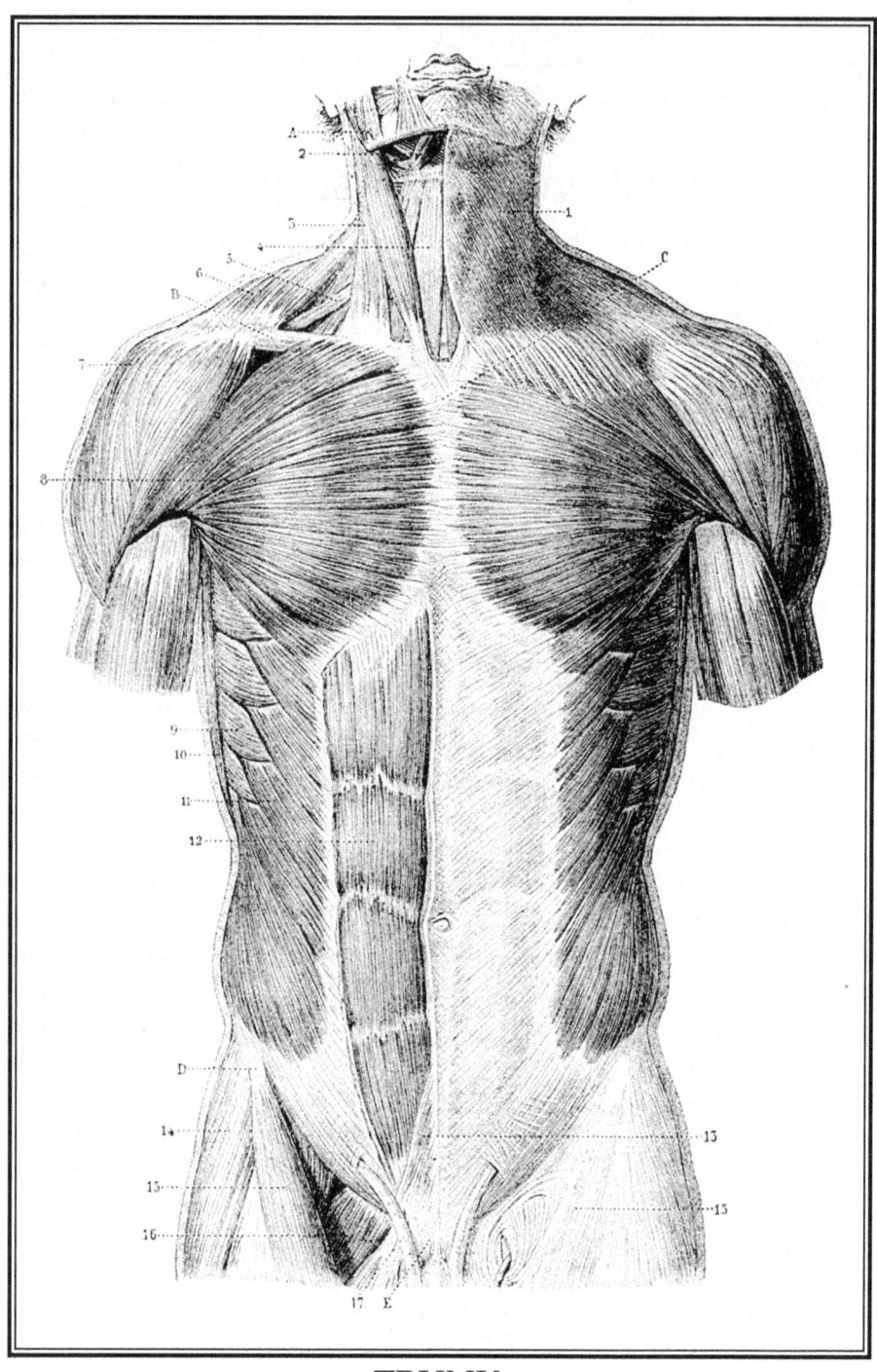

TRUNK
Front View[46]

46 Anatomy in Art, Jonathon Scott Hartley, New York, 1891

TRUNK.

Side view.

A. Clavicle.

B. Crest of the ilium.

C. Great trochanter.

1. Lower extremity of the Sternocleido mastoid.

2. Lower extremity of the trapezius.

3. Deltoid.

4. Pectoralis major.

5. Serratus magnus. (a.)

6. Rectus abdominis covered with the aponeurosis.

7. Great oblique. (b.)

8. Dorsalis magnus.

9. Gluteus maximus.

10. Gluteus medius.

11. Tensor of the fascia lata aponeurosis.

12. Sartorius.

13. Rectus femoris.

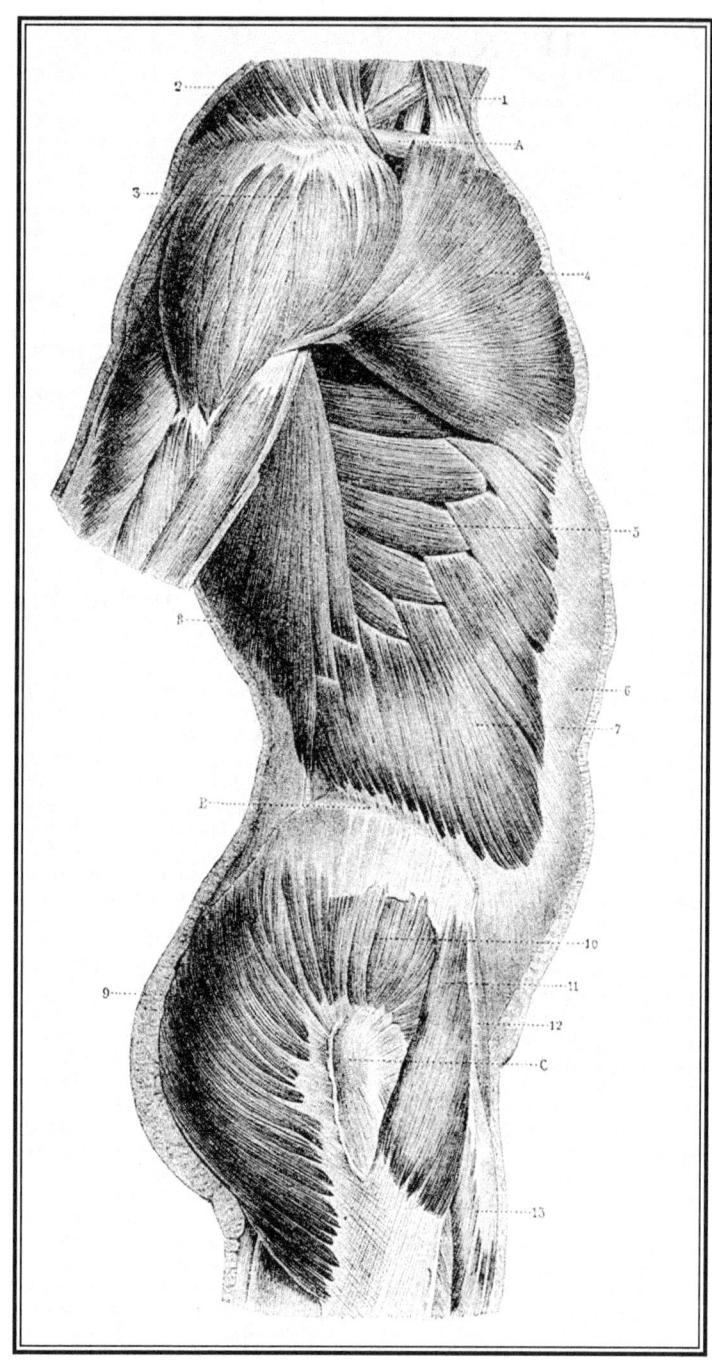

TRUNK
Side View

TRUNK.

Back view.

A. Seventh cervical vertebra.

B. Spine of the scapula.

C. Iliac bone.

D. Great trochanter.

1. Occipital.

2. Sterno-cleido mastoideus.

3. Splenius.

4. Trapezius. (a.)

5. Deltoid.

6. Triceps.

7. Iufra spinatus. (b.)

8. Teres minor. (c.)

9. Teres major. (a'.)

10. Rhomboid. (e.)

11. Latissimus dorsi. (f.)

12. Fleshy sacro-lumbar masses, composed of the muscles called sacro-lumbar, longissimus dorsi, and transverse spinous. (g.)

13. Great oblique.

14. Gluteus maximus.

15. Gluteus medius.

16. Tensor of the aponeurosis.

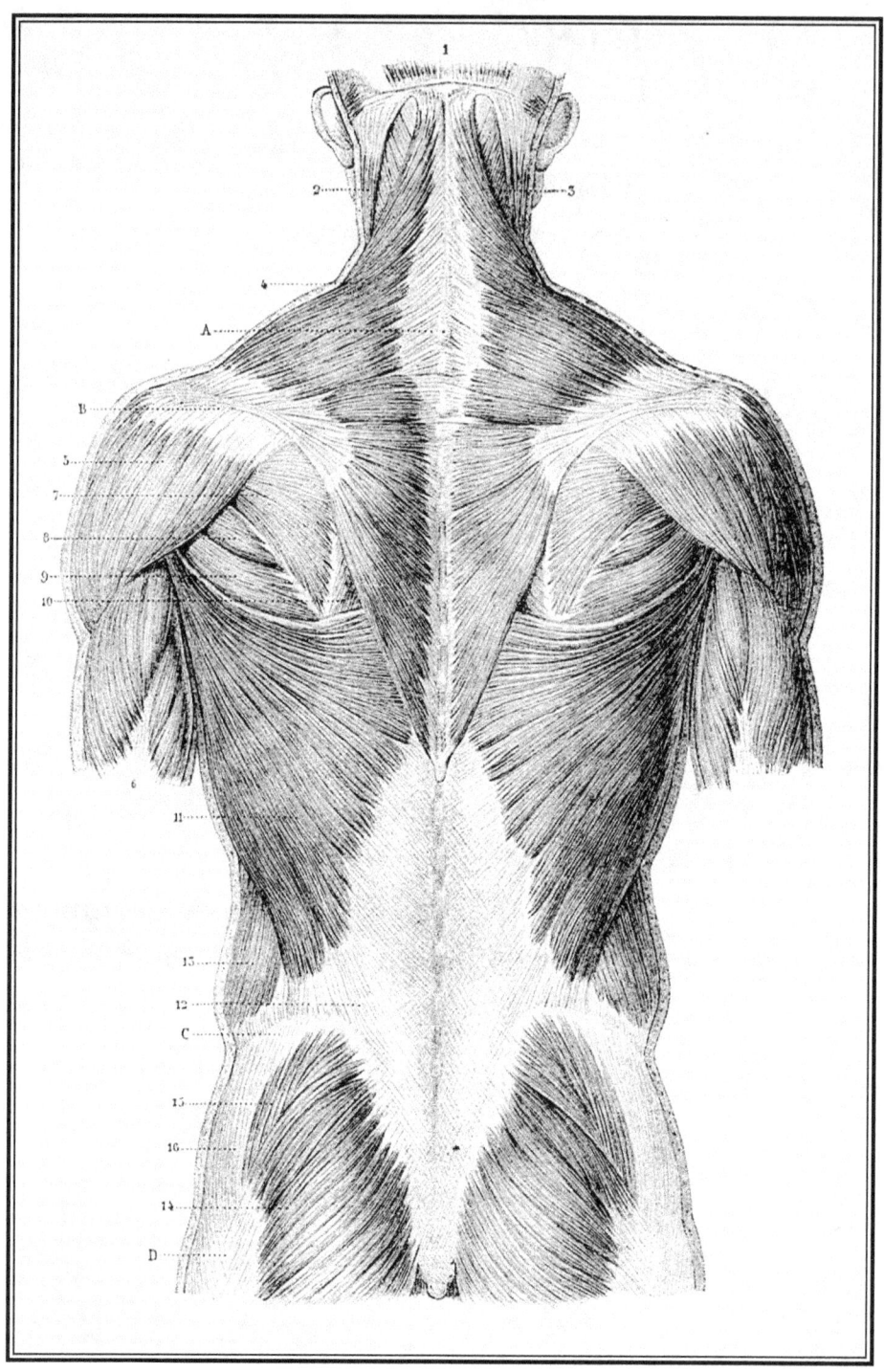

TRUNK.
Back view.

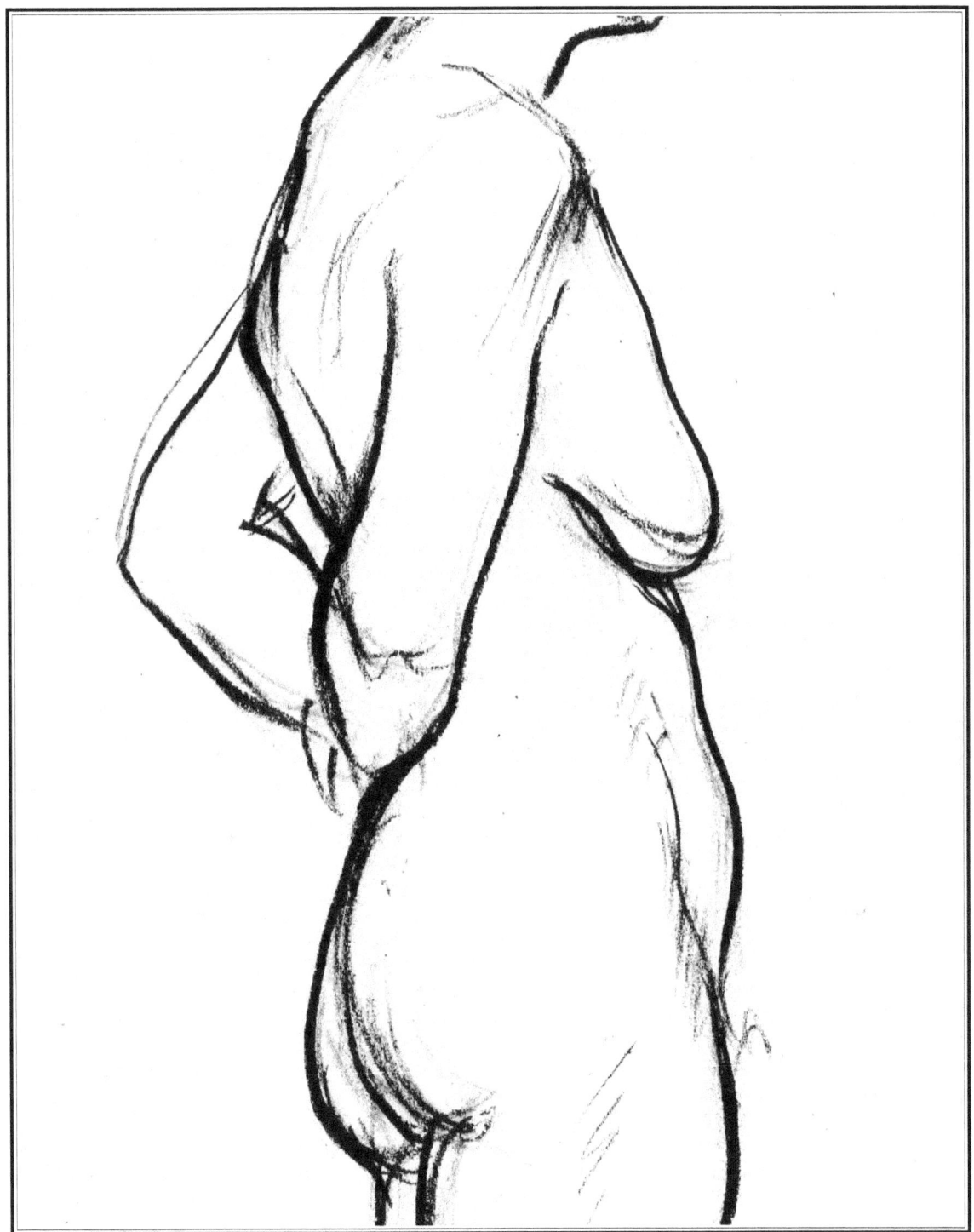

Grace Young

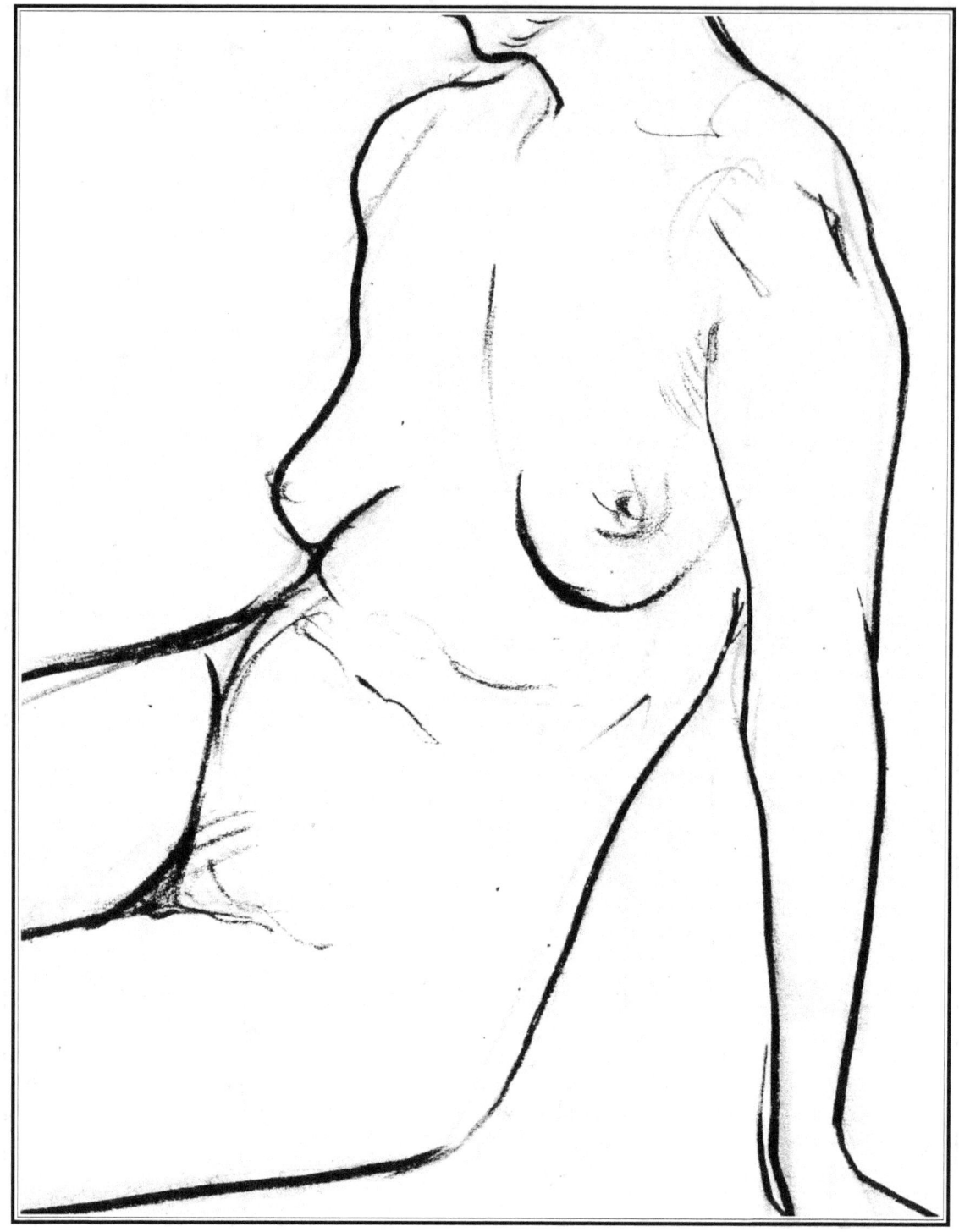

Grace Young

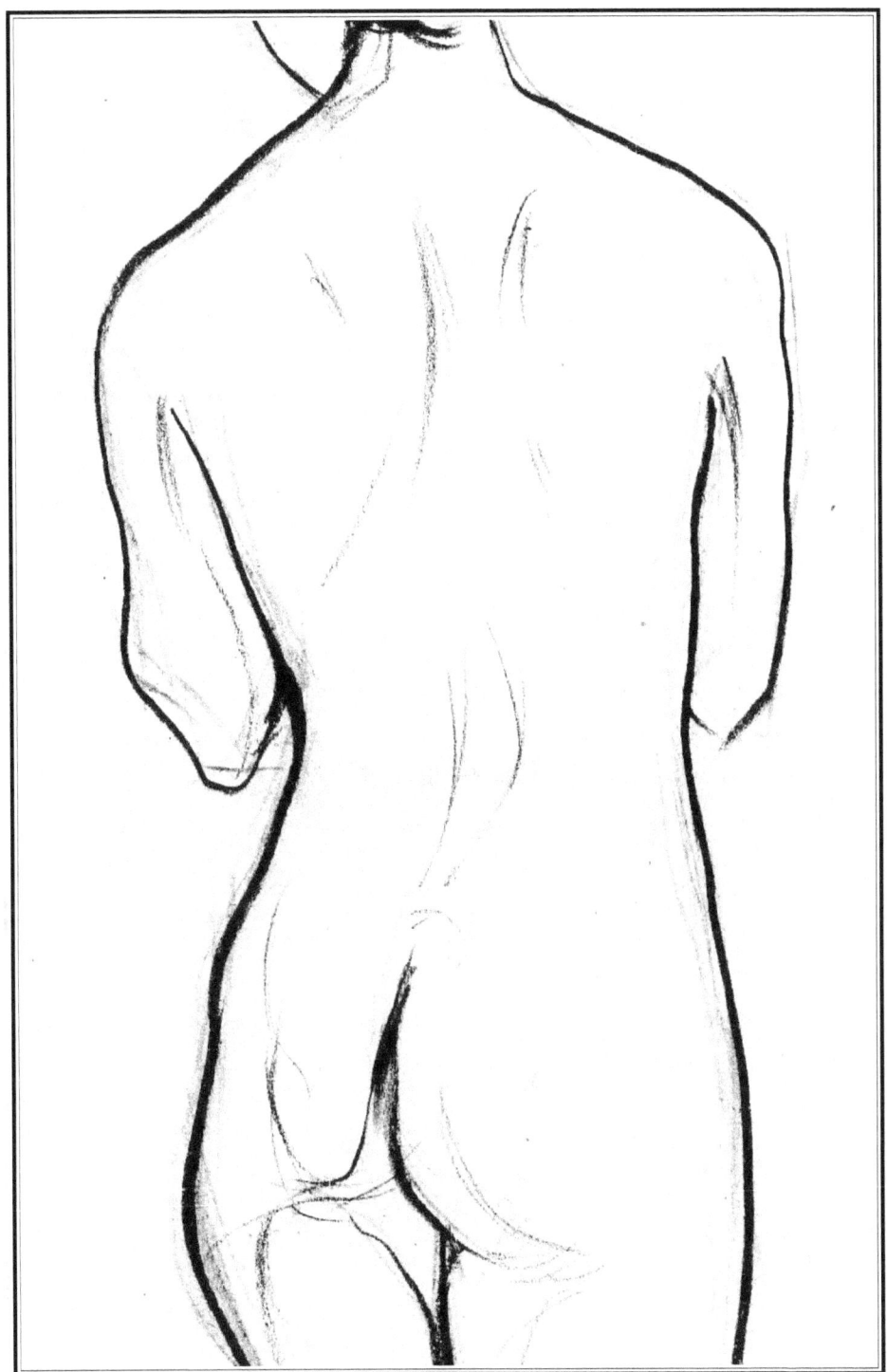

Grace Young

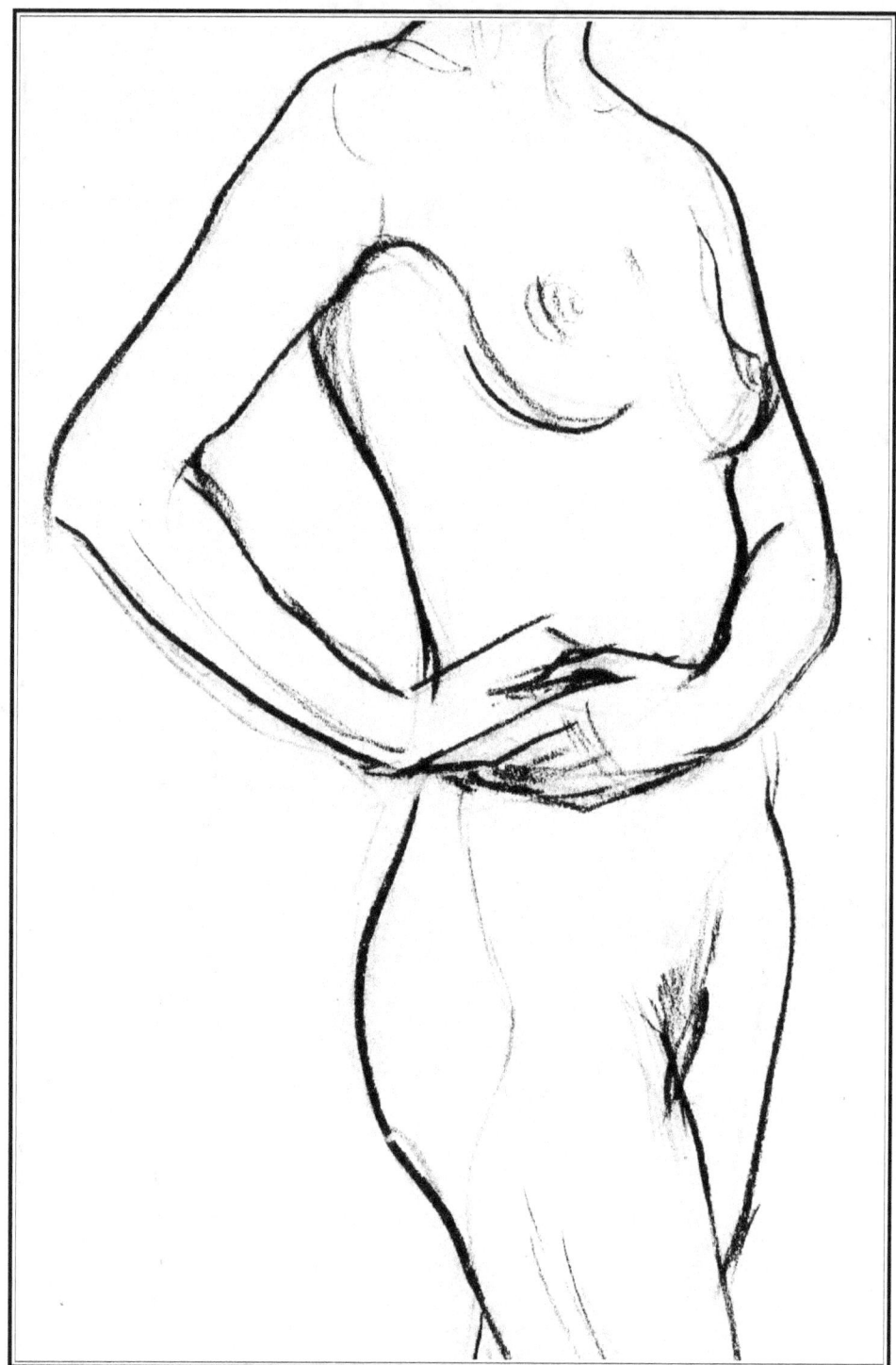

Grace Young

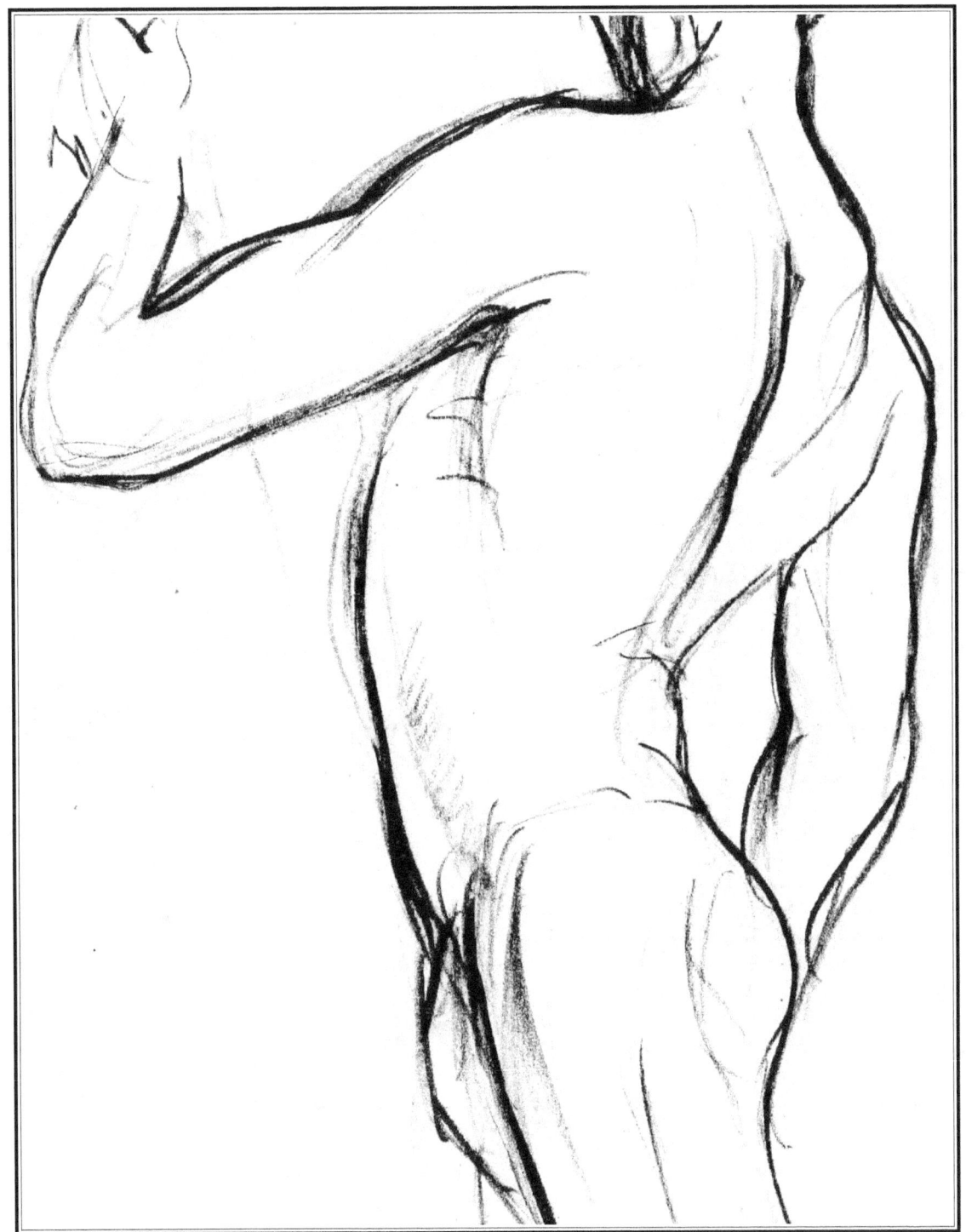

Grace Young

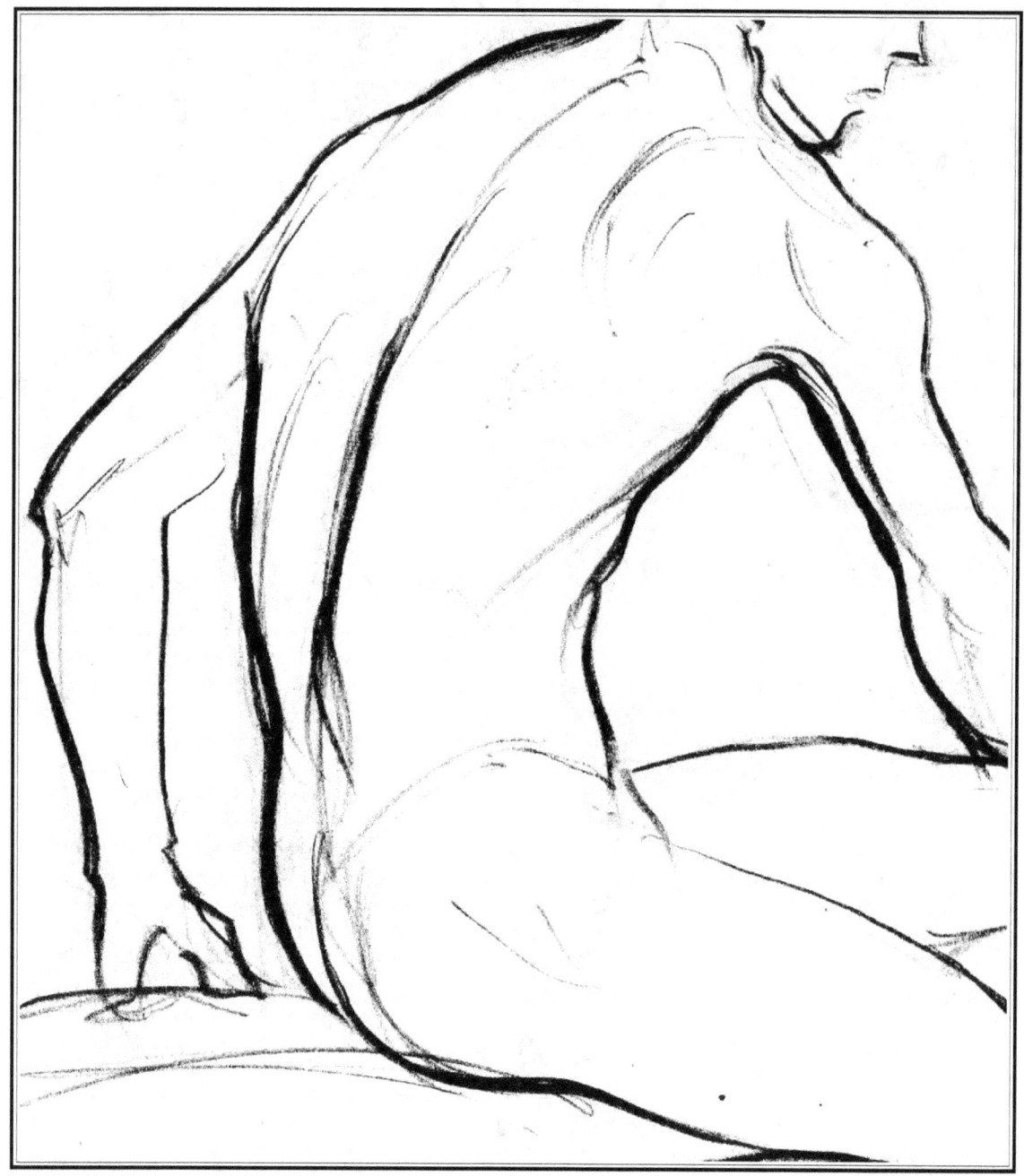

Grace Young

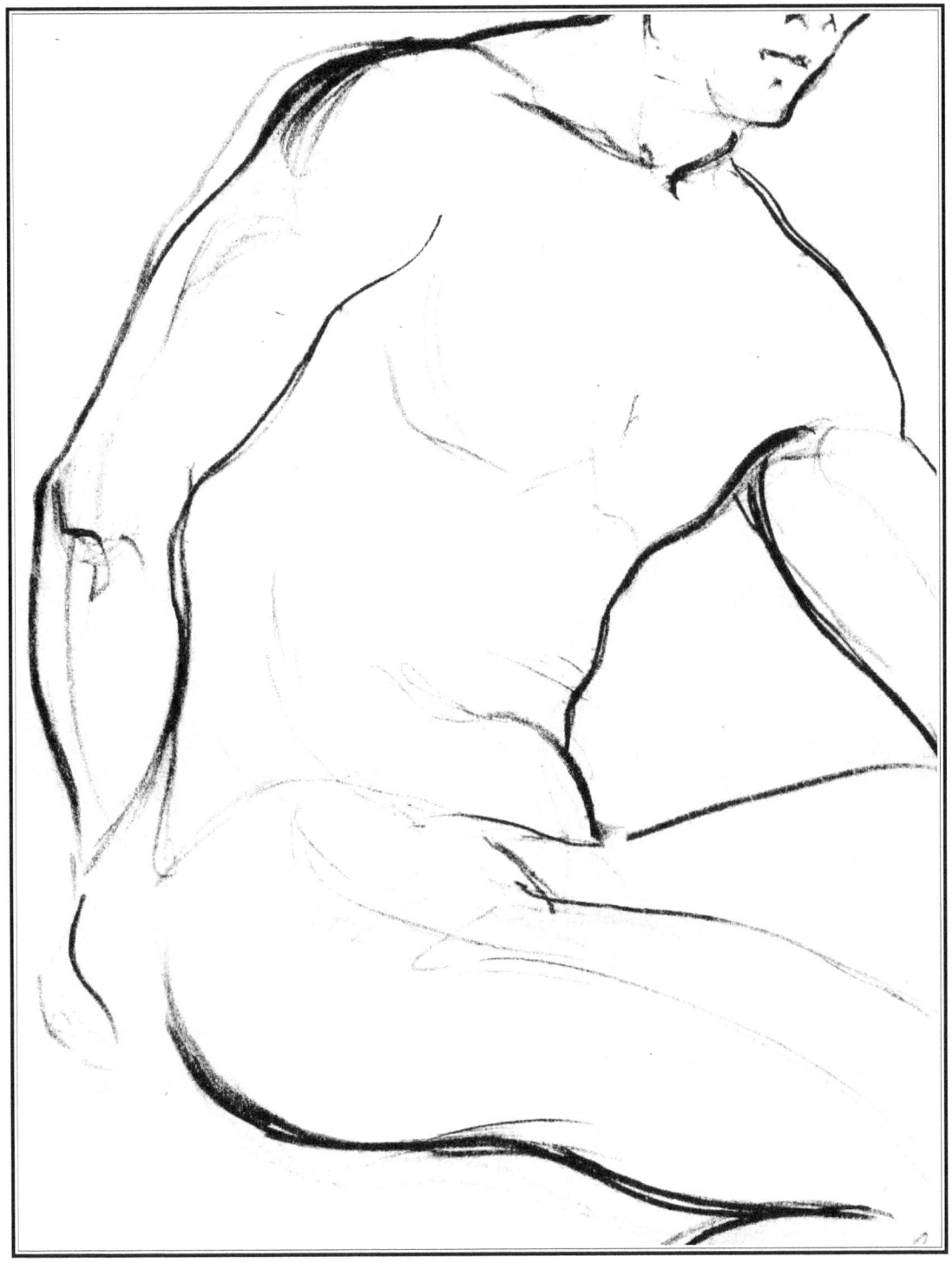

Grace Young

.

DRAWING THE HUMAN FIGURE USING AN OUTLINE

In 1916 Adolphe Armand Braun published a book called the *Hieroglyphic or Greek Method of Life Drawing* which was an argument for the use of the live model, the observation of the model in movement or action, an understanding of anatomy, and choosing a pose relevant to the subject intended.

There is no evidence that Grace Young was familiar with the work but it did go into several editions and captured the spirit of the times and describes the course of education that most students encountered.

Here is what Braun says about the art master's dilemma, "...Once a student can draw satisfoctorily from the cast he is allowed to draw from the living modeland the same routine continues for years, for the systems of tuition are similar and progress is slow. It is only the fun of it all that remains ever fresh. Of late certain schools have adopter the method of quick memory sketches from life, alternating with work which requires time and patience, but the practice of imparting knowledge is neither general nor systemic enough..."

"...reverting to the subject of my book, it is my contention that Life Drawing should rank with experimental studies in order to be profitable, studies such as Chemistry, Botany, etc. Before attempting Life Drawing the student ought to possess a thorough knowledge of the construction and proportions of the human body and be equipped to see more in the model before him than a still mass of flesh and to achieve something more then a mere representation of a shape possessing threee dimensions in a diagram of two."

"In order to understand the construction of the human body it will be useful to proceed from the fact that only a few number of bones and muscles
influence the outward form. As a rule , the study of anatomy is derived from skeletons, casts, plates, often demonstrated on living subjects and sometimes on the dissected body. Without despising any of these aids, let us for our immediate advancement utilize the nearest means at our disposal, namely ourselveses. Your own body...and a hand-mirror will form the simple apparatus upon which to base the study."

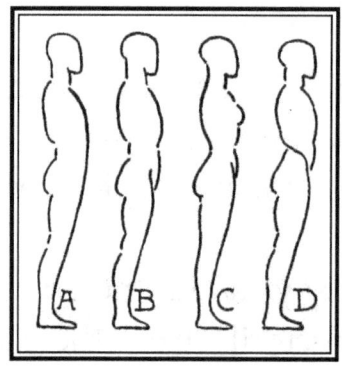

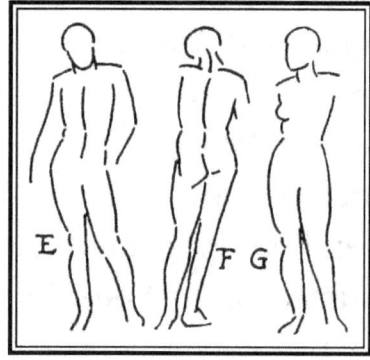

SIMPLEST FORM OF THE FIGURE[47]

---

47 Practical Drawing, E. G. Lutz, Philadelphia, 1915

Notice how Grace Young seeks the dominant line in her drawings, the front line, the back line, the line of the legs, the arch of the back, and the lines which indicate the distribution of weight. After the basic structure is worked out the details can be added without disturbing the proportion of the figure. The following illustrations are from Braun's book showing how a pose can be reduced to lines.

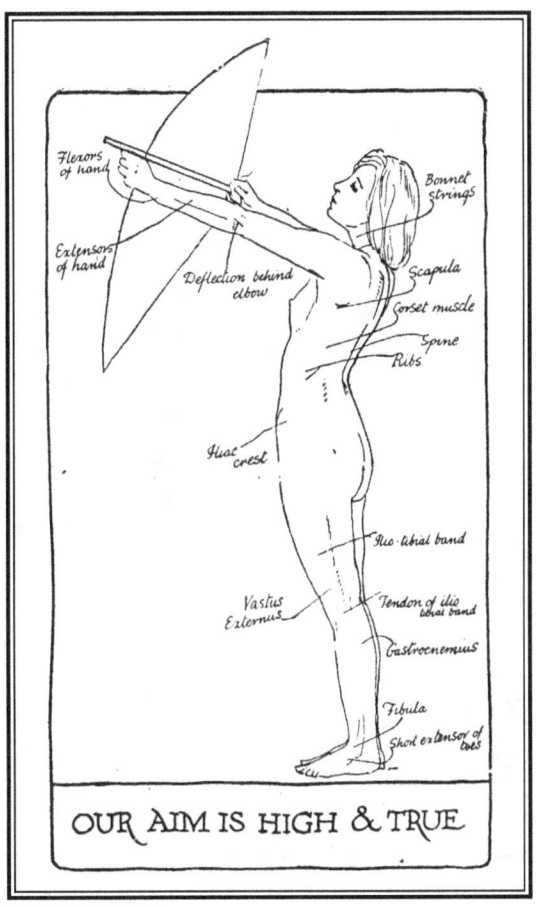

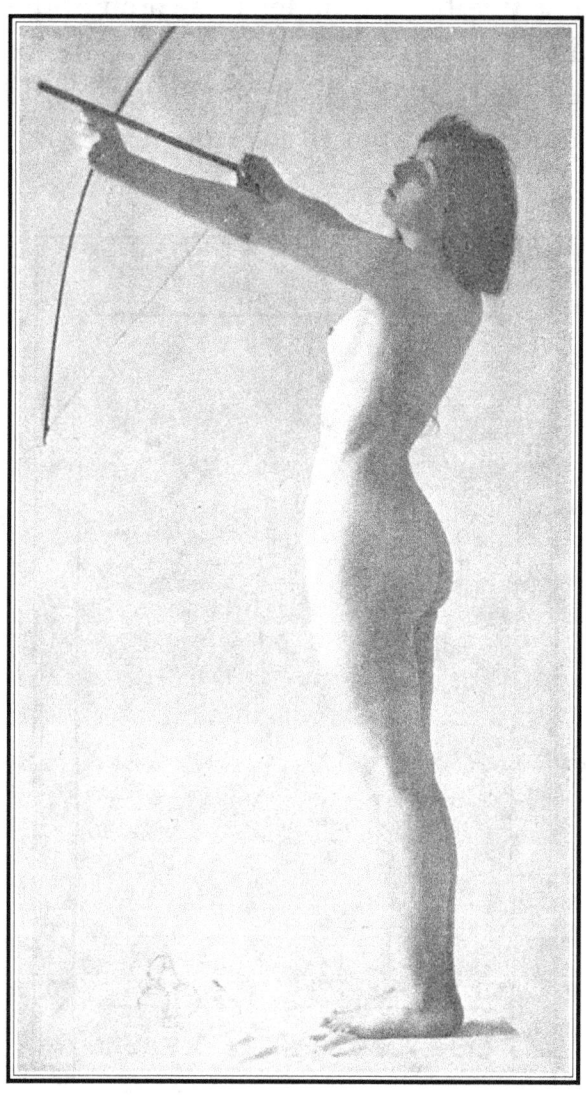

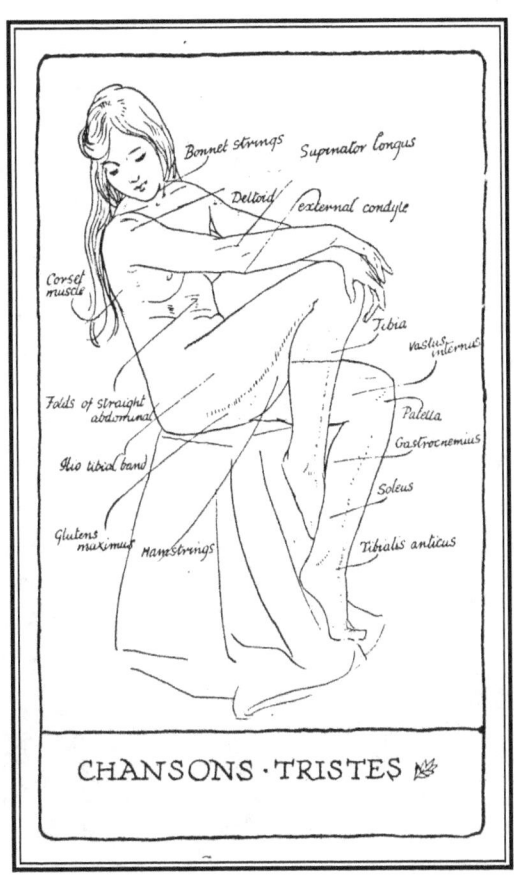

CHANSONS · TRISTES

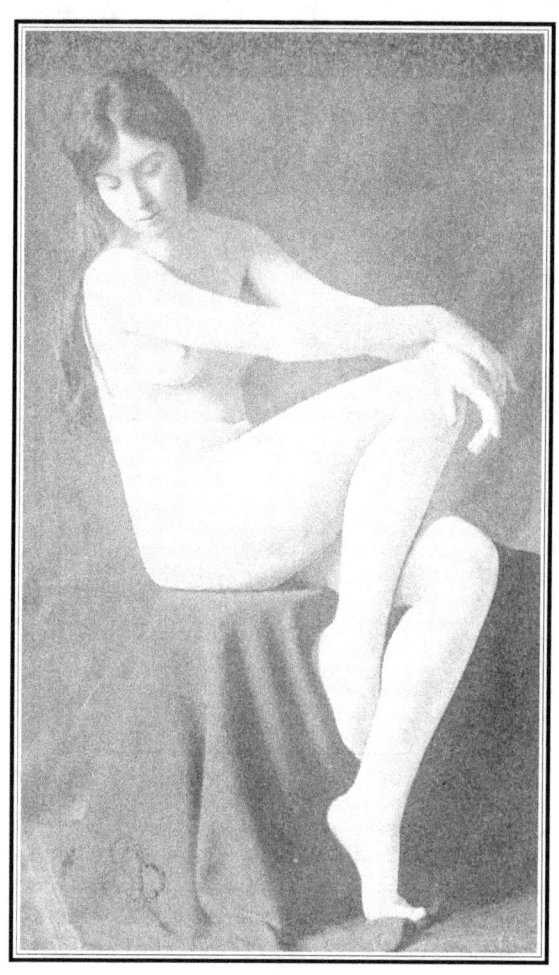

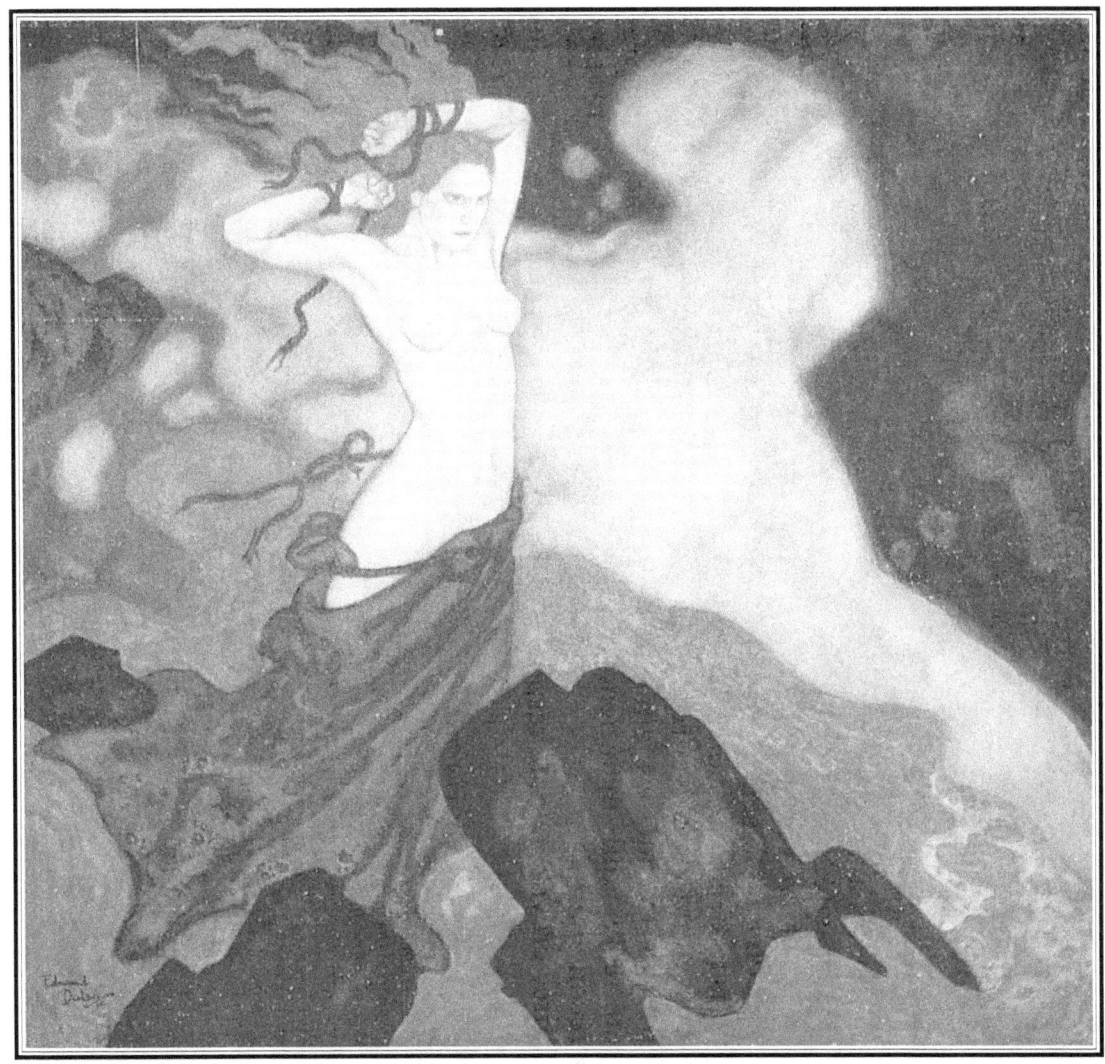

EDMUND DULAC'S CONTRIBUTION TO KING ALBERT'S BOOK[48]

This image is Edmund Dulac's contribution to ***King Albert's Book*** which was sold for the benefit of the Daily Telegraph's Belgian Fund at the beginning of World War I. Notice that Dulac achieves the form largely through the use of outline using his immense drafting technique to produce a powerful image.

---

48 King Albert's Book, London, 1914

DRAWING ACTION FIGURES

The following pages show a series of photographs from Yerbury and Ellwood[49] compared with similar memory action drawings by Grace Young.

---

49 Studies of the Human Figure, G. M. Ellwood and F. R. Yerbury, London 1918 and The Human Form and Its Use in Art, 1924

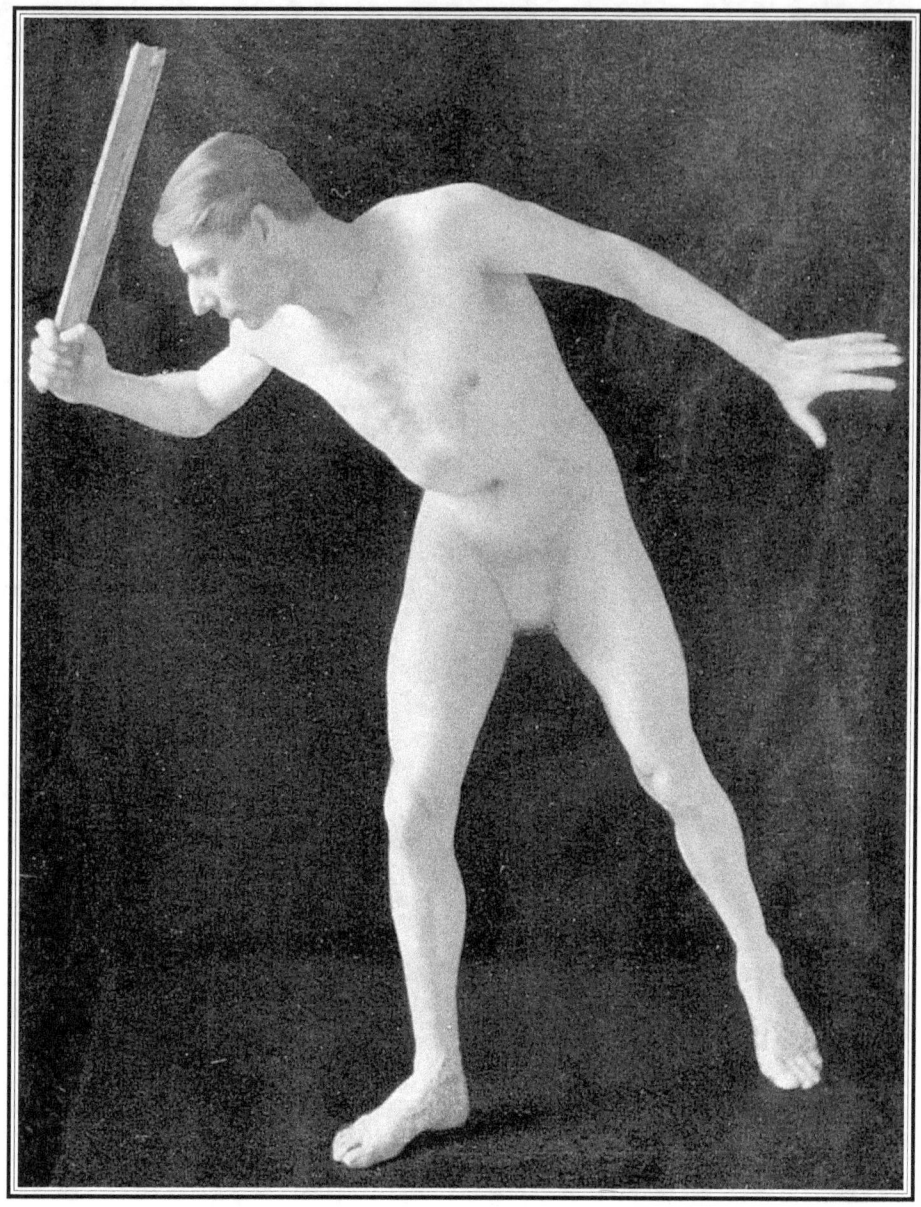

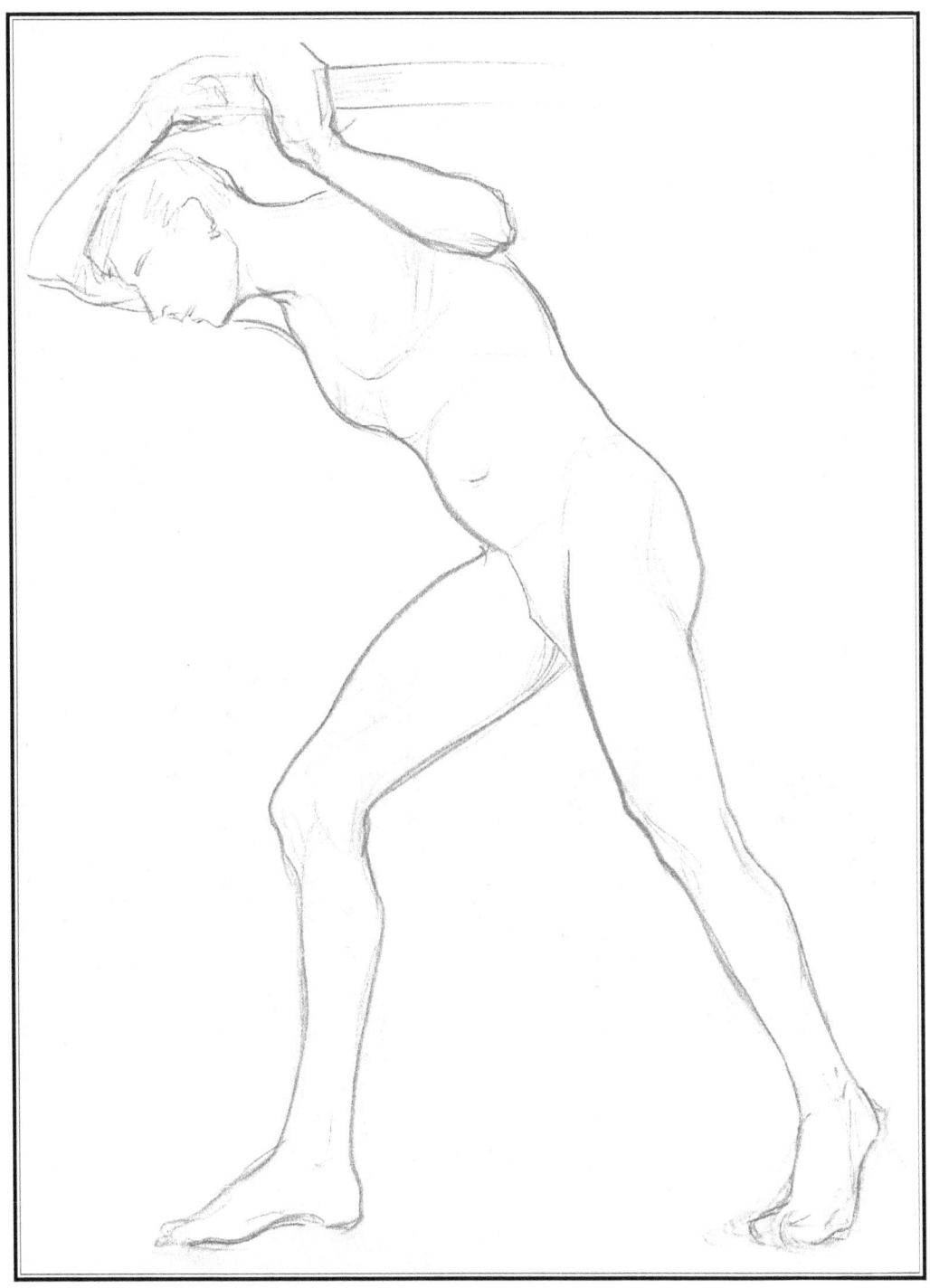

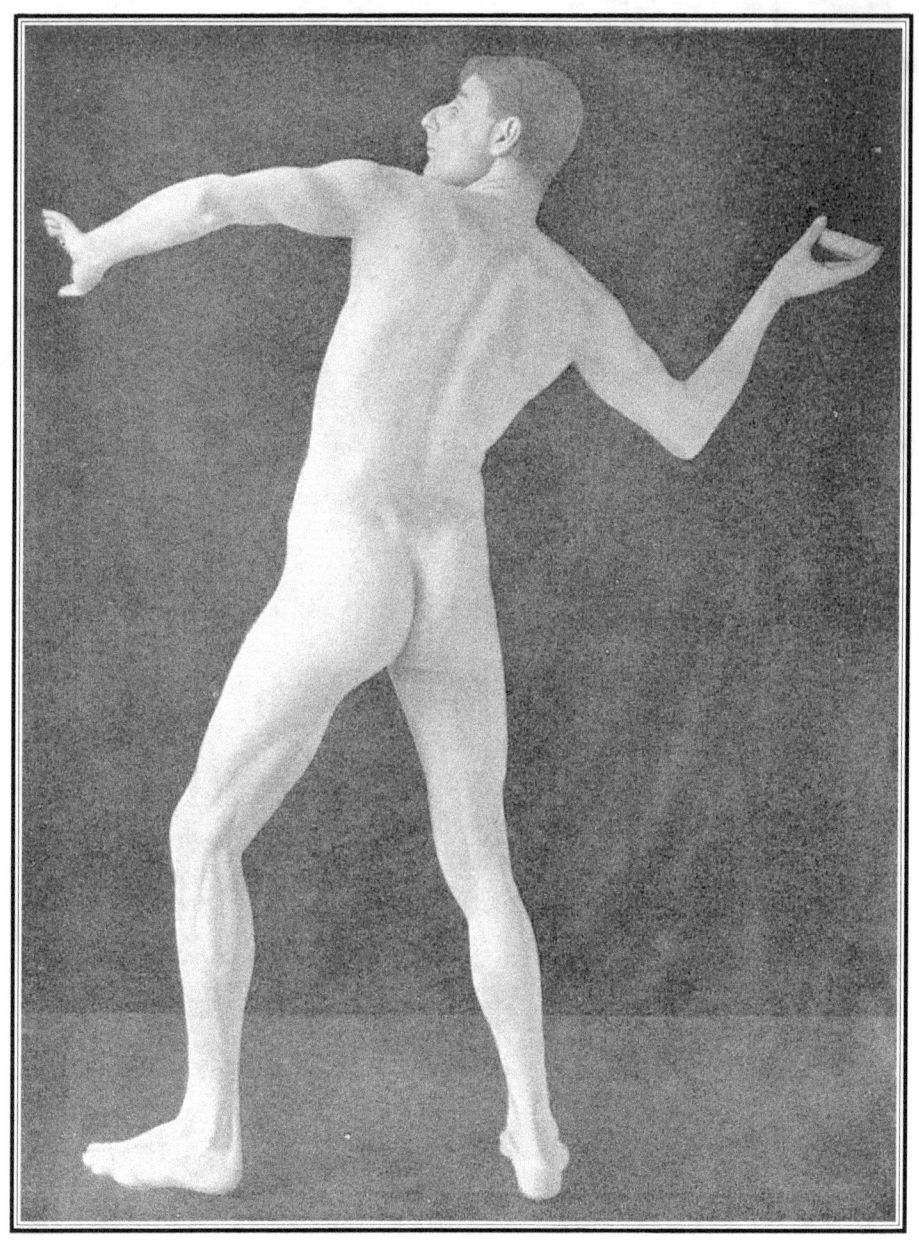

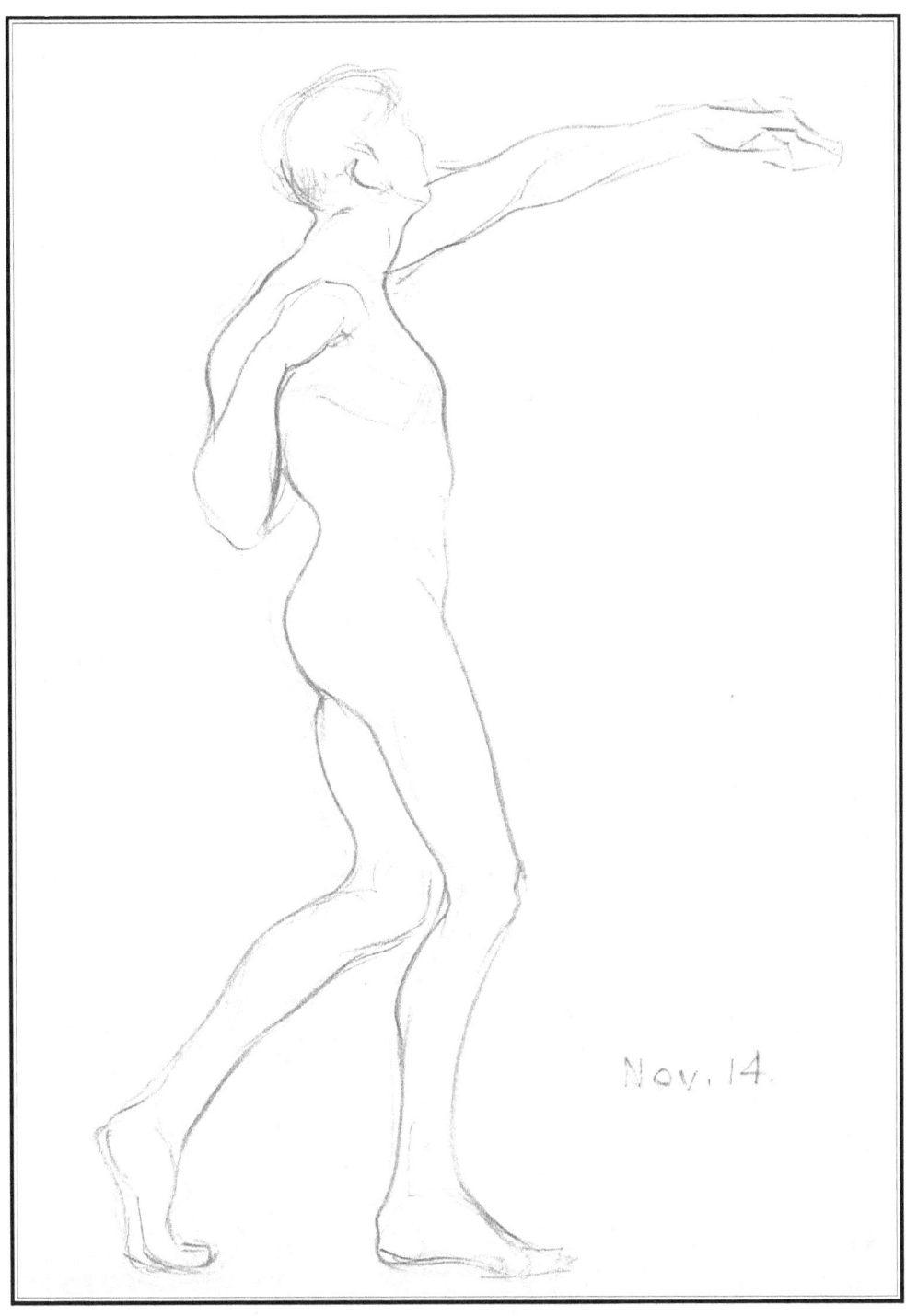

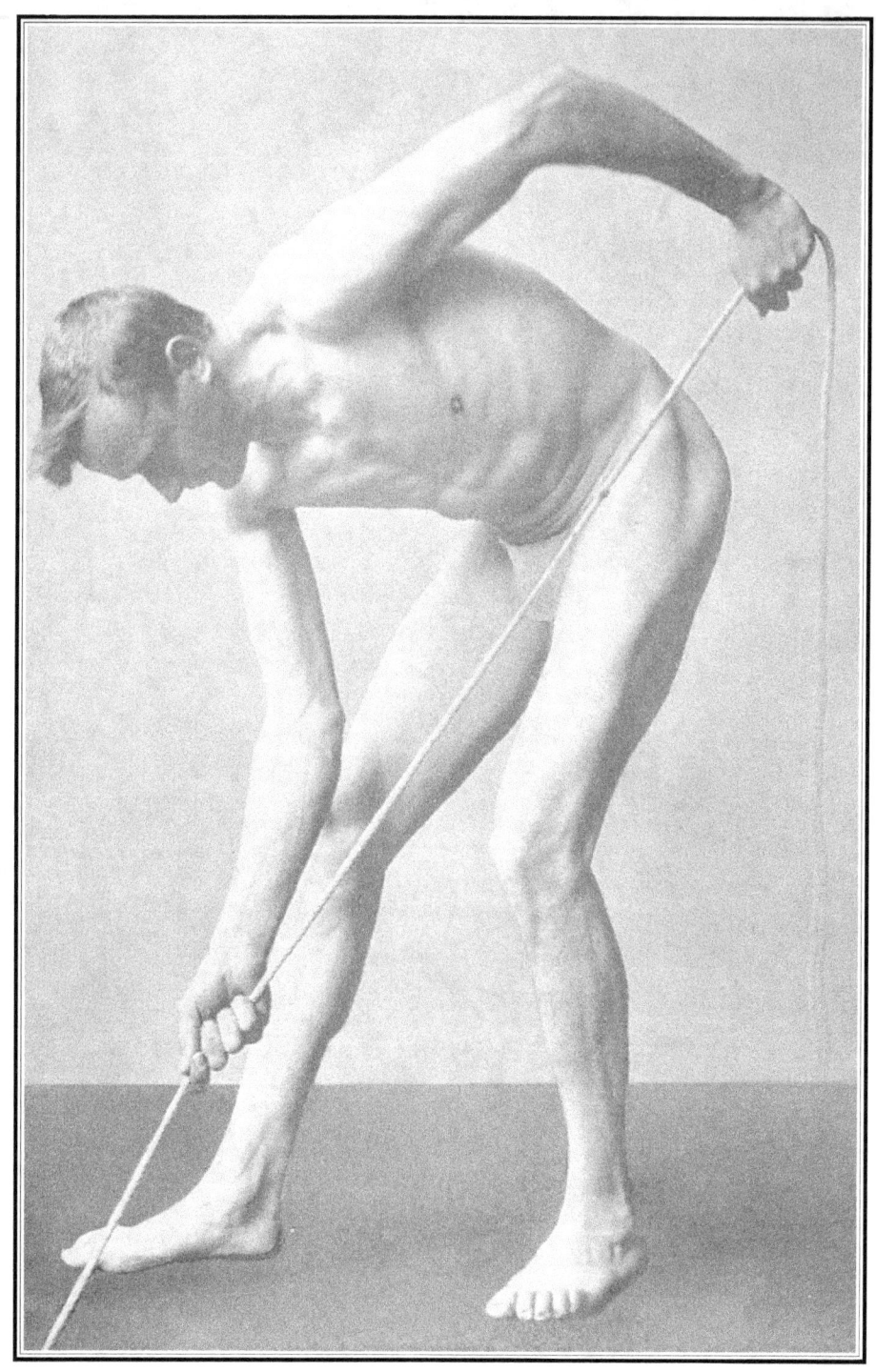

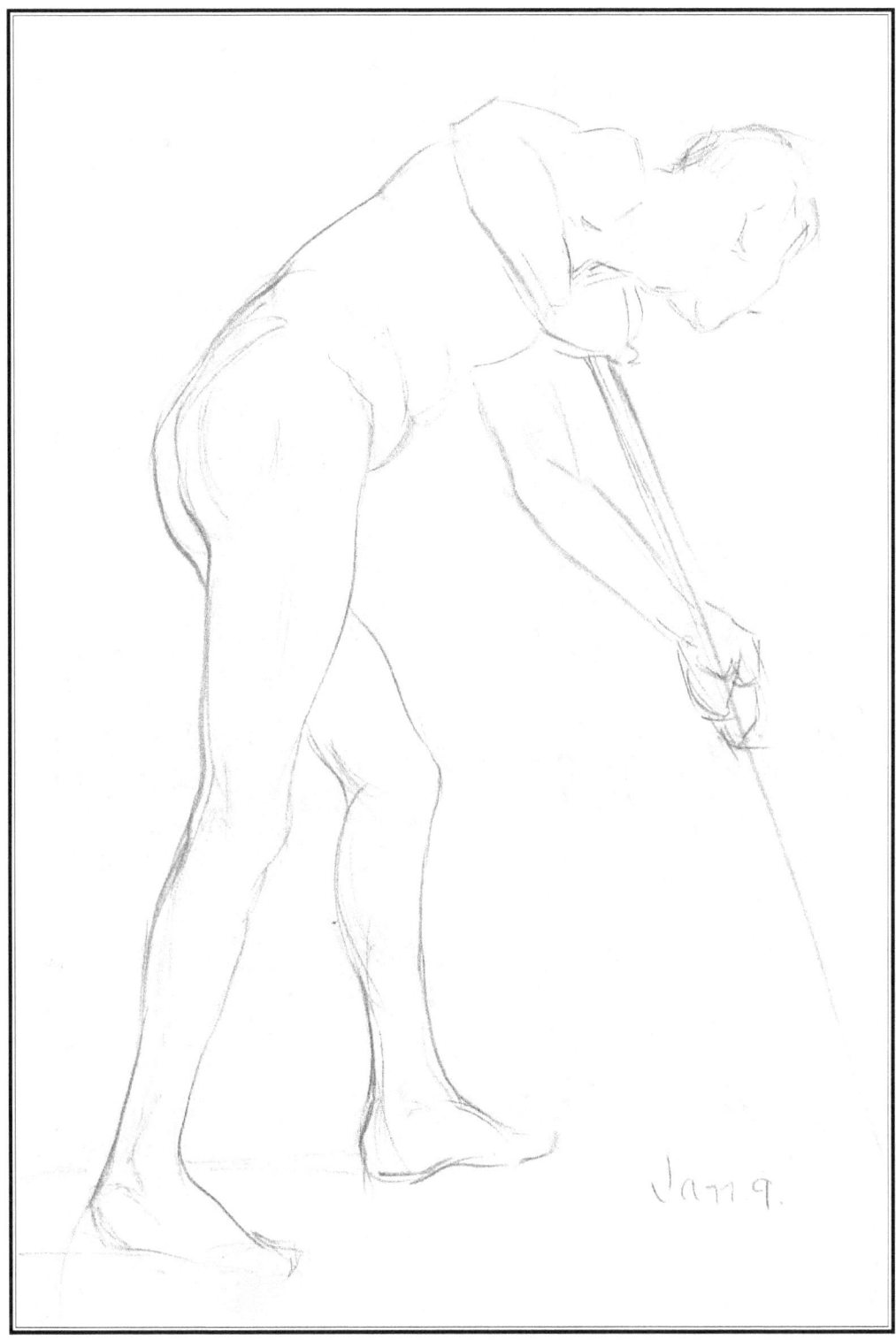

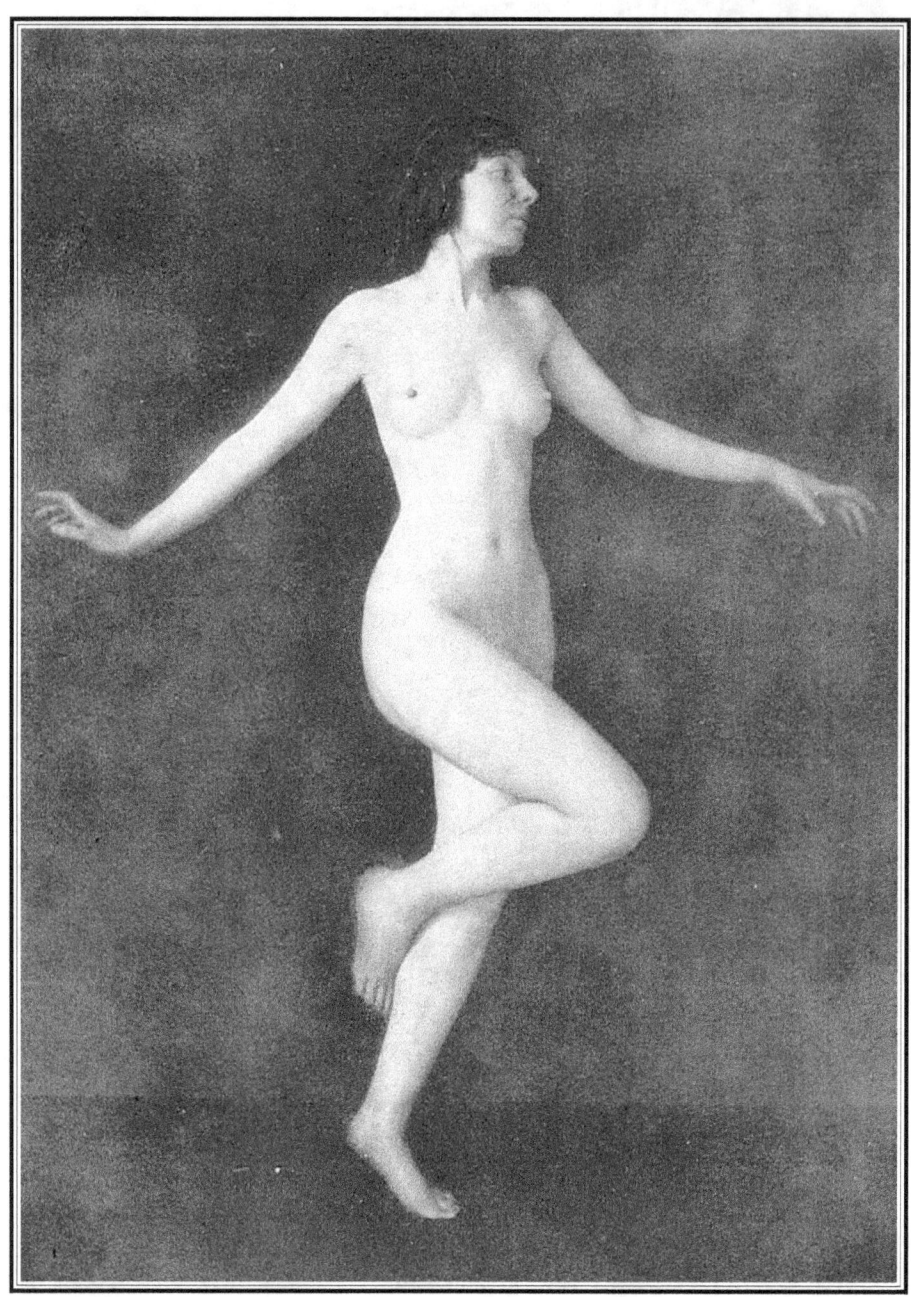

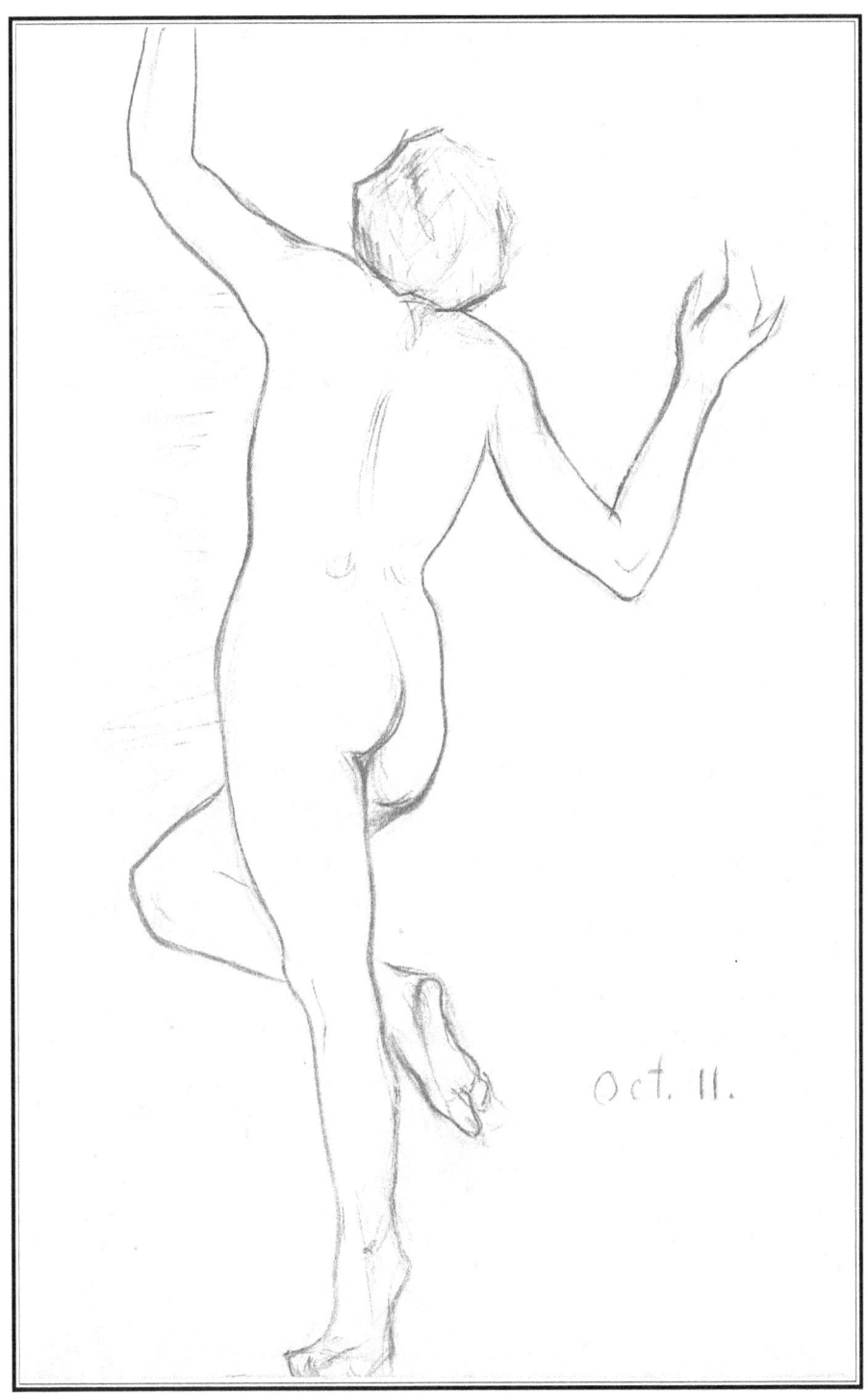

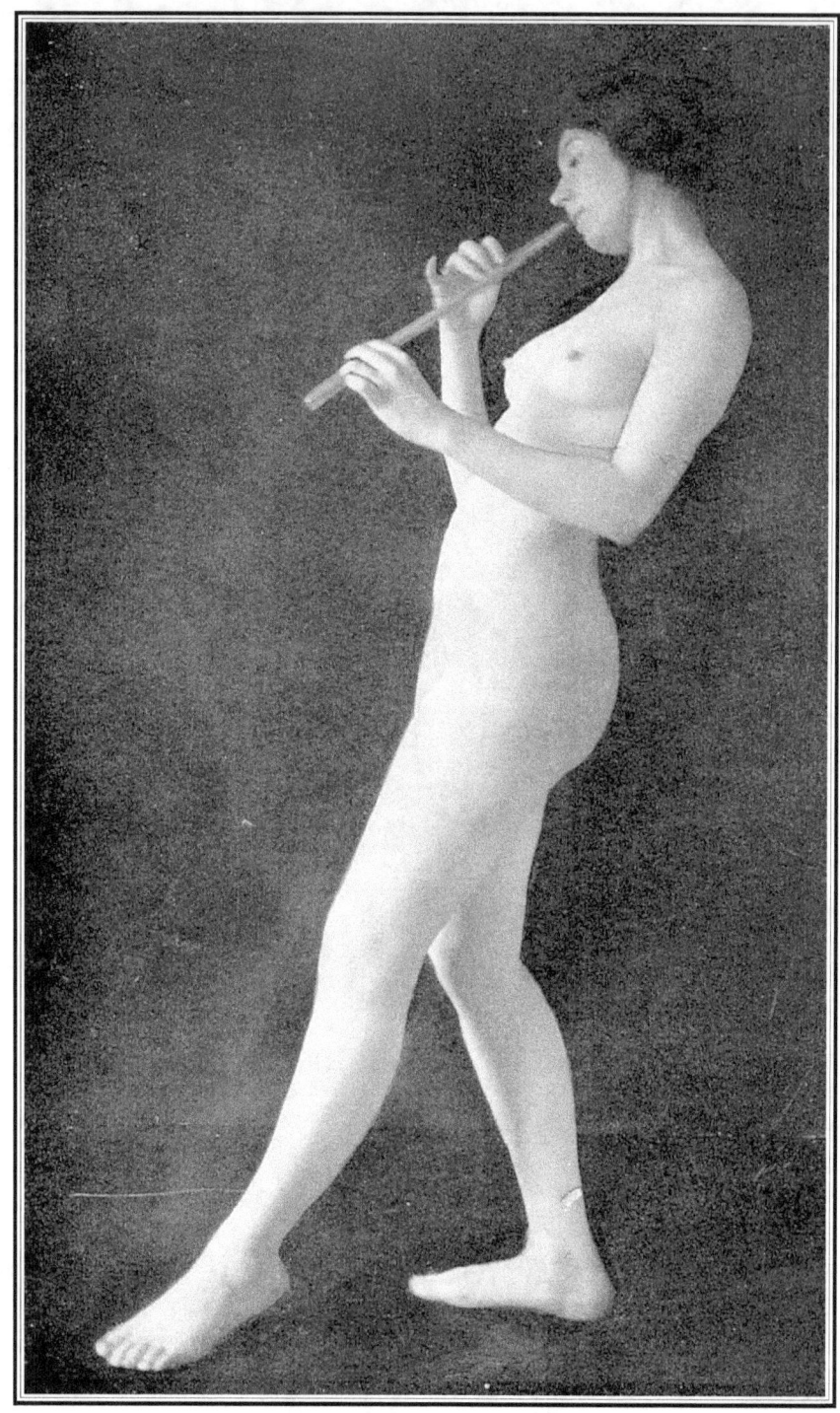

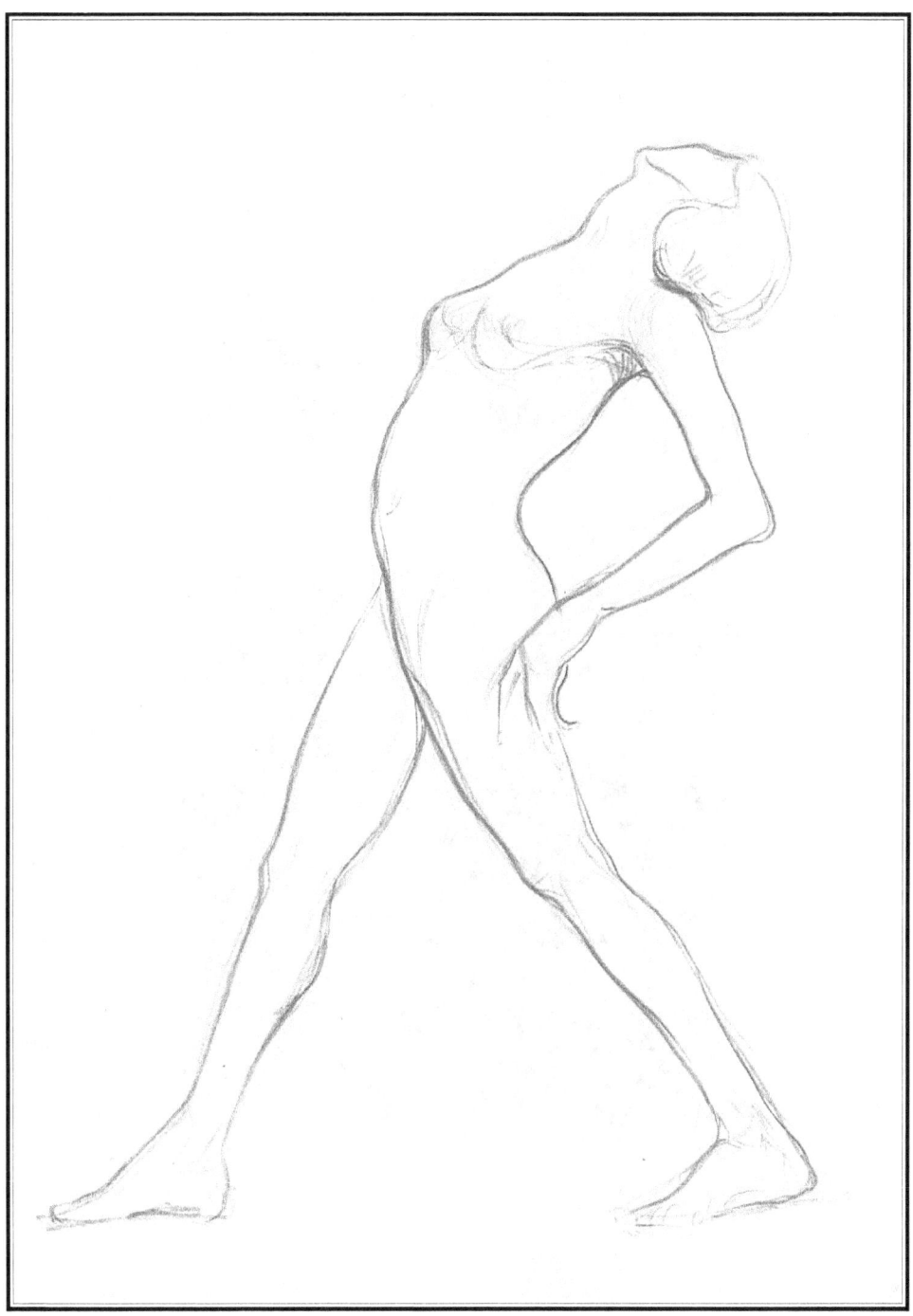

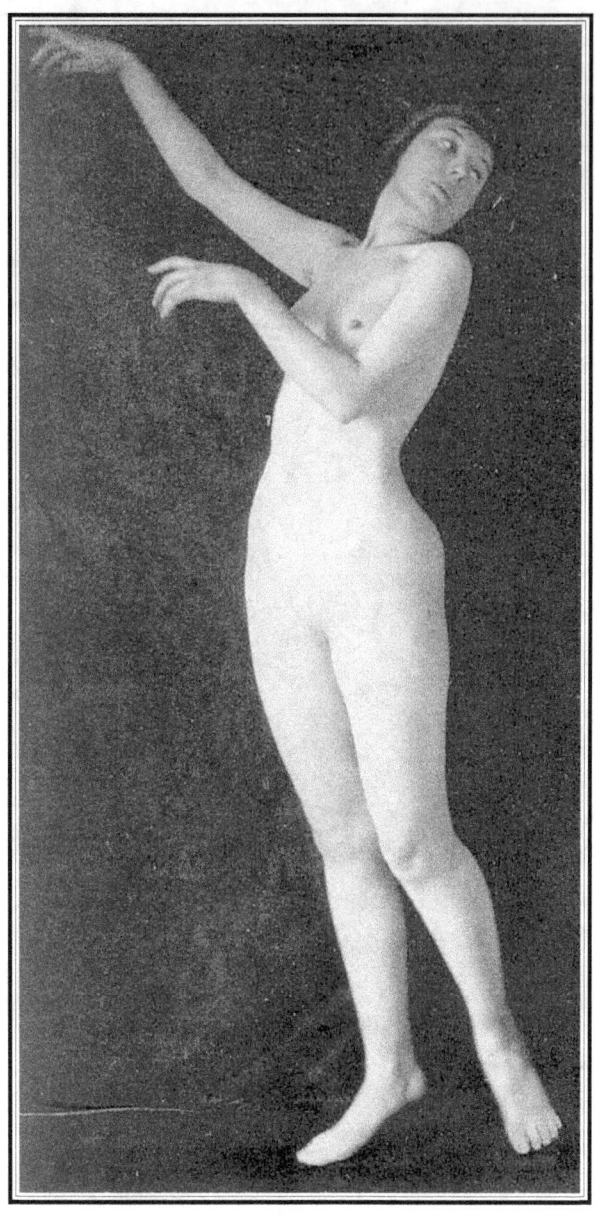

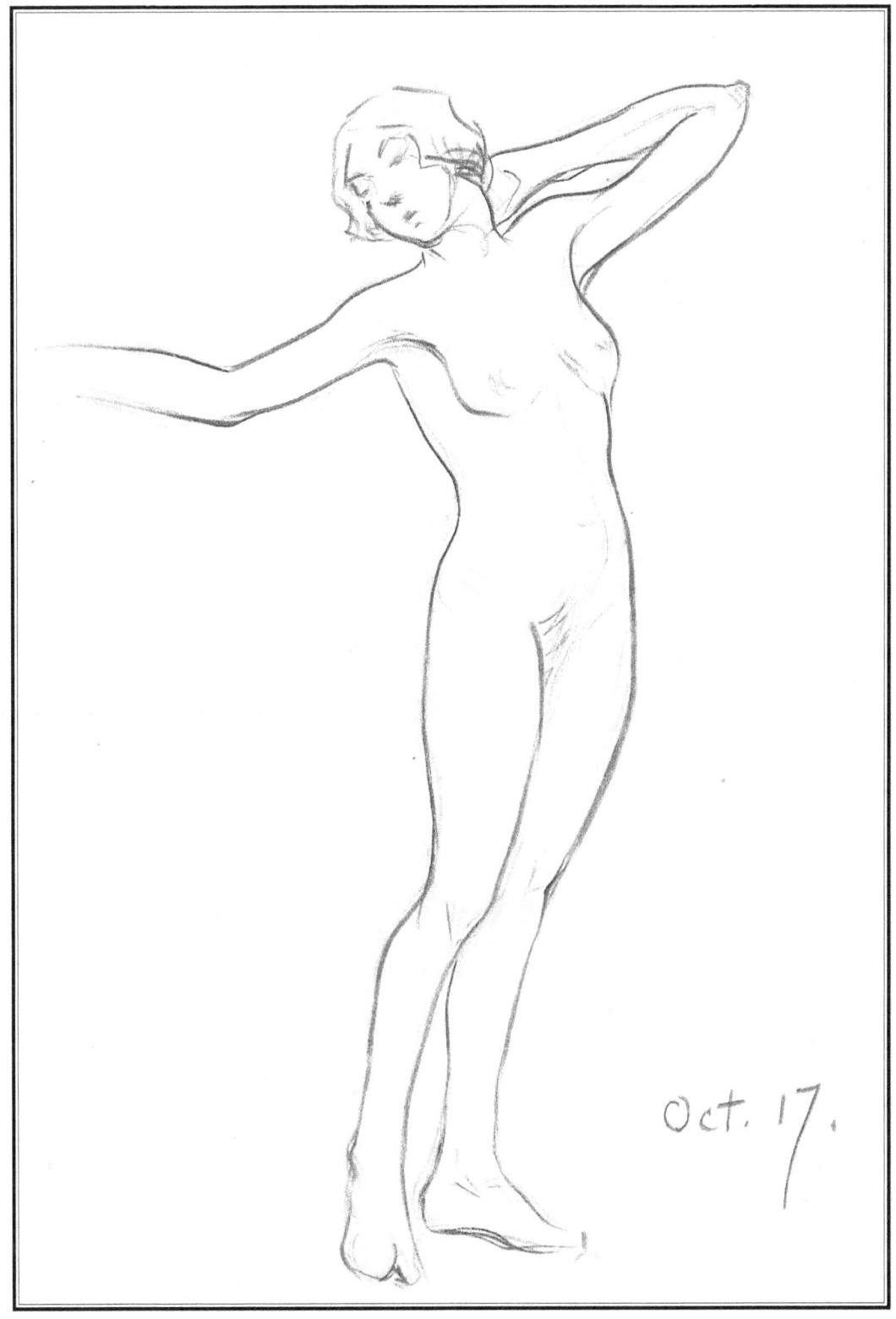

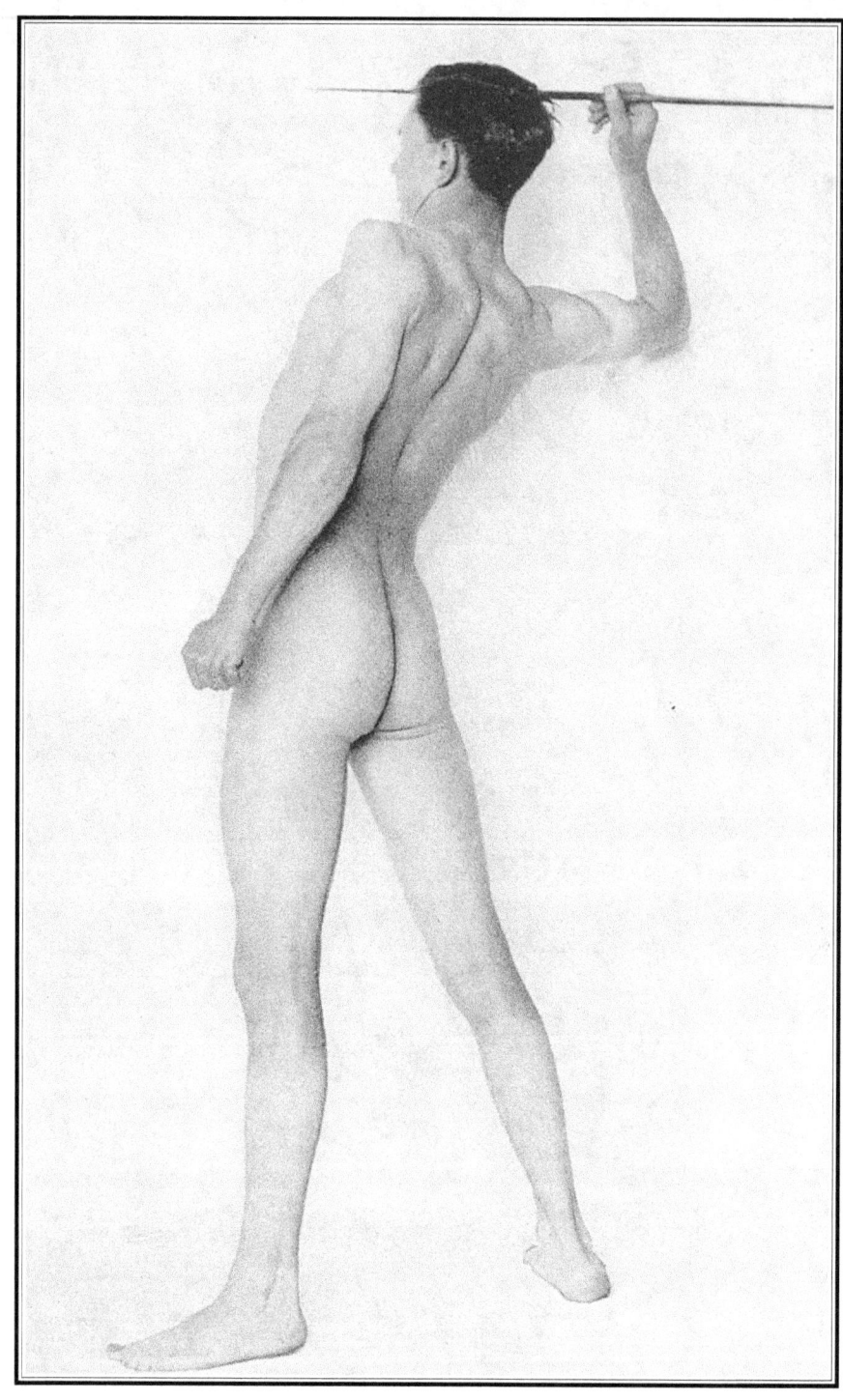

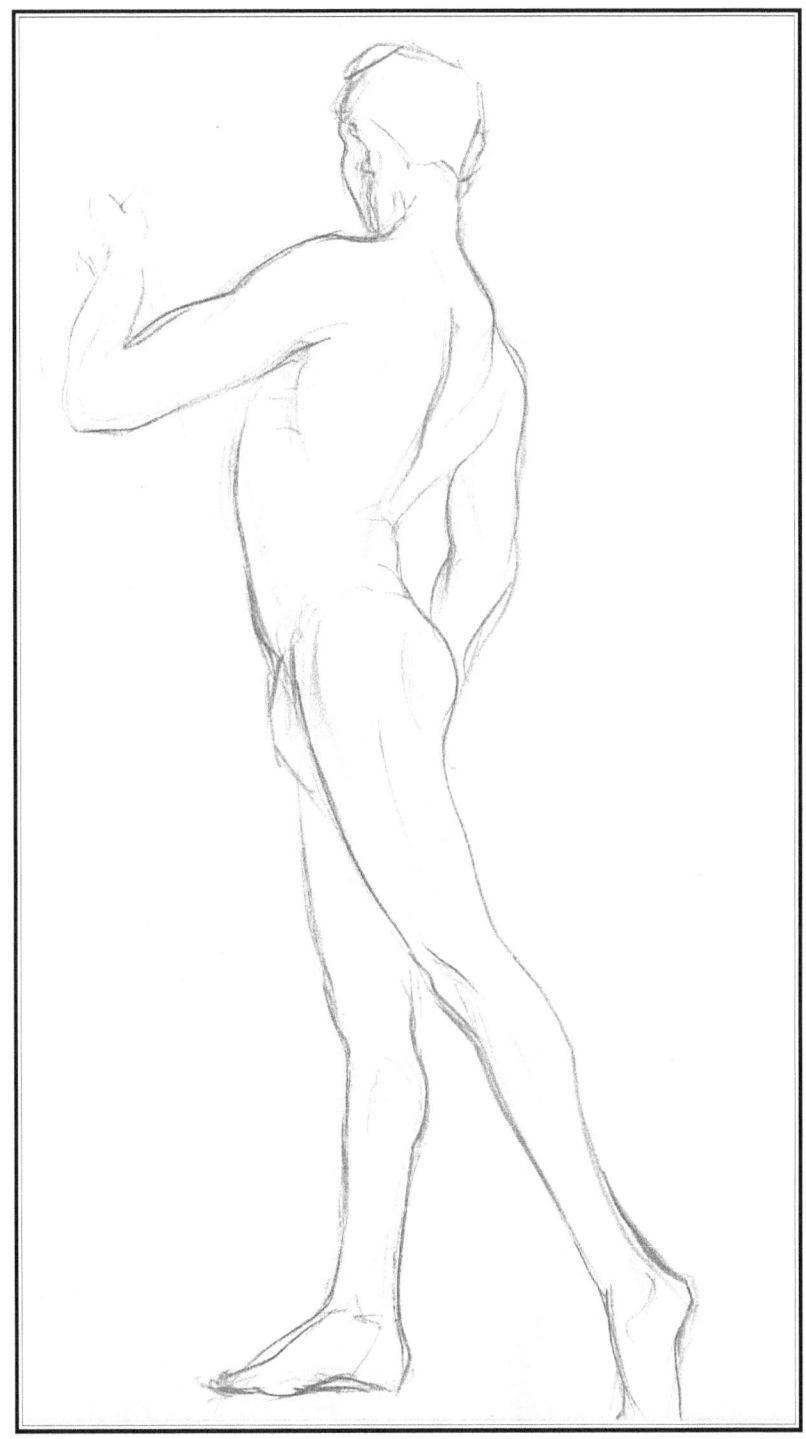

SHADOWS

The next pages show examples of shadows making the form. The photographs are form Yerbury and Ellwood.[50]

Look carefully at the examples from Grace Young, although the drawings are not shaded, she includes lines which delineate the placement of the shadow.

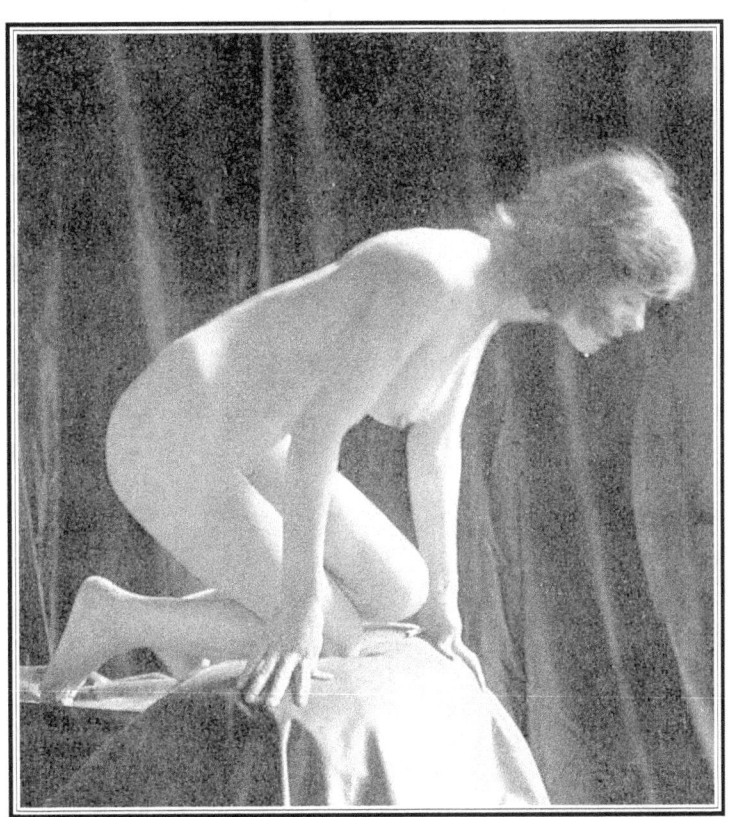

---

50 The Humand Form and Its Use in Art F. R. Yerbury and G. M. Ellwood, London 1924

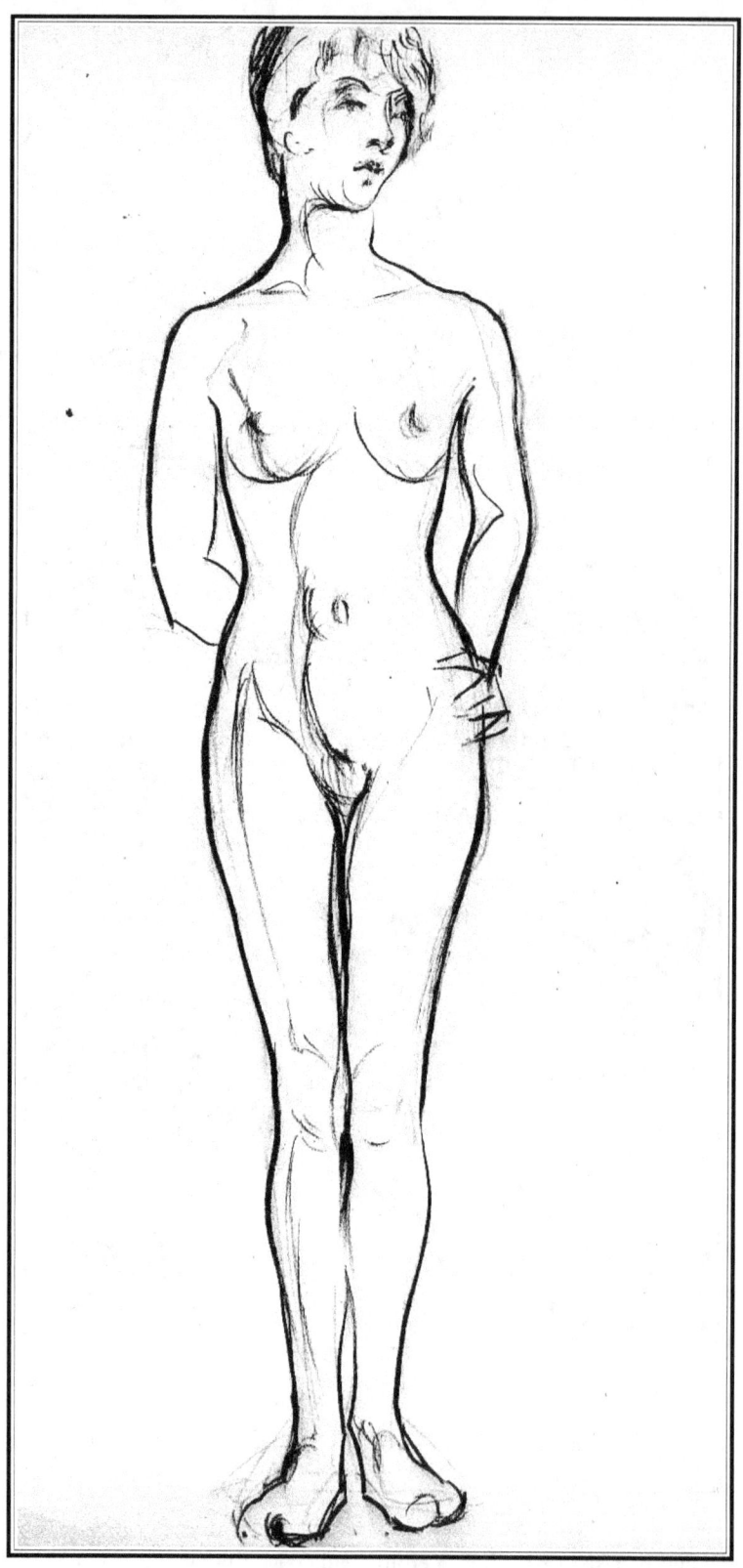

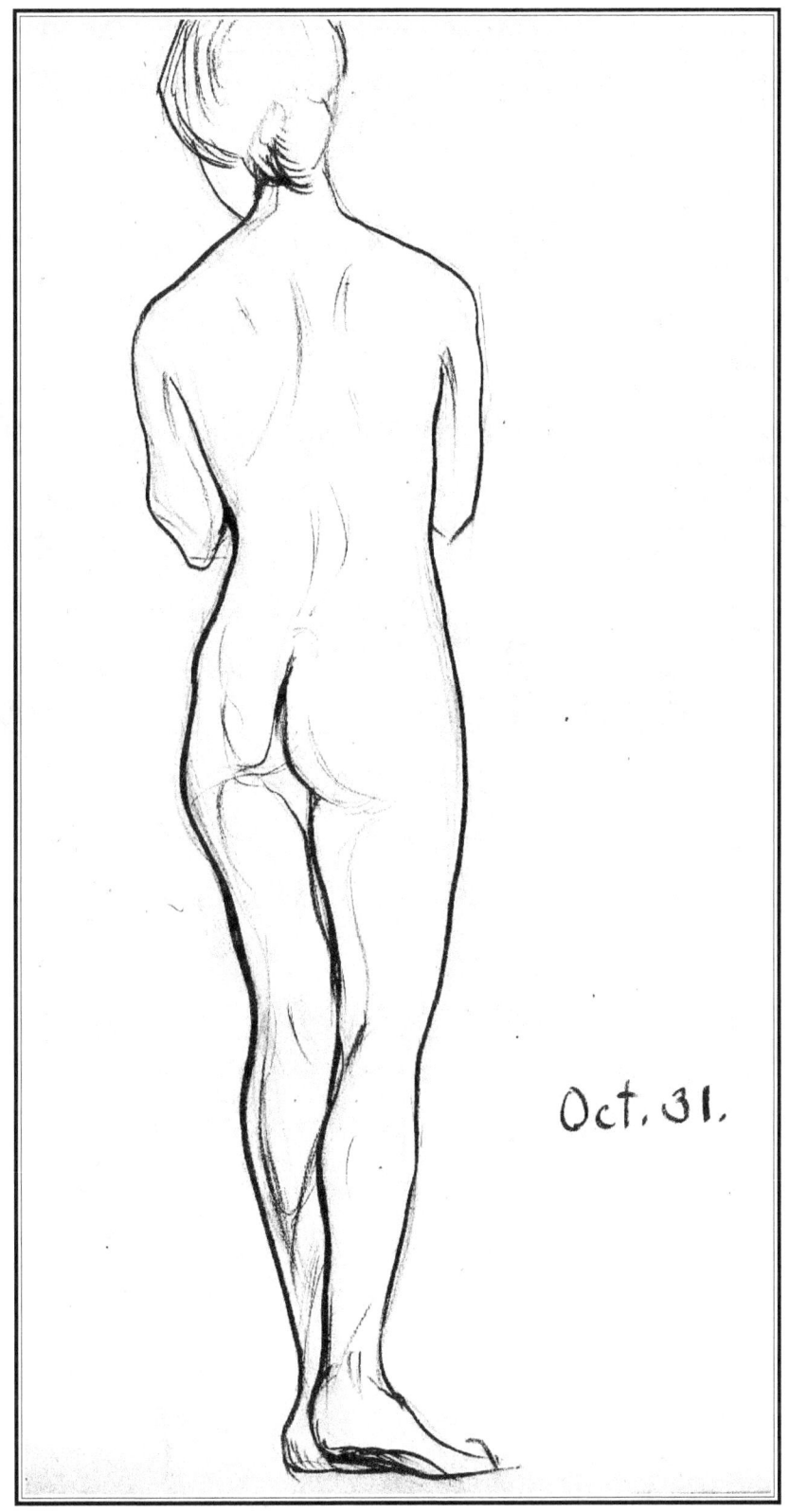

Oct. 31.

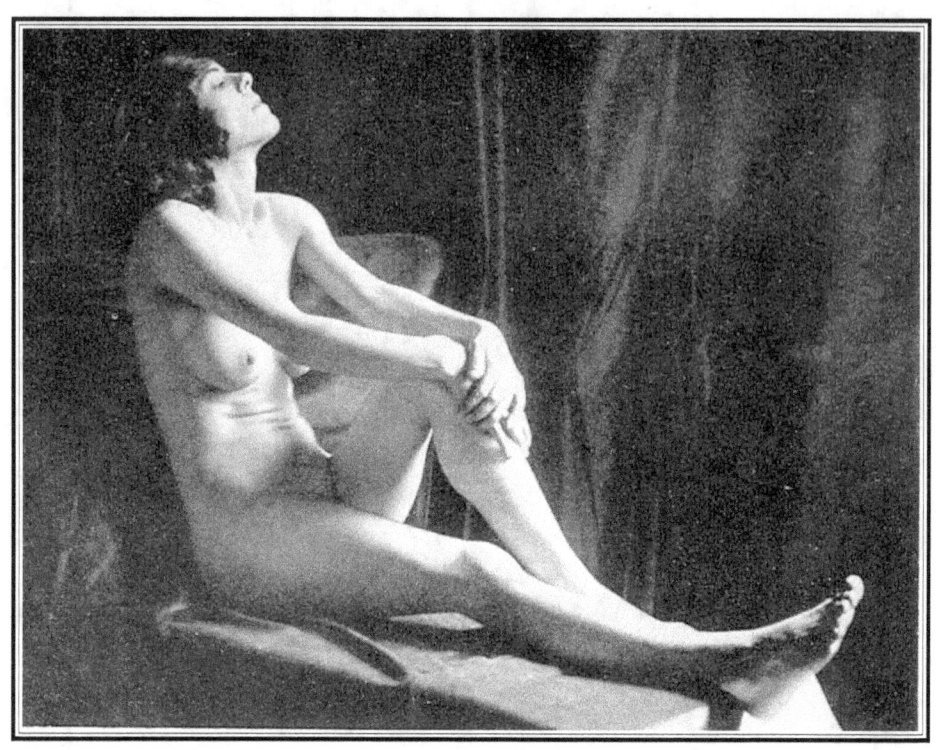

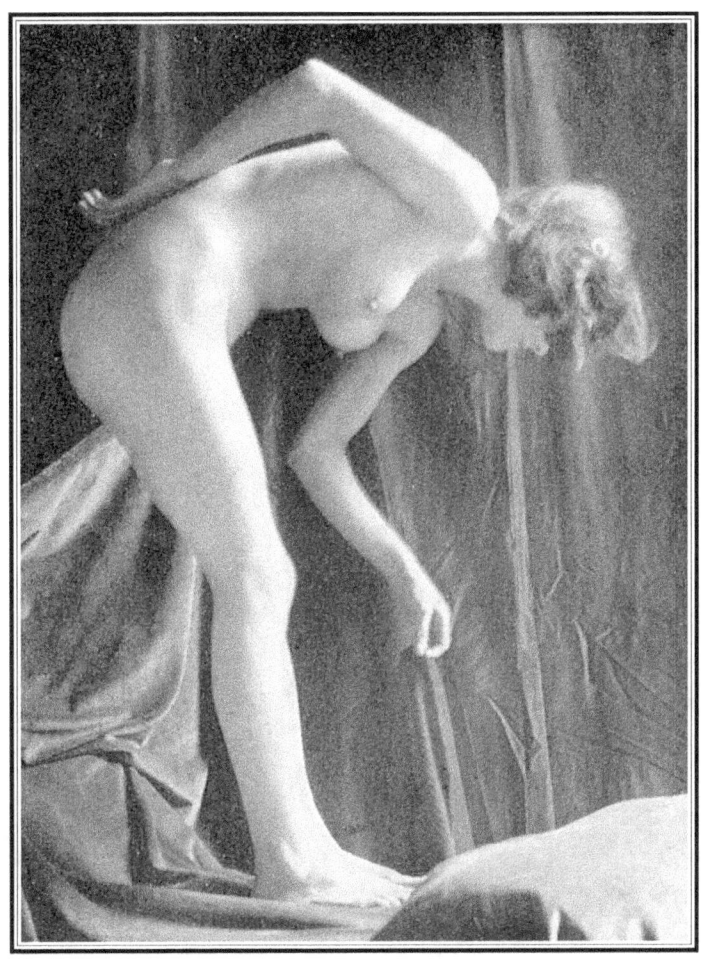

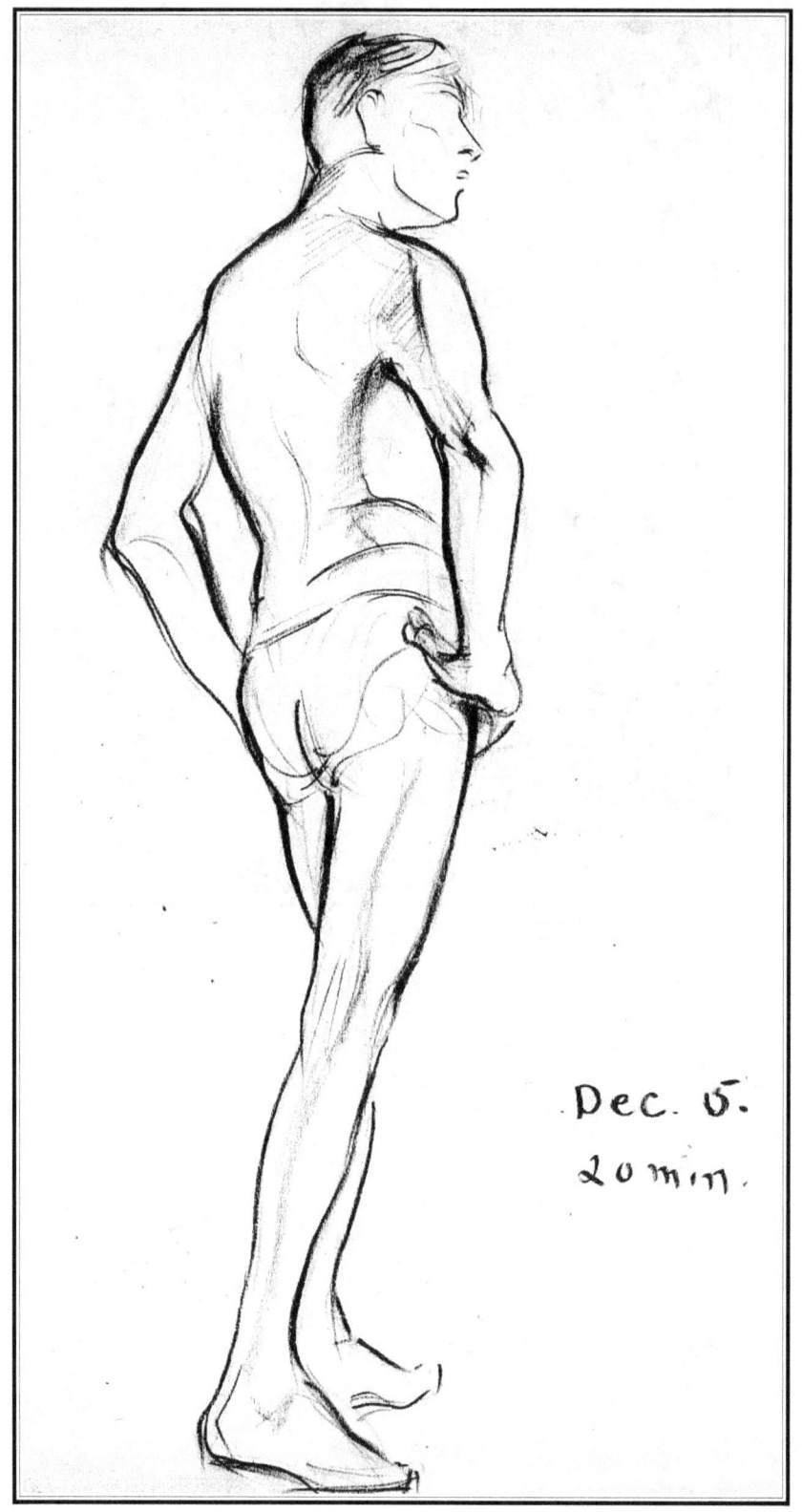

Dec. 5.
20 min.

GRACE YOUNG

20 MINUTES

SEPT. - DEC.

1927

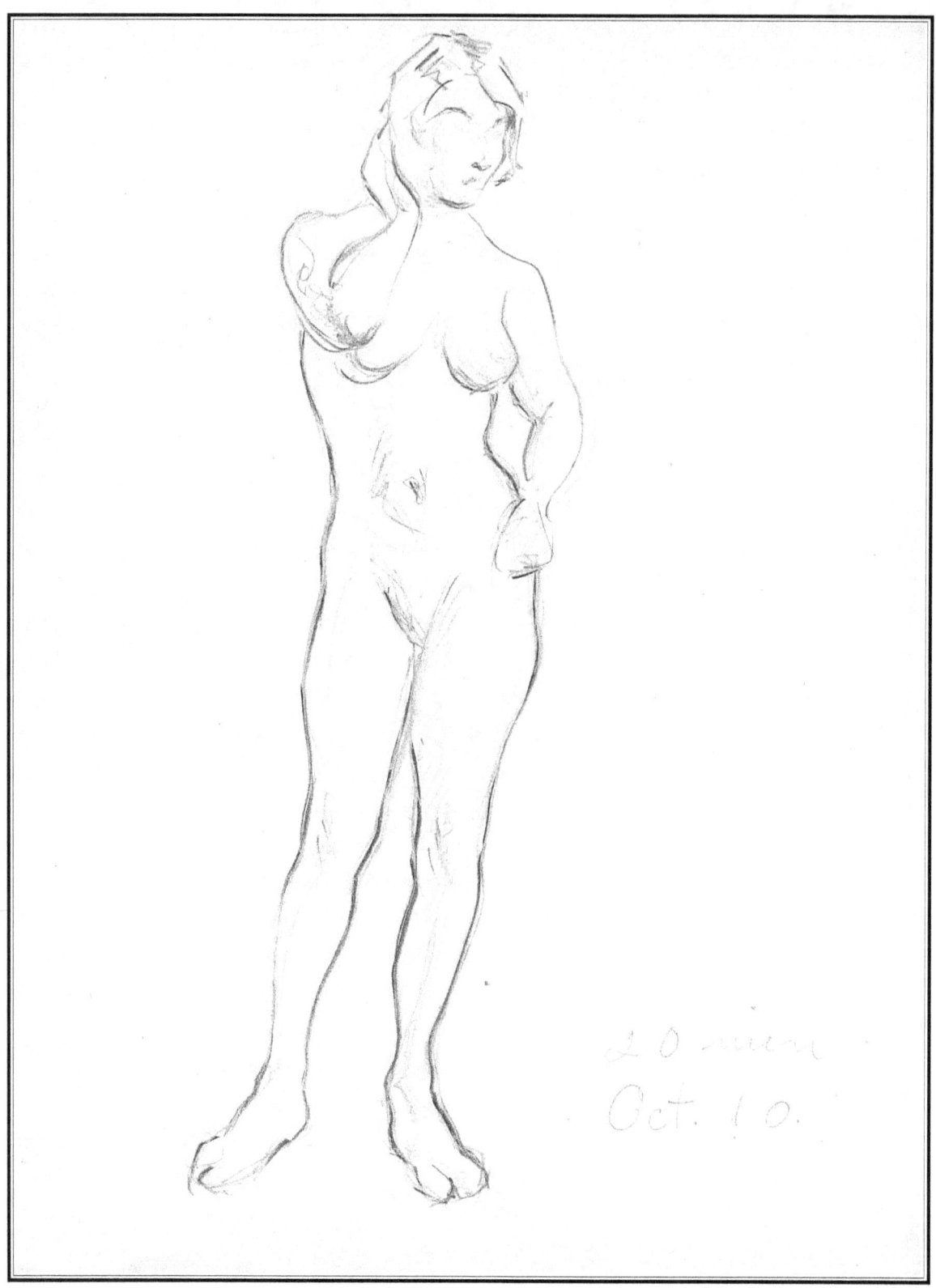

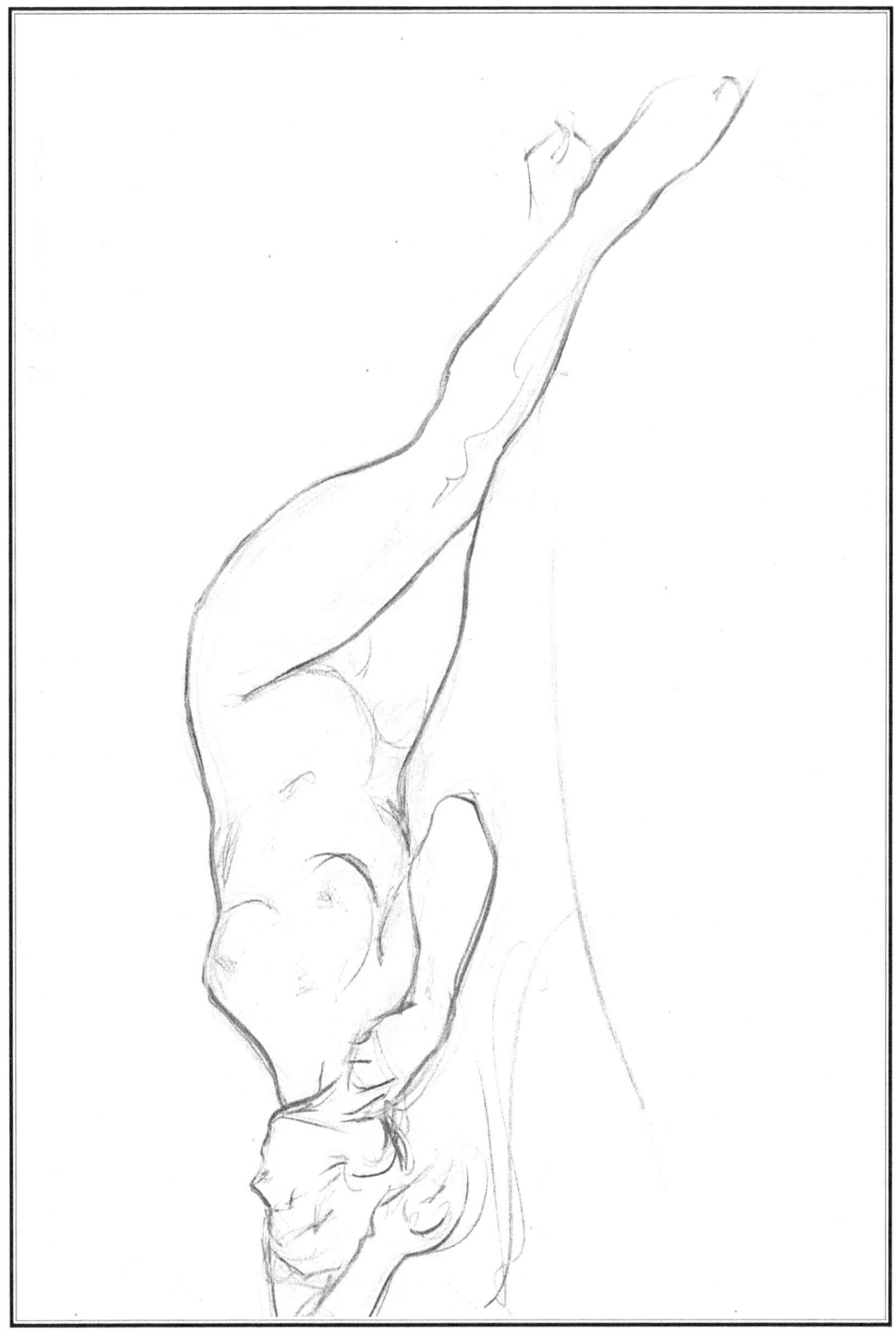

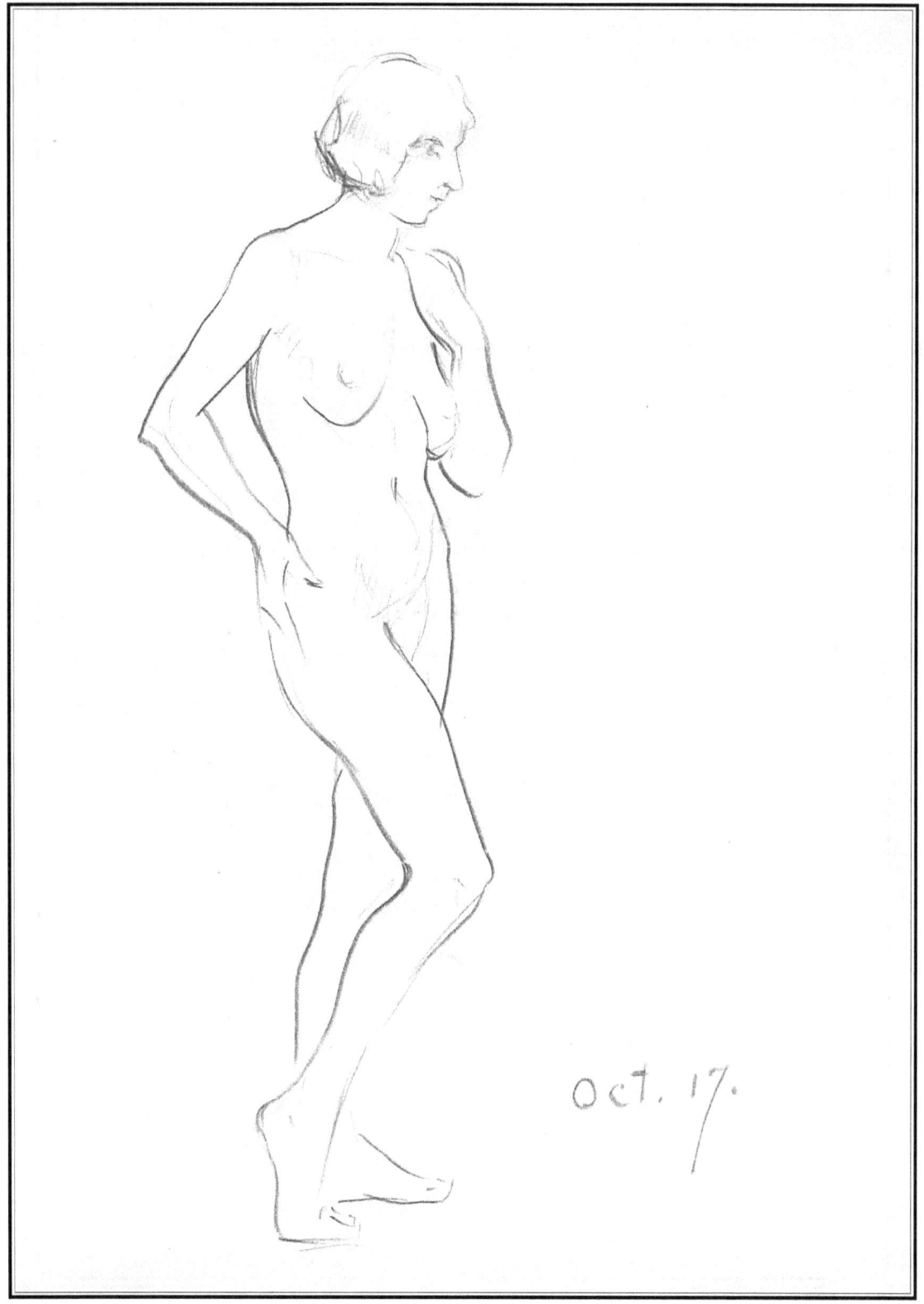

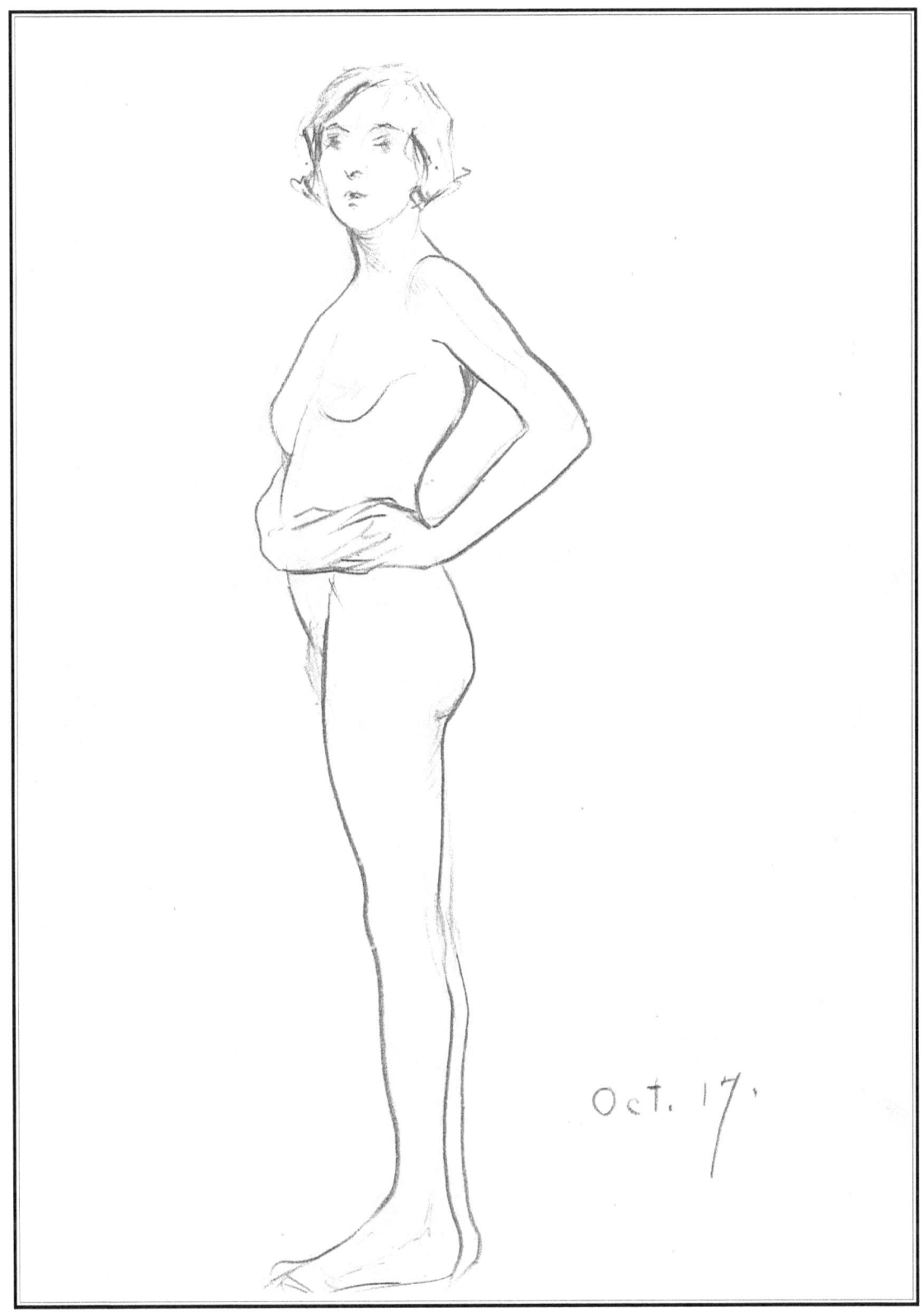

Oct. 17

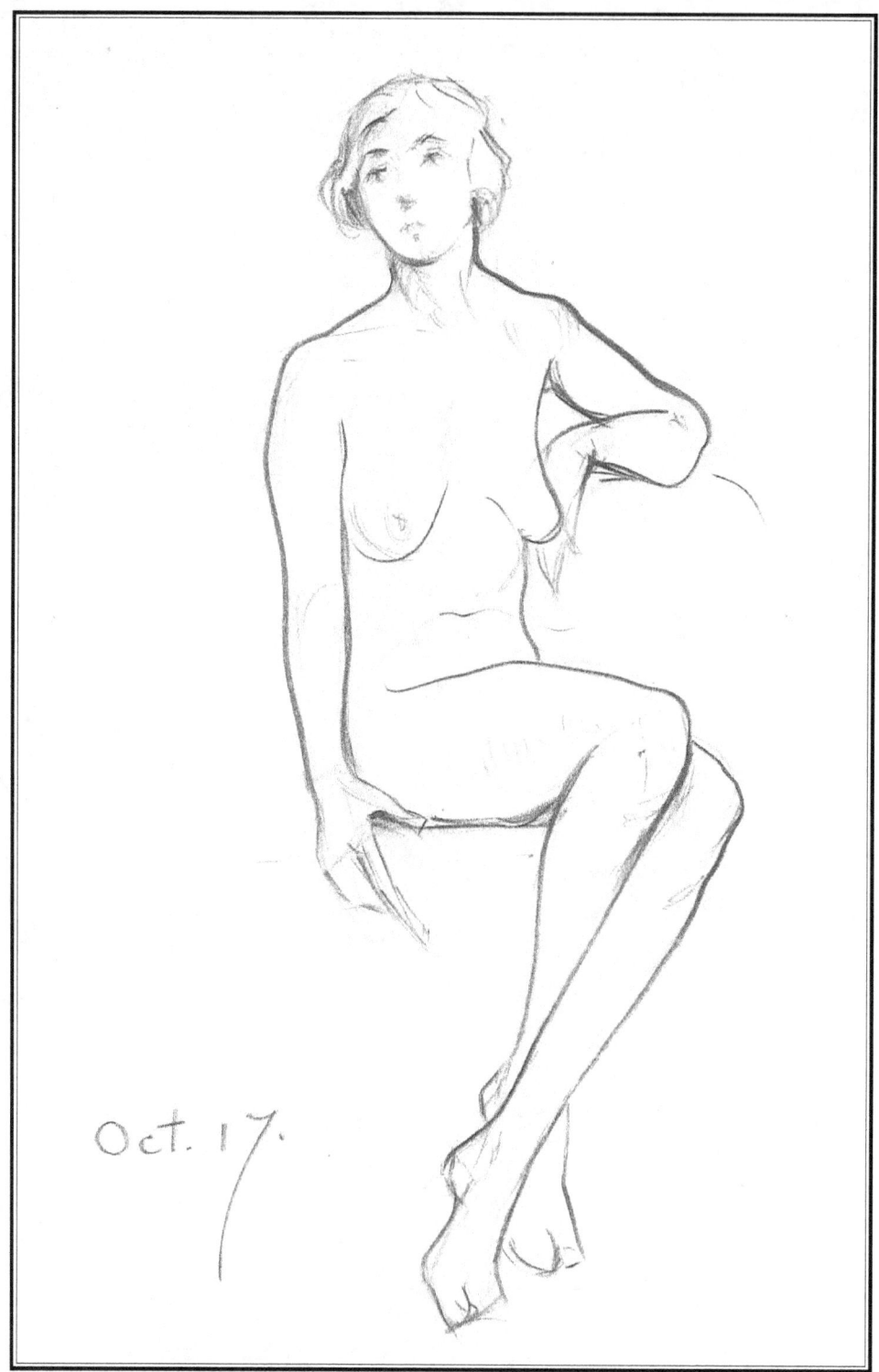

Oct. 17.

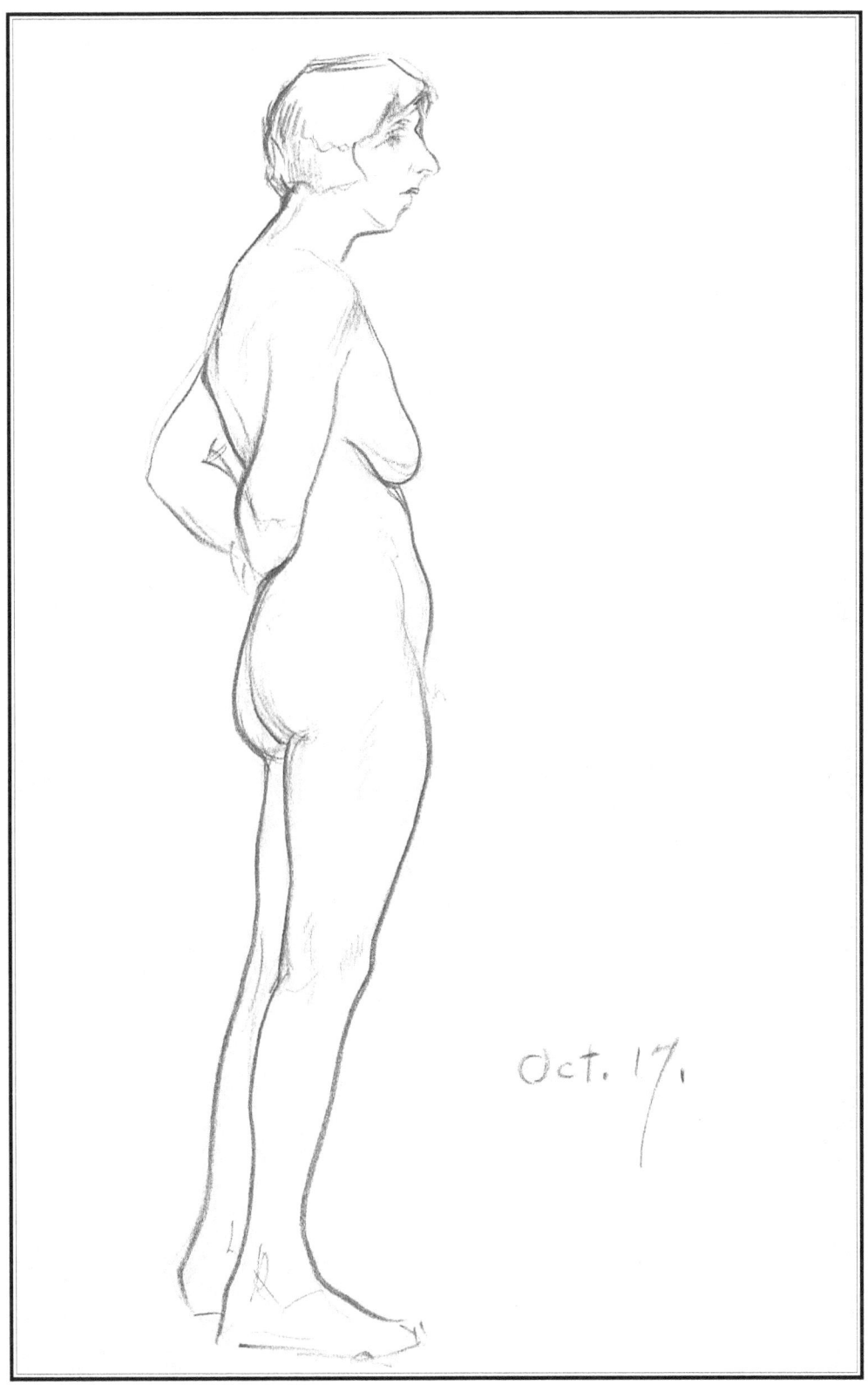

Oct. 17.

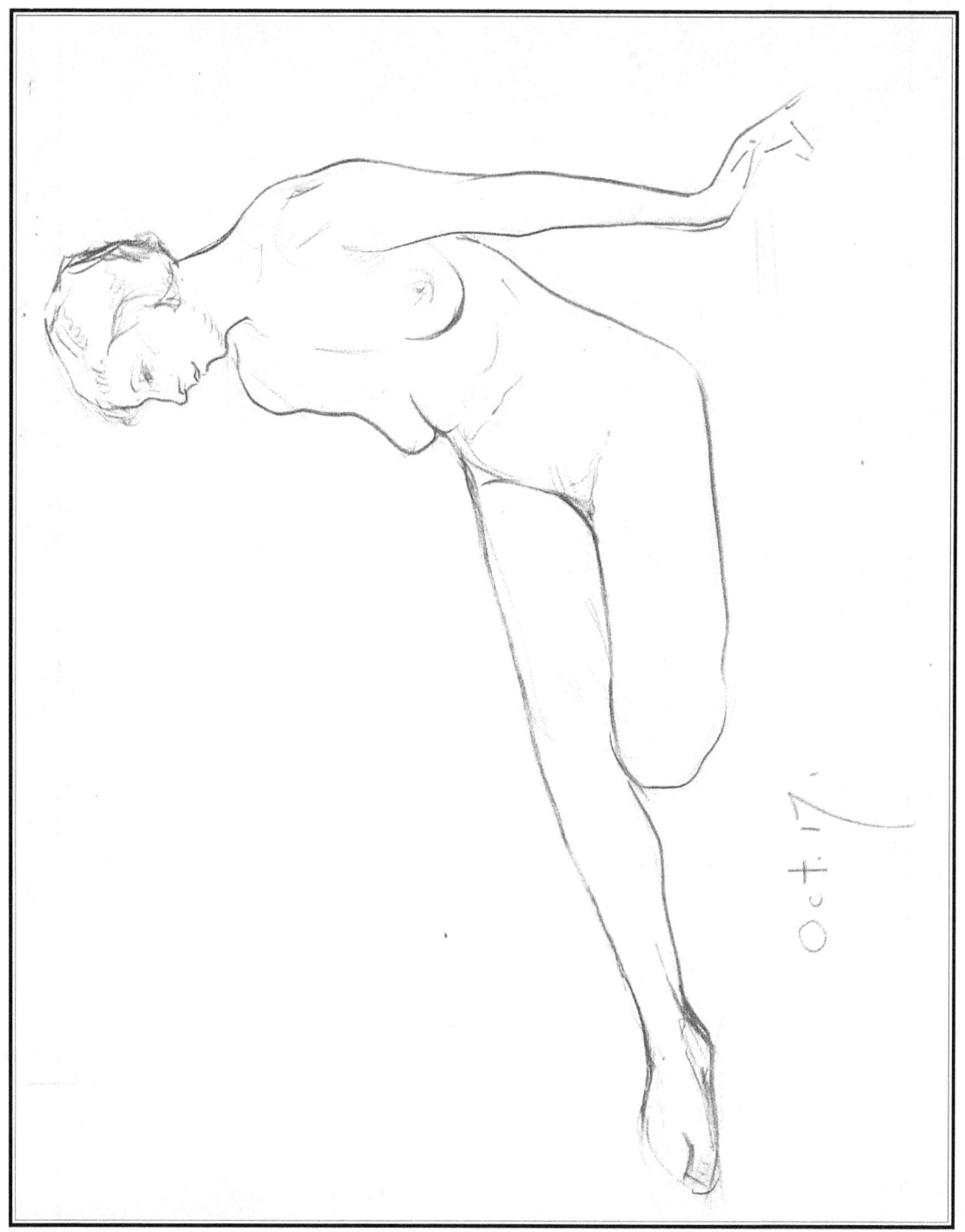

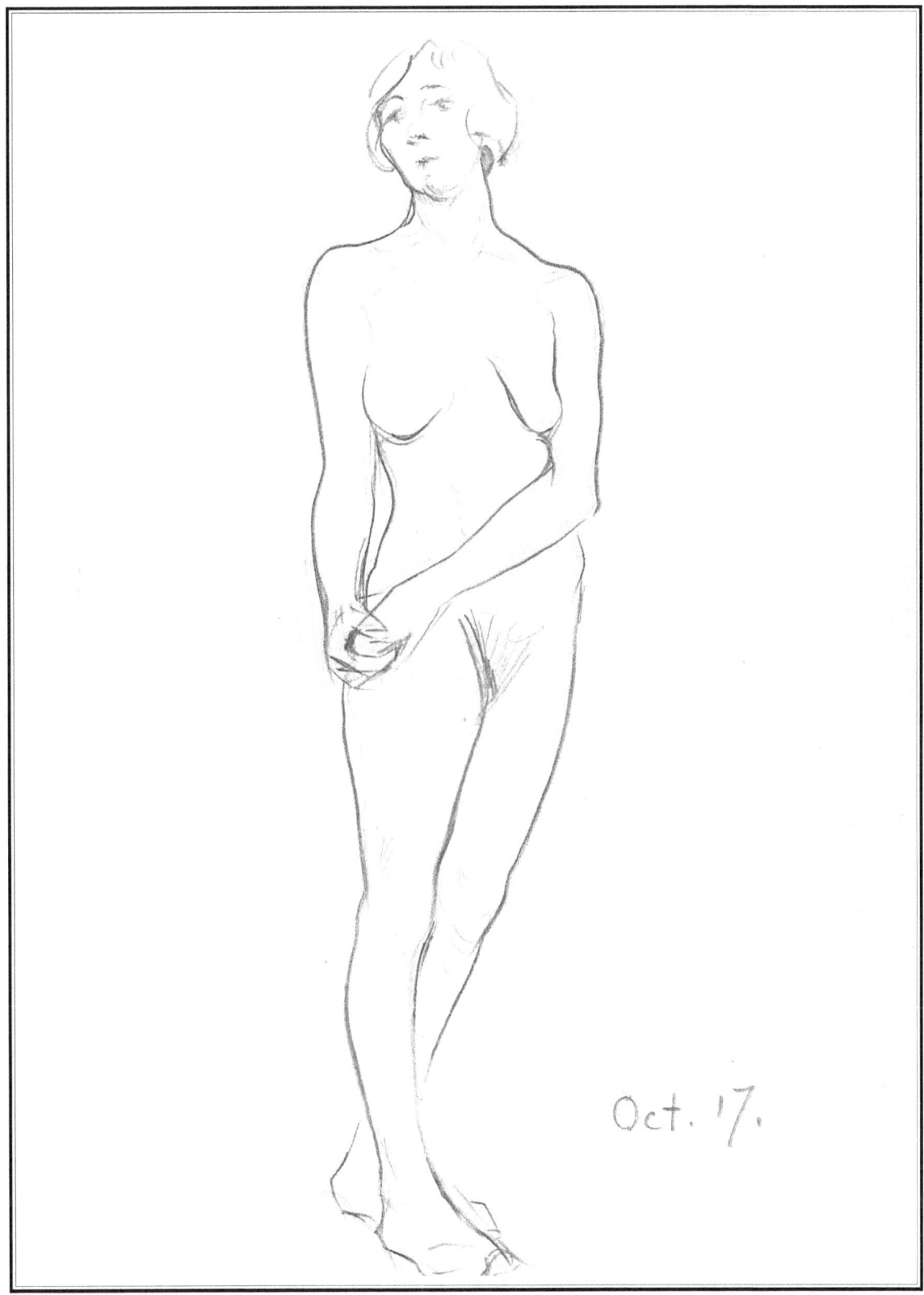

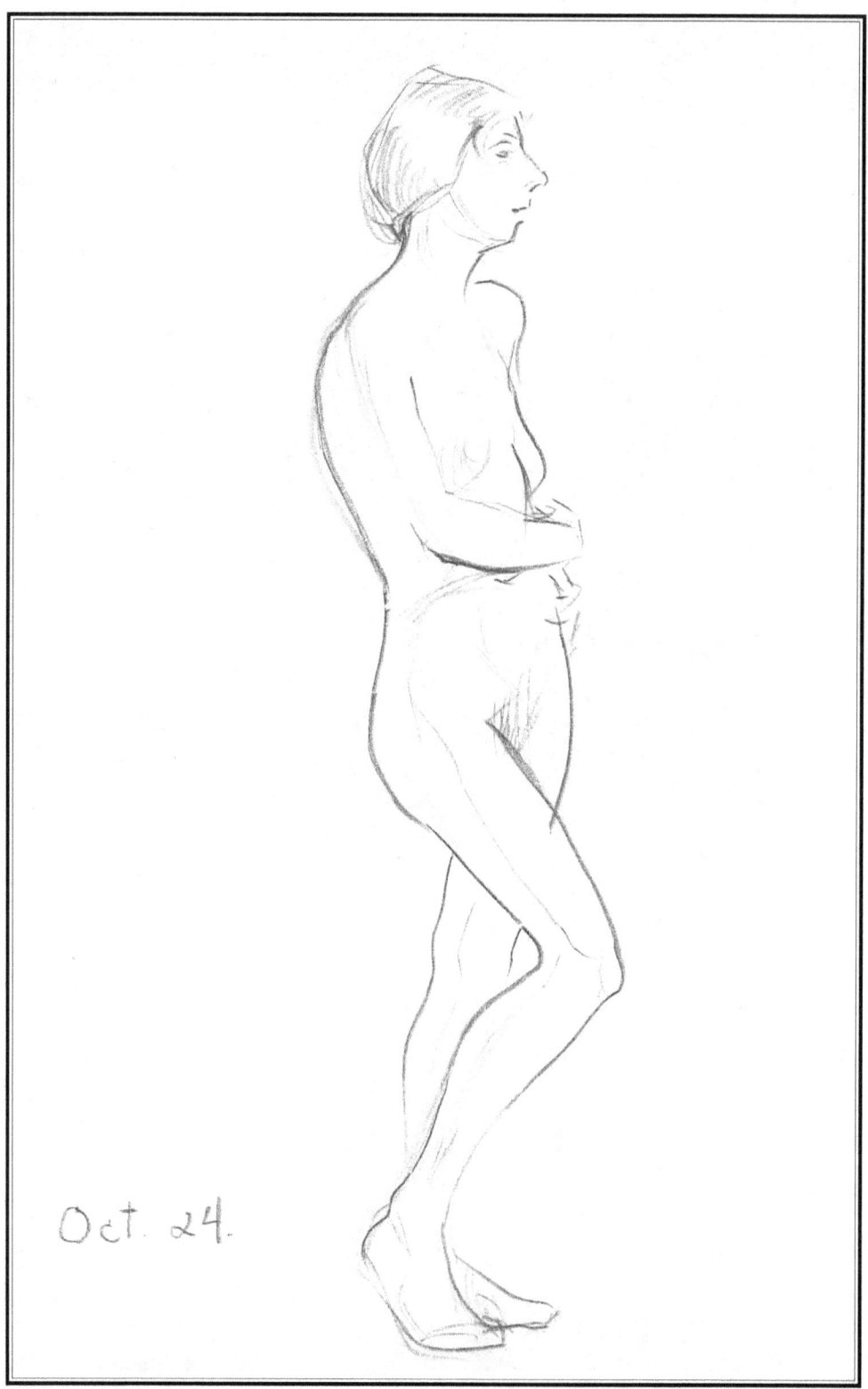

Oct. 24.

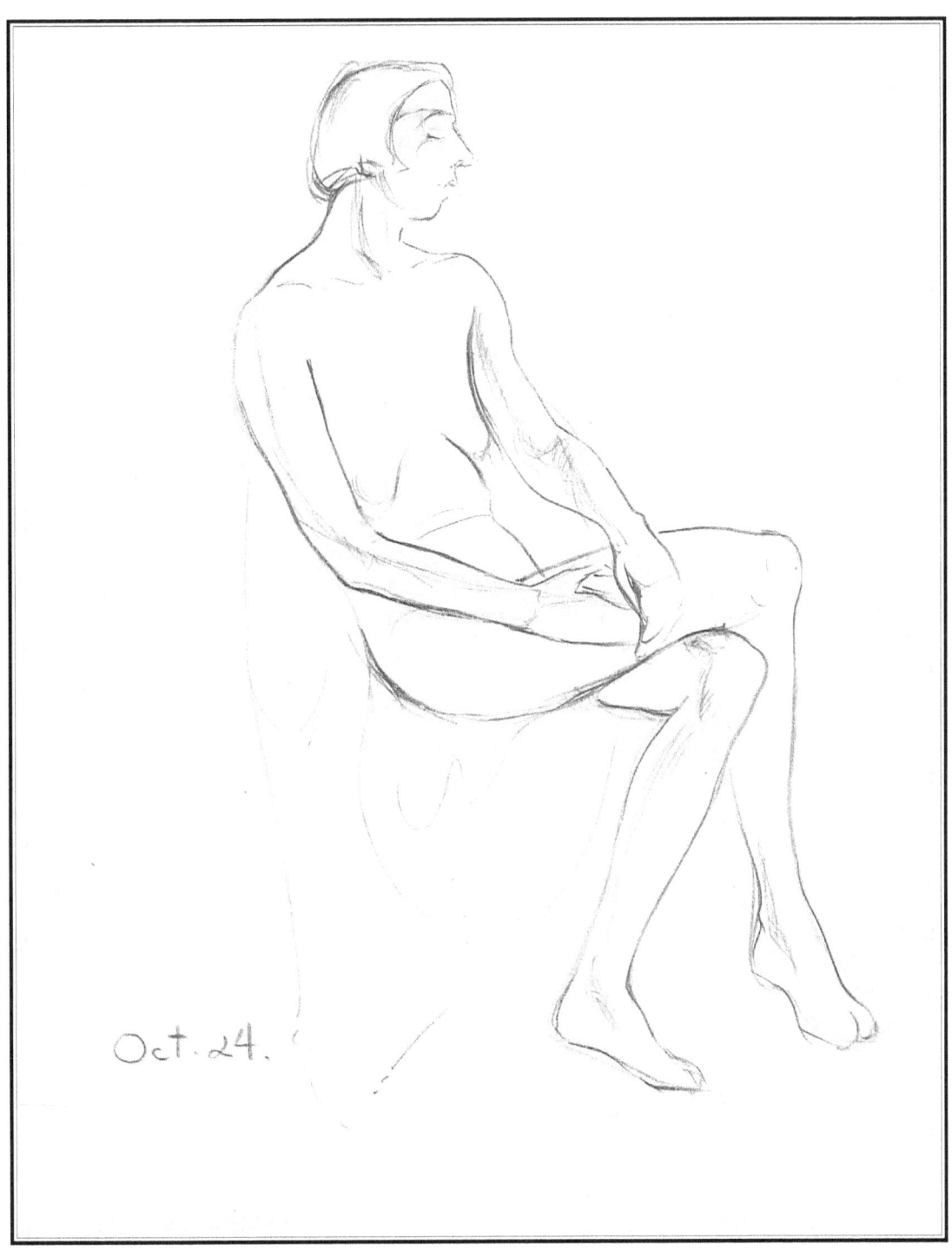

Oct. 24.

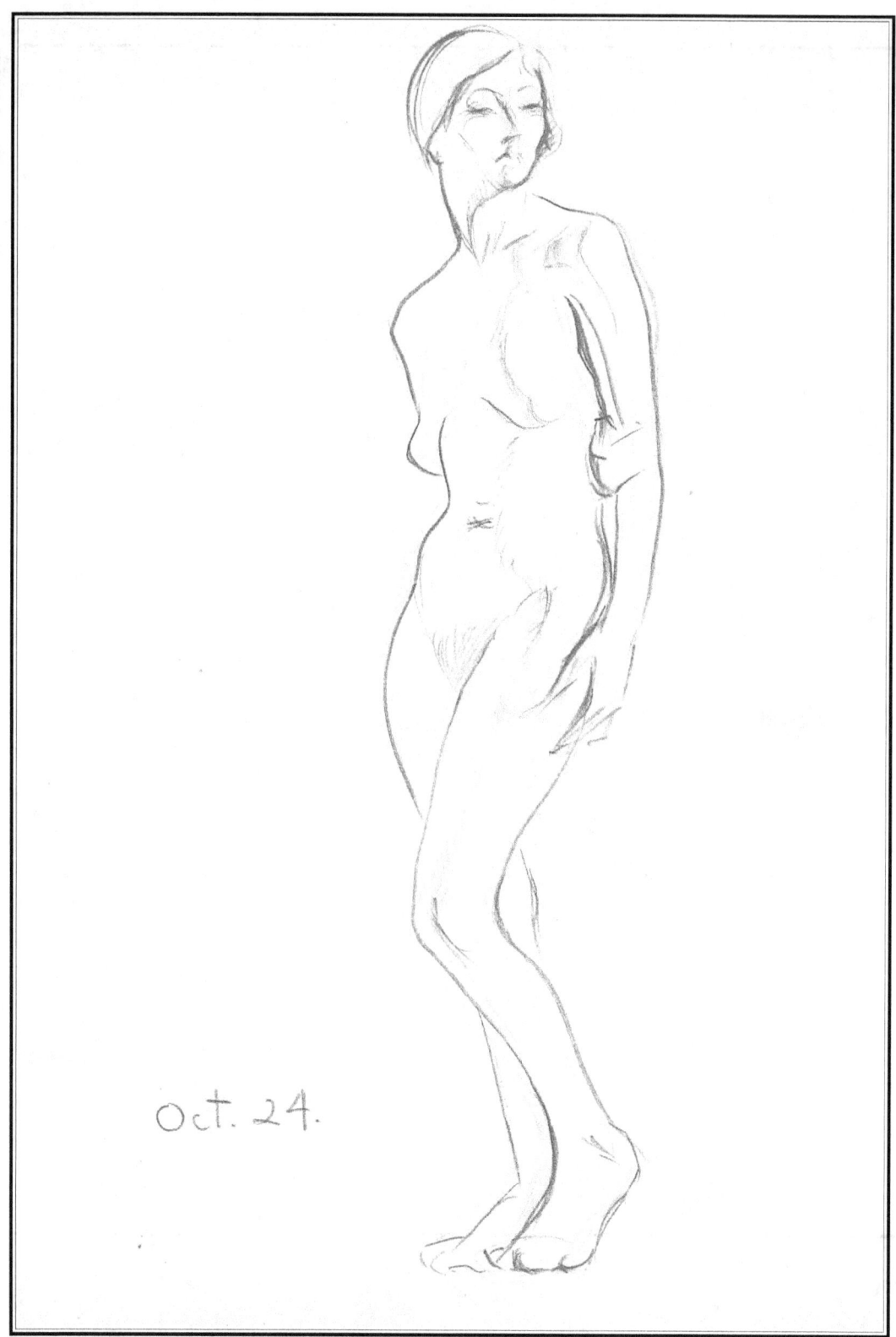

Oct. 24.

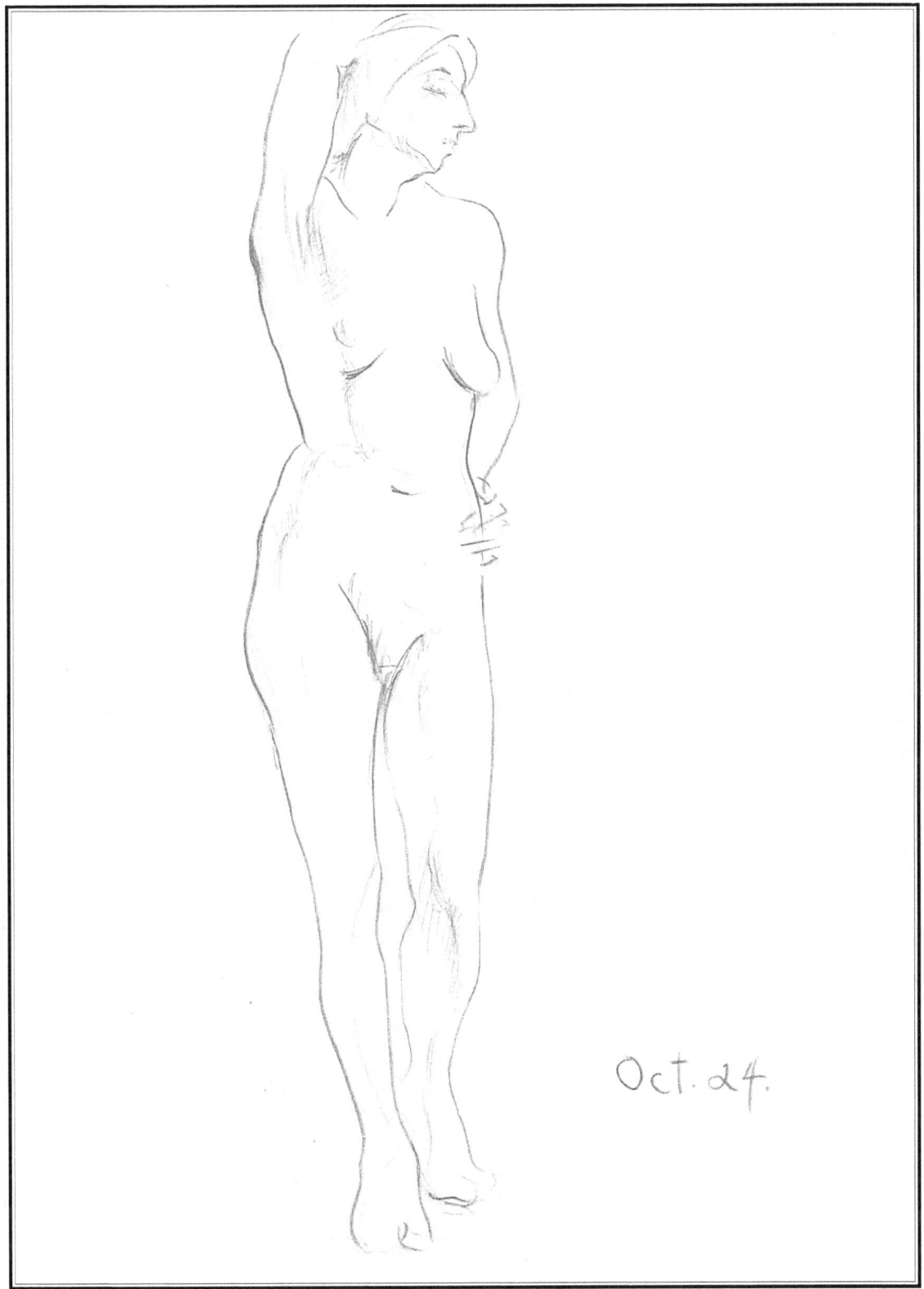

Oct. 24.

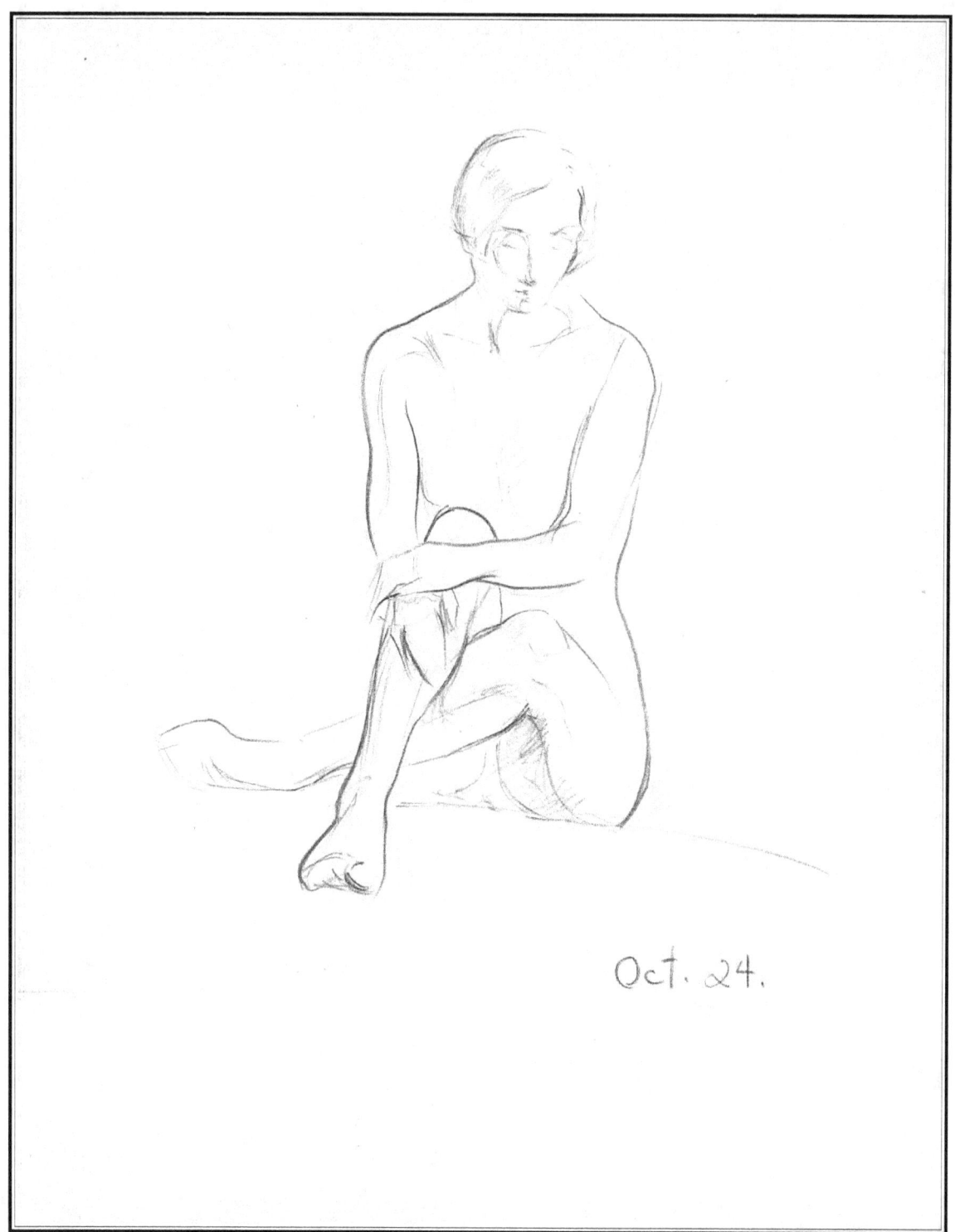

Oct. 24.

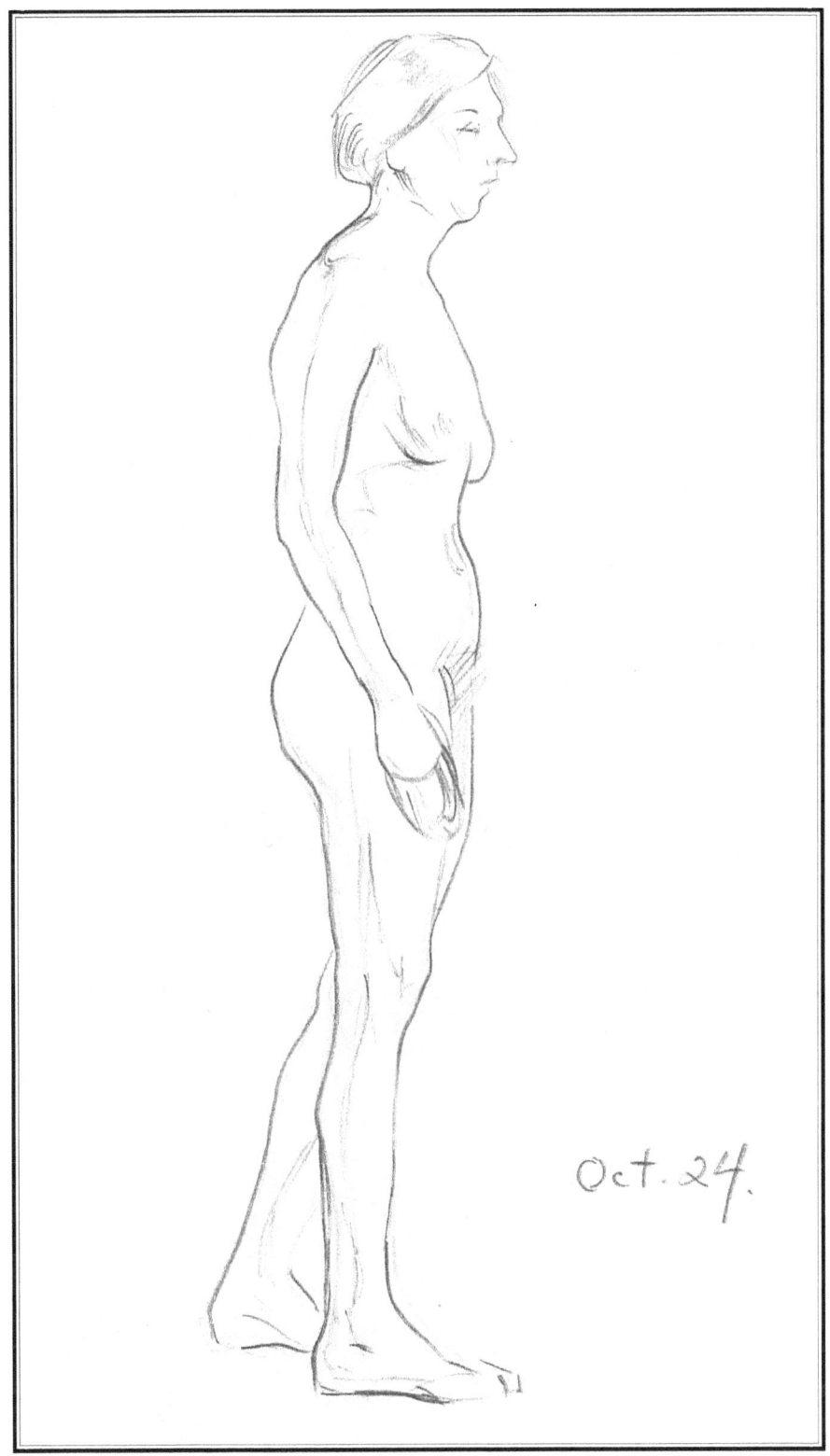

Oct. 24.

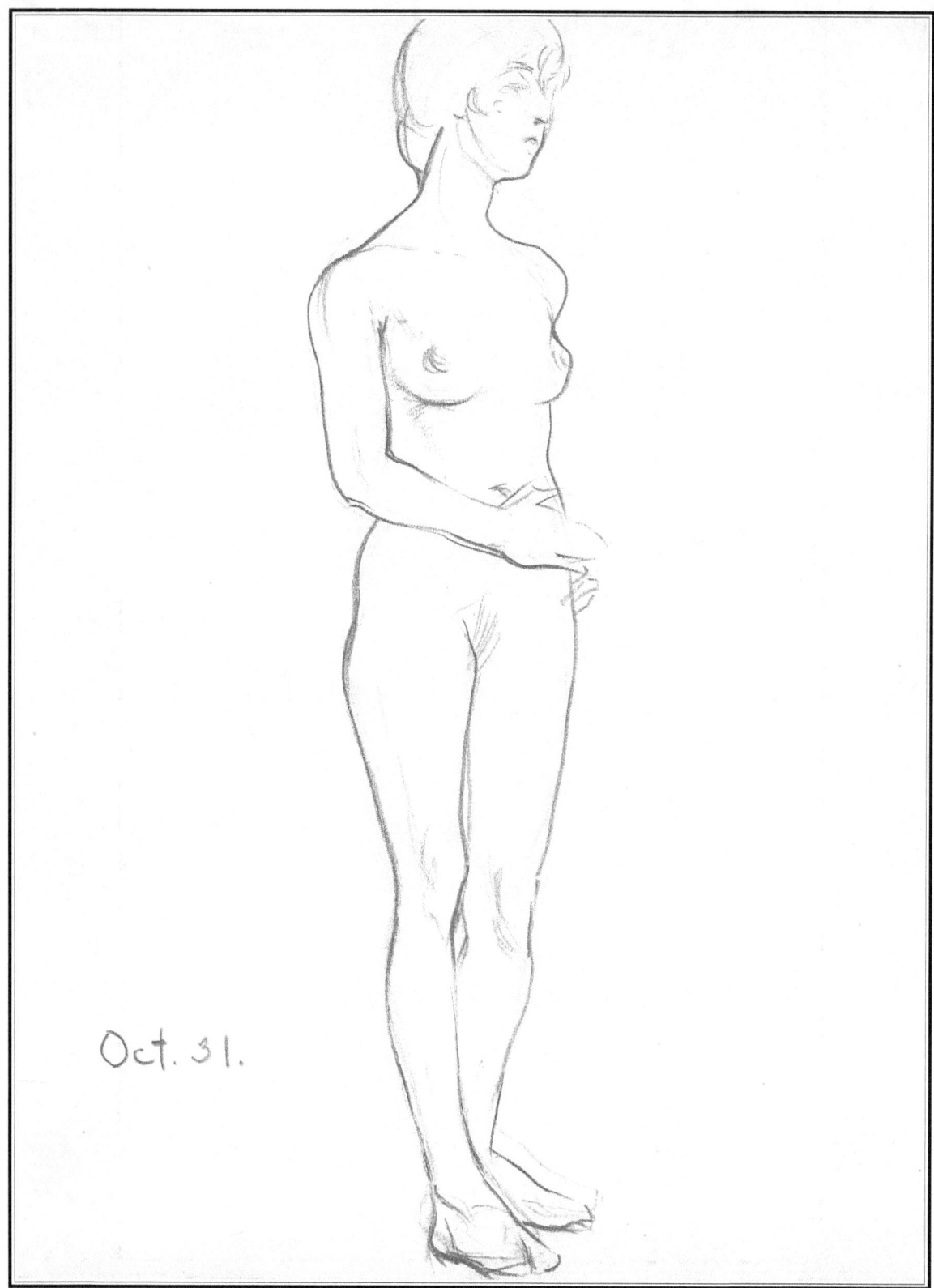

Oct. 31.

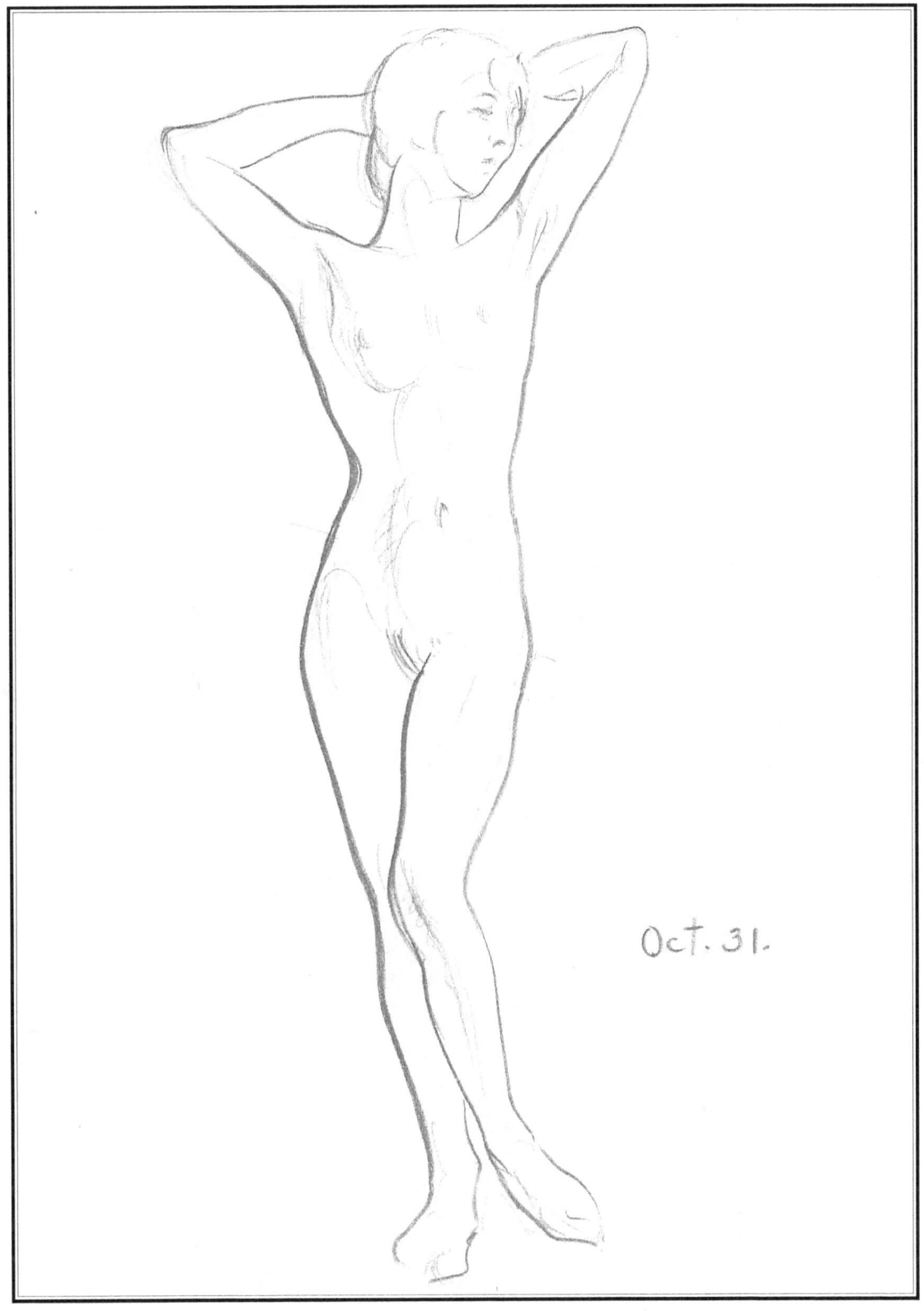

Oct. 31.

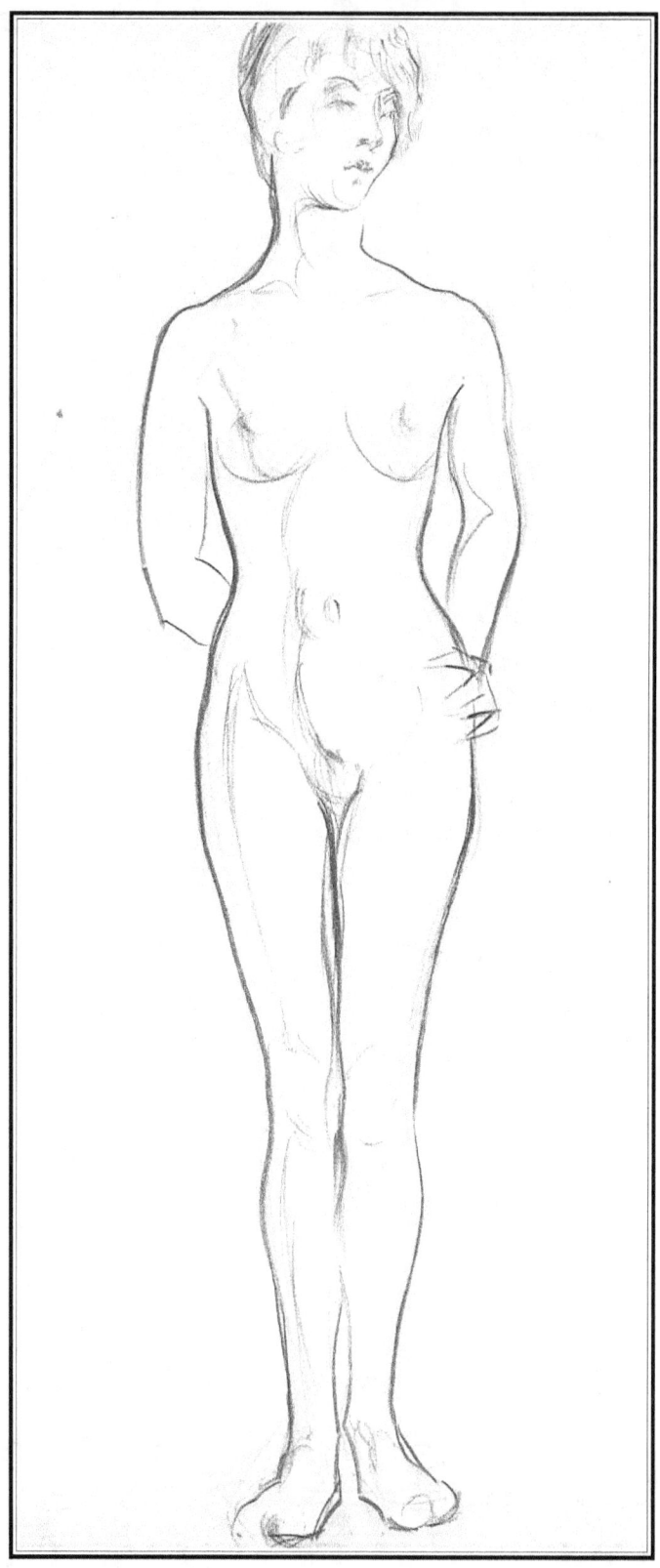

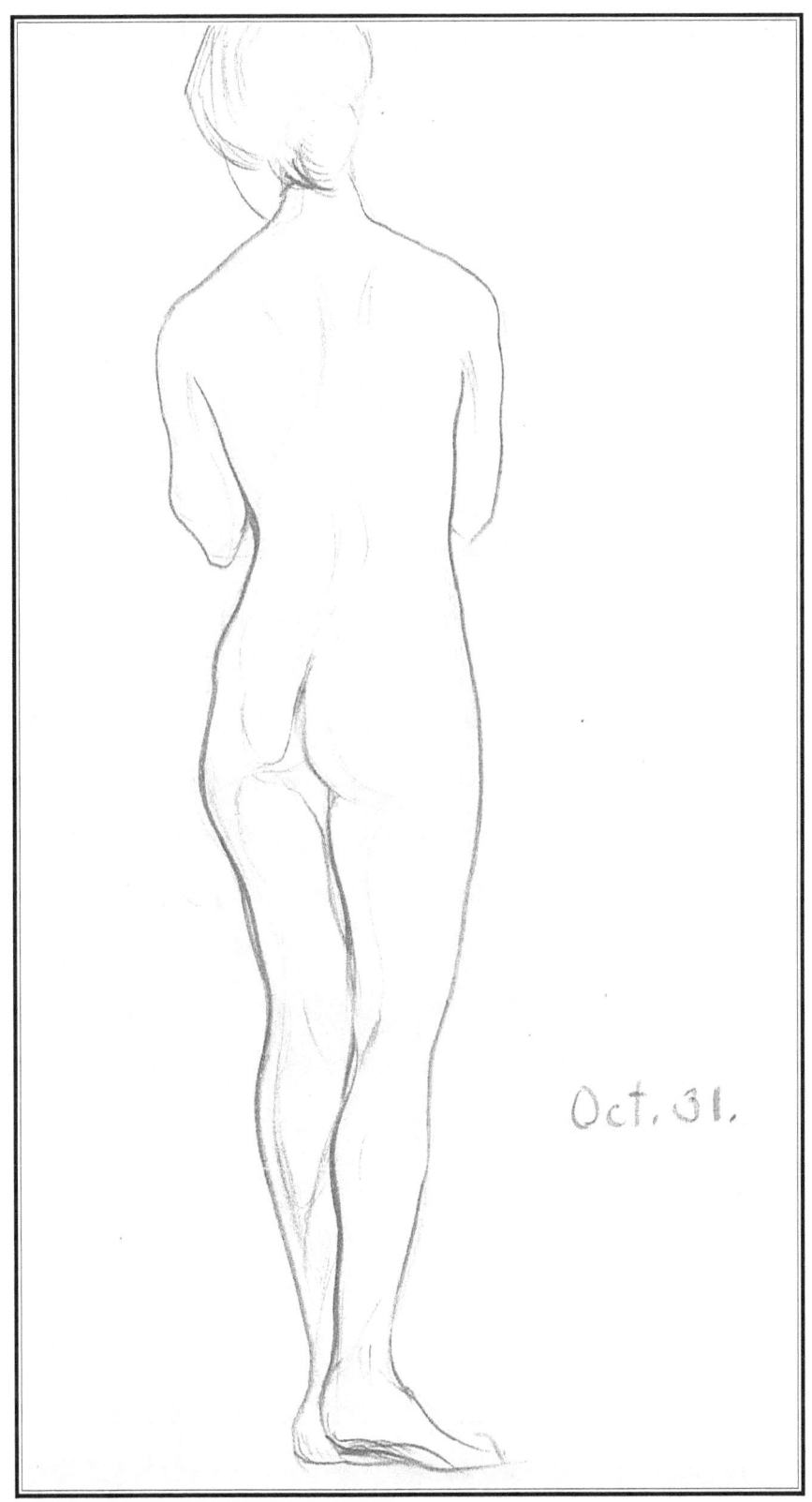

Oct. 31.

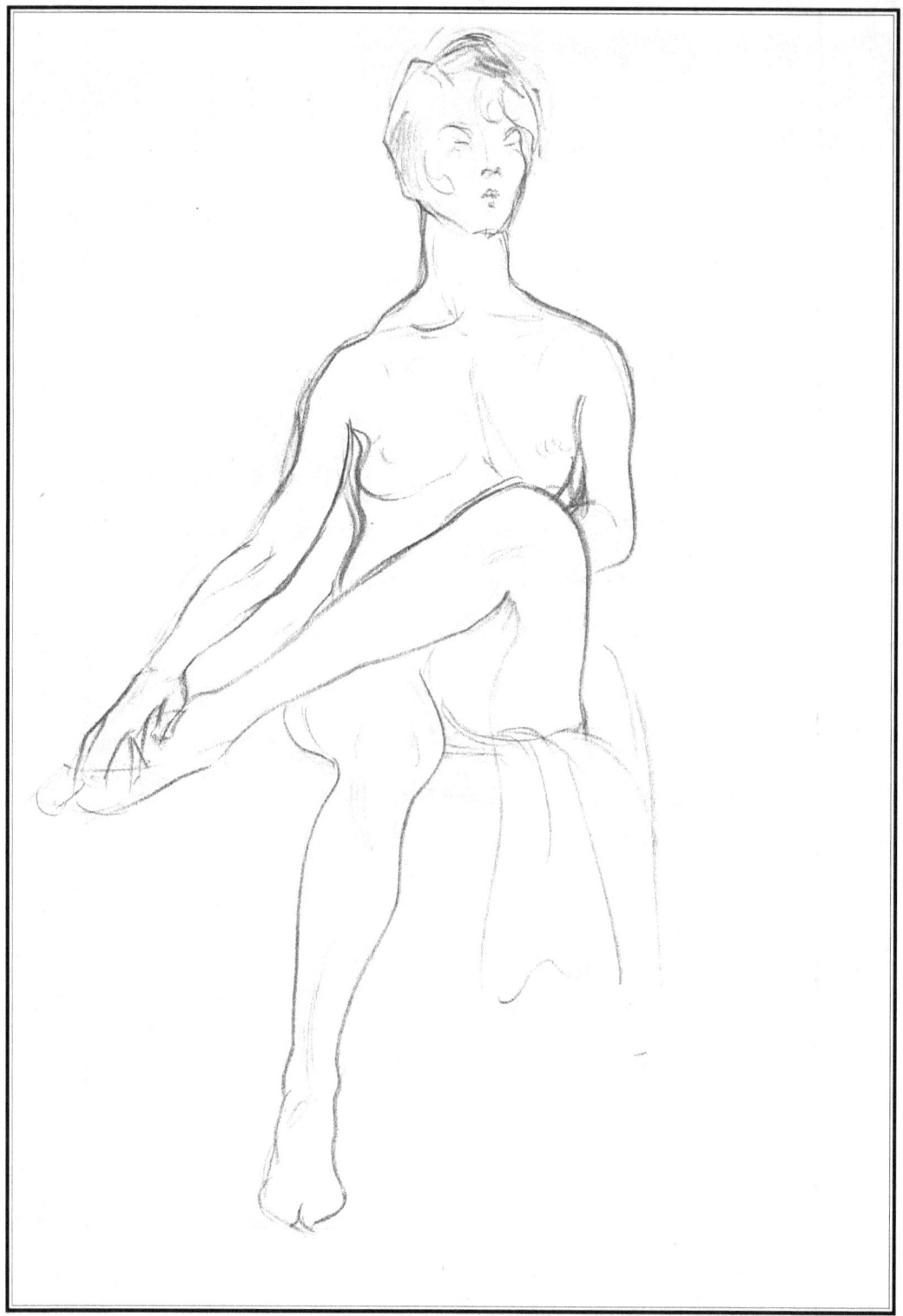

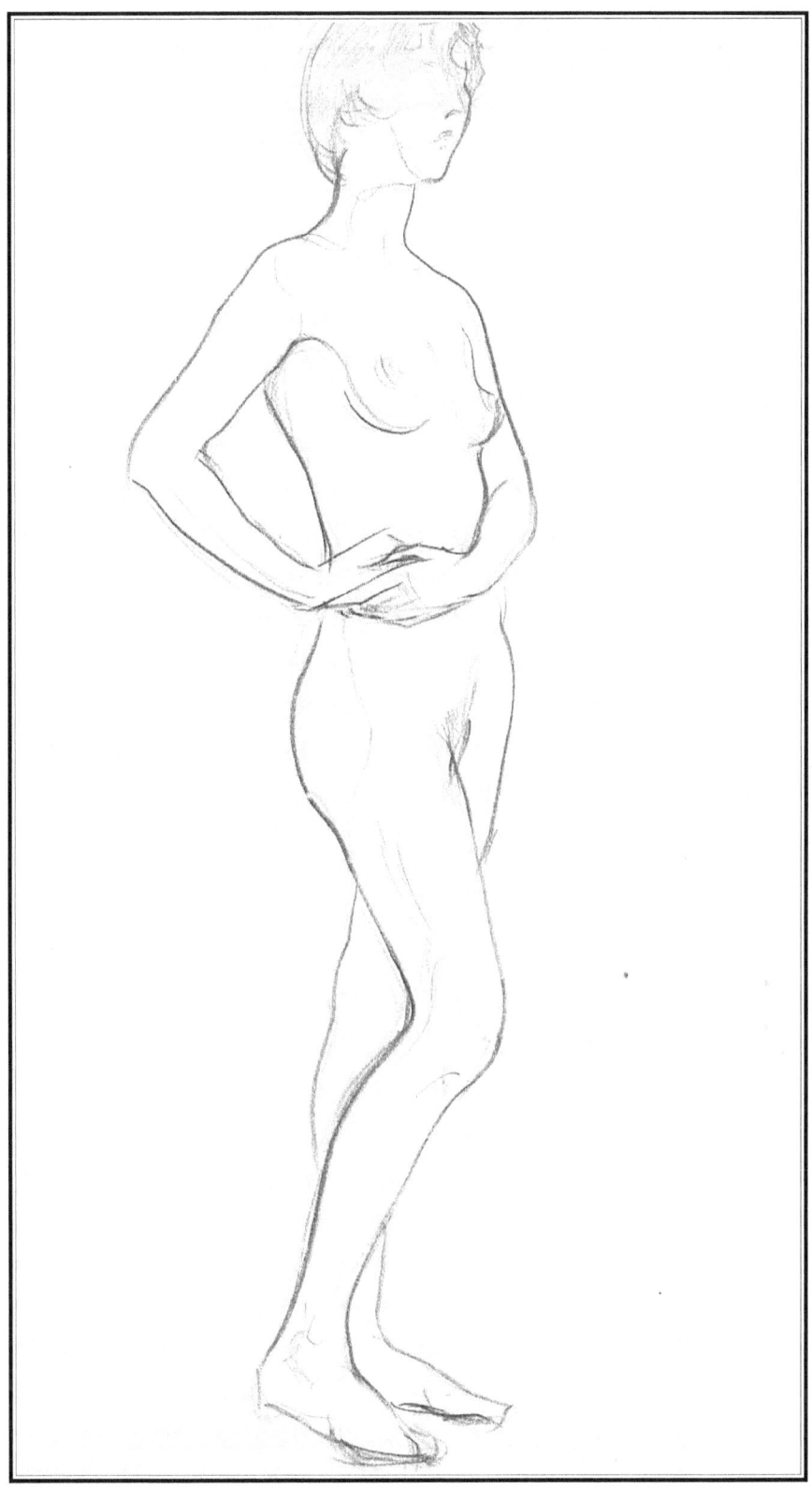

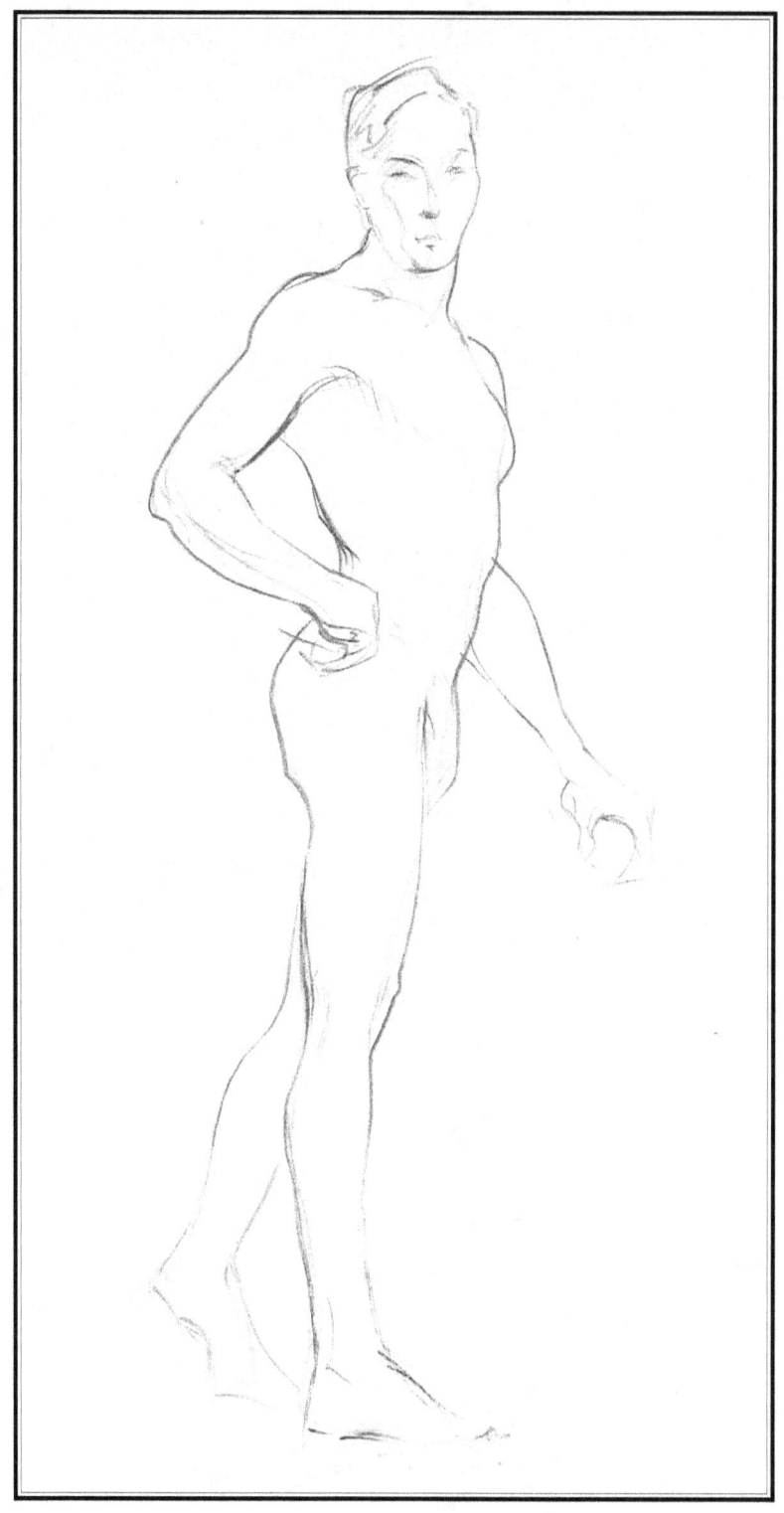

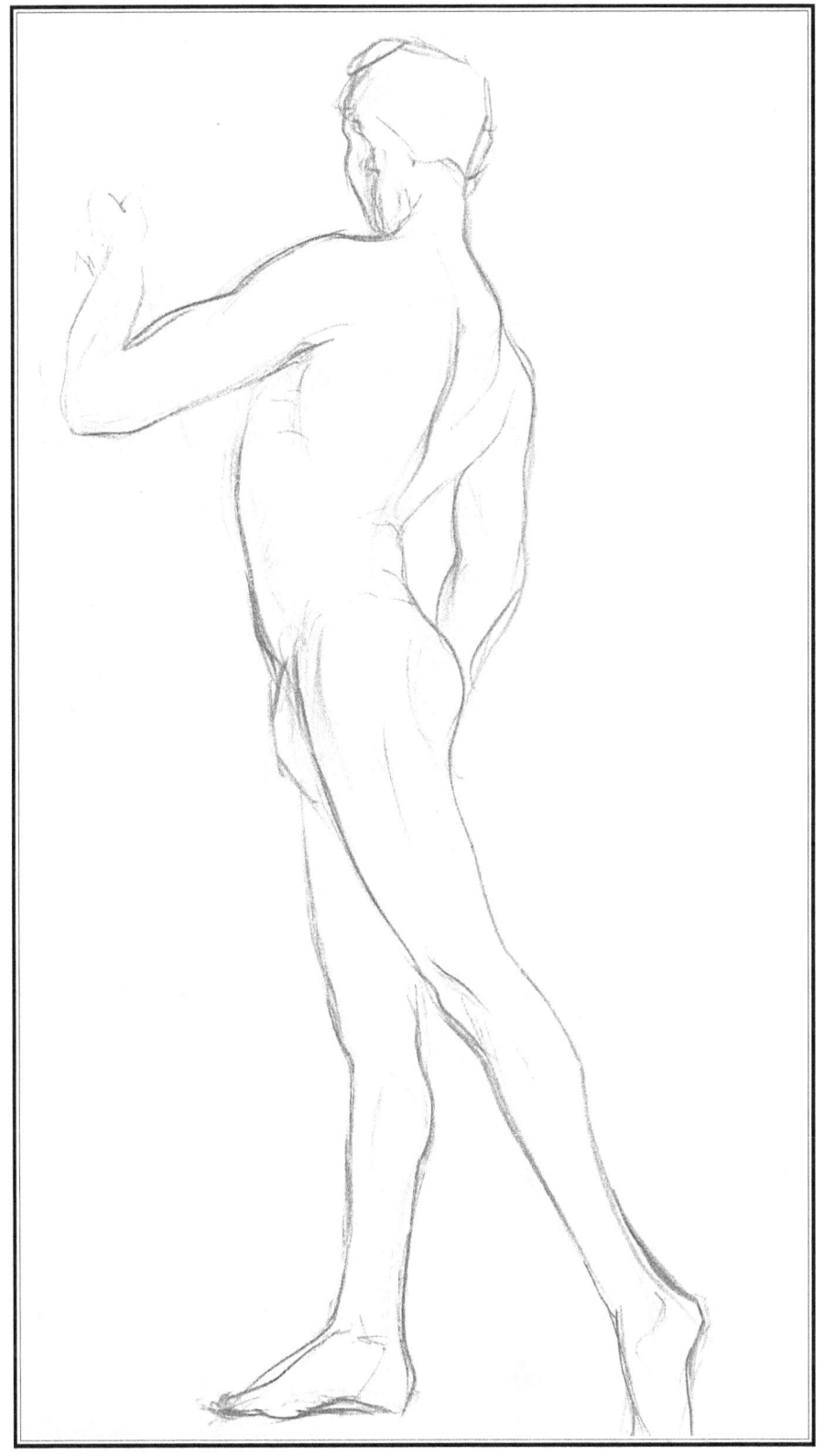

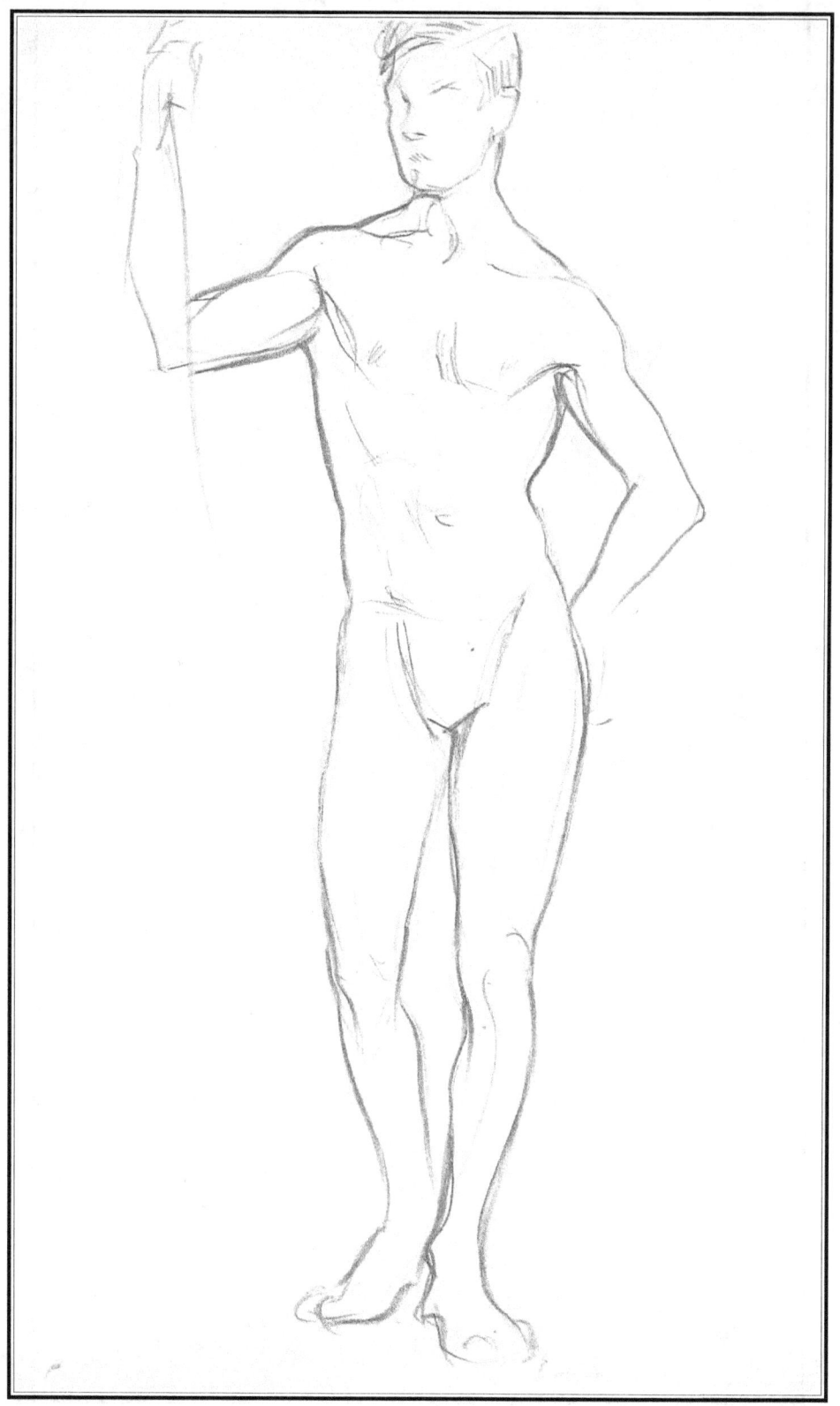

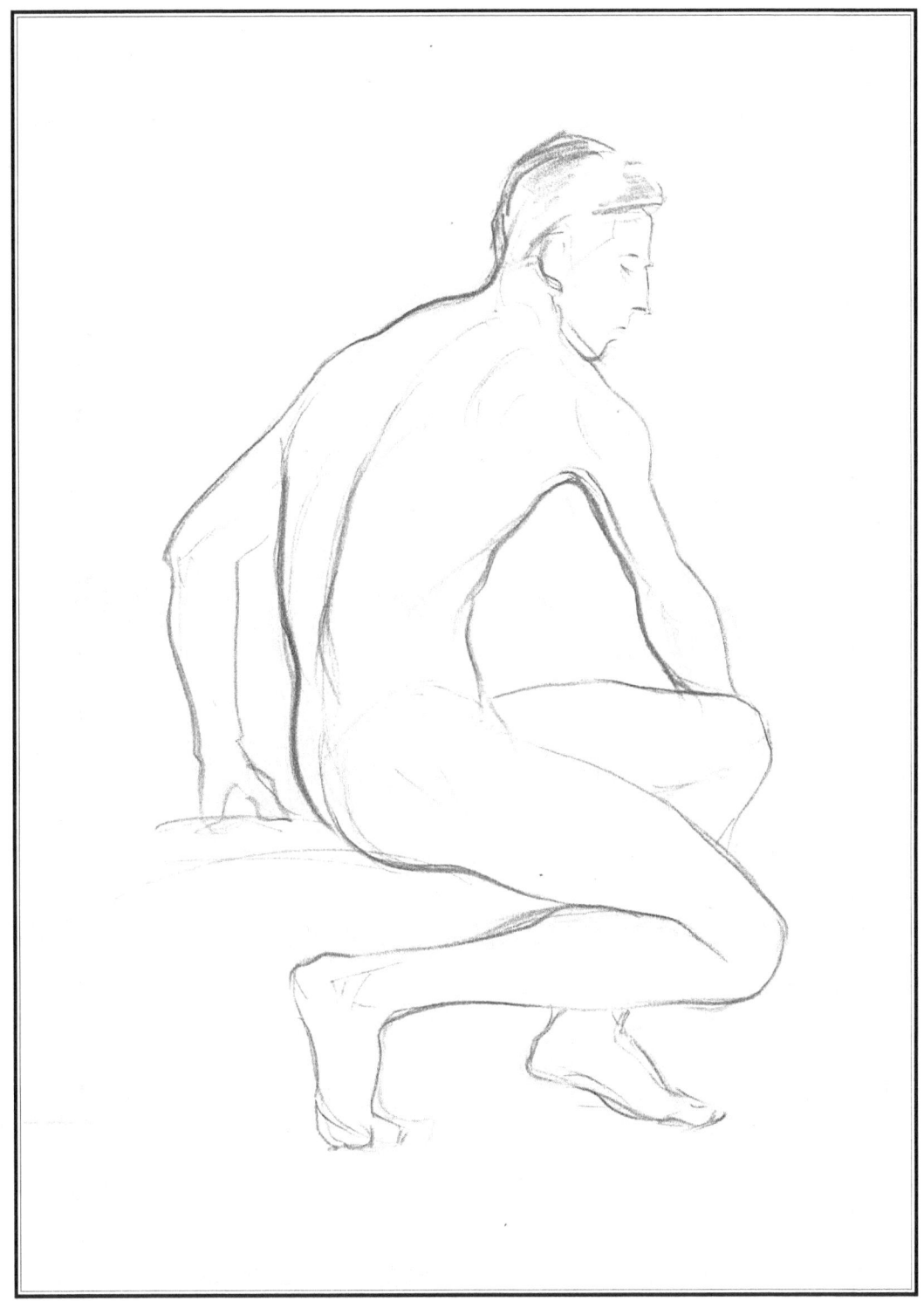

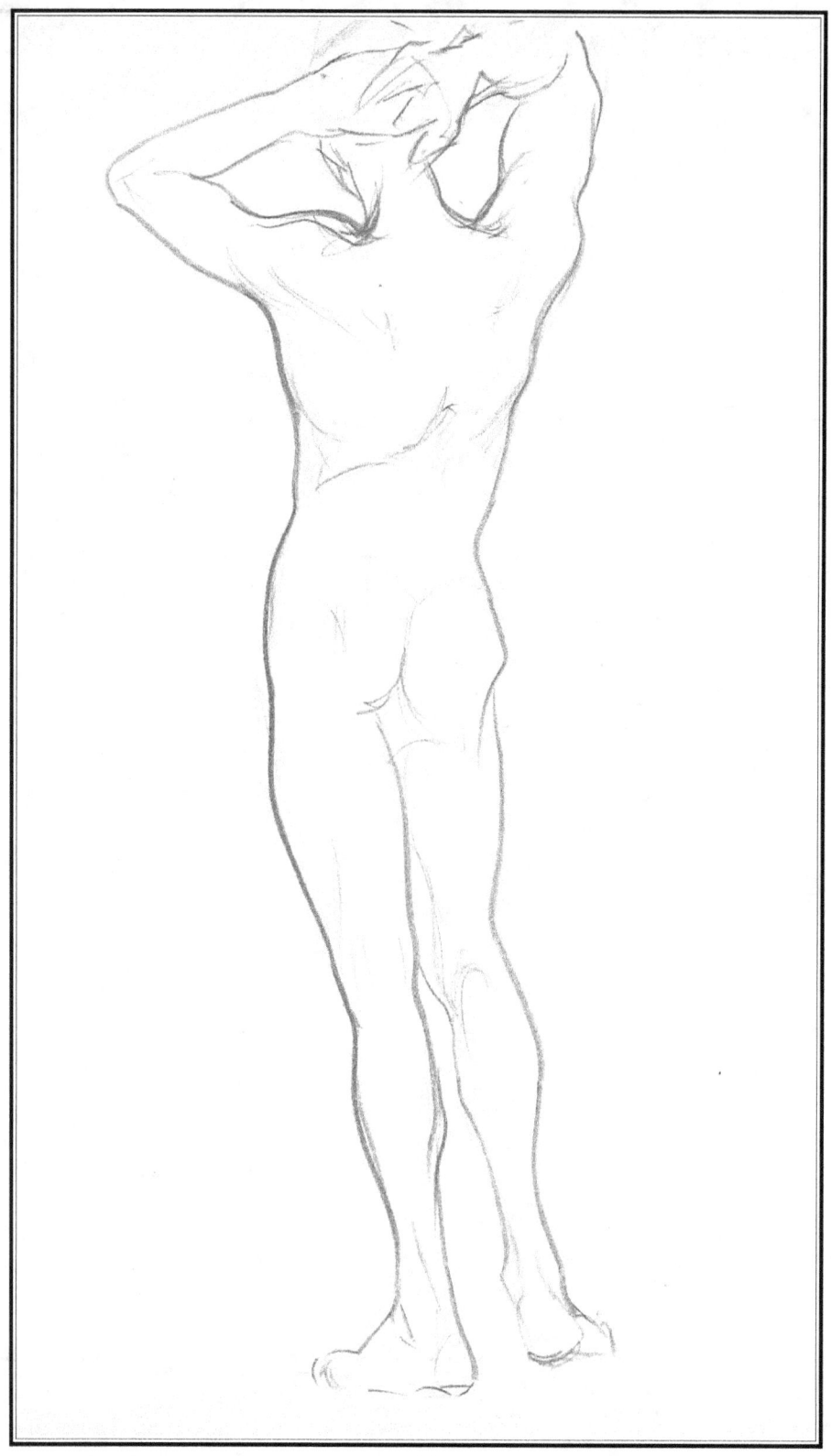

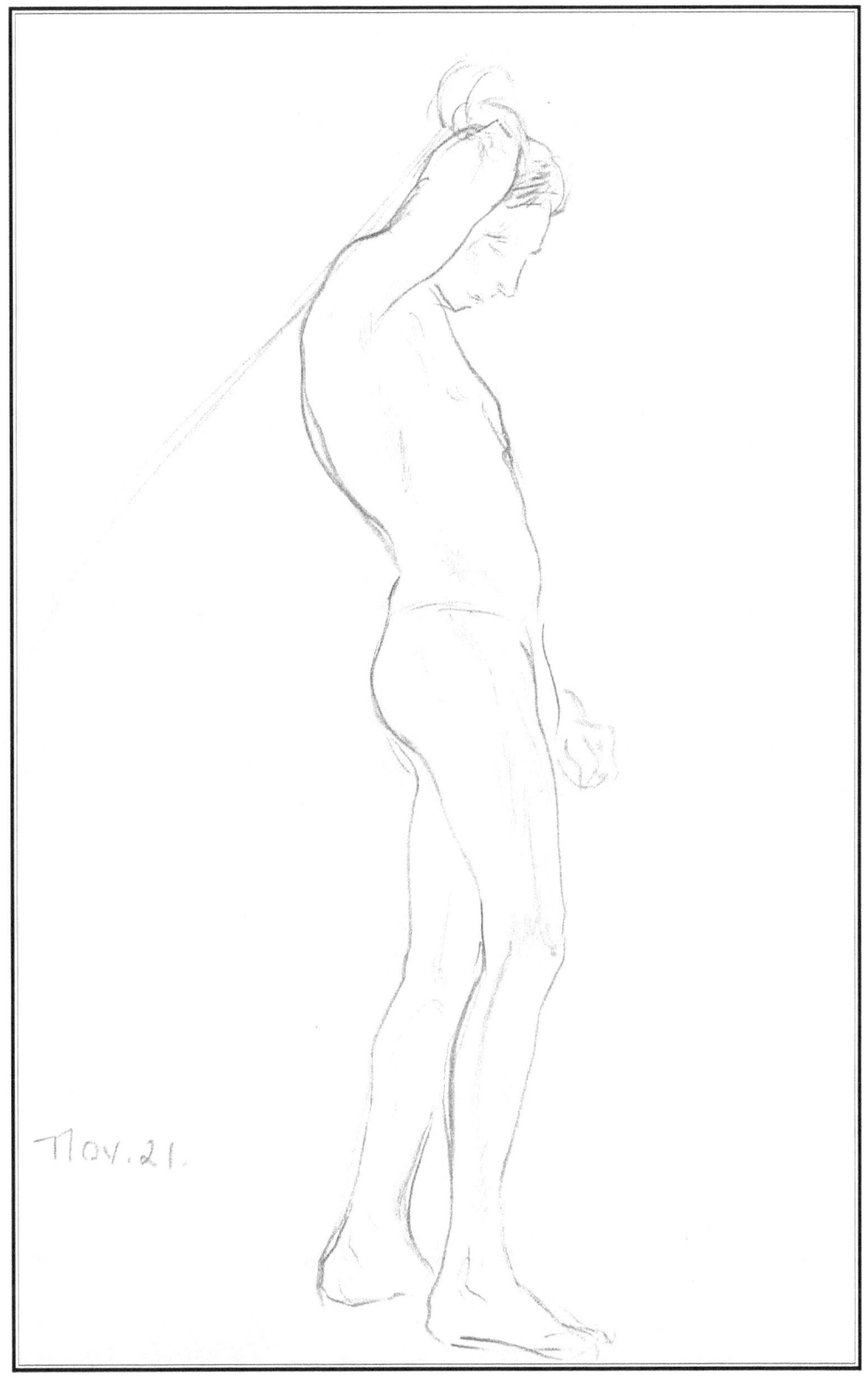

Nov. 21.

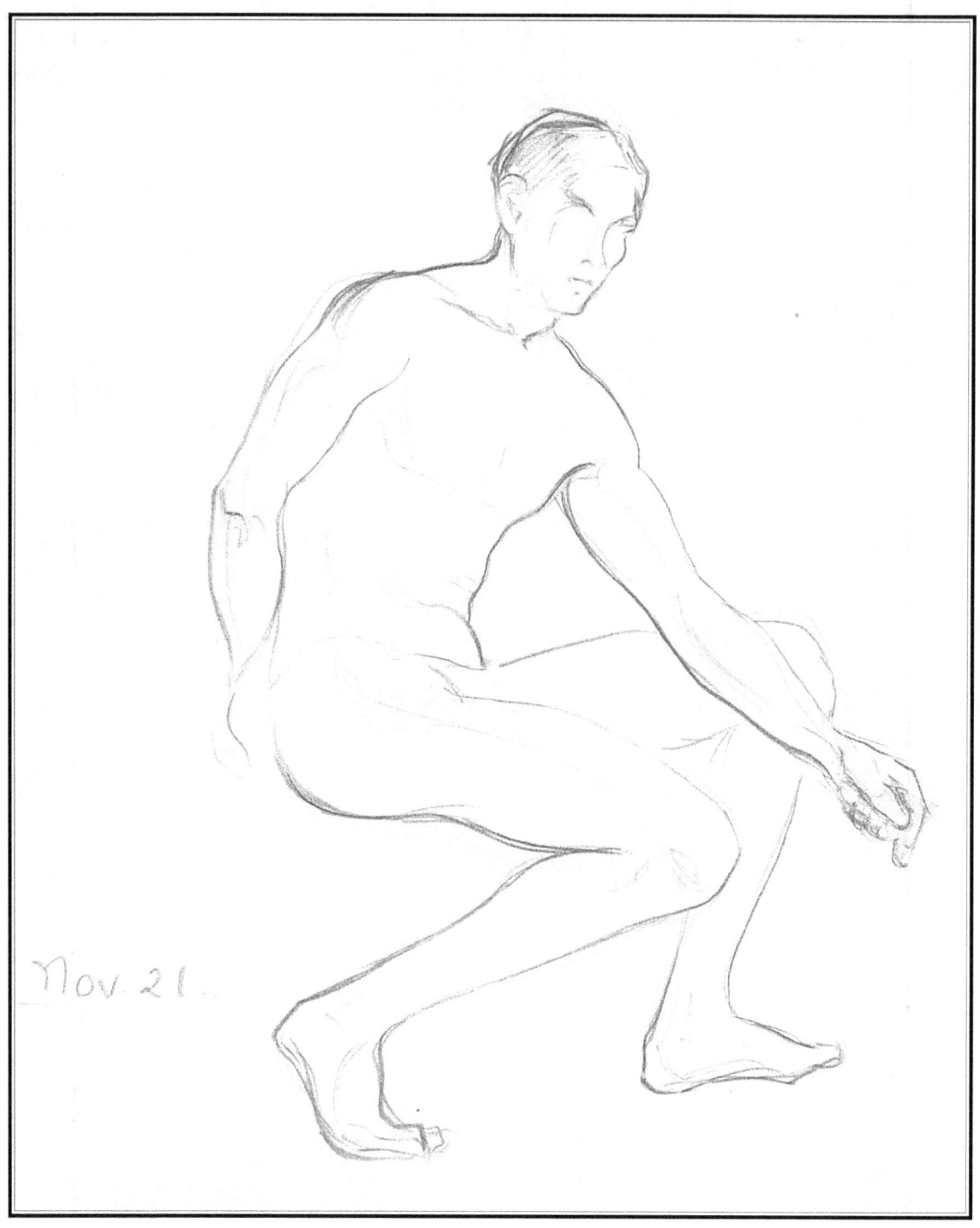

Nov. 21.

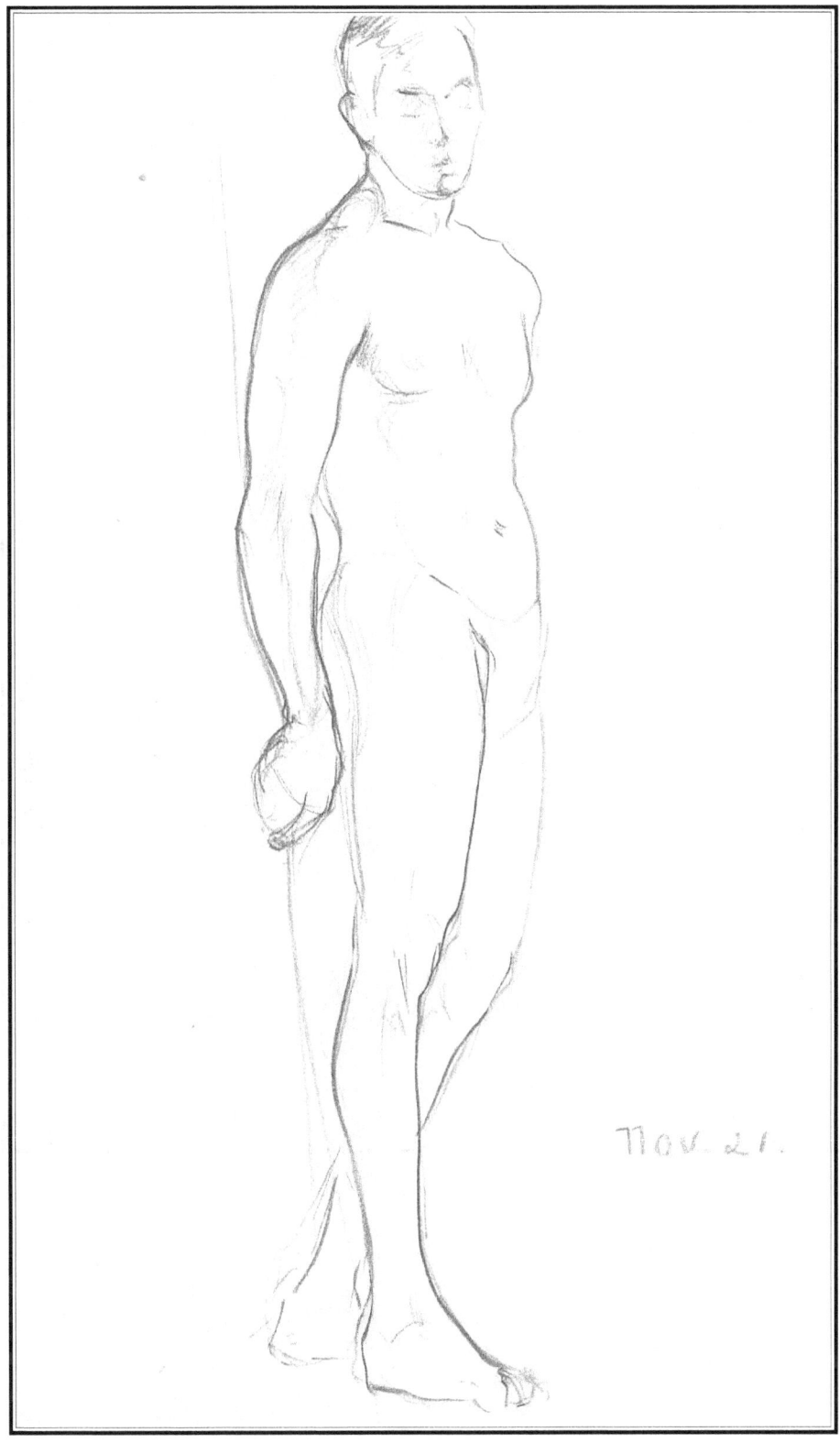

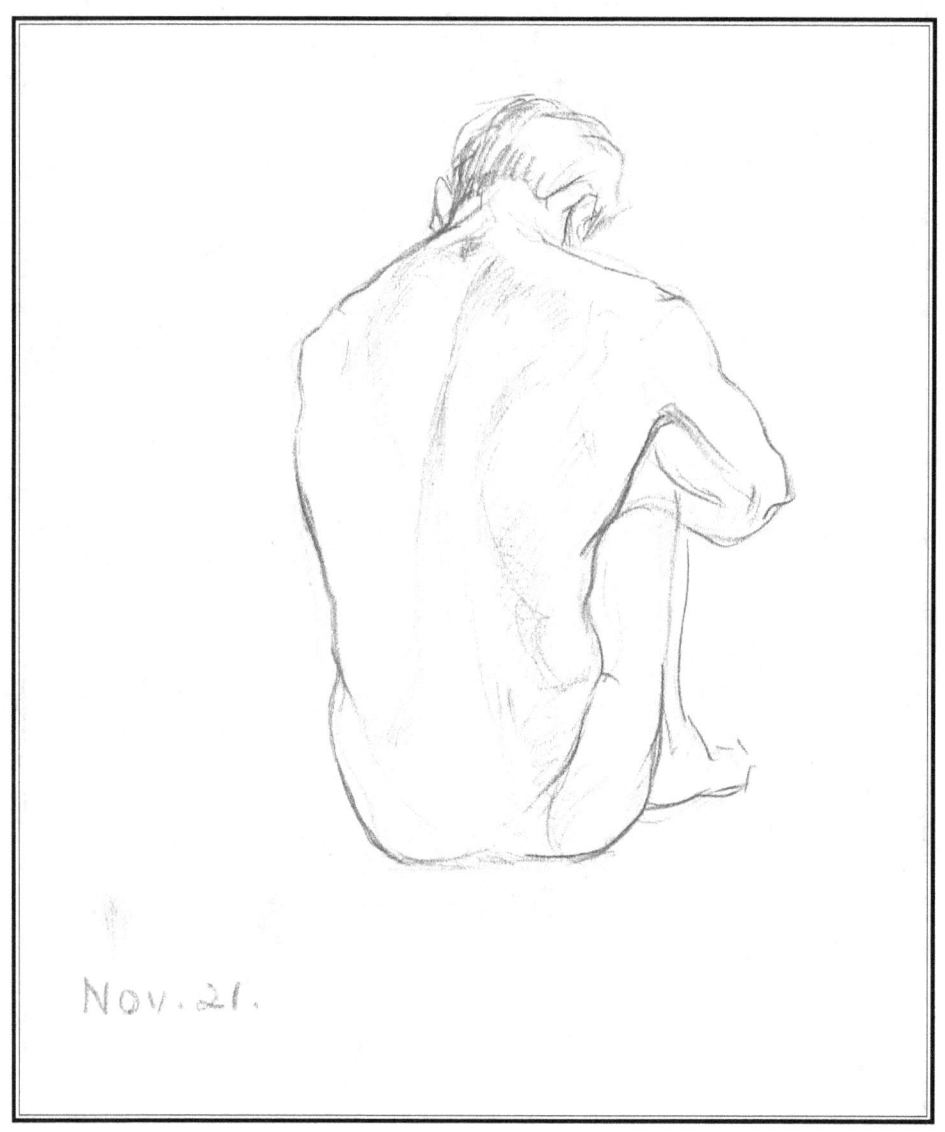

Nov. 21.

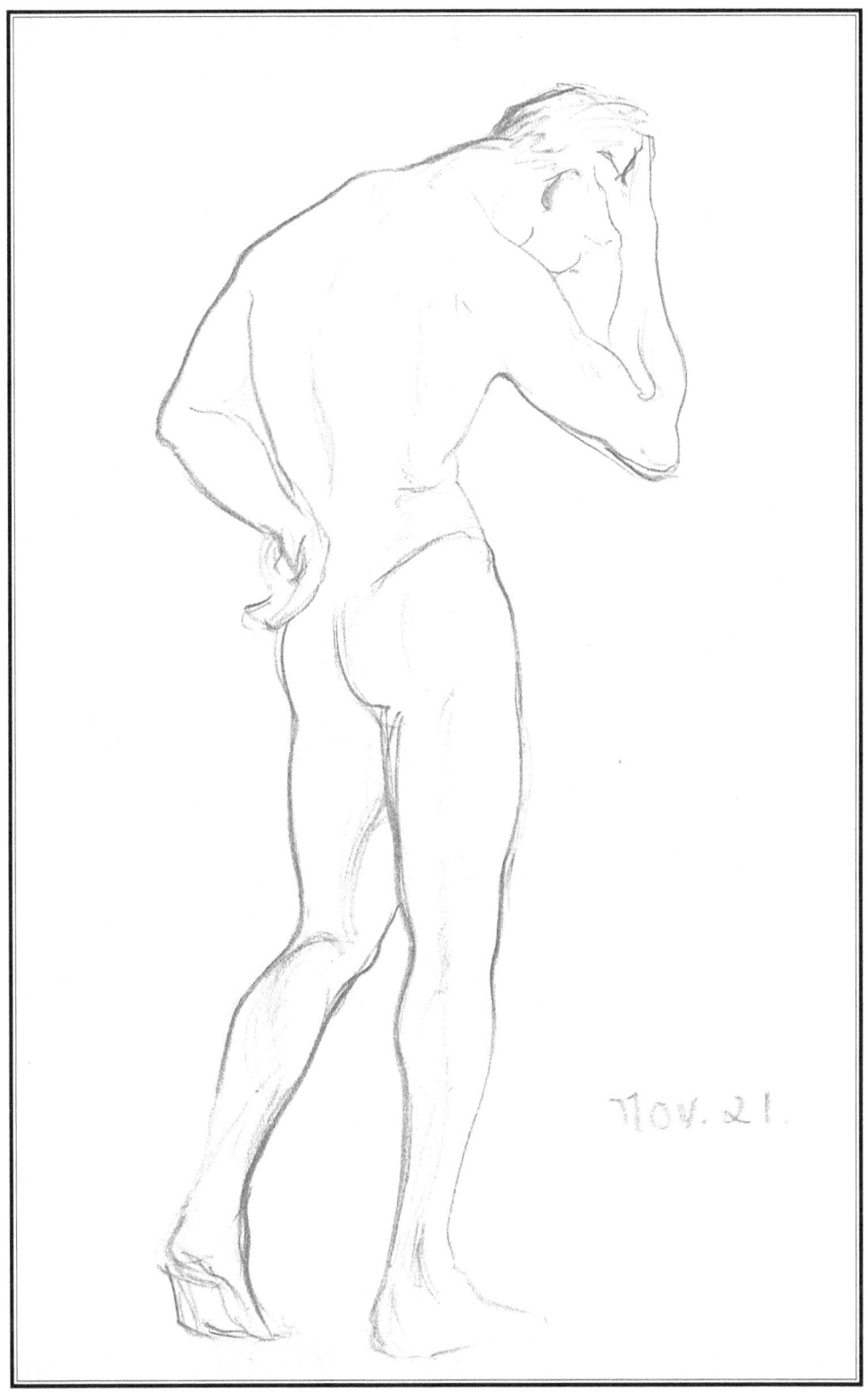

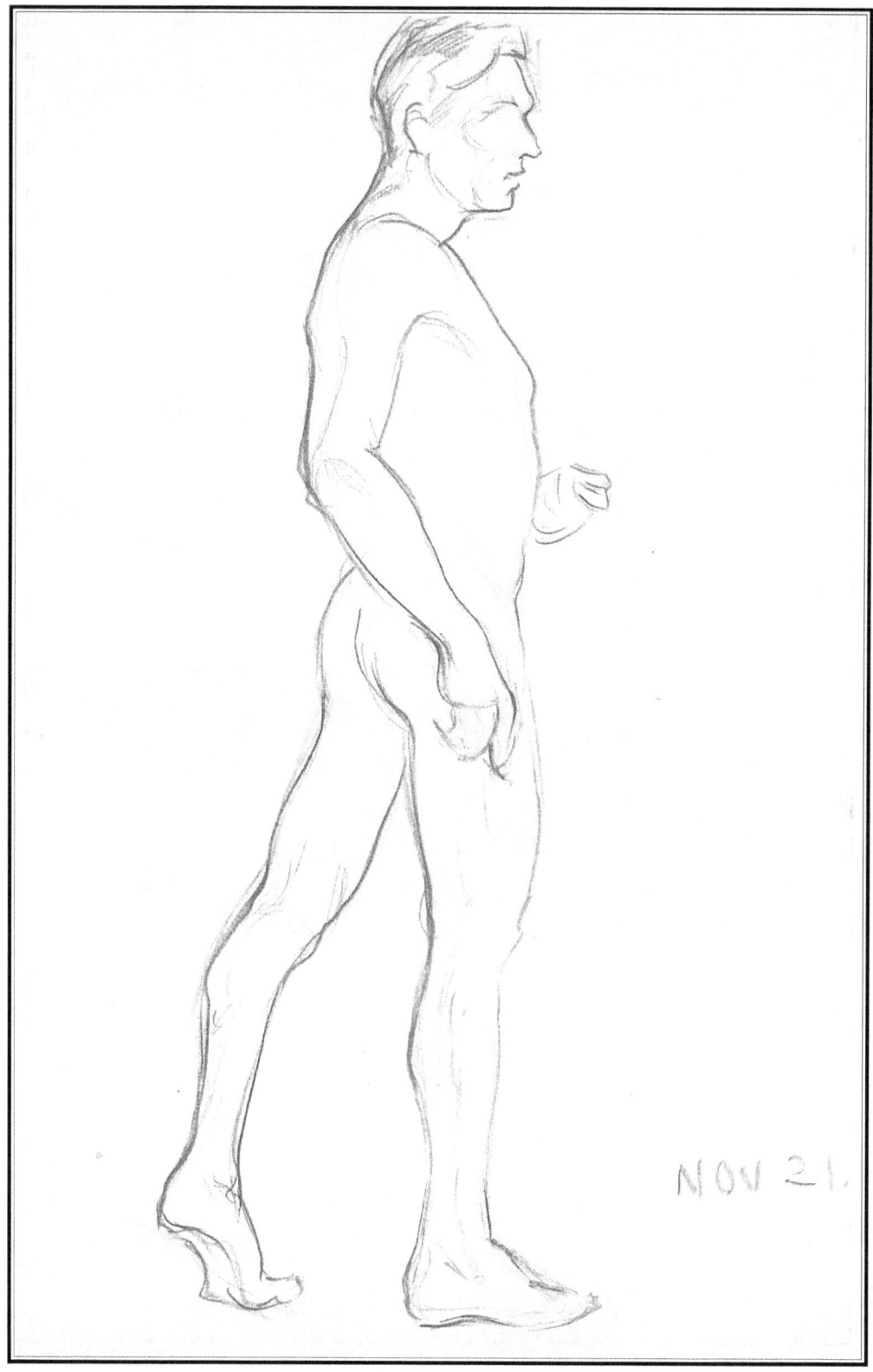

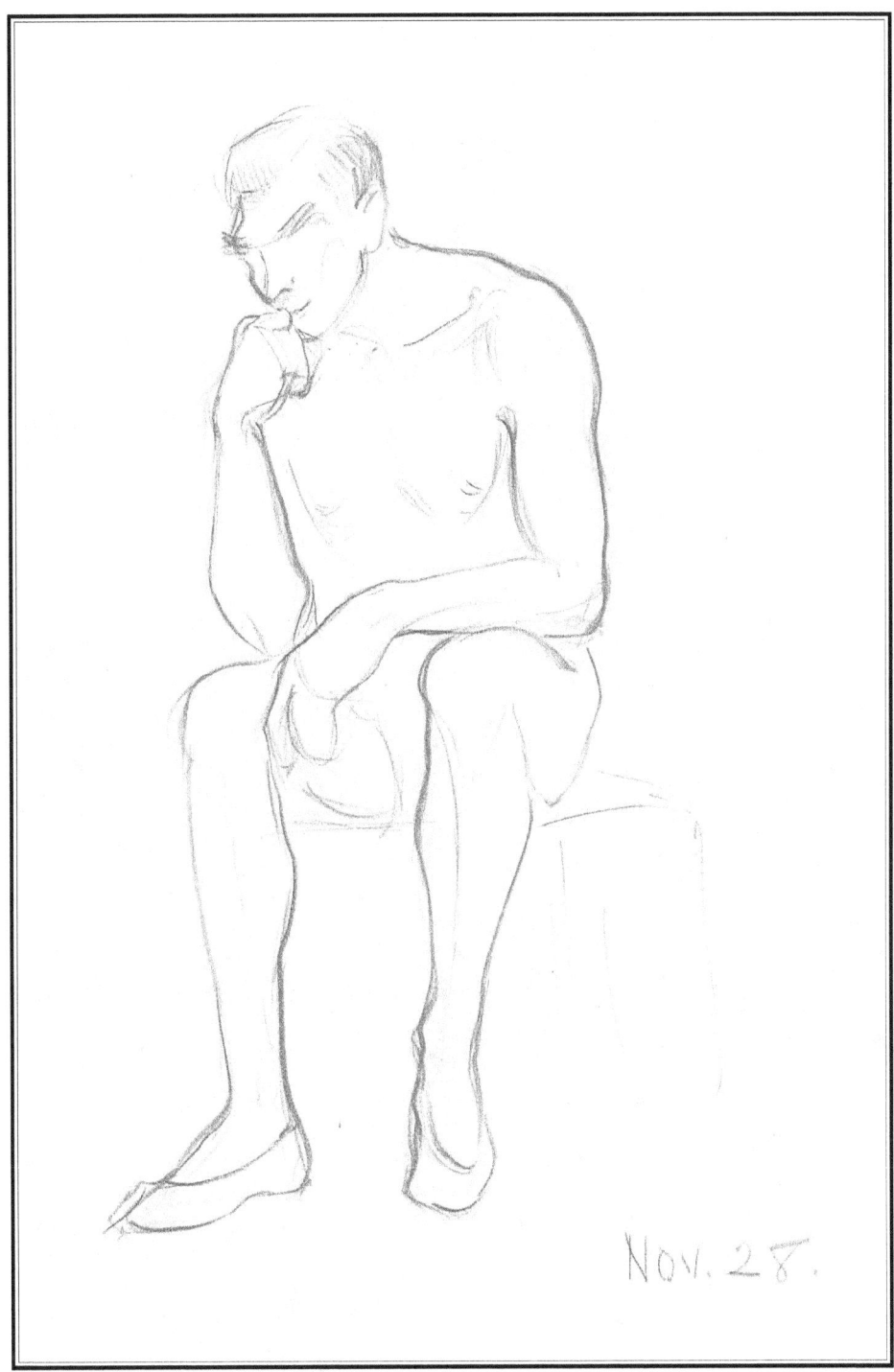

Nov. 28.

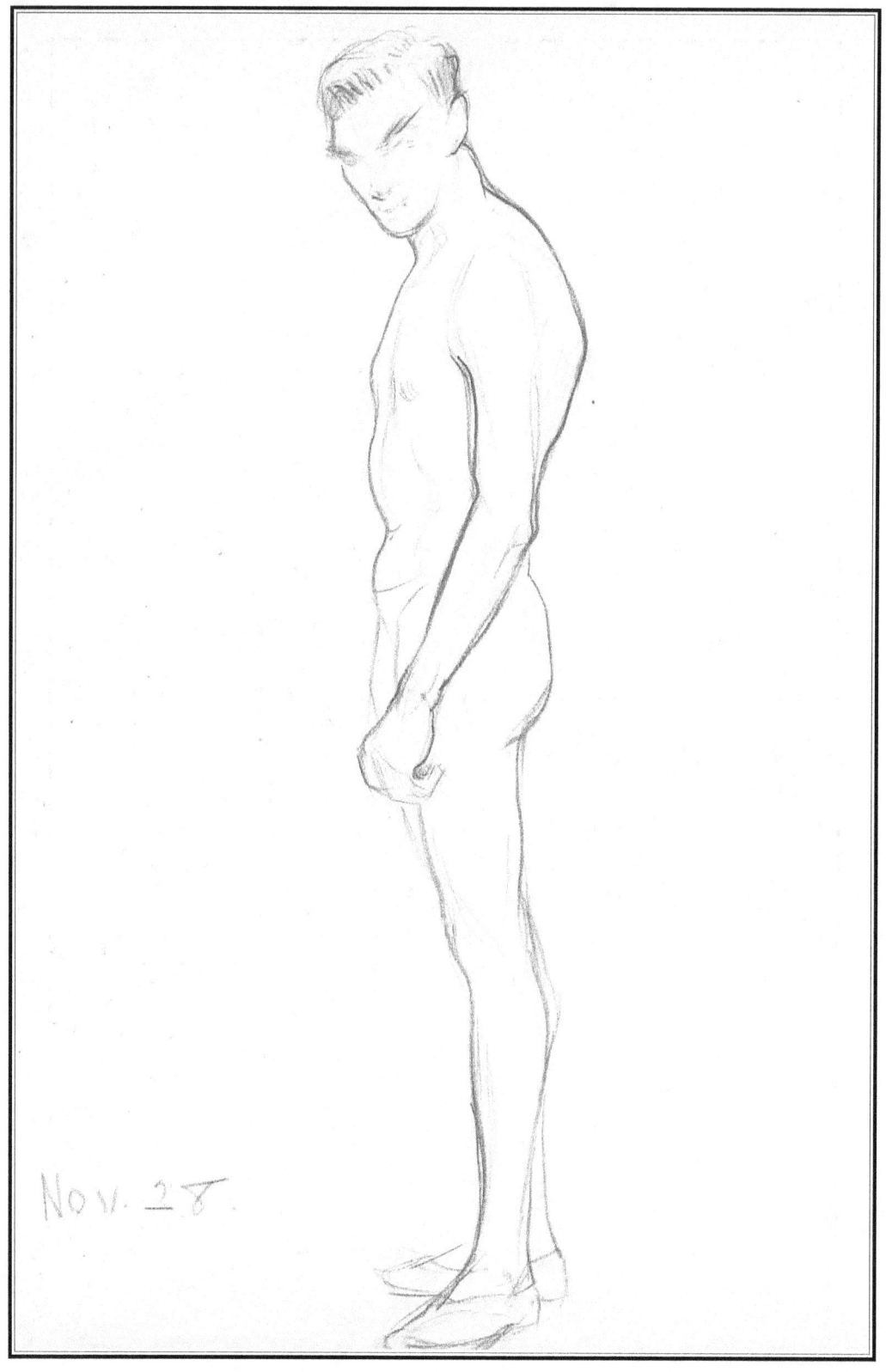

Nov. 28.

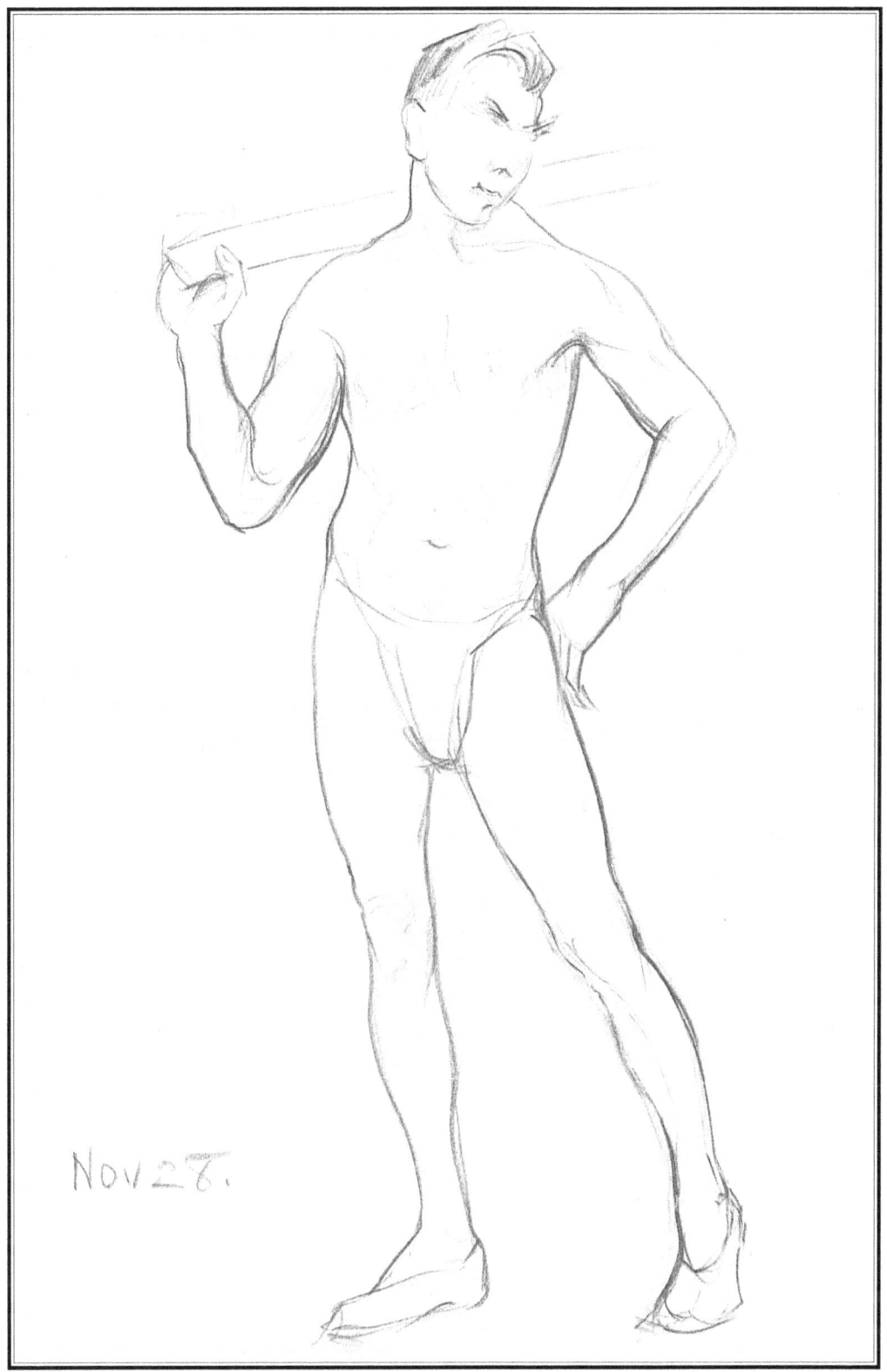

Nov 28.

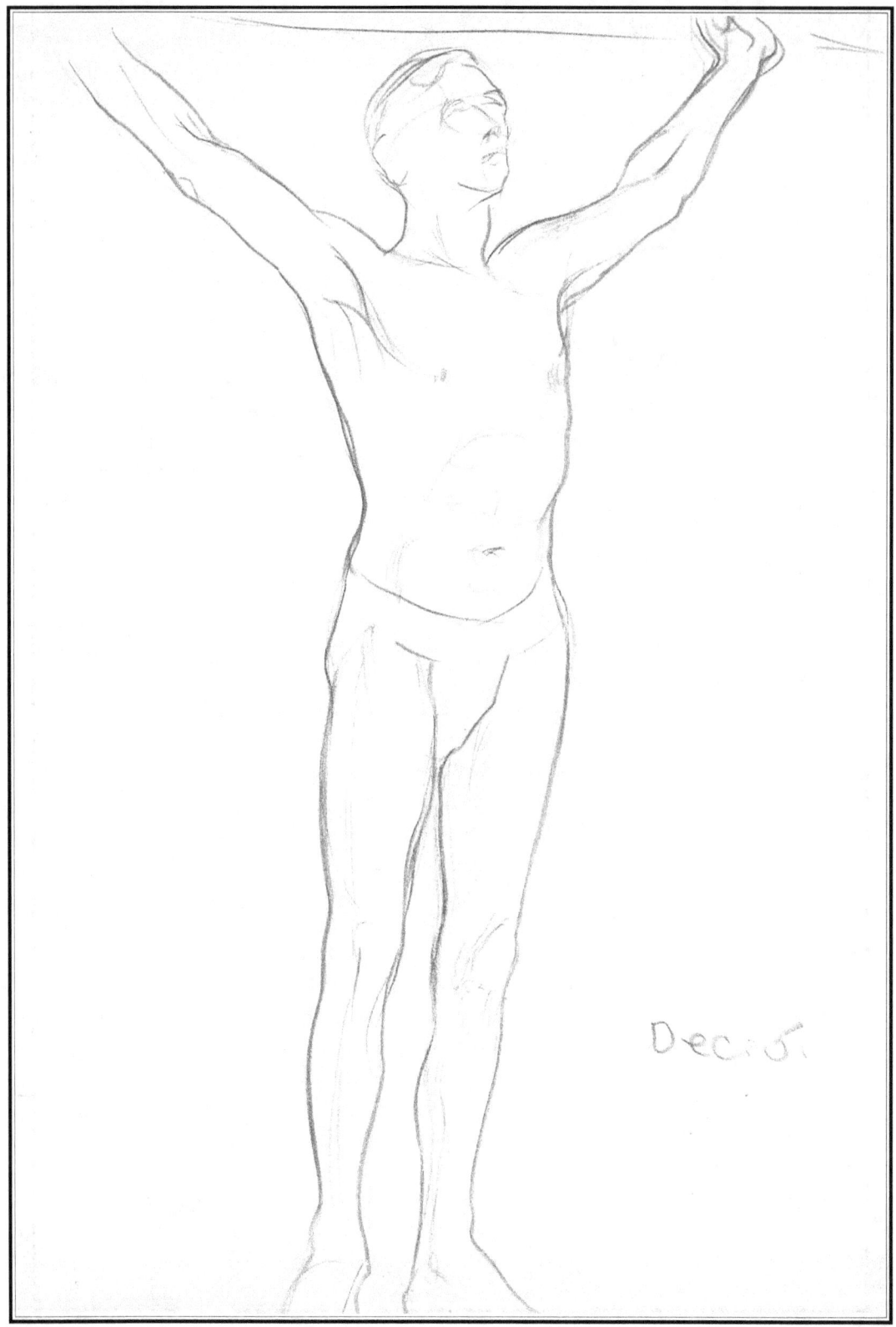

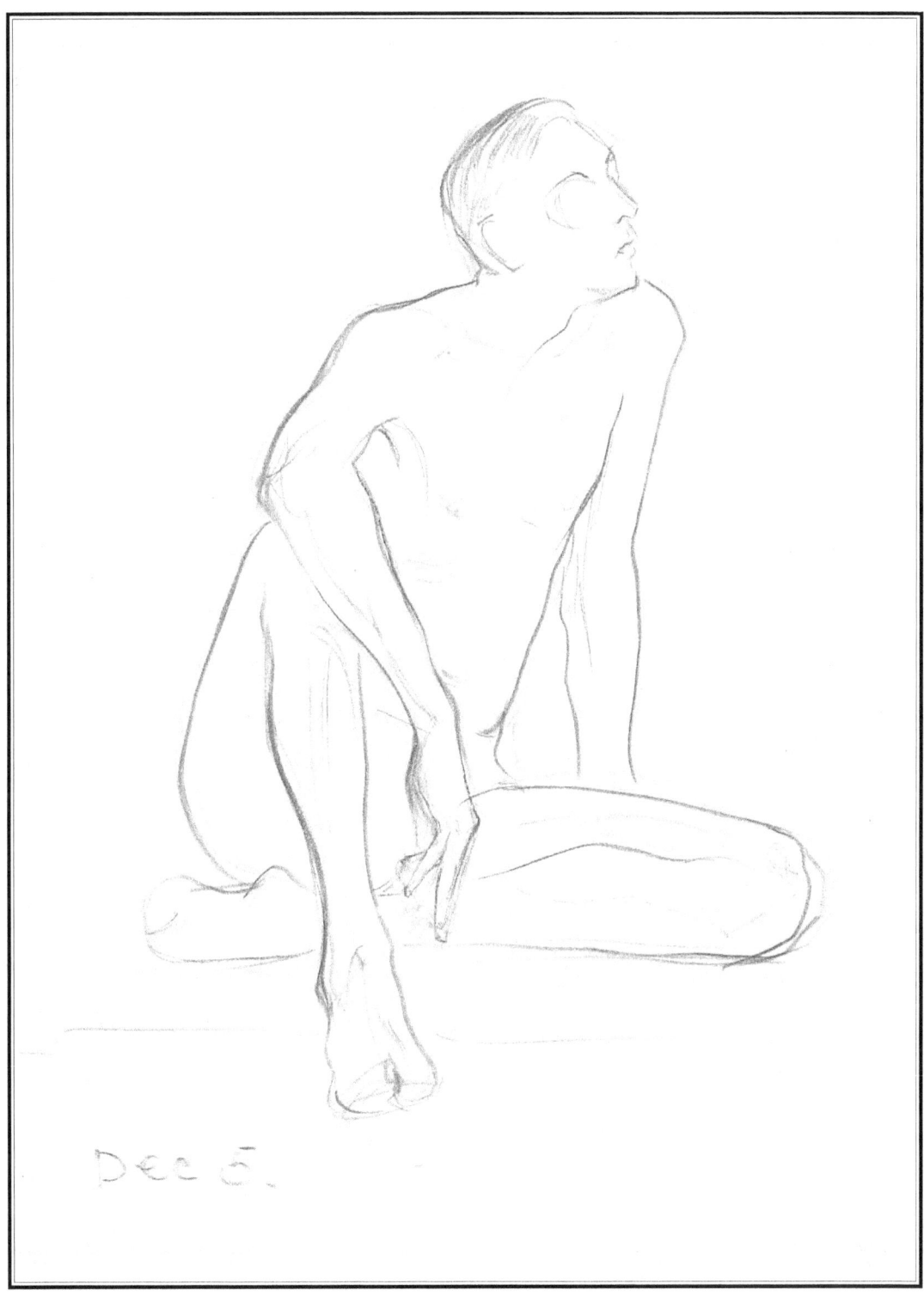

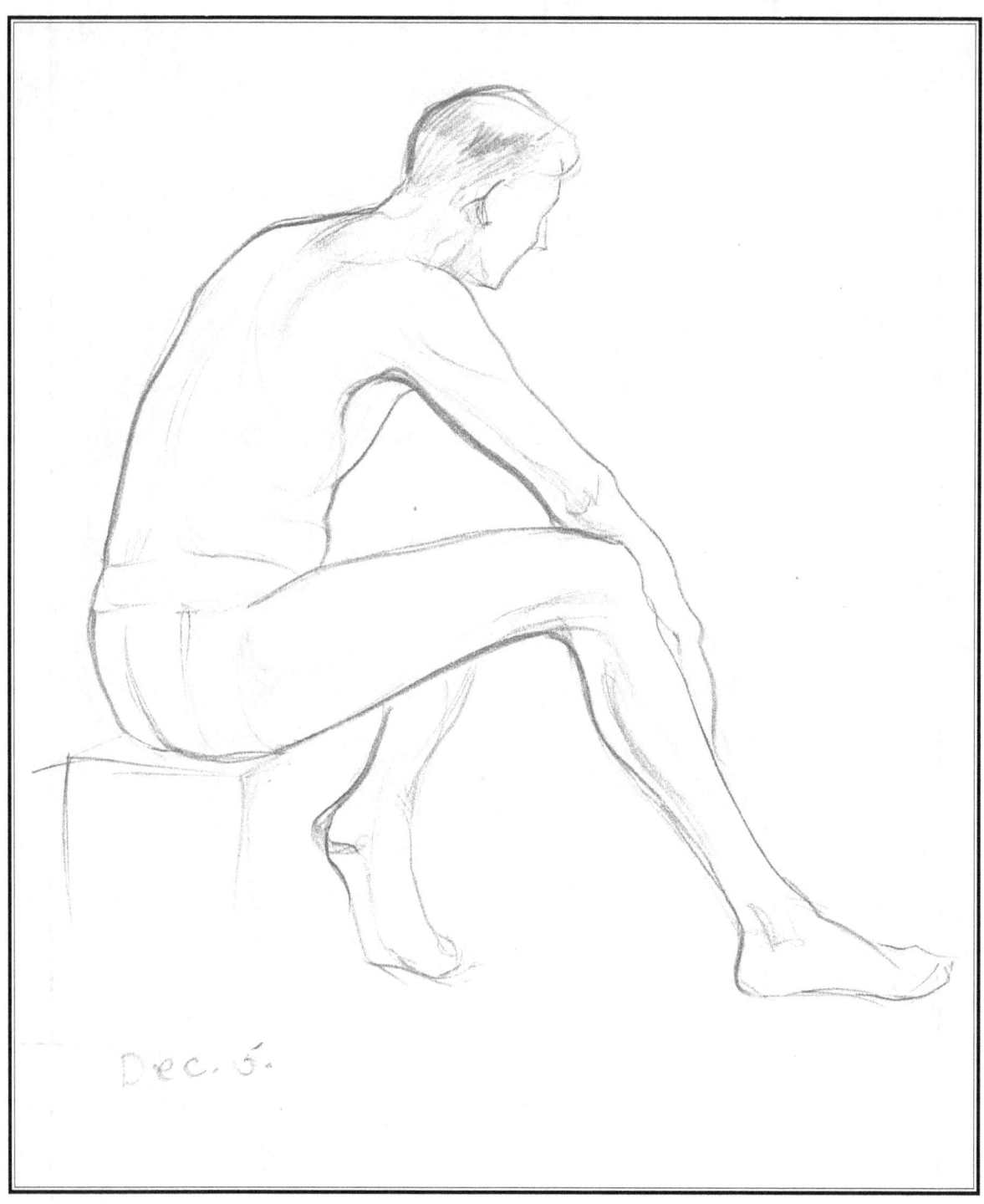

Dec. 5.

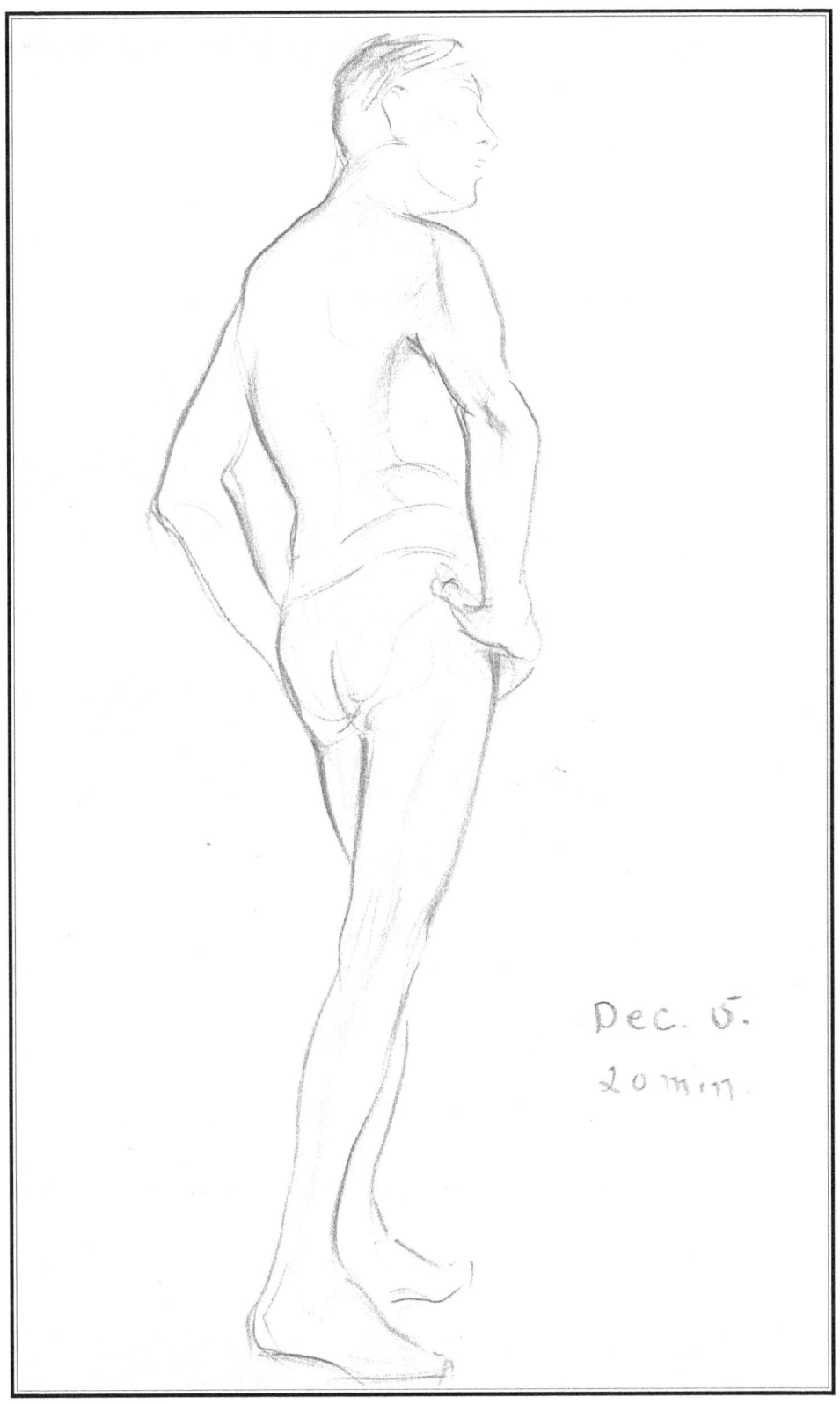

Dec. 5.
20 min.

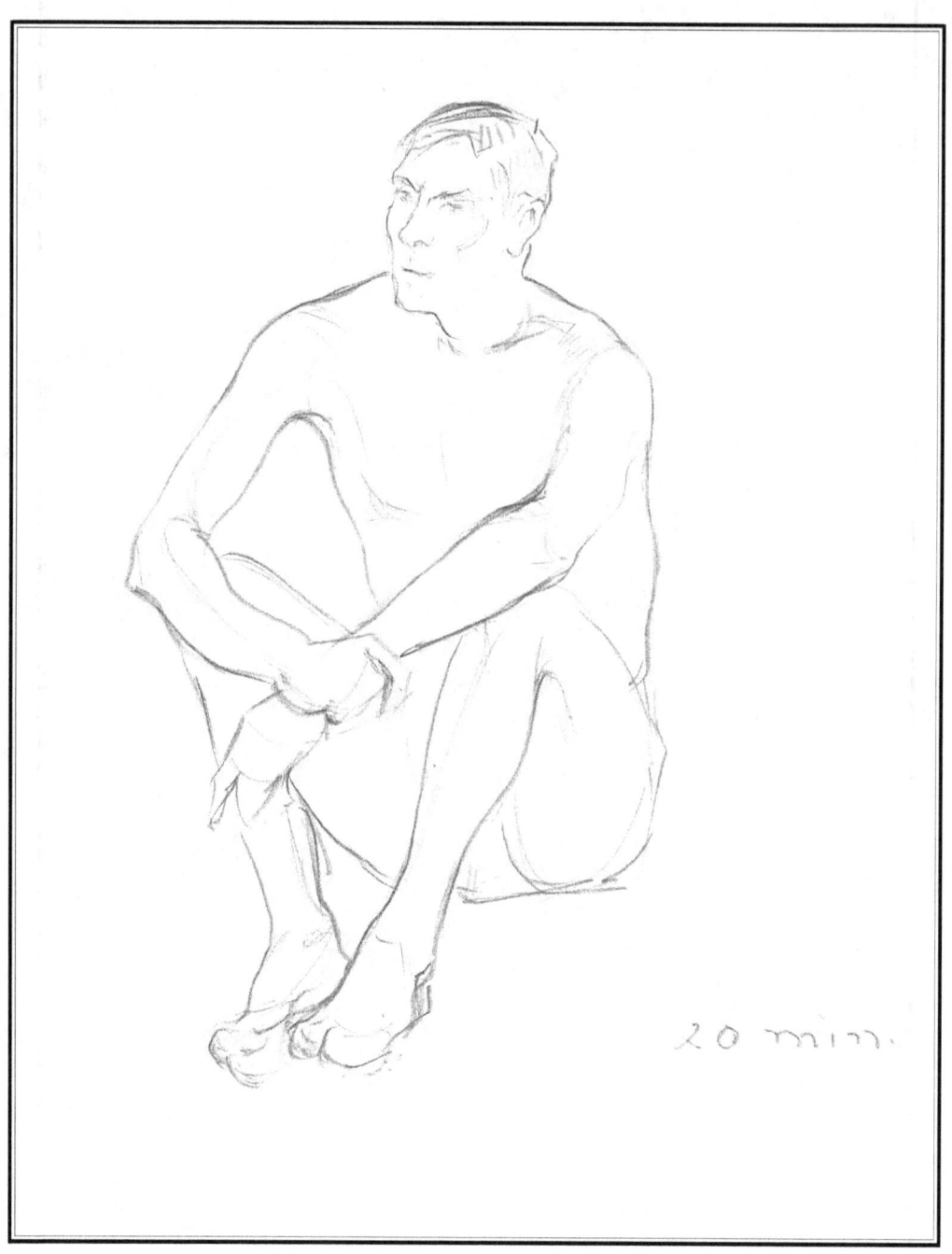

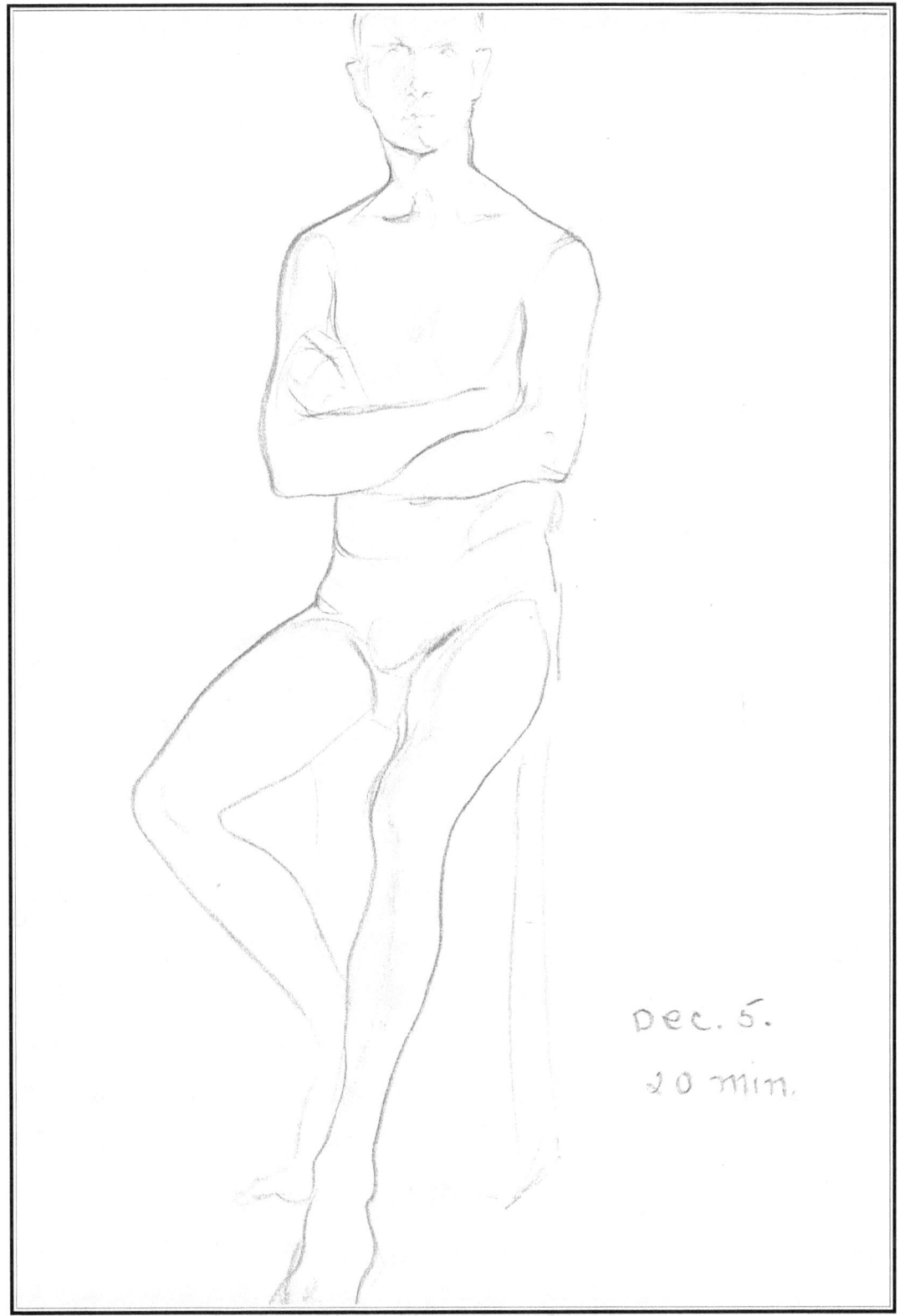

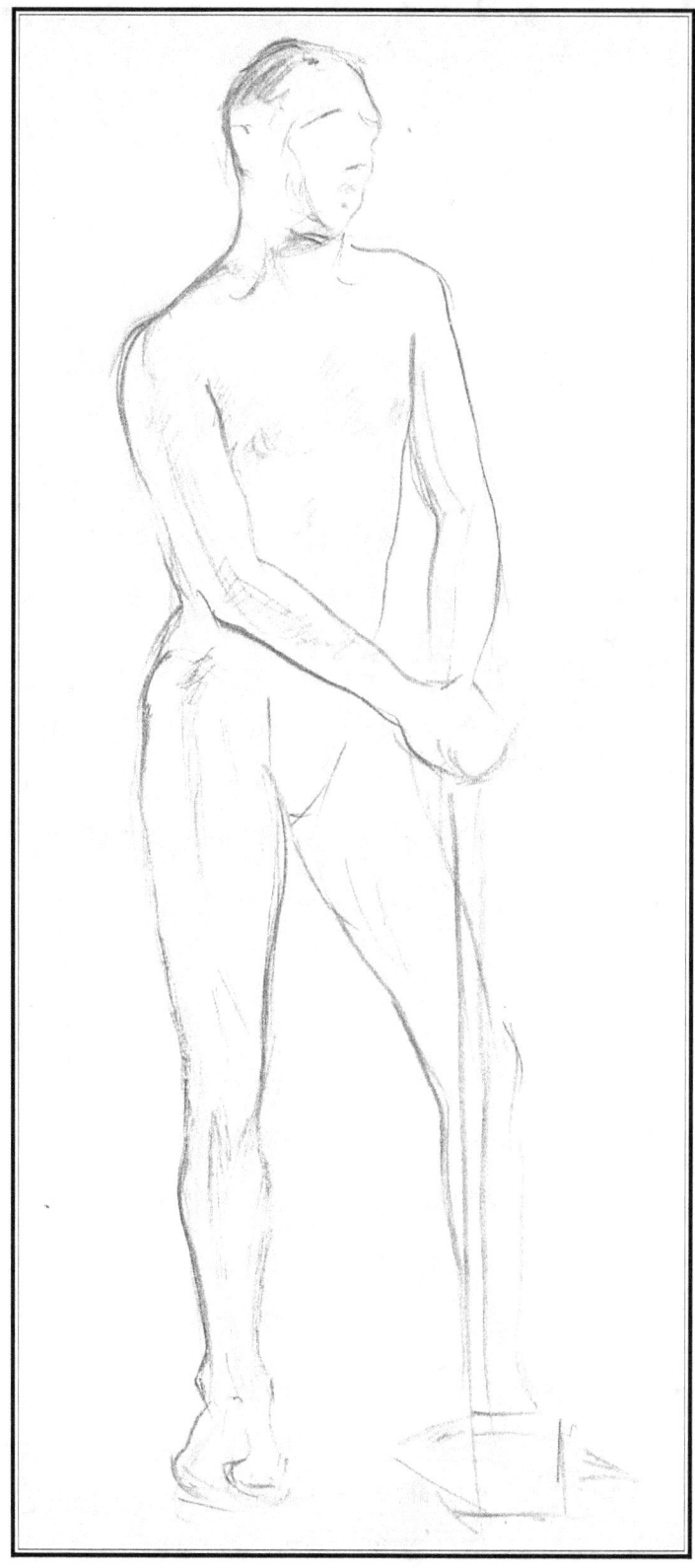

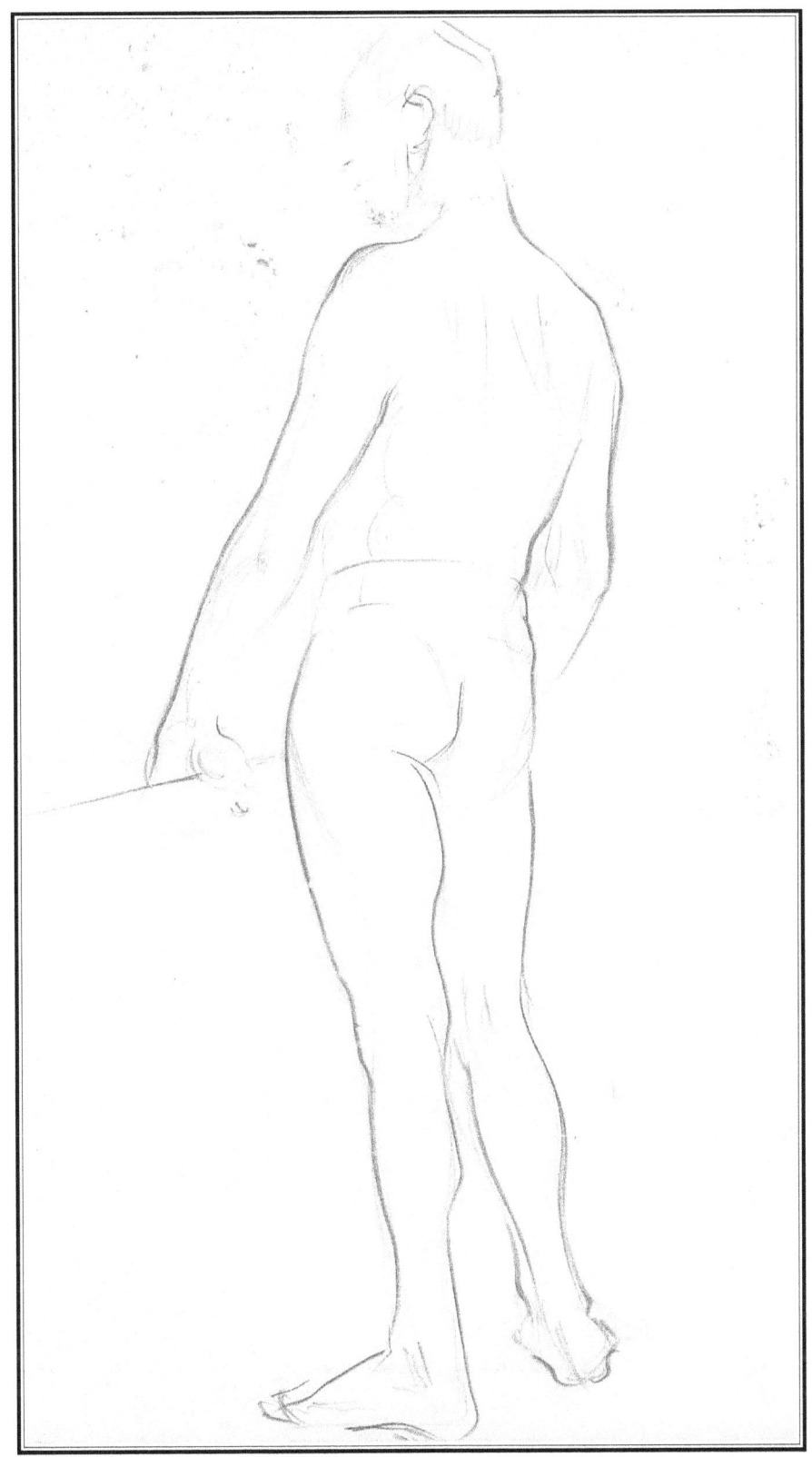

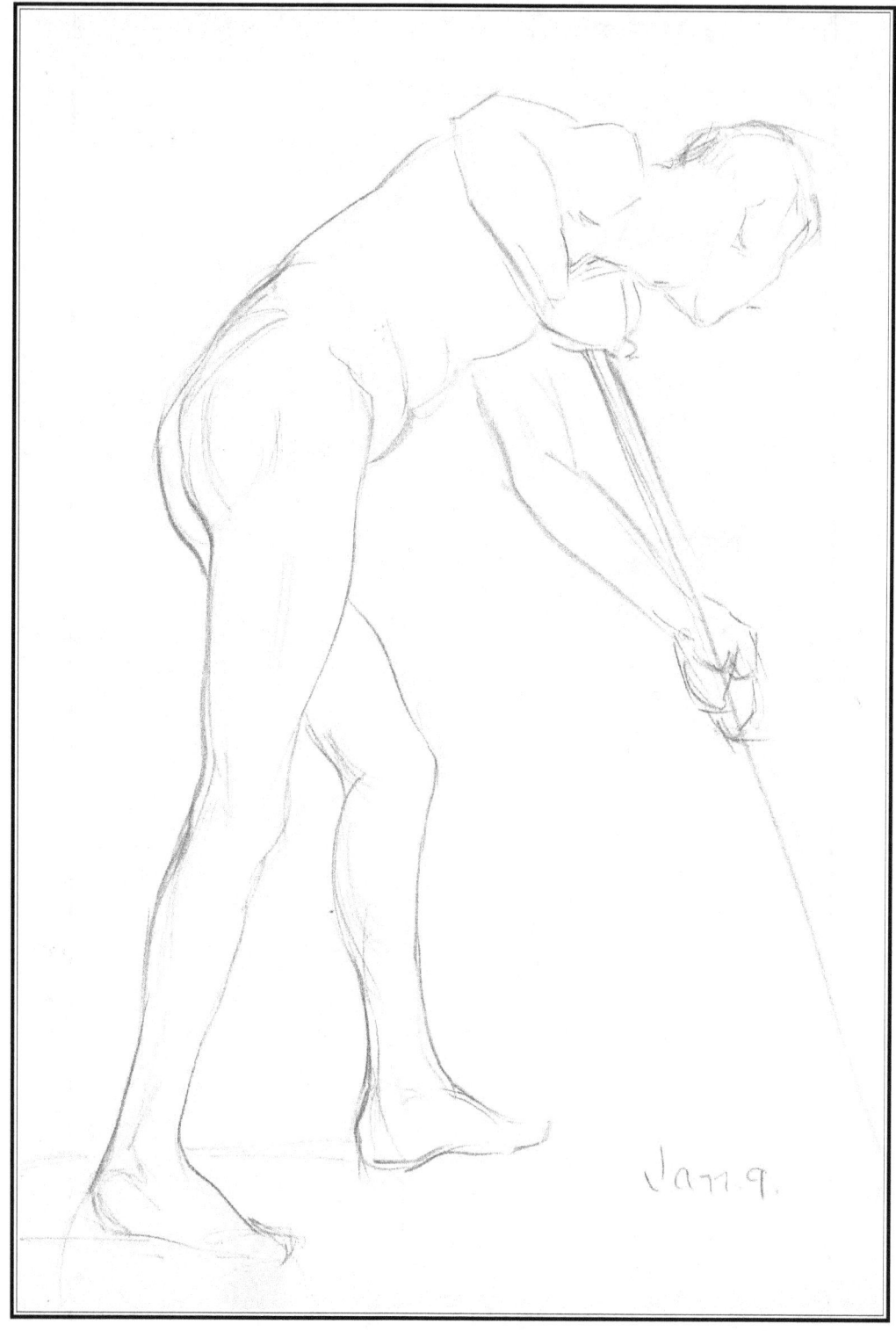

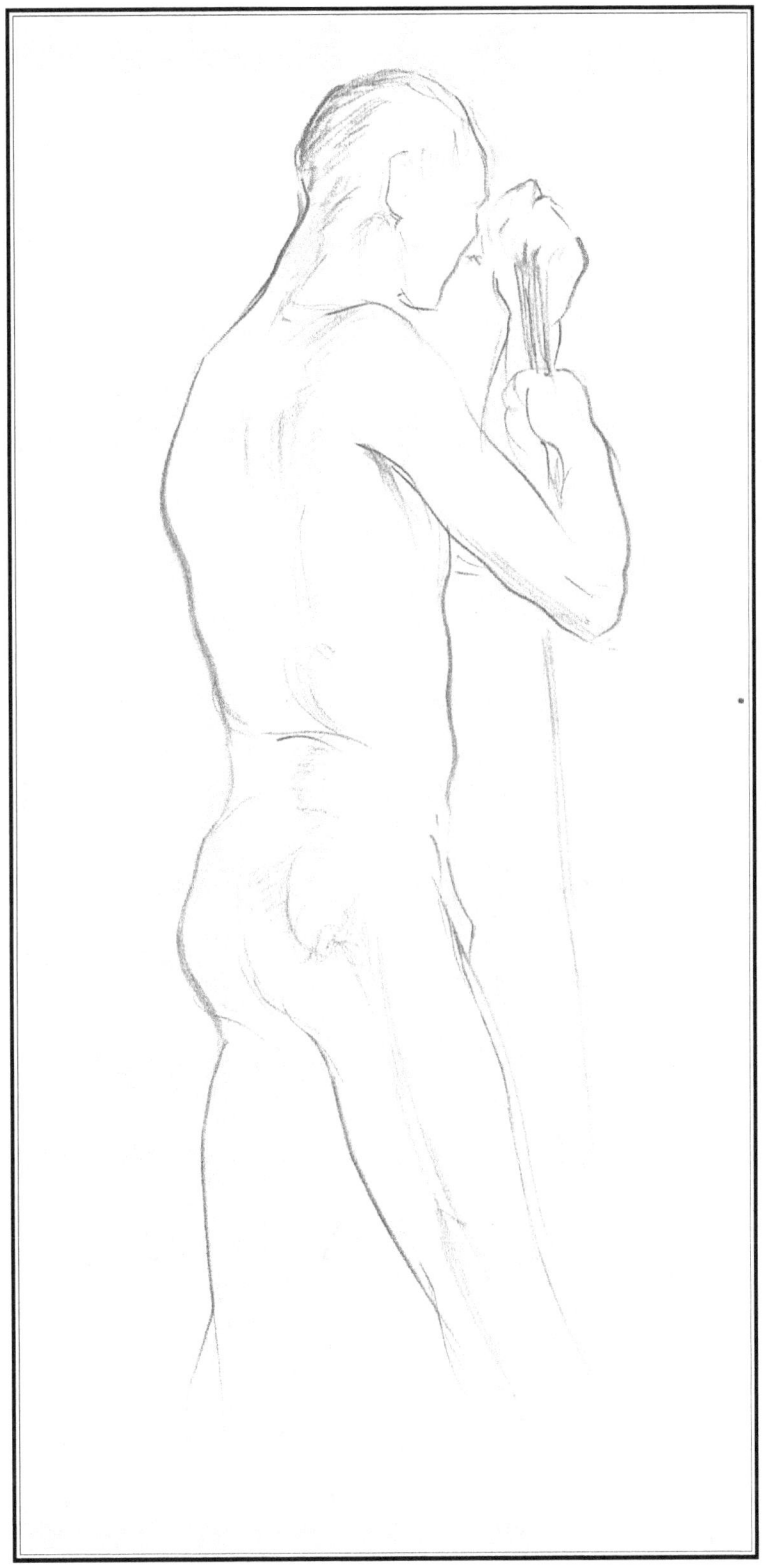

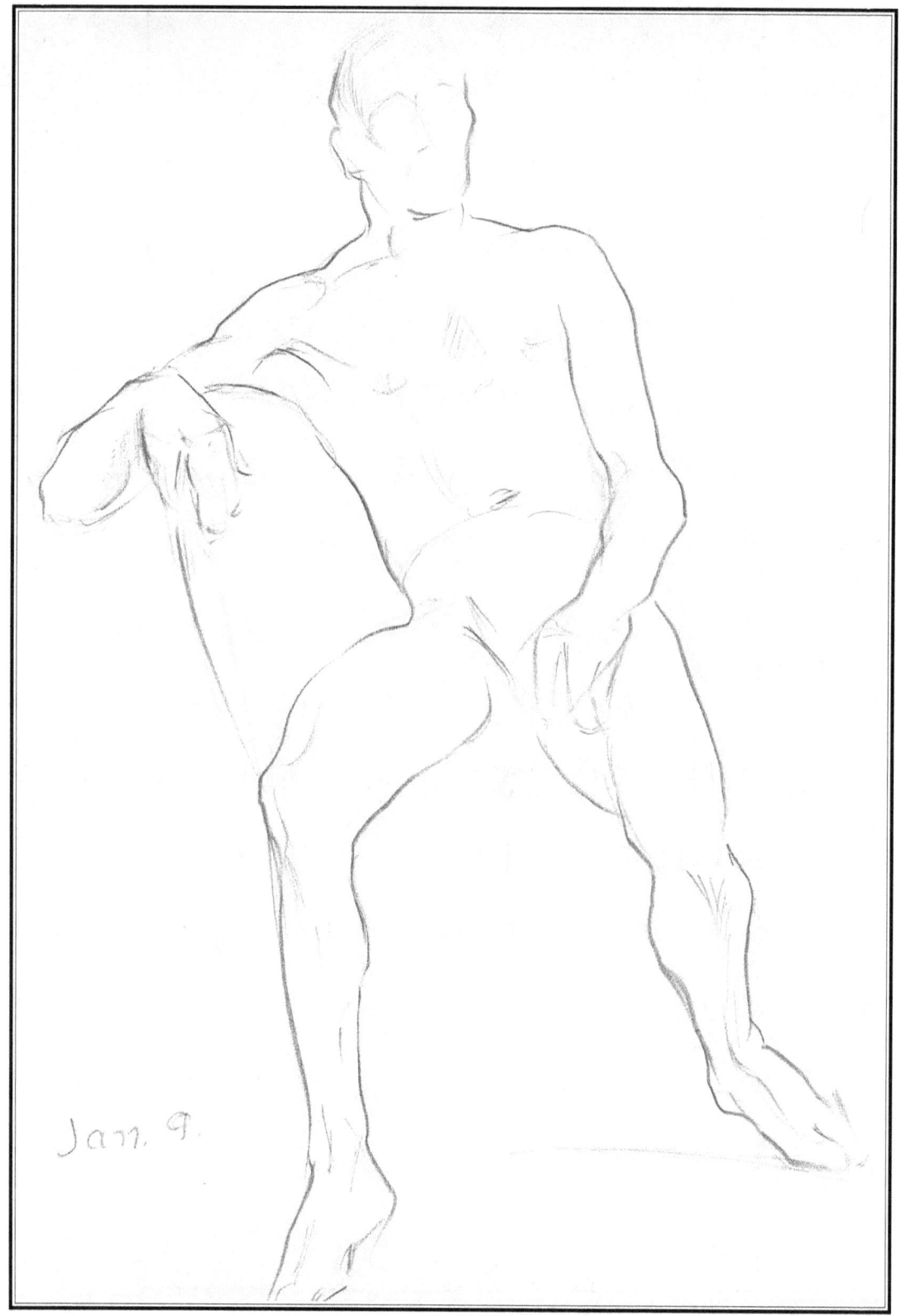

Jan. 9.

HOW TO DRAW THE HUMAN FIGURE

GRACE YOUNG

MEMORY ACTION

SEPT. - DEC.

1927

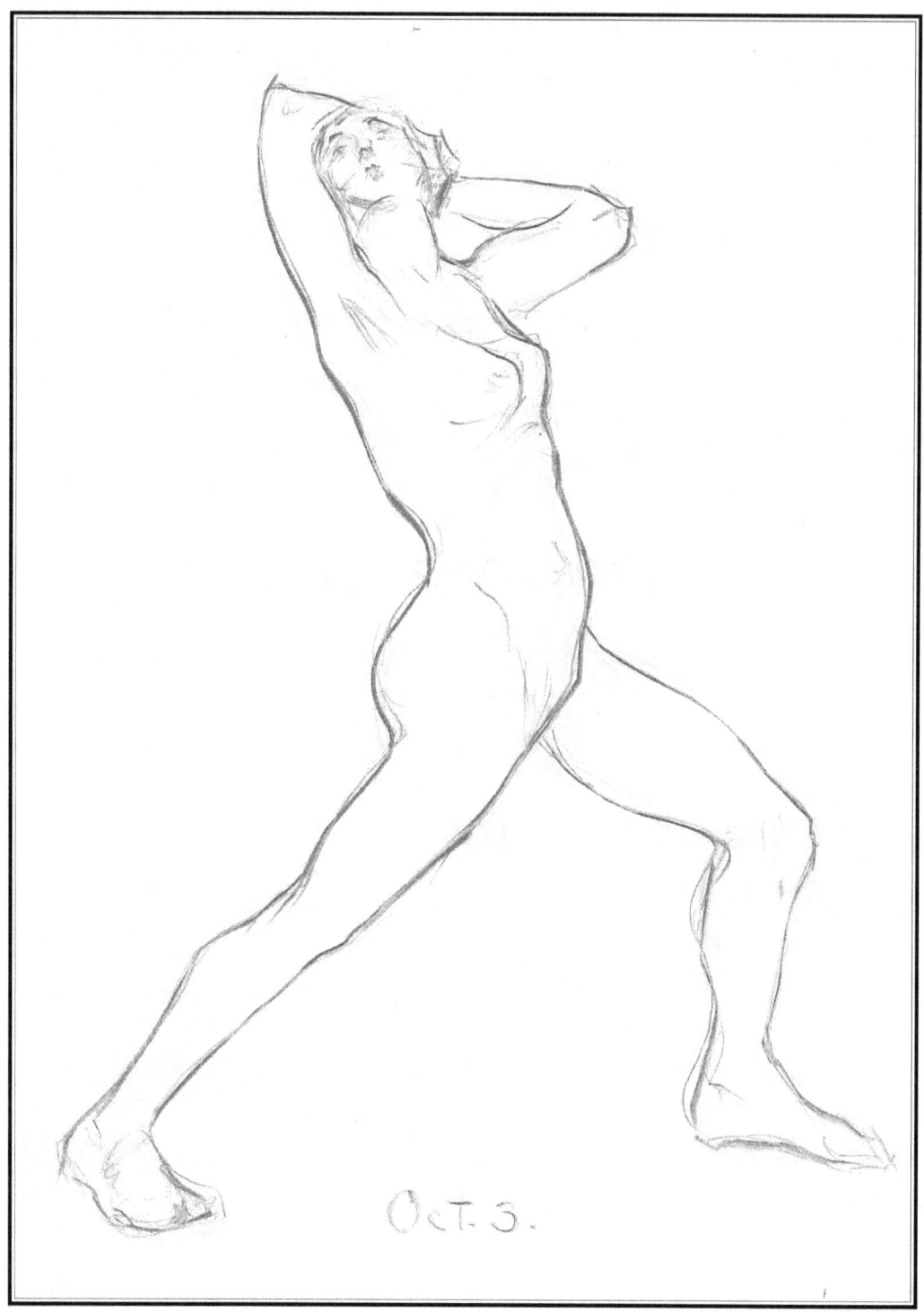

Oct. 3.

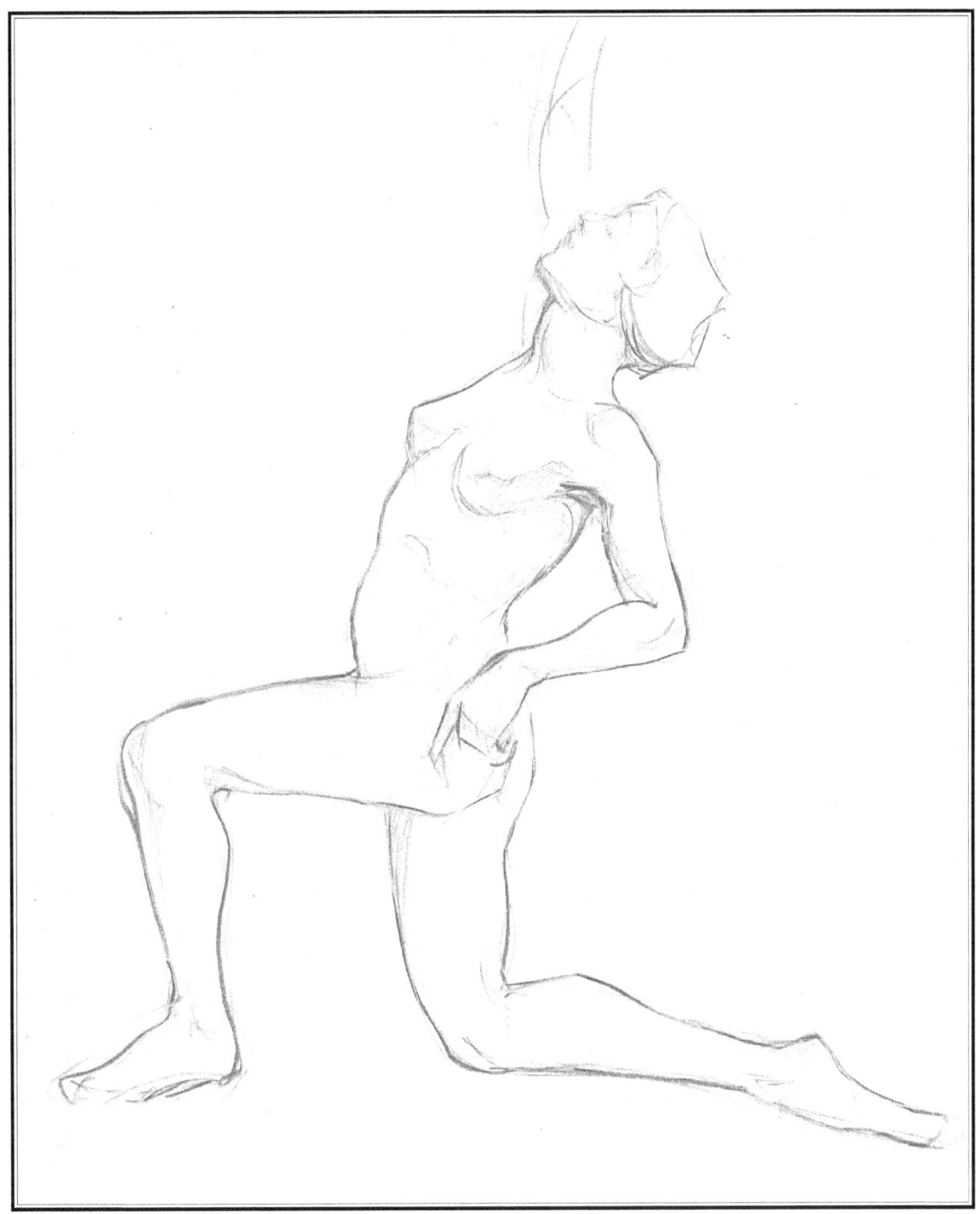

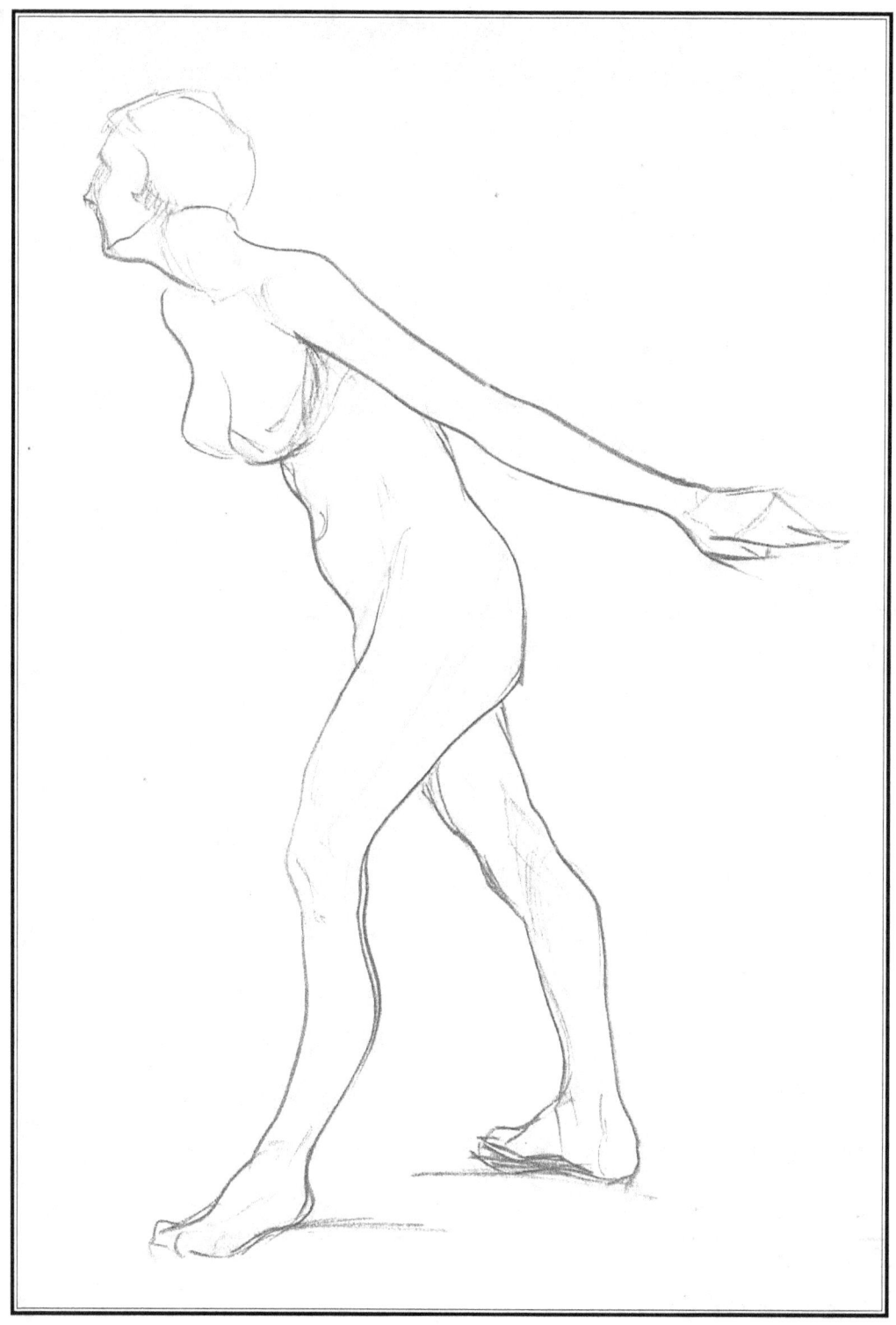

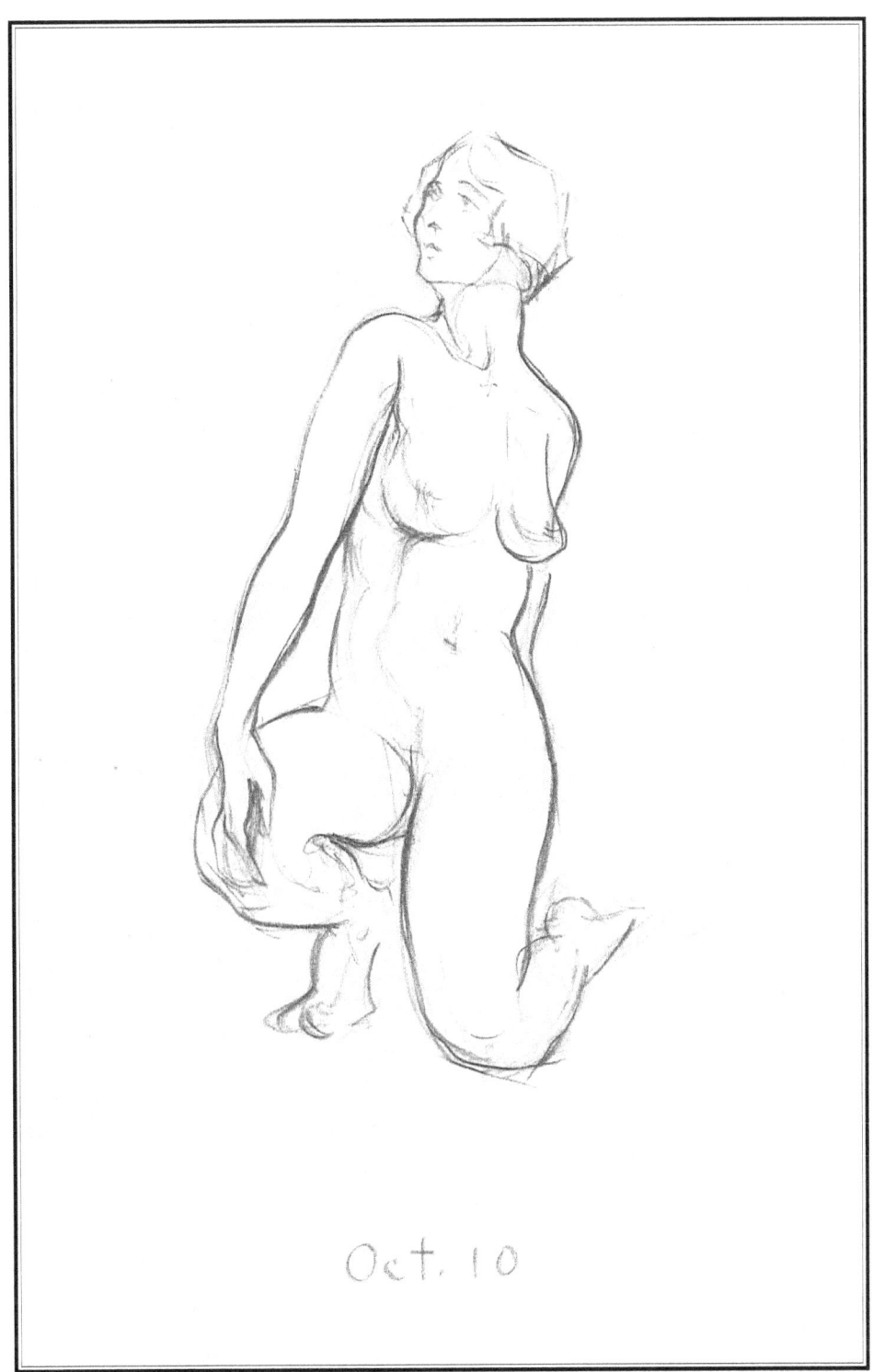

Oct. 10

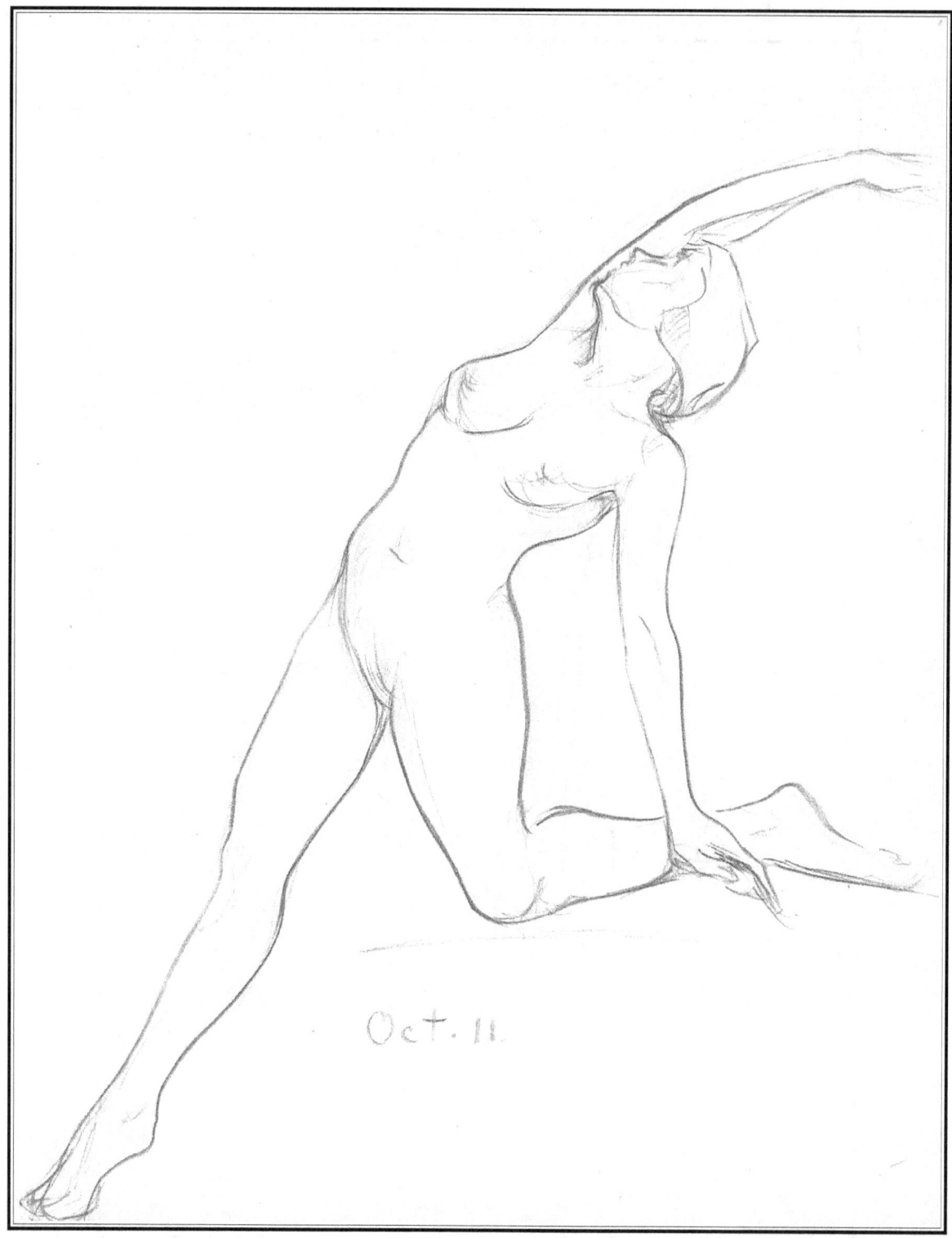

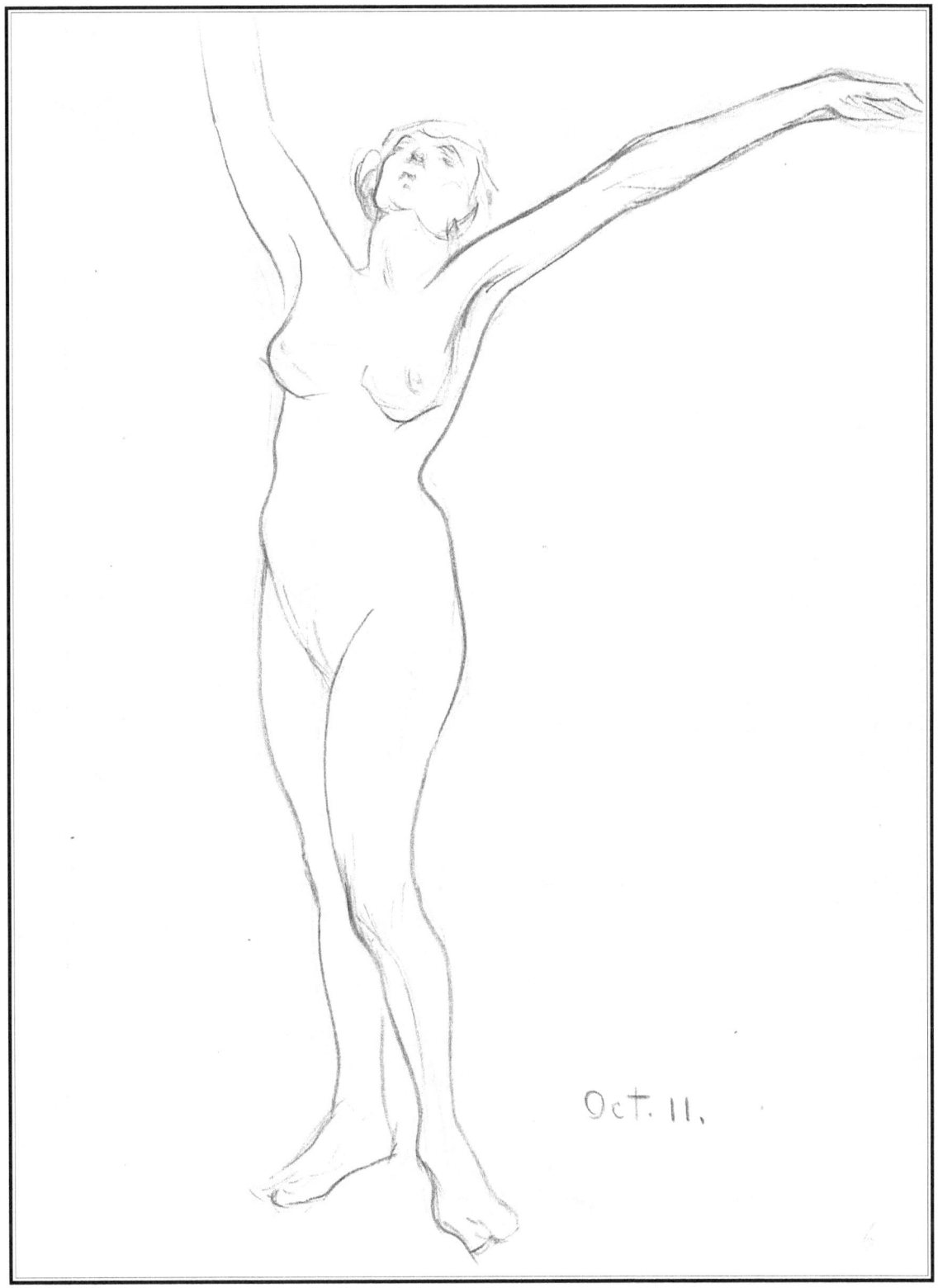

Oct. 11.

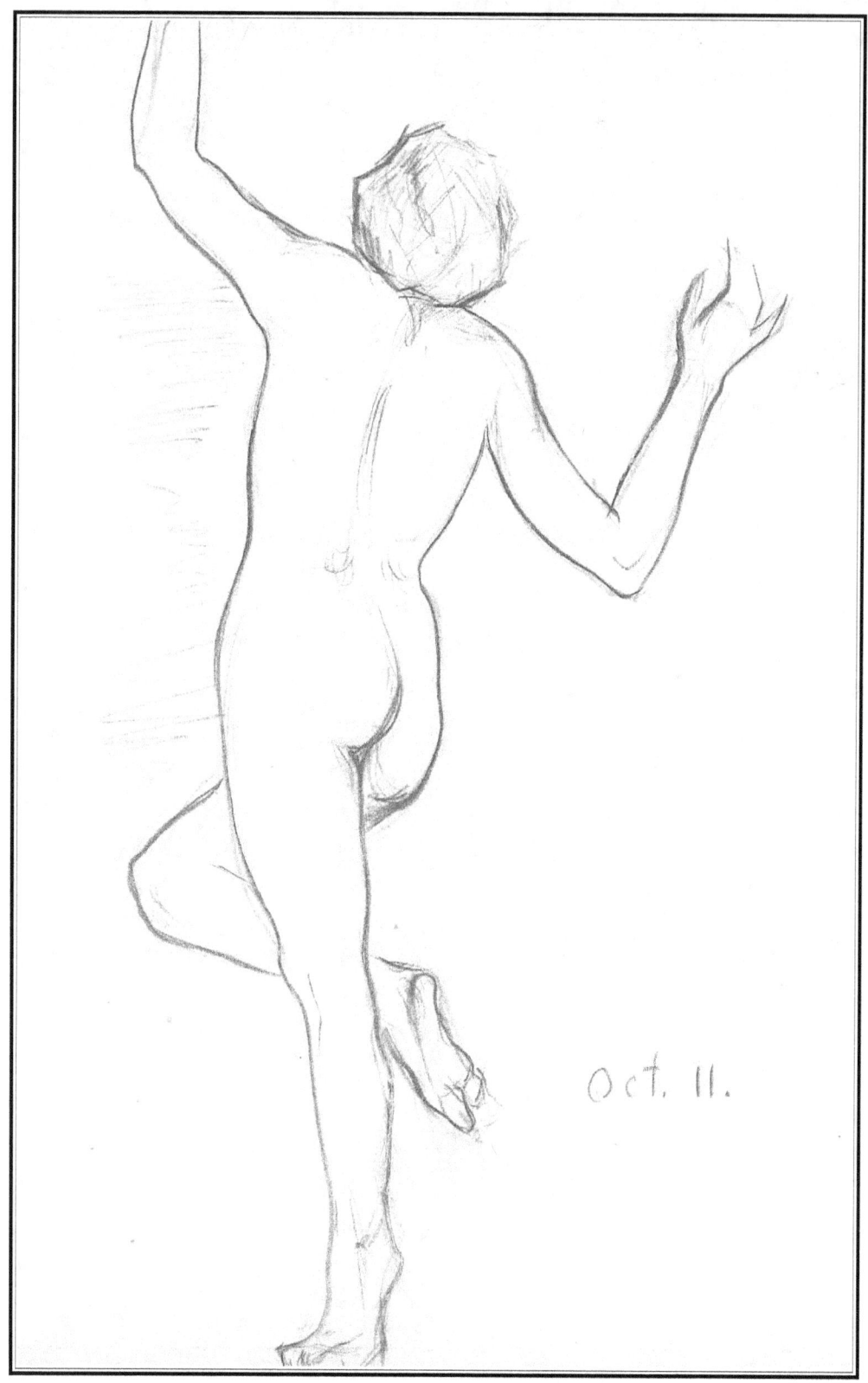

Oct. 11.

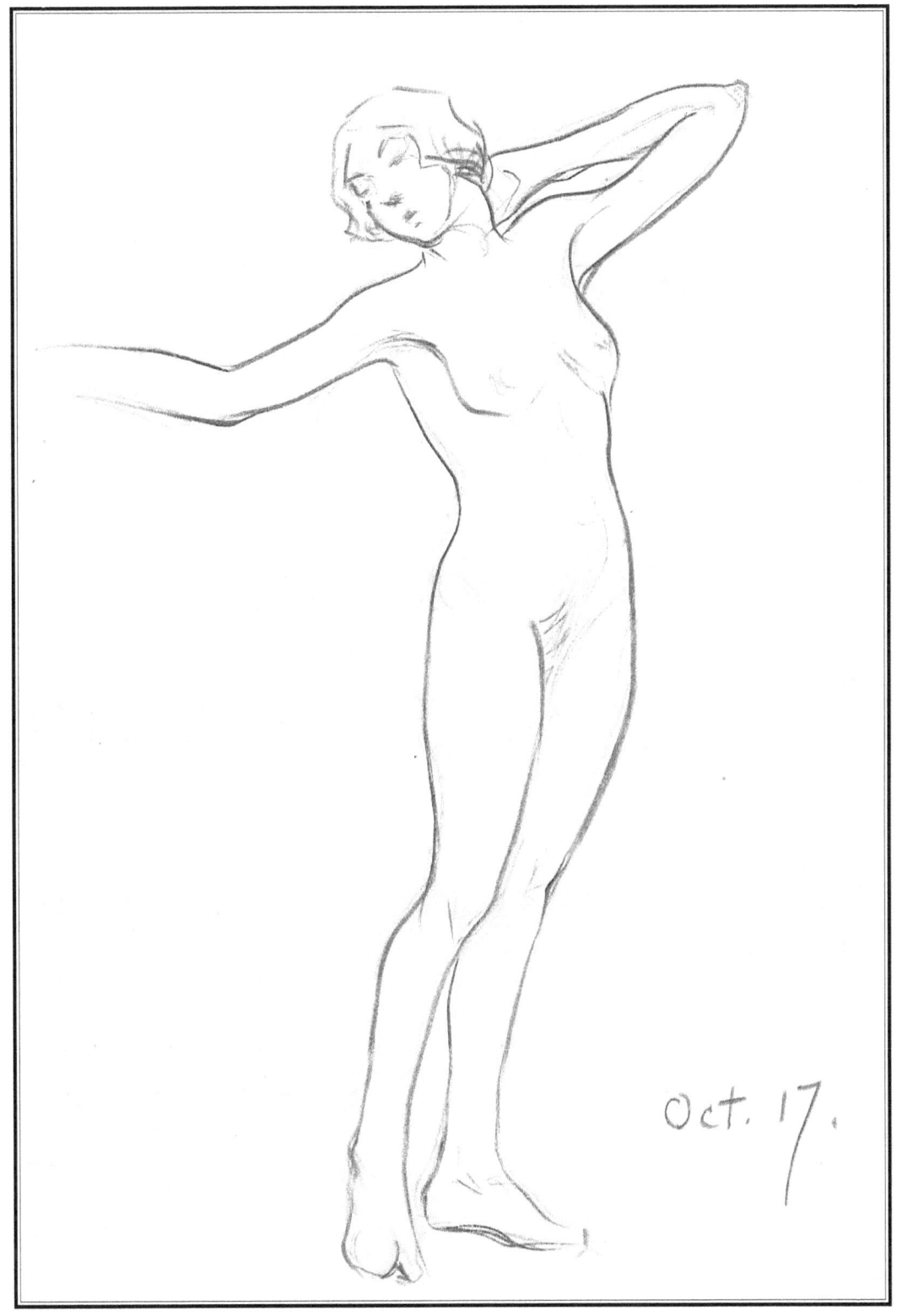

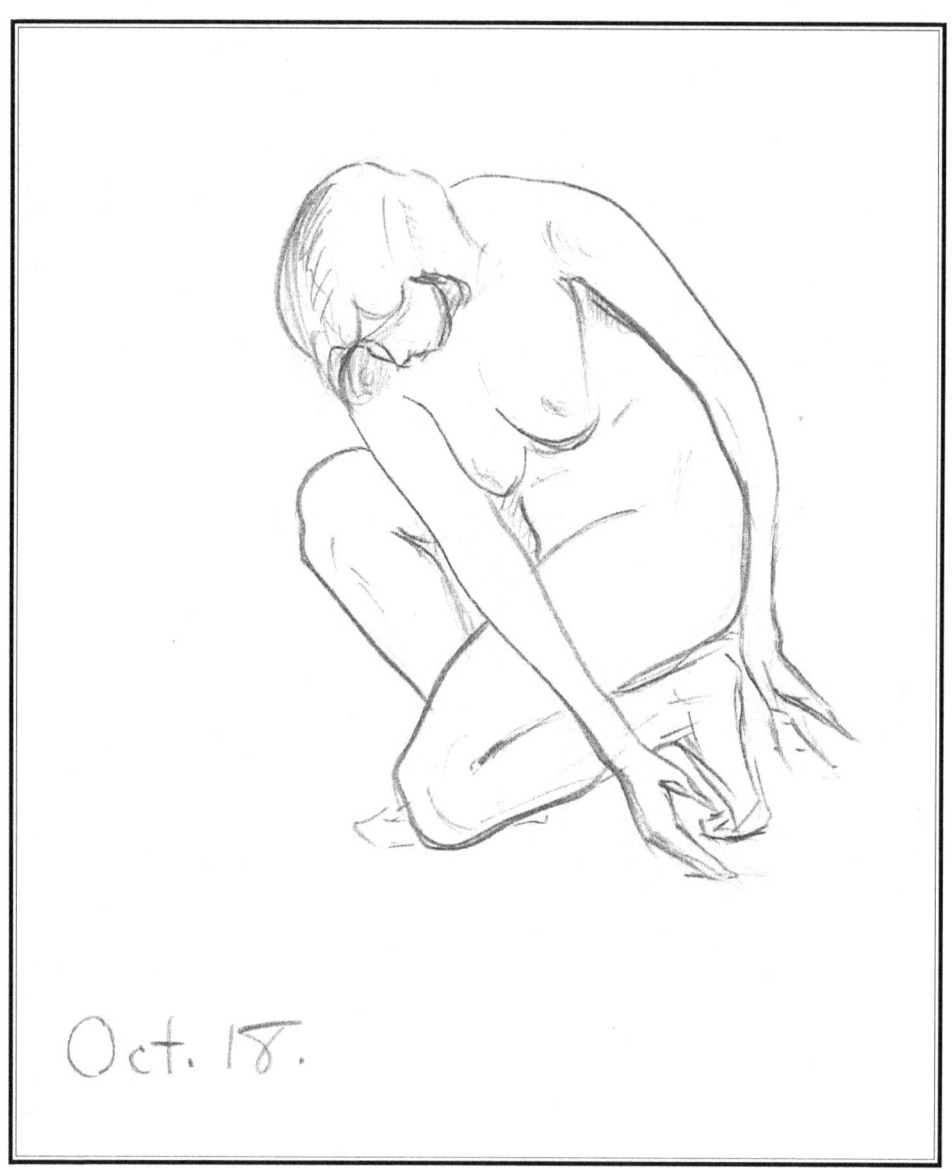

Oct. 18.

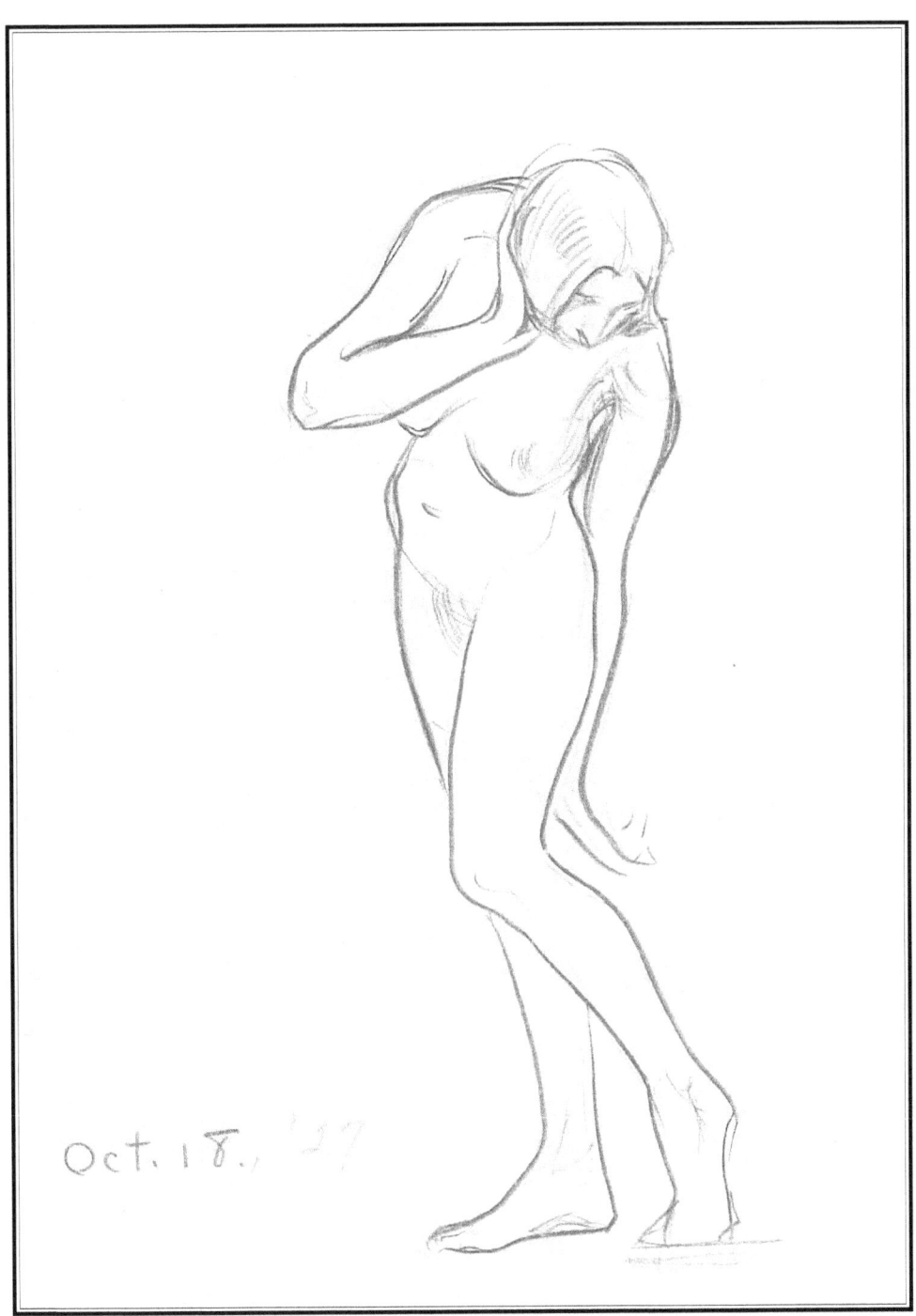

Oct. 18, '47

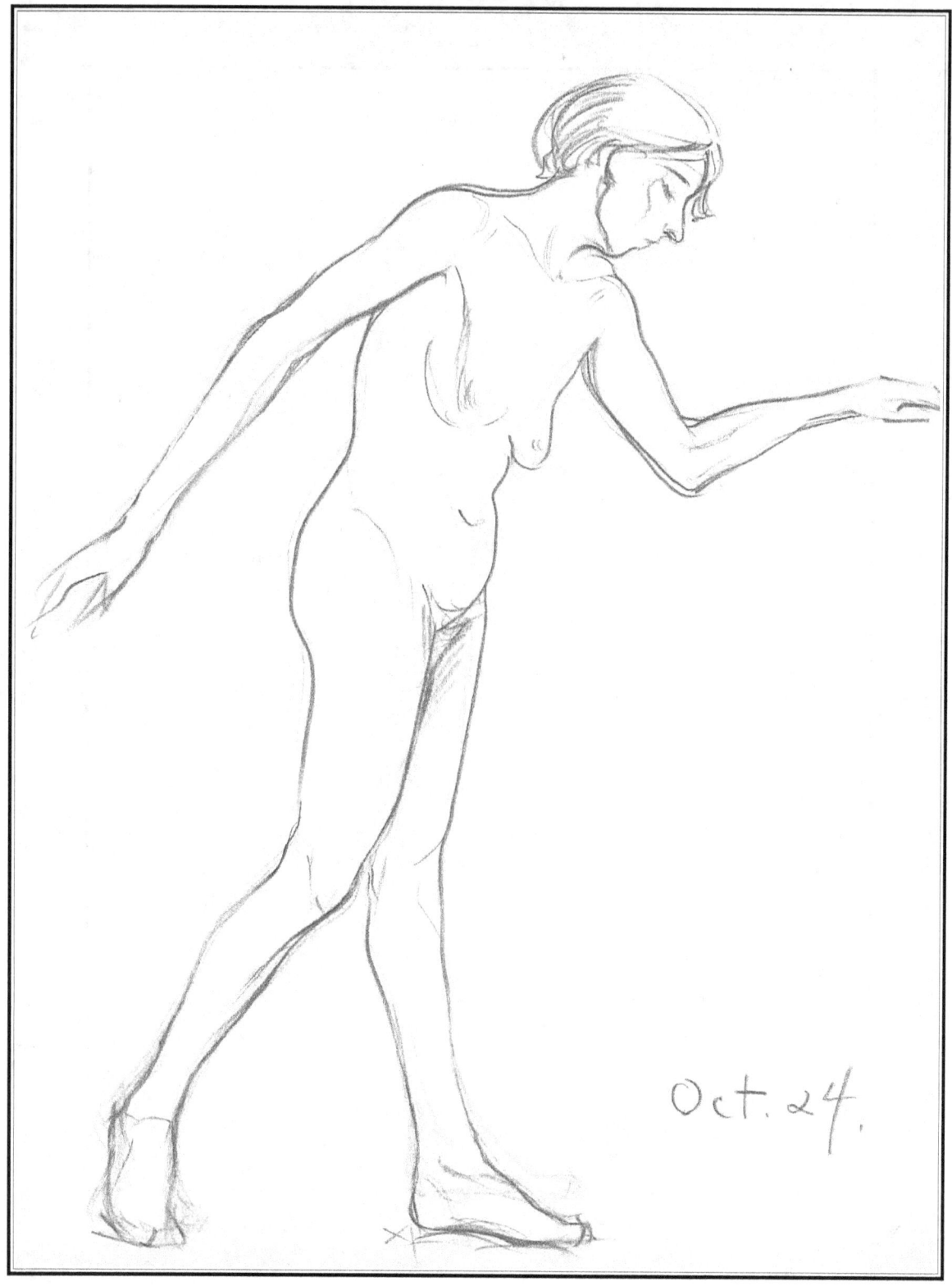

Oct. 24.

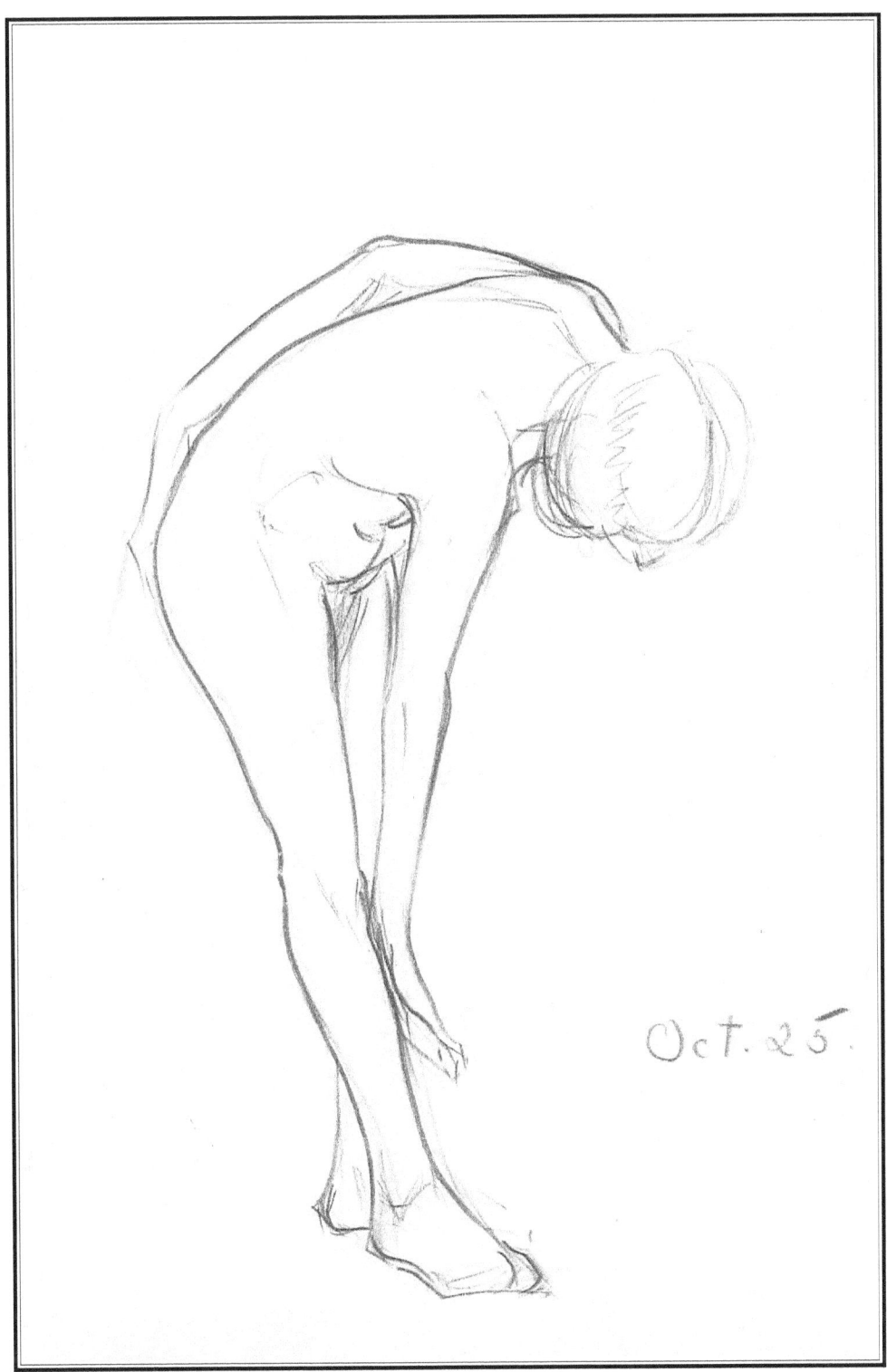

Oct. 25.

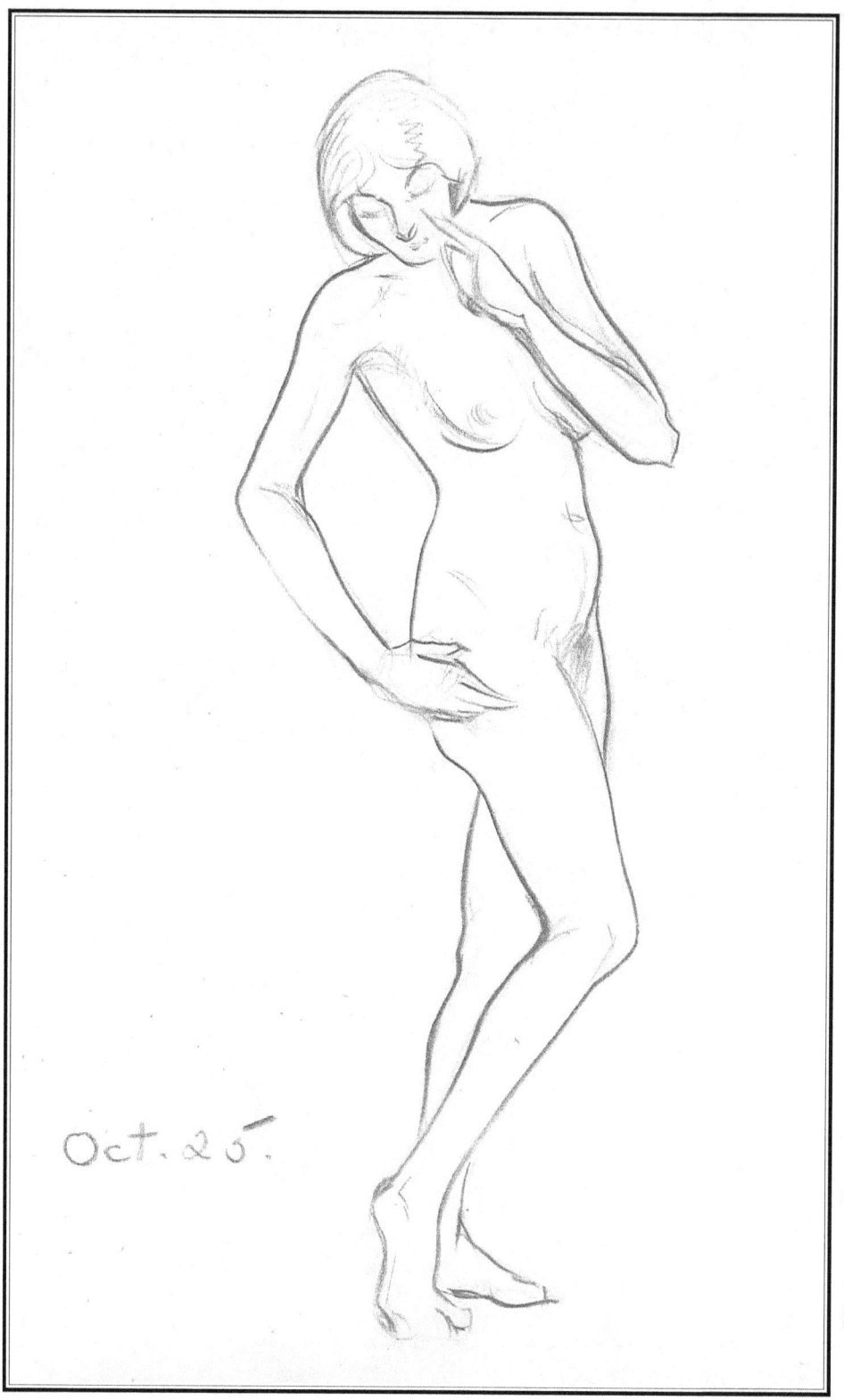

Oct. 26.

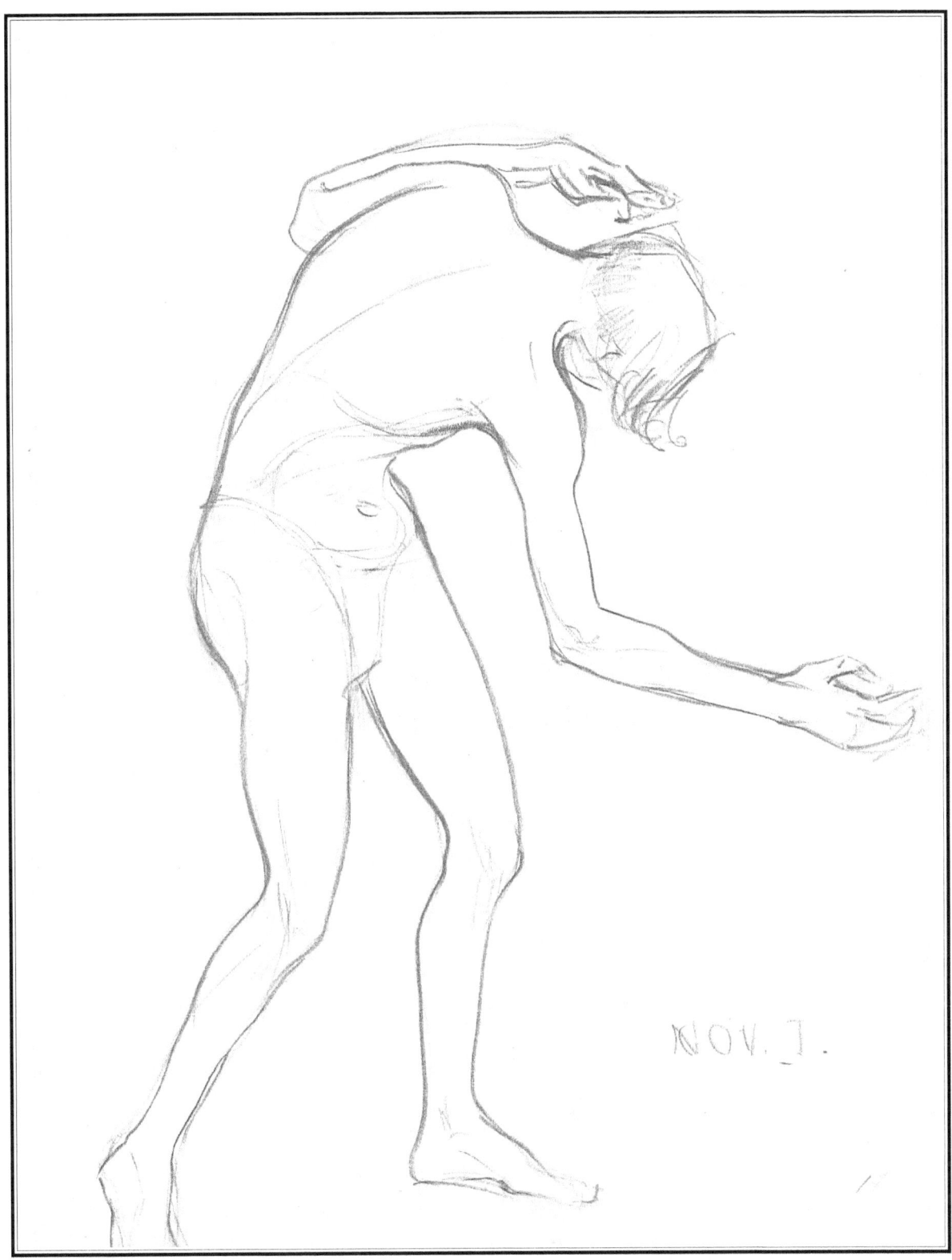

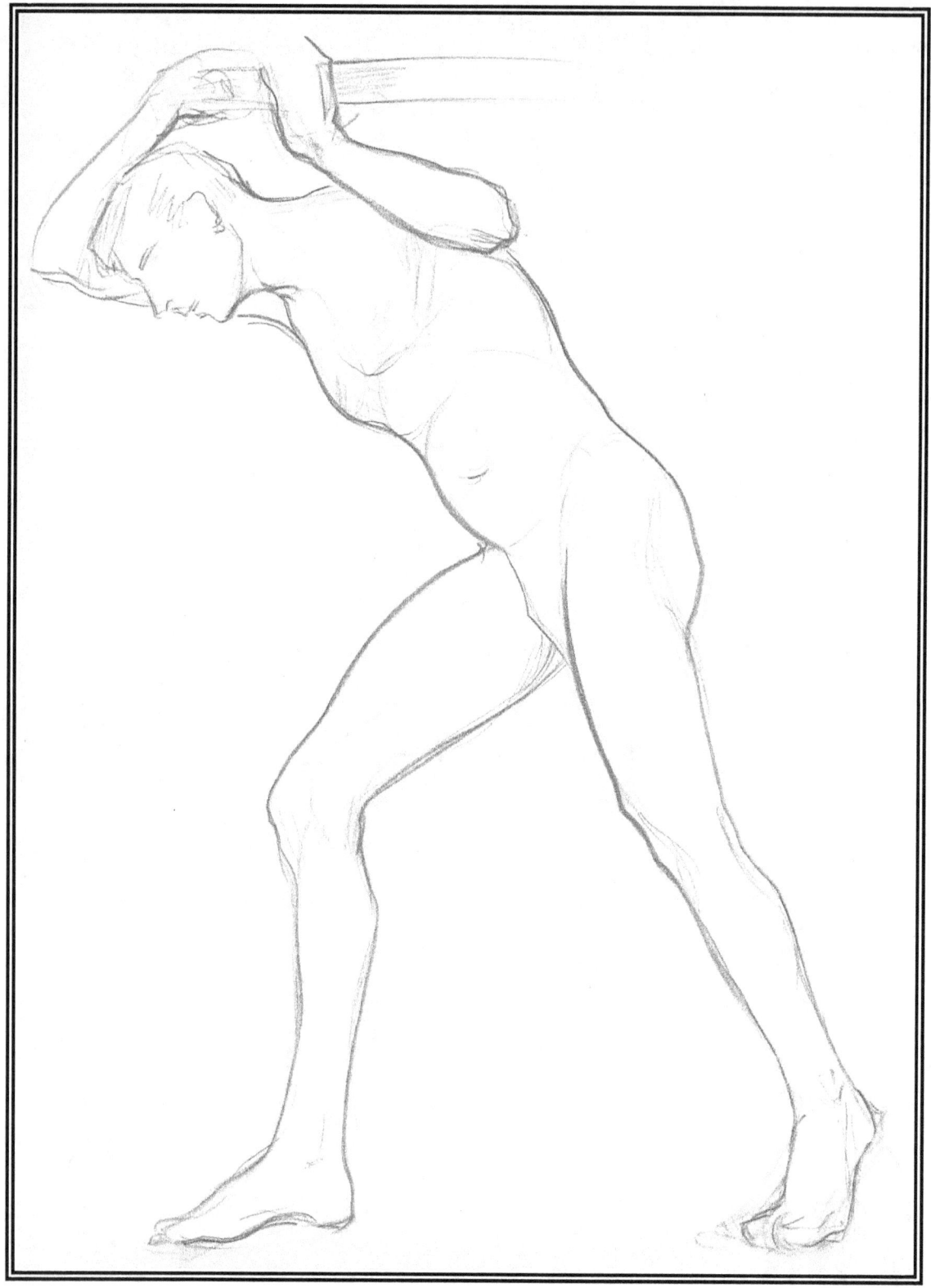

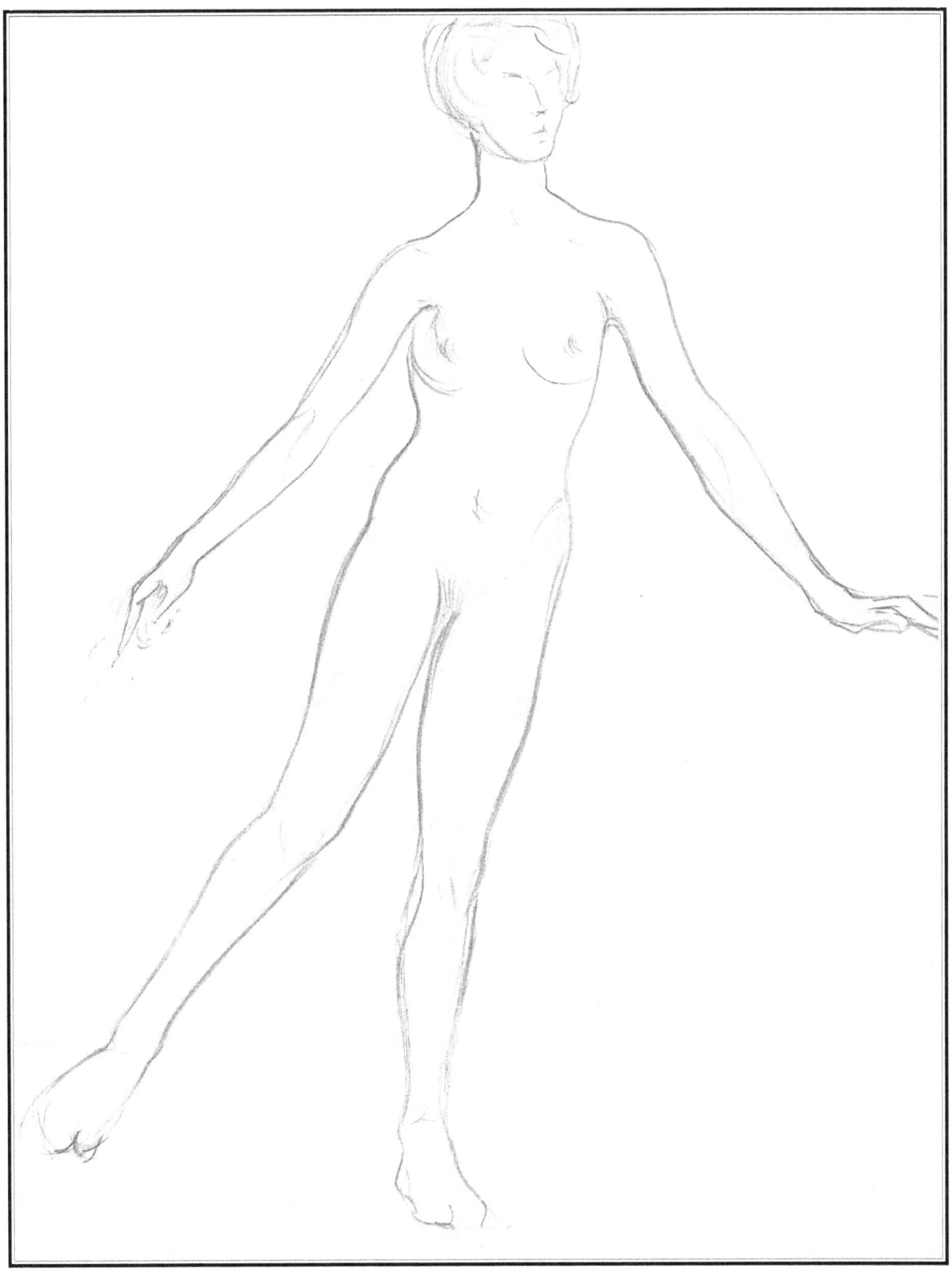

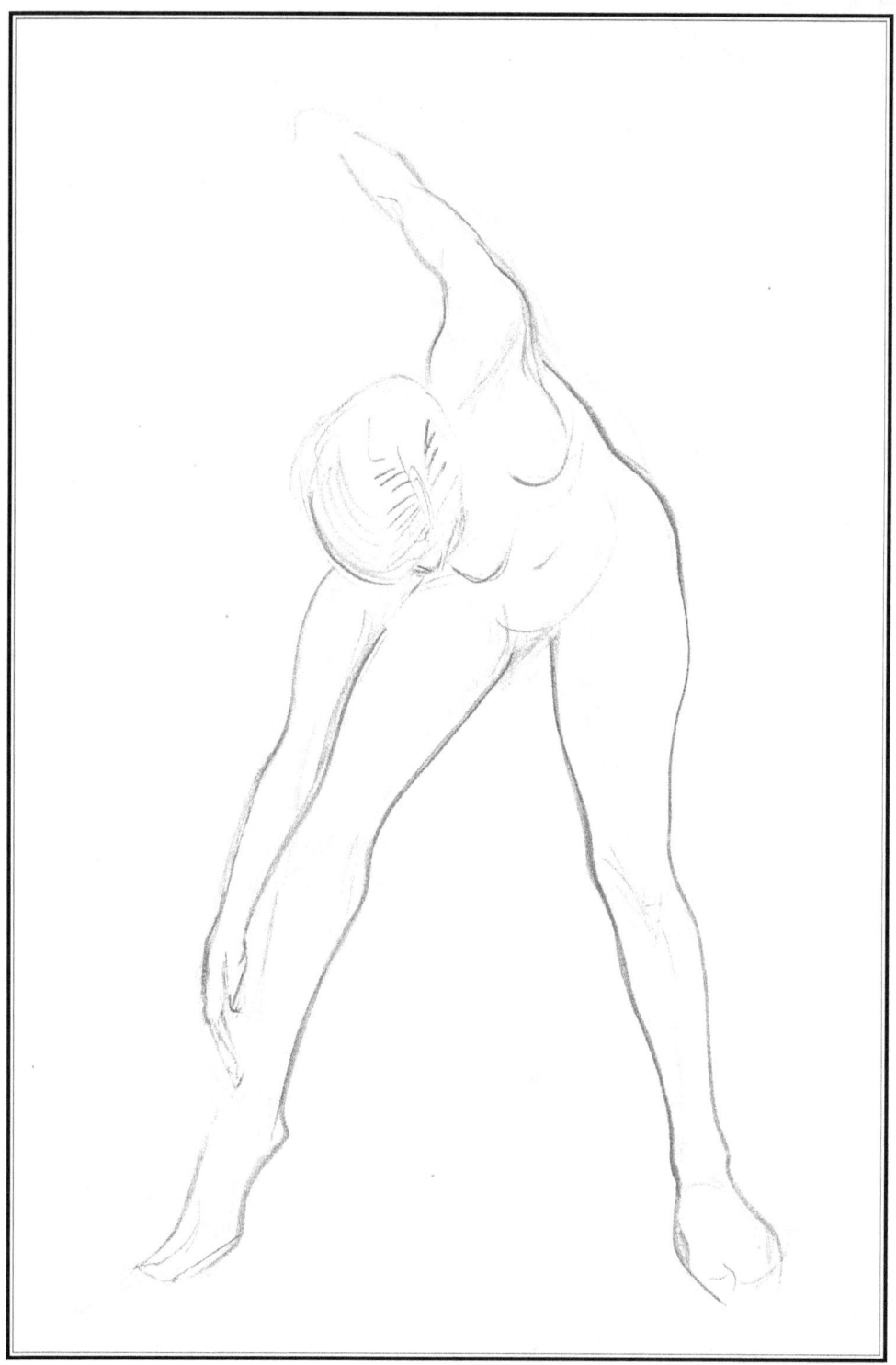

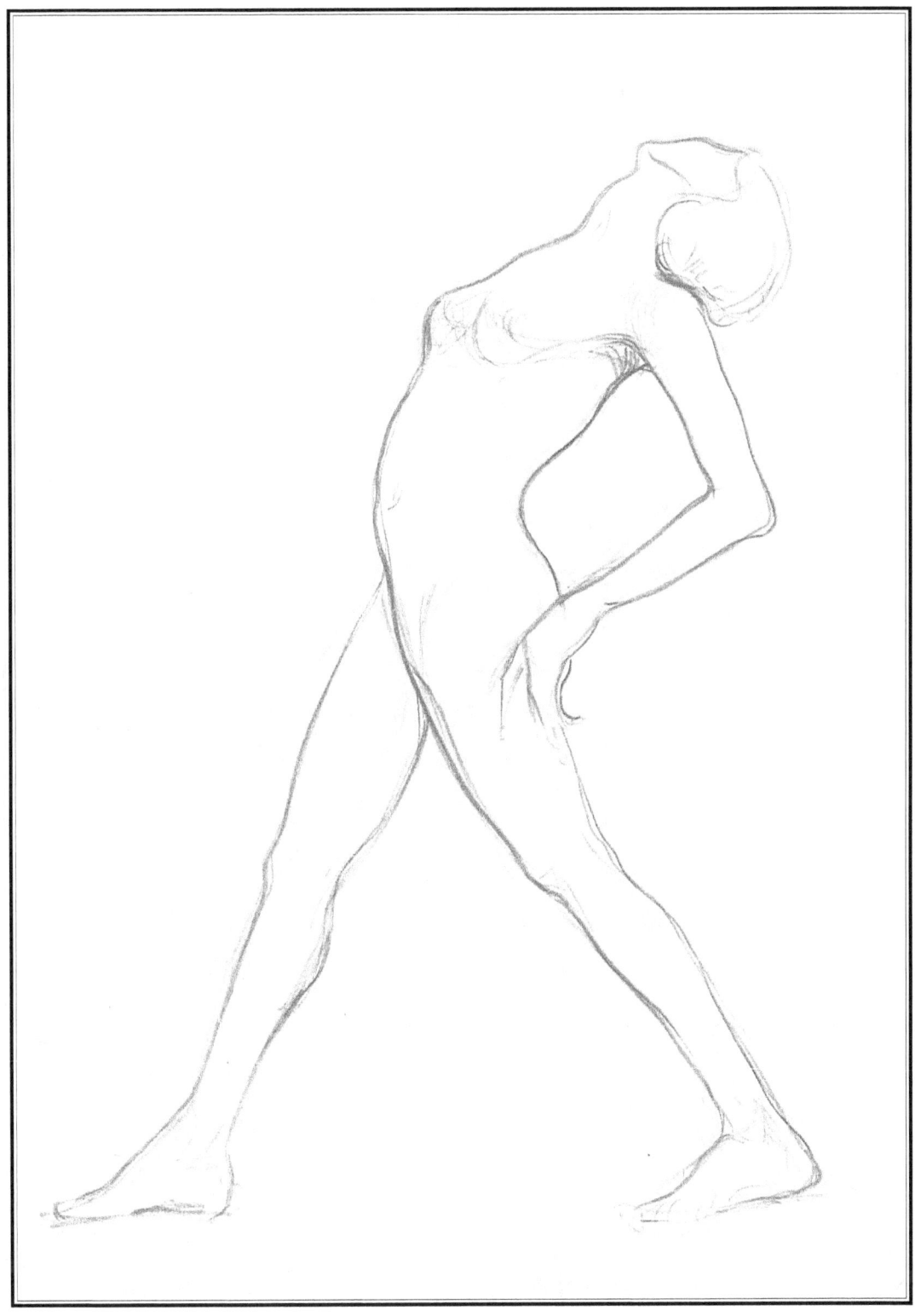

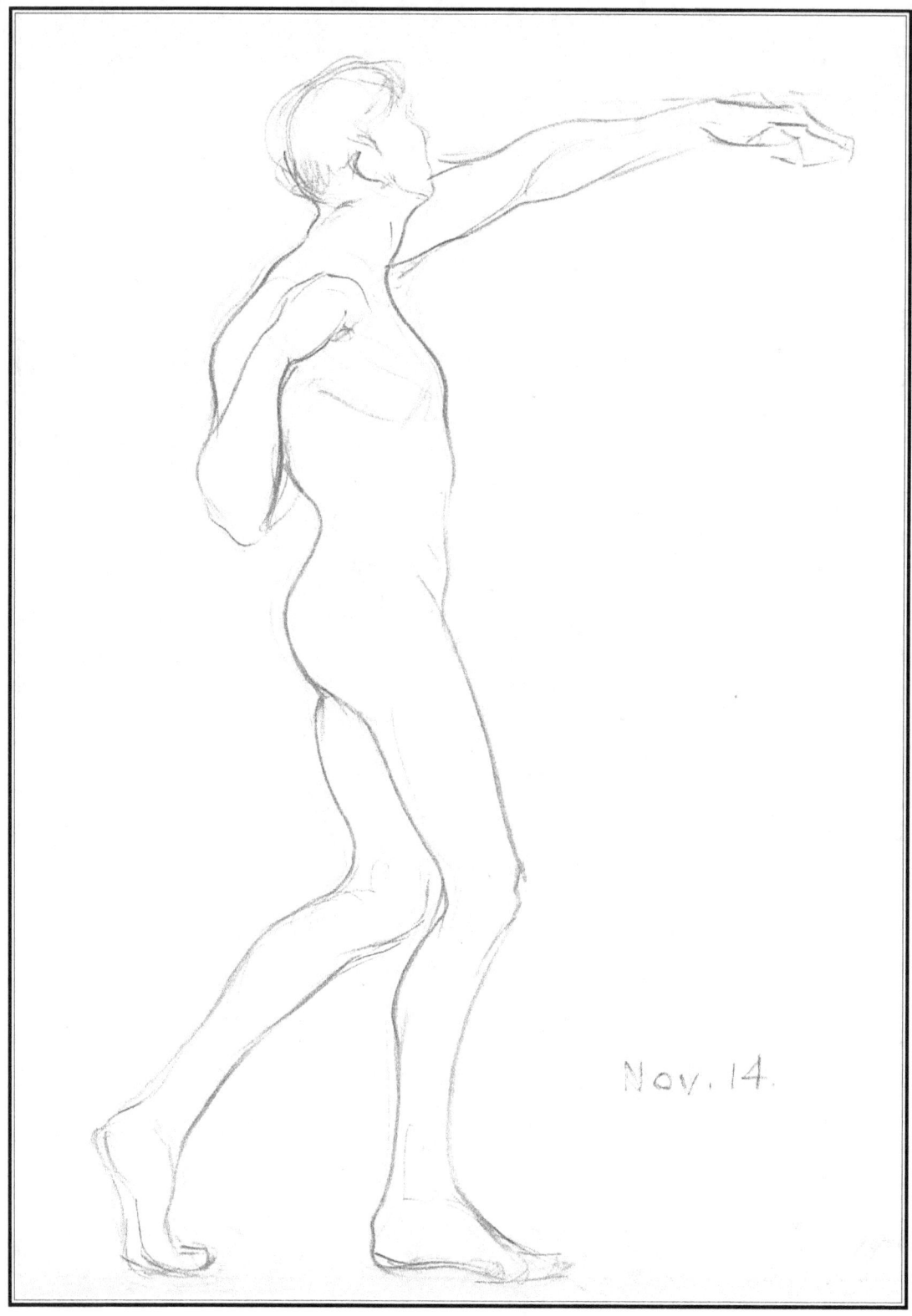

Nov. 14.

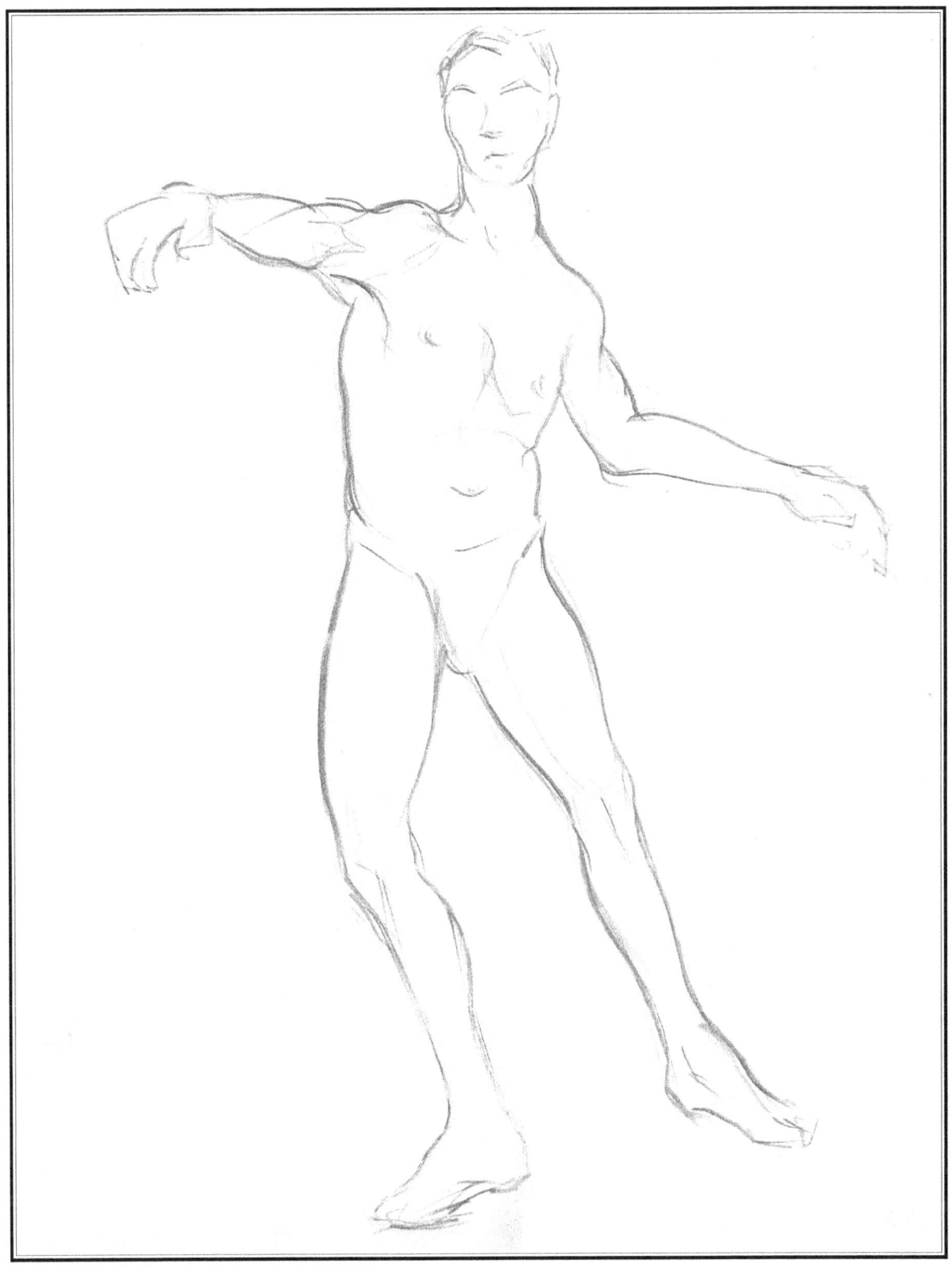

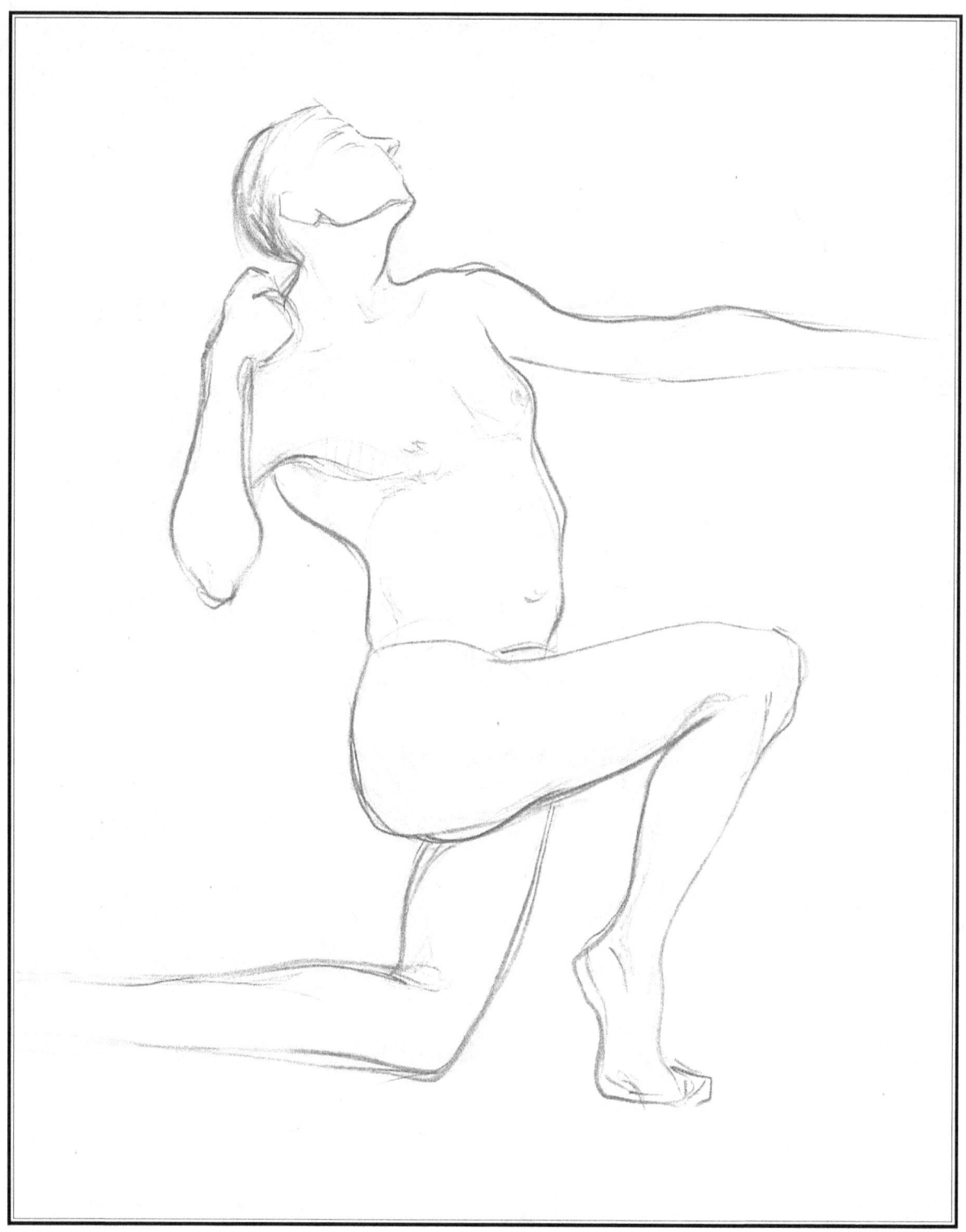

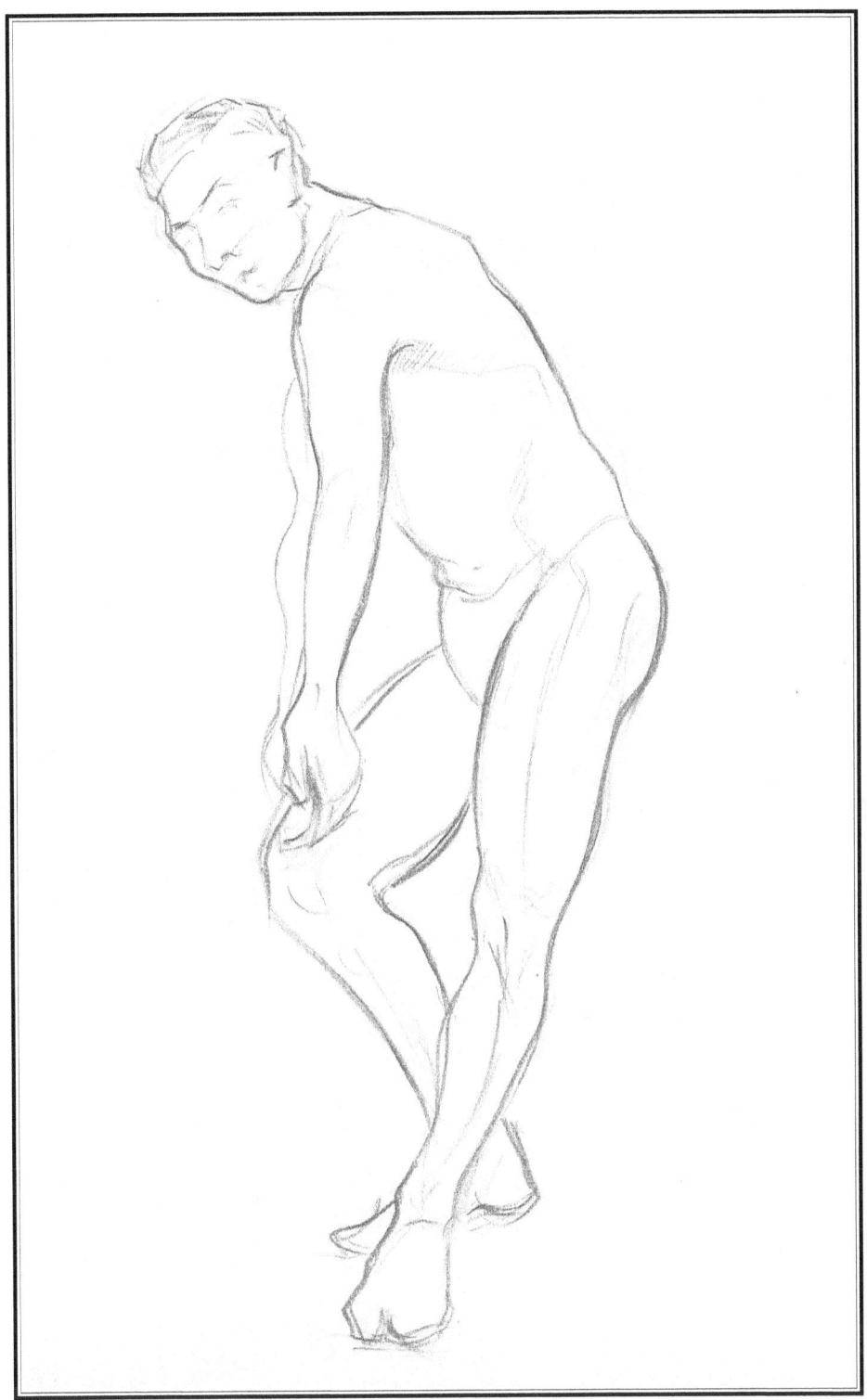

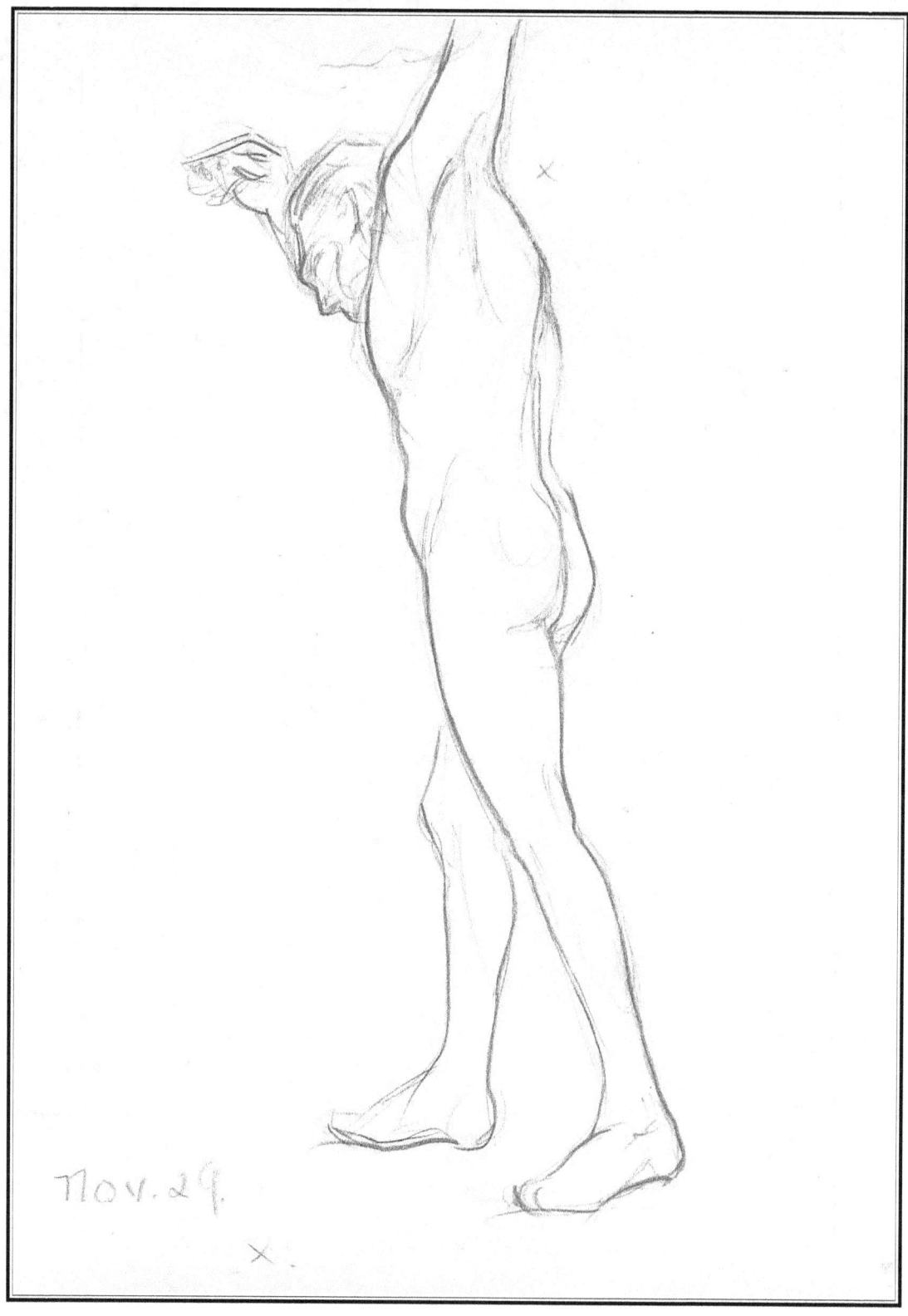

Nov. 29.

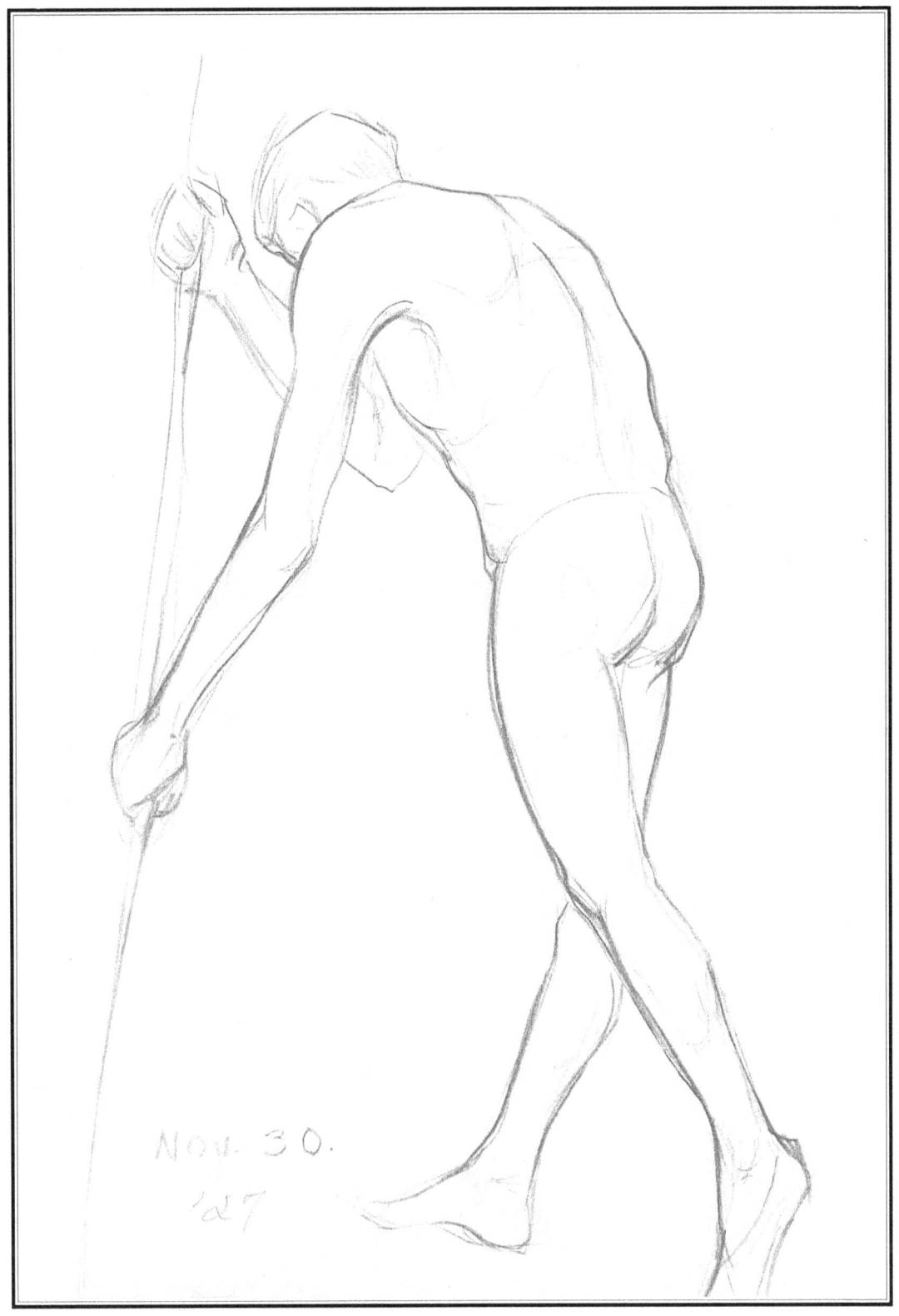

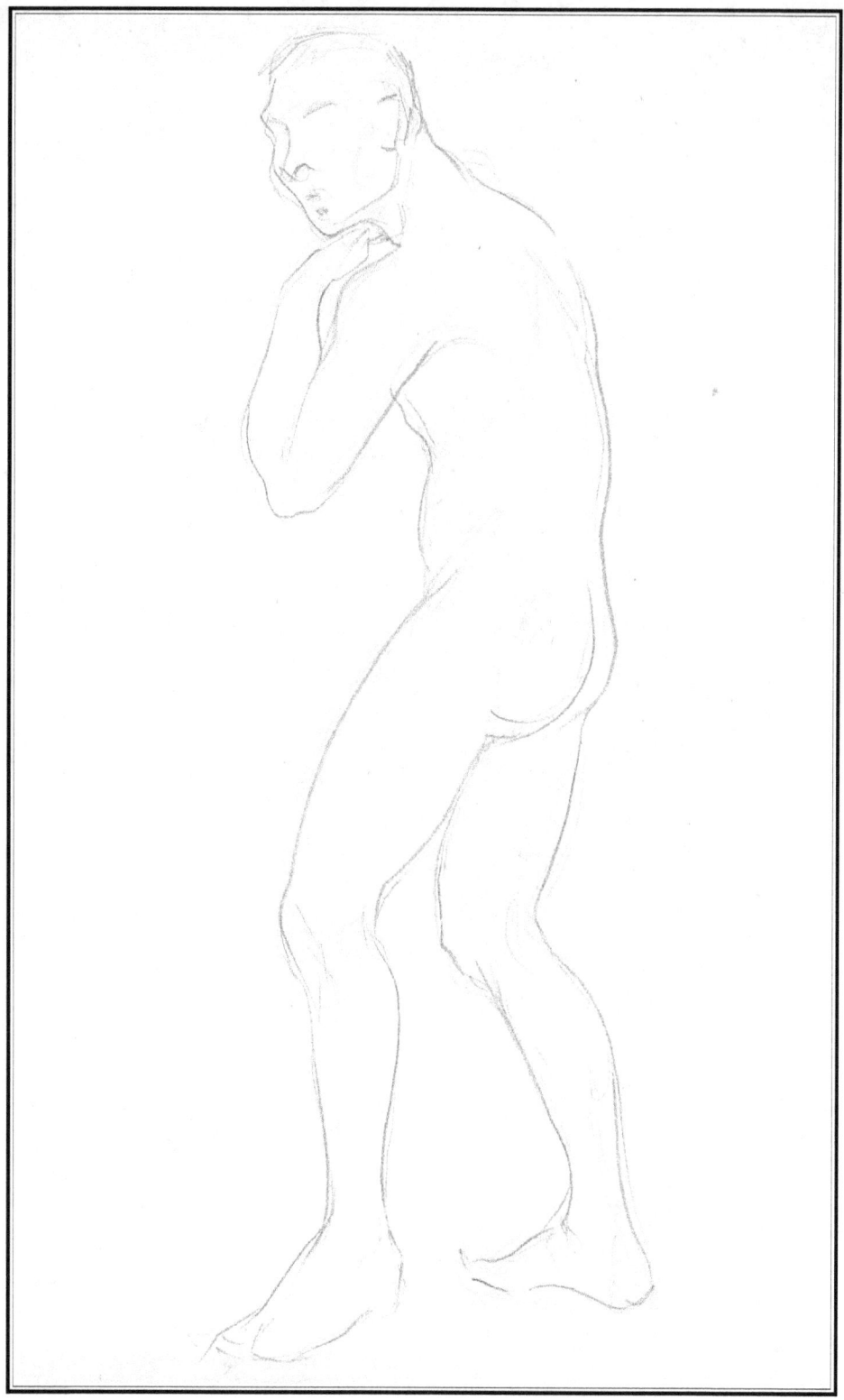

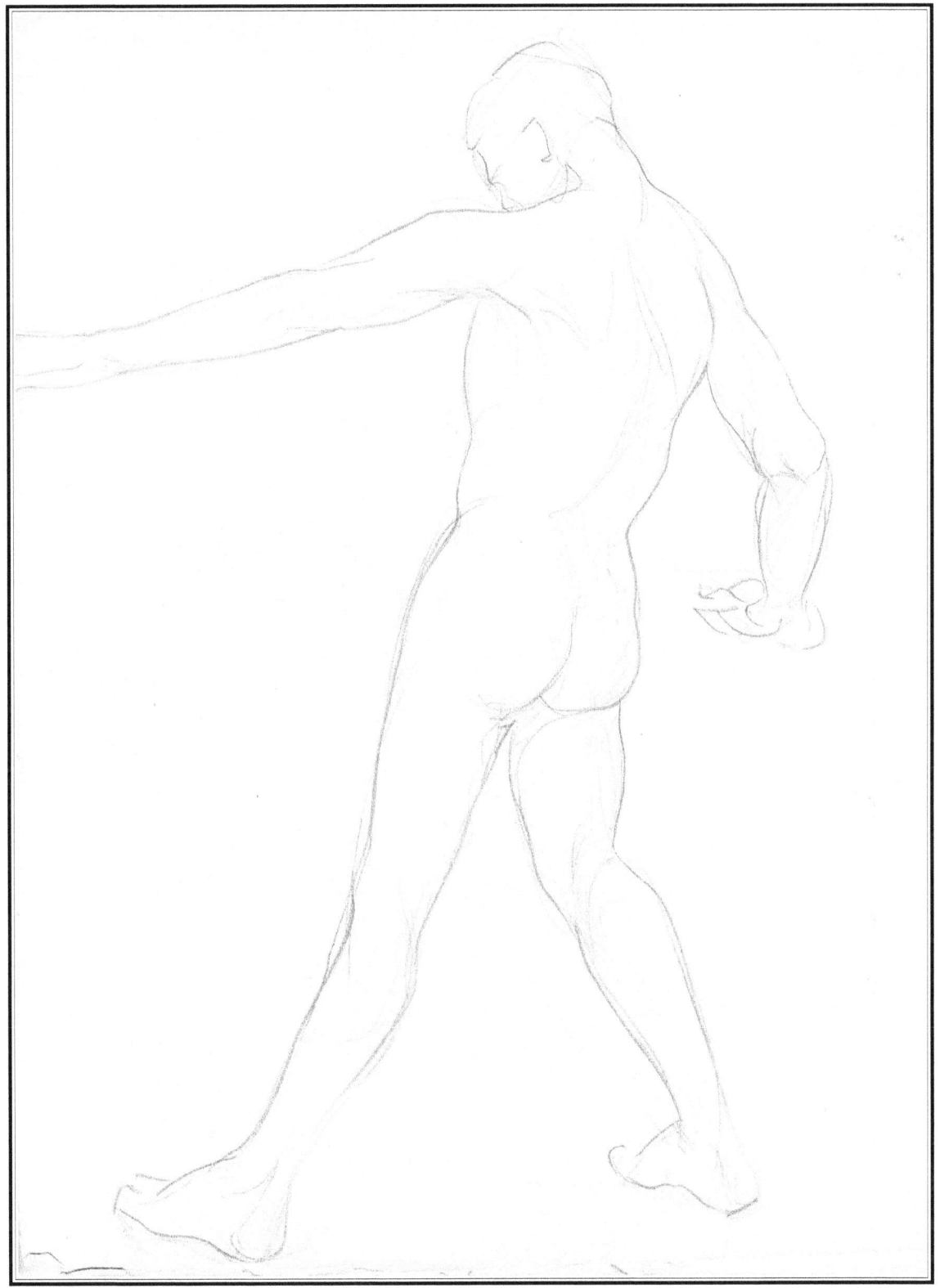

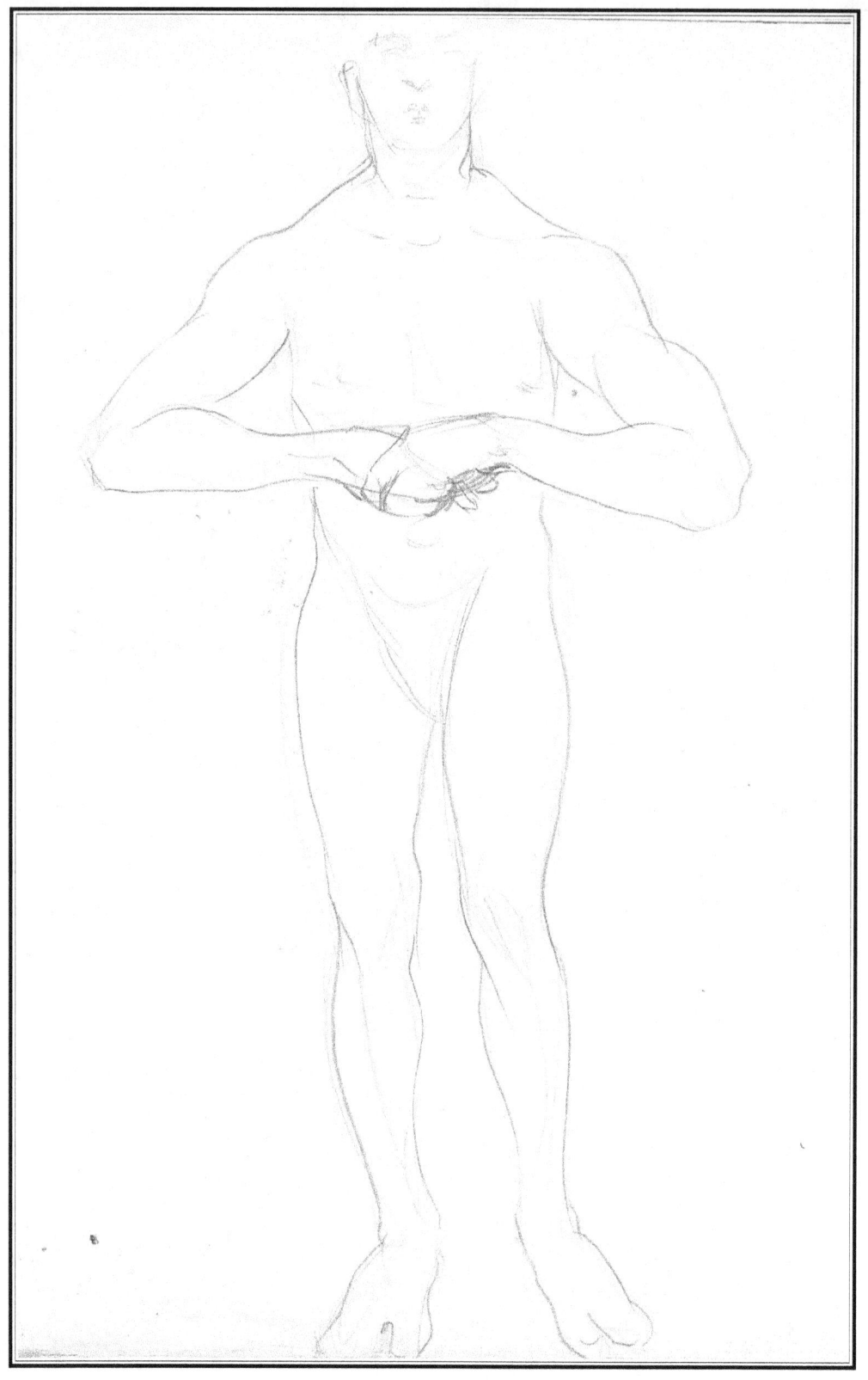

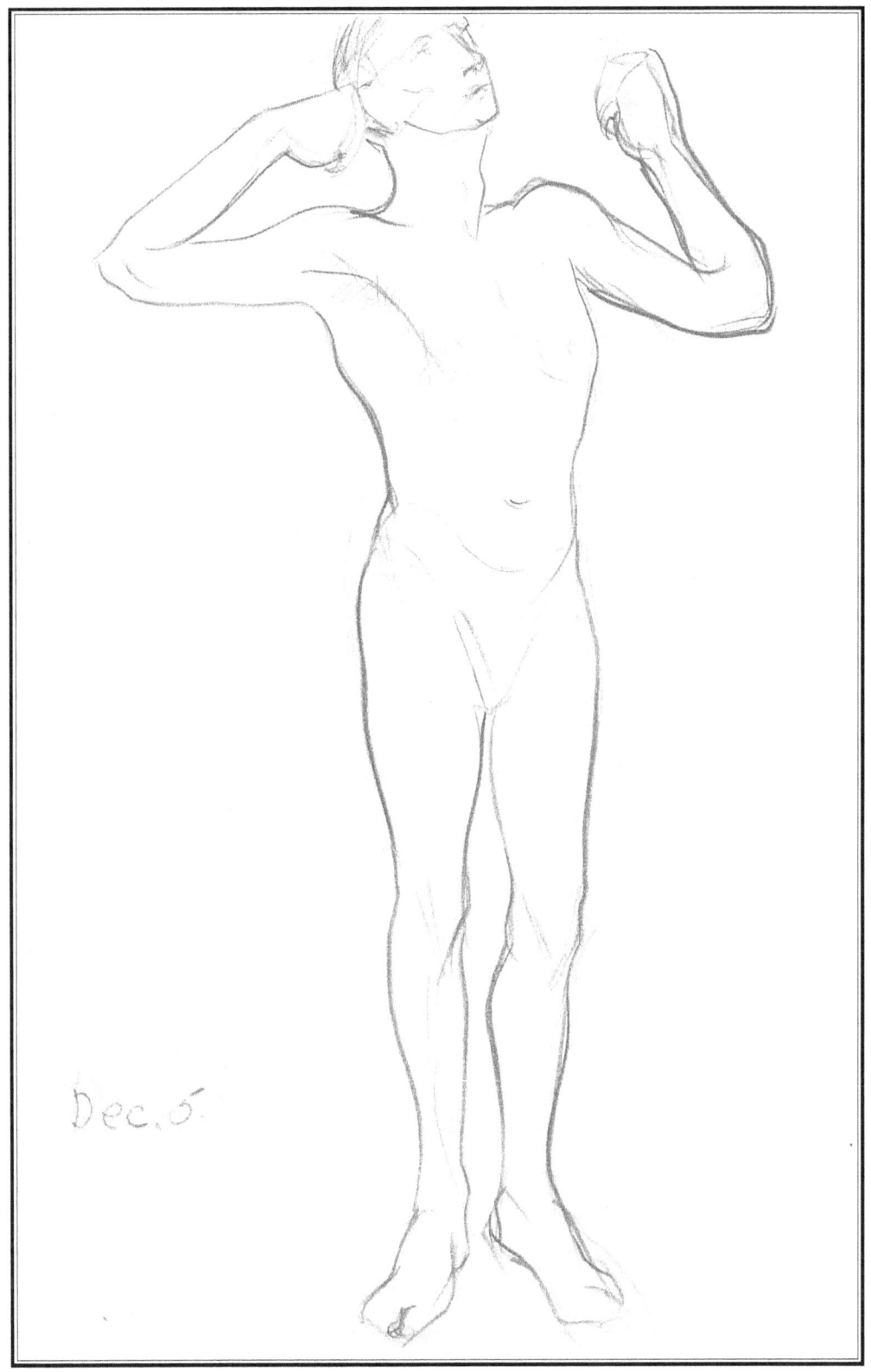

Dec. 5.

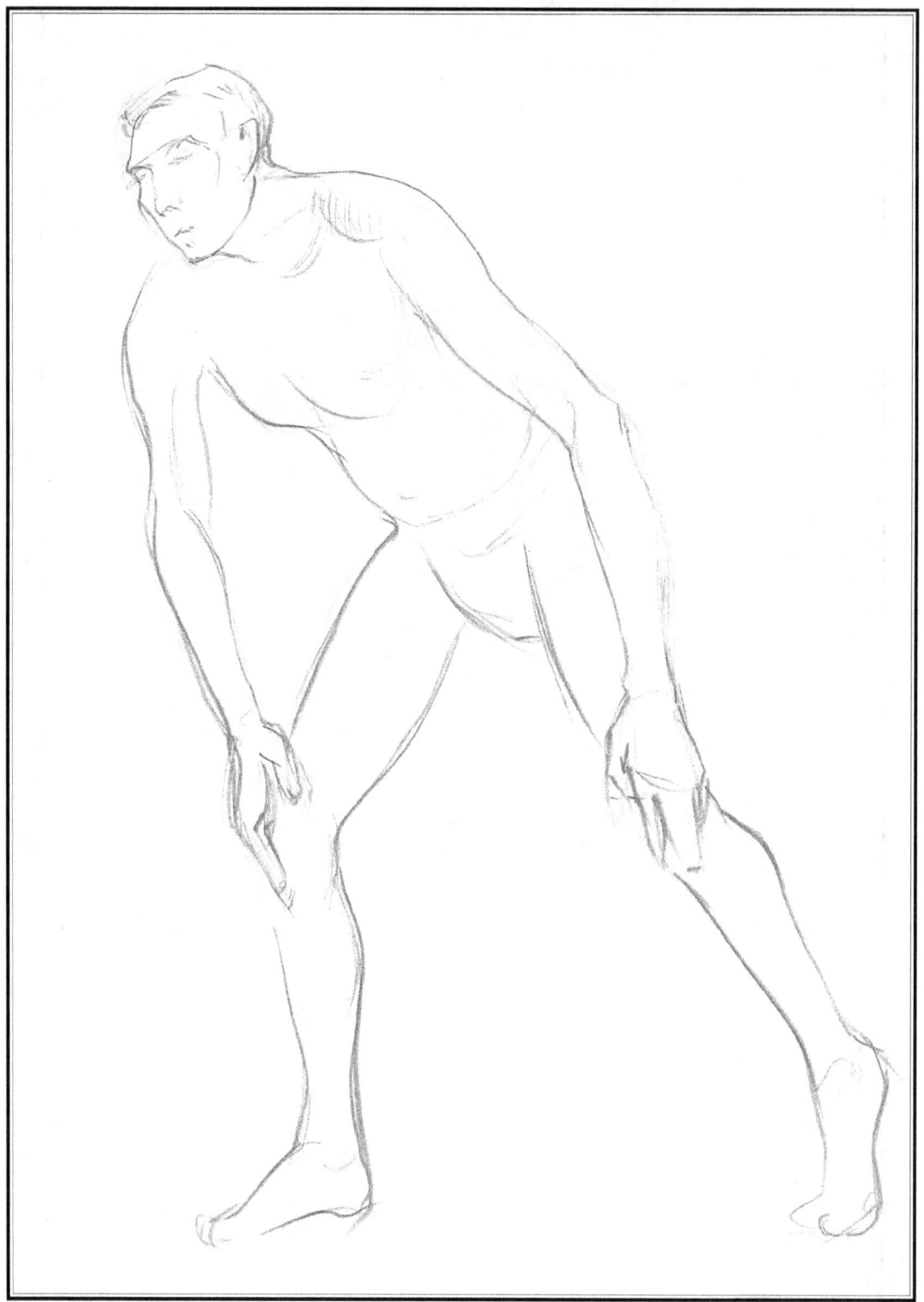

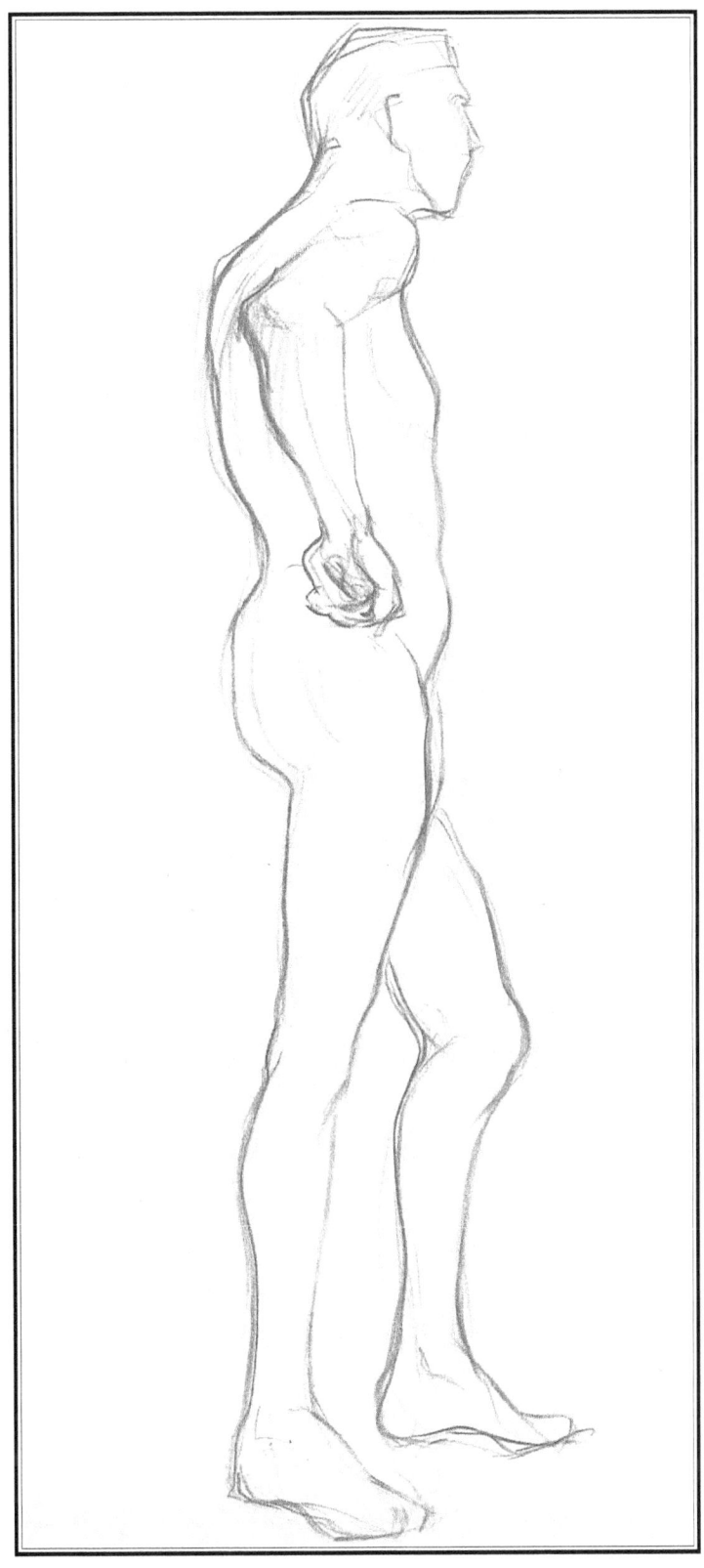

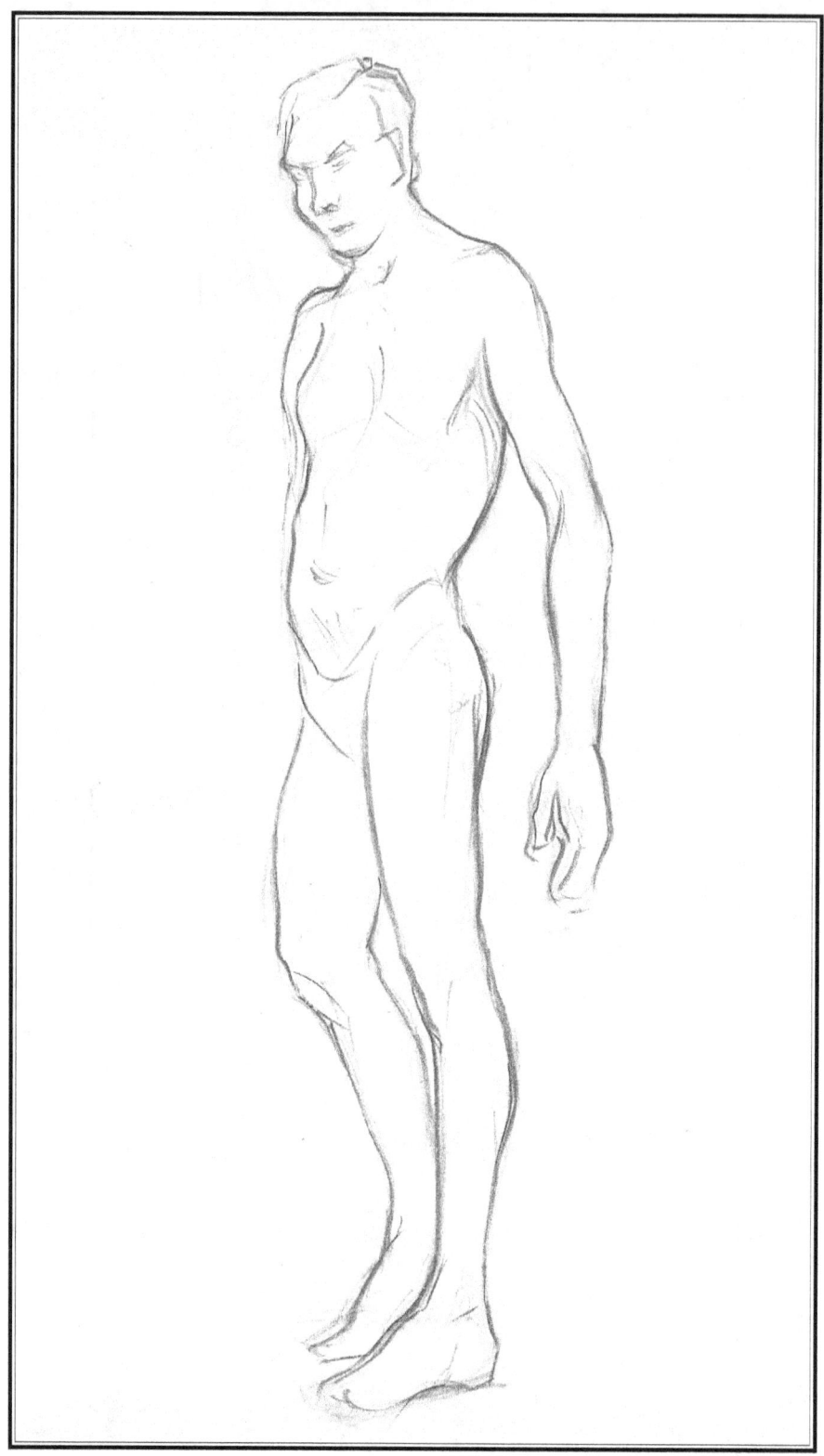

GRACE YOUNG

SECOND SEMESTER

1928

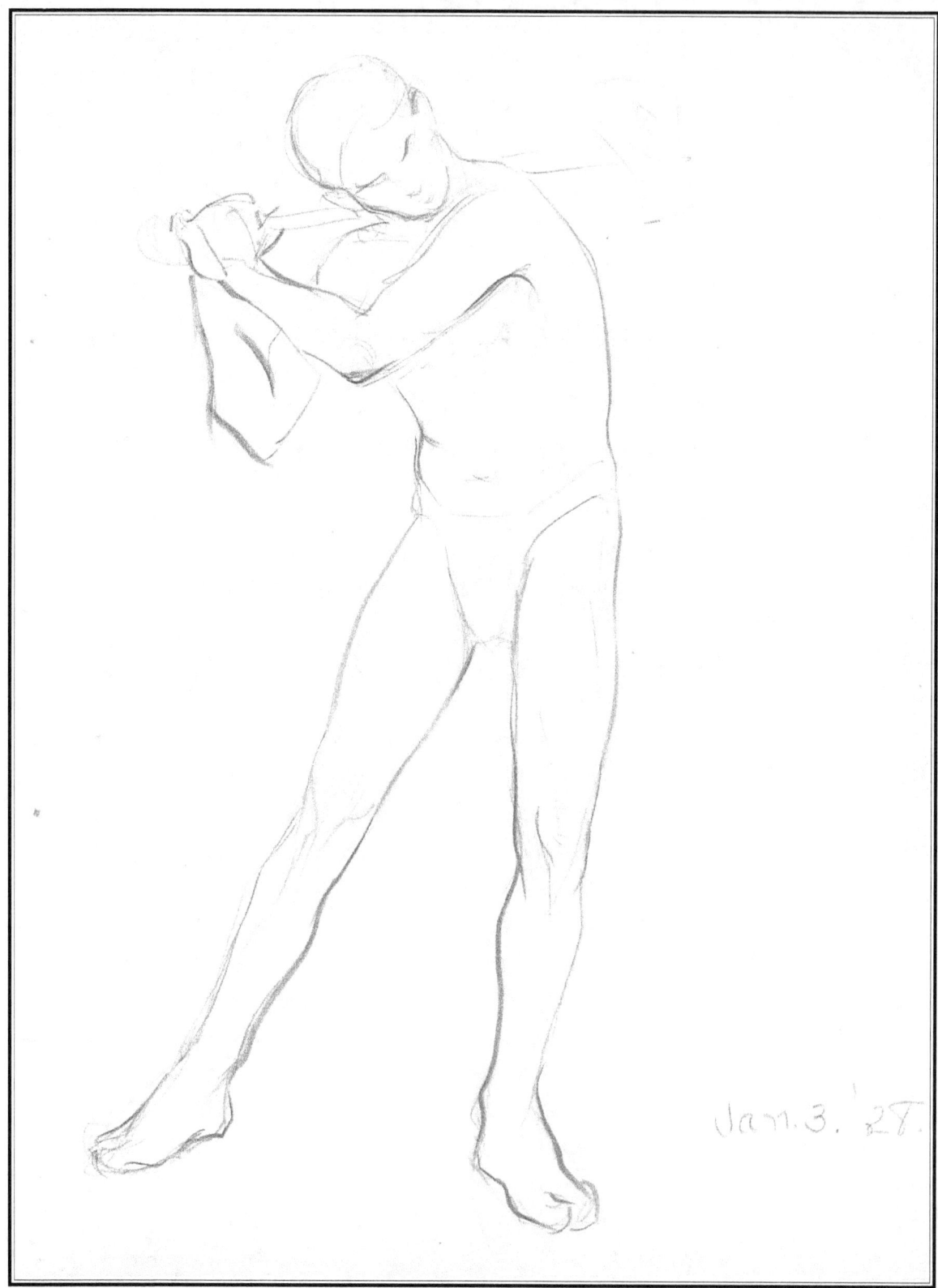

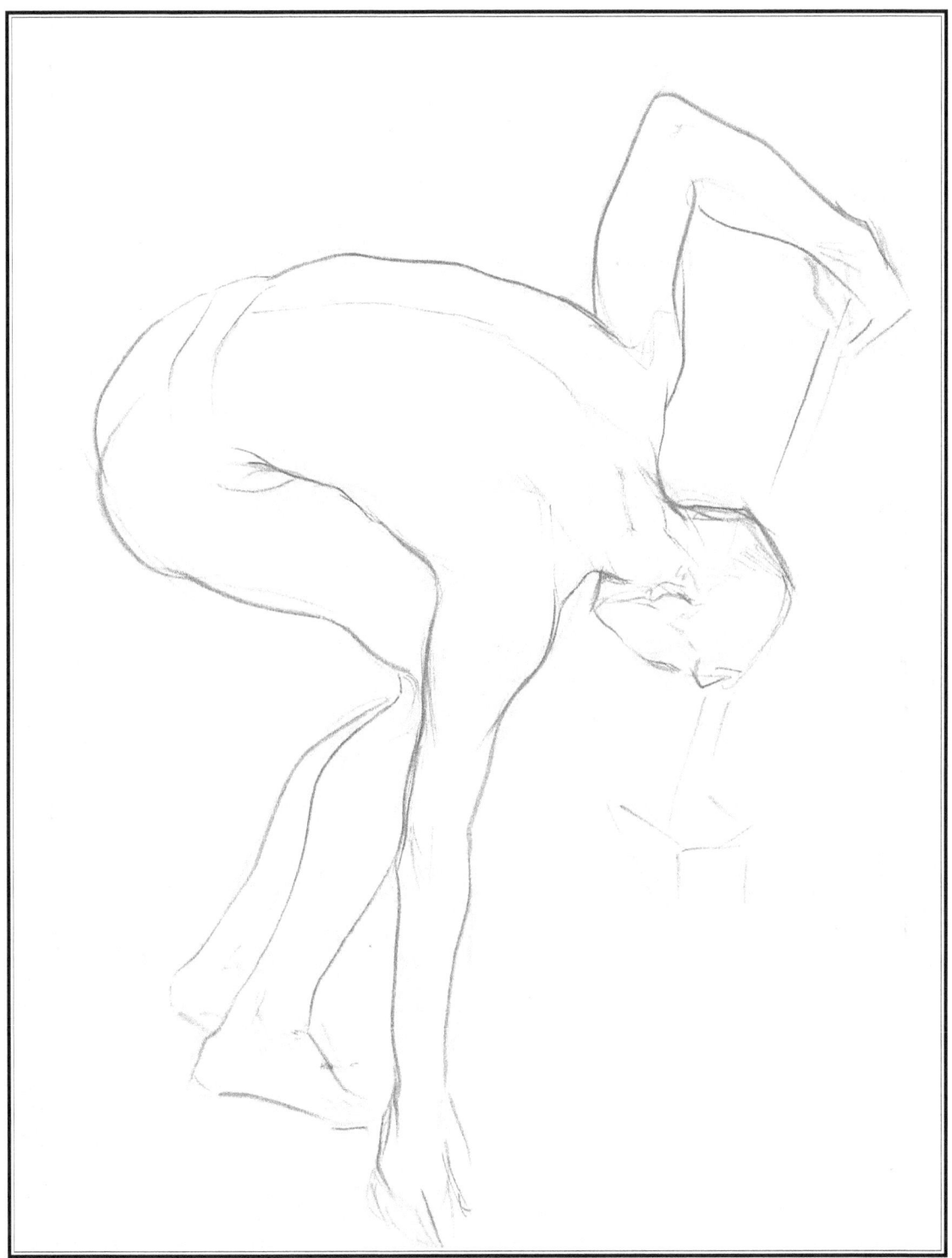

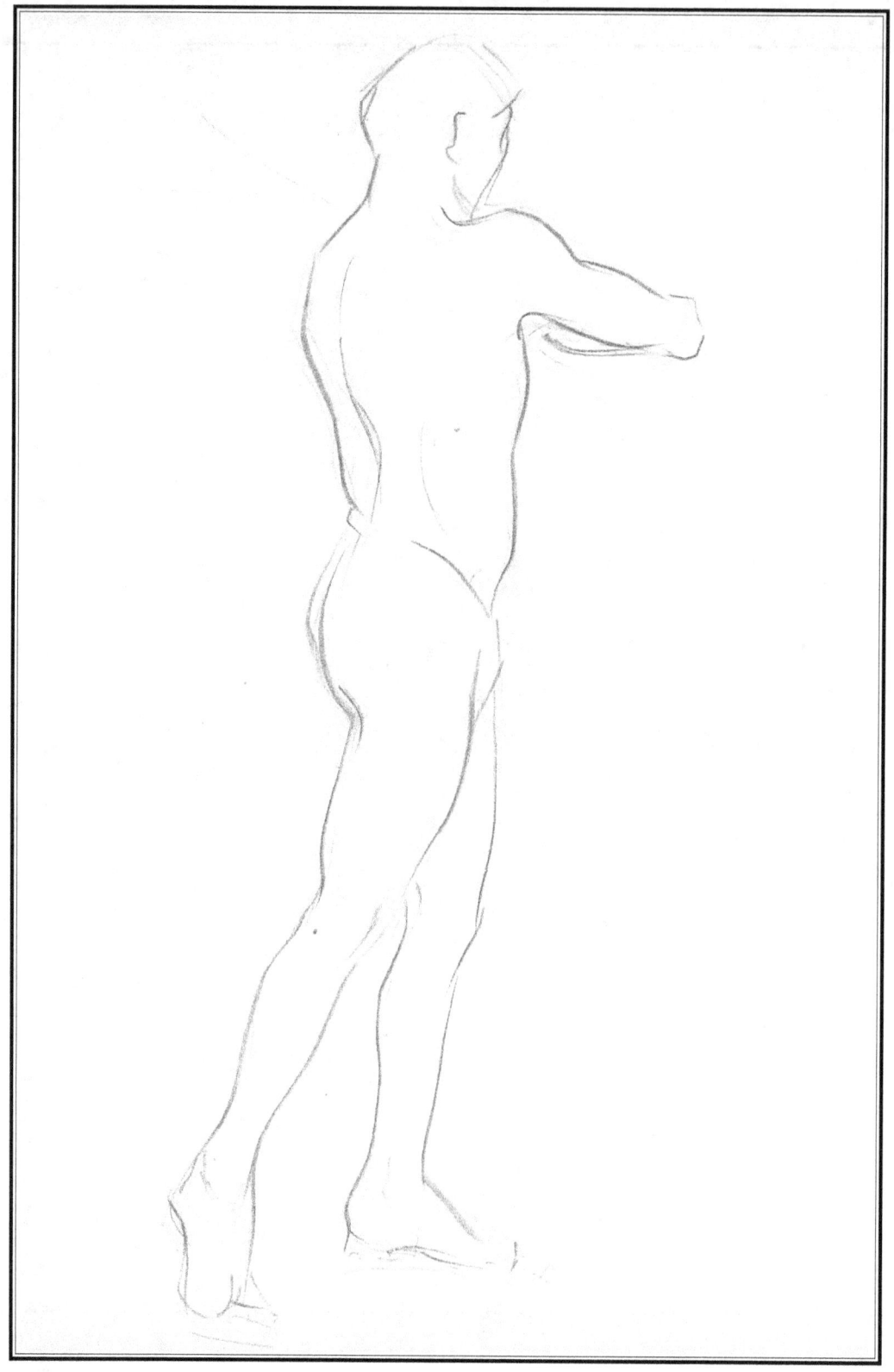

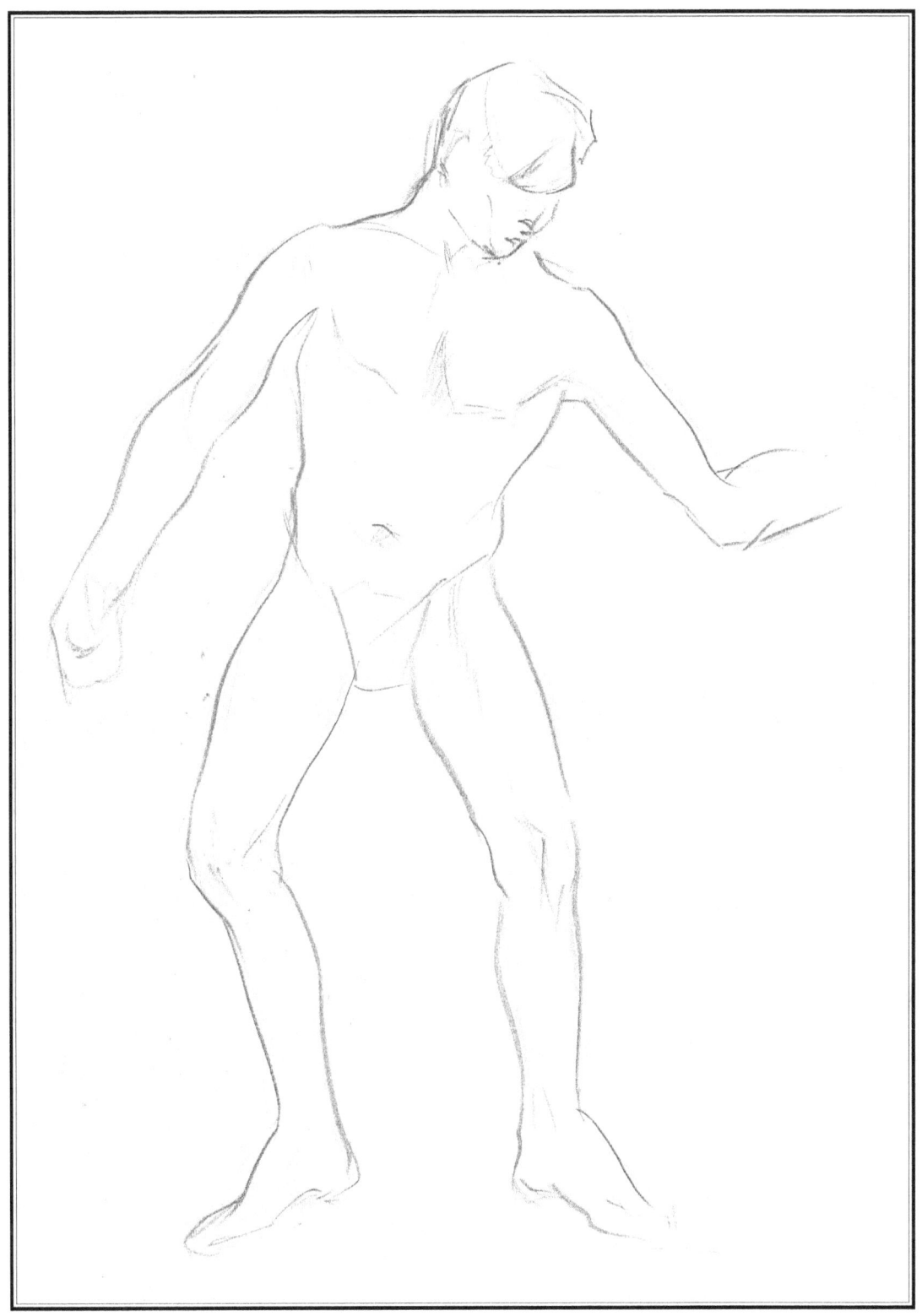

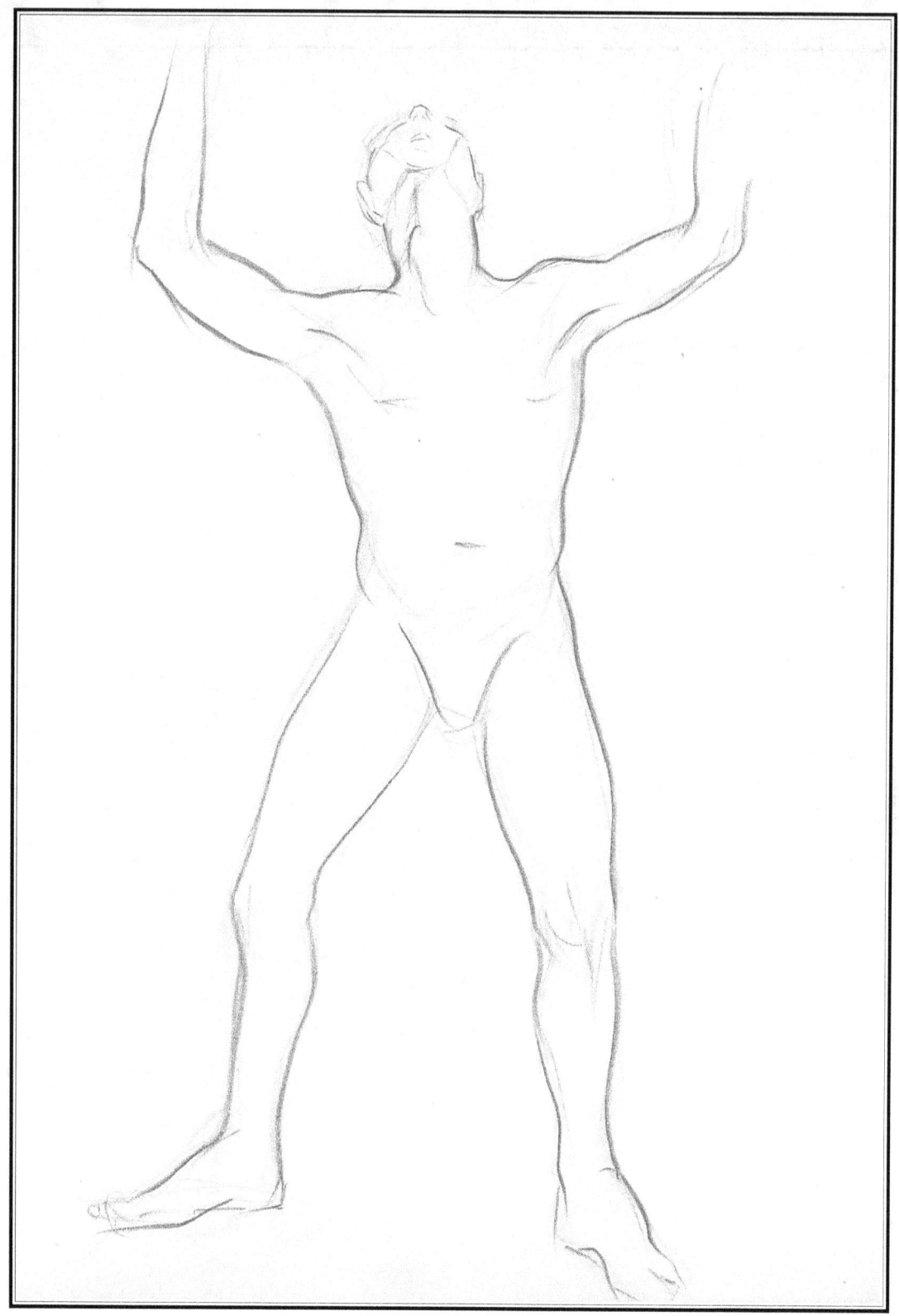

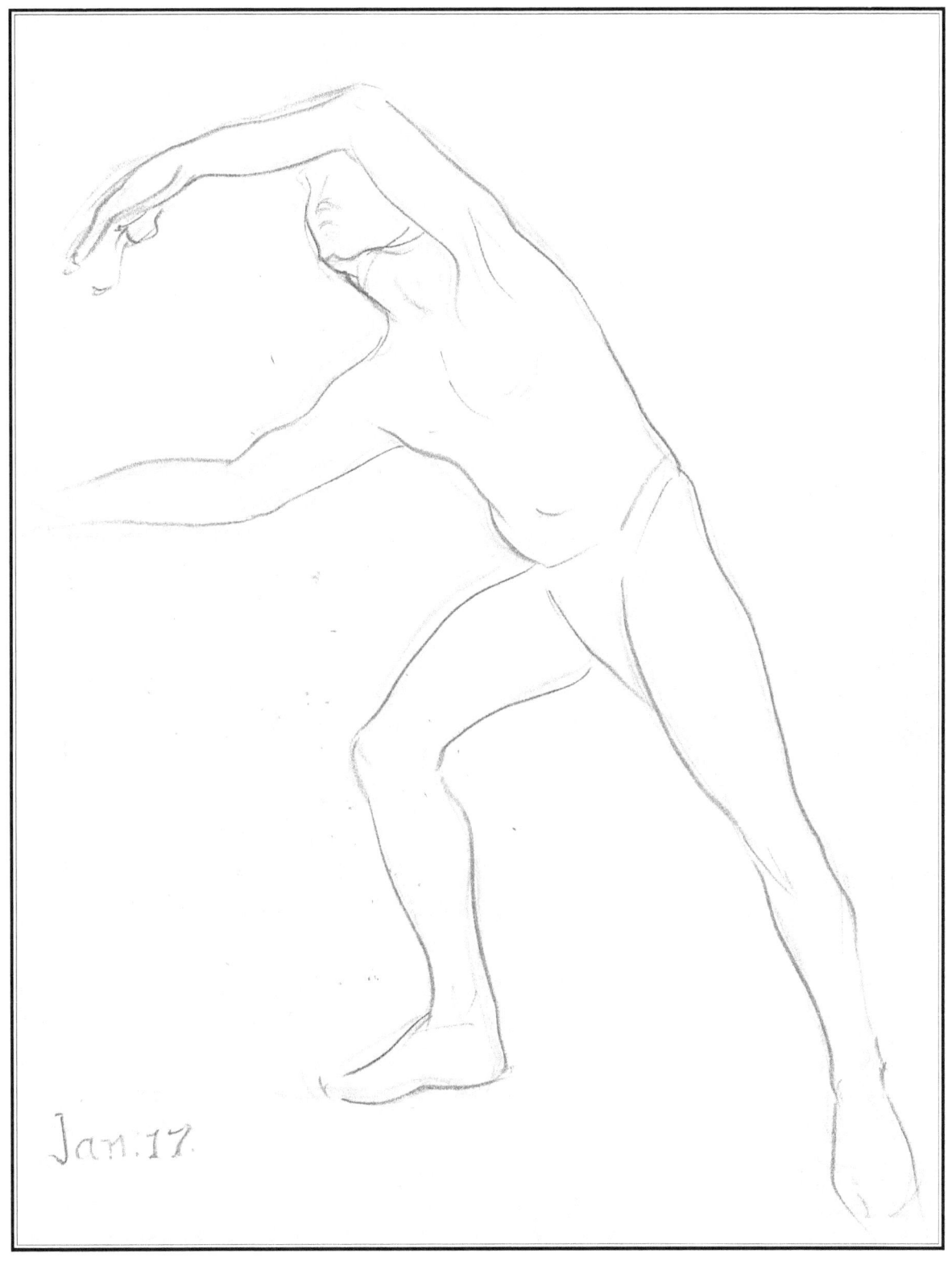

Jan.17

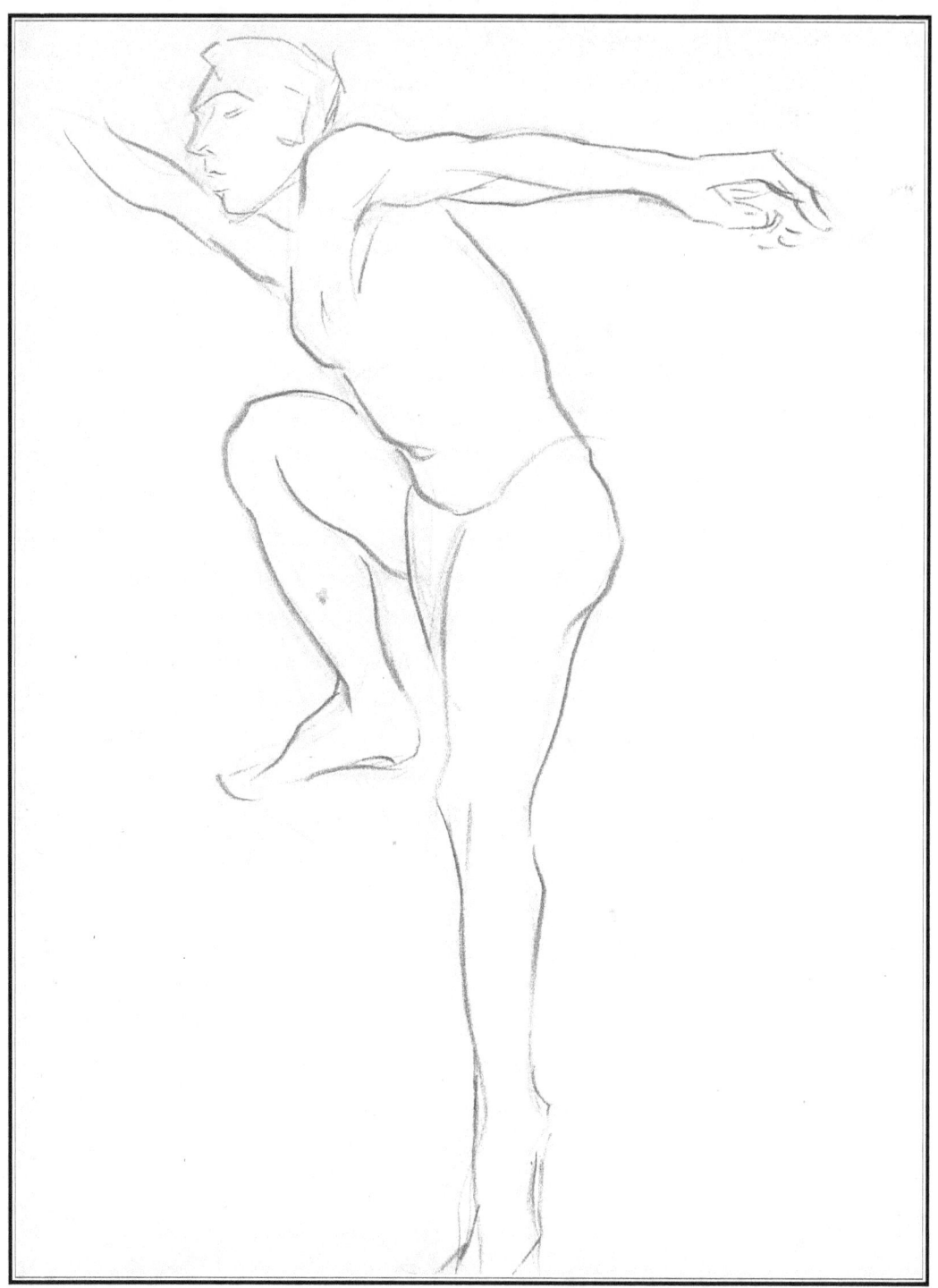

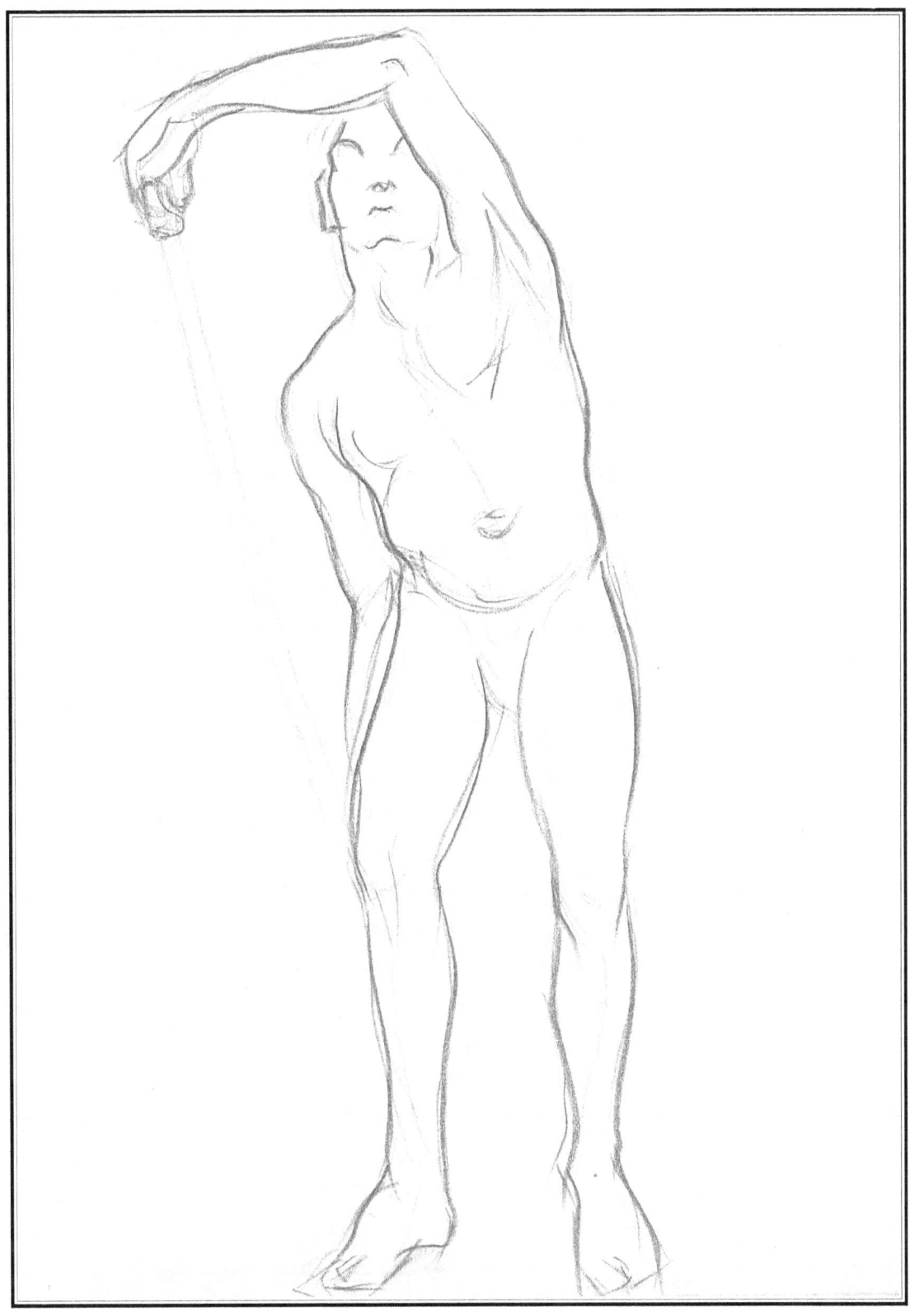

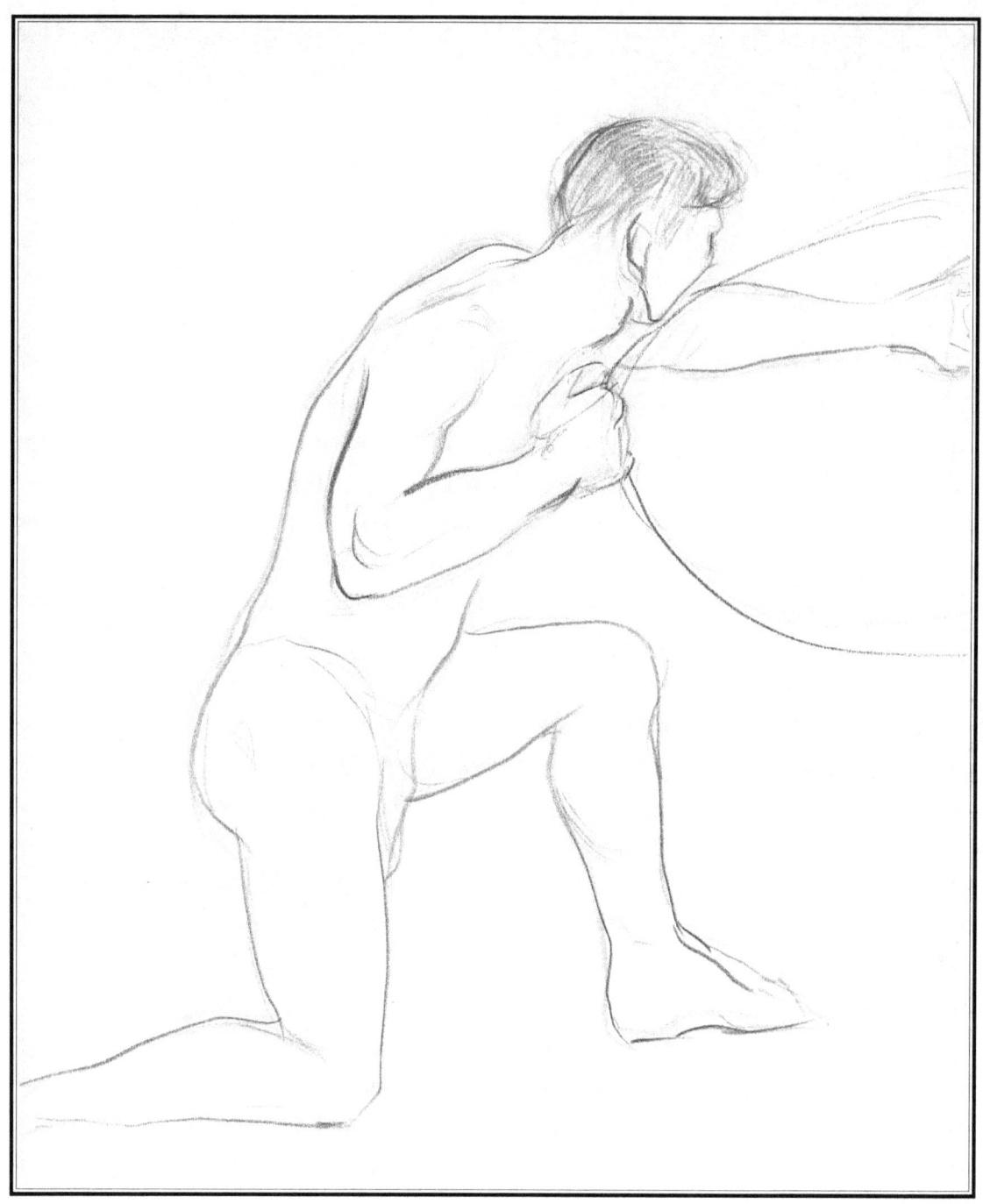

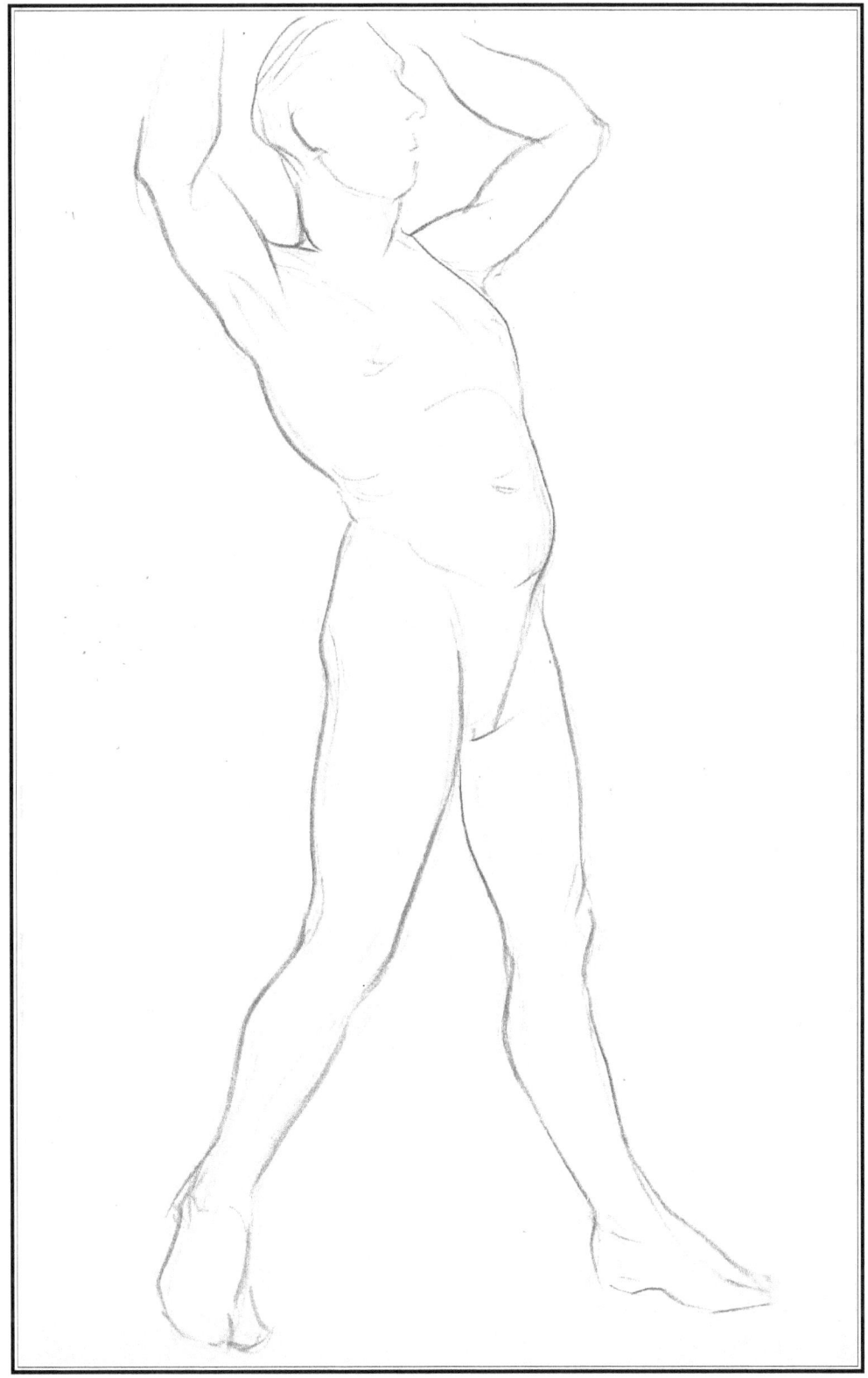

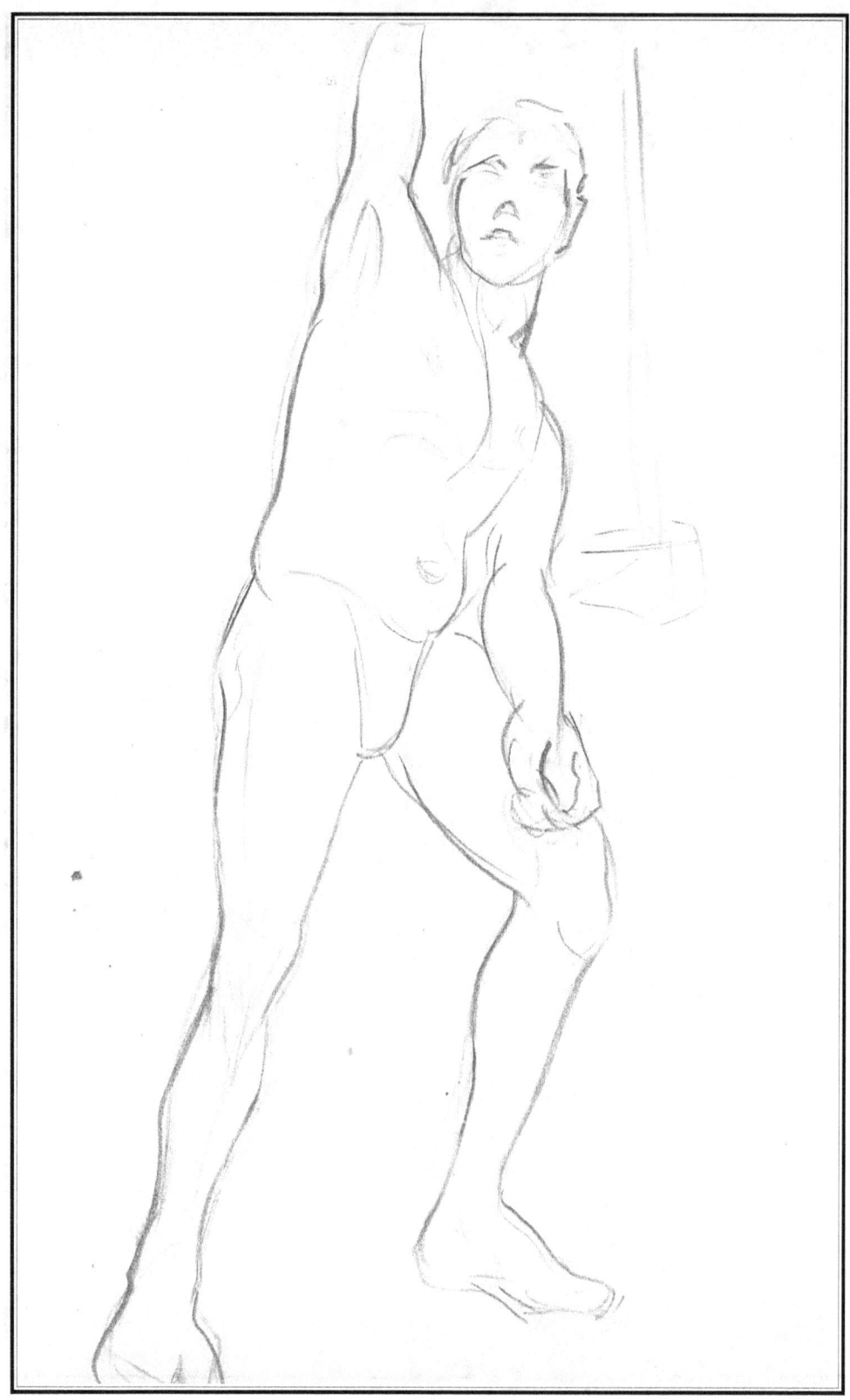

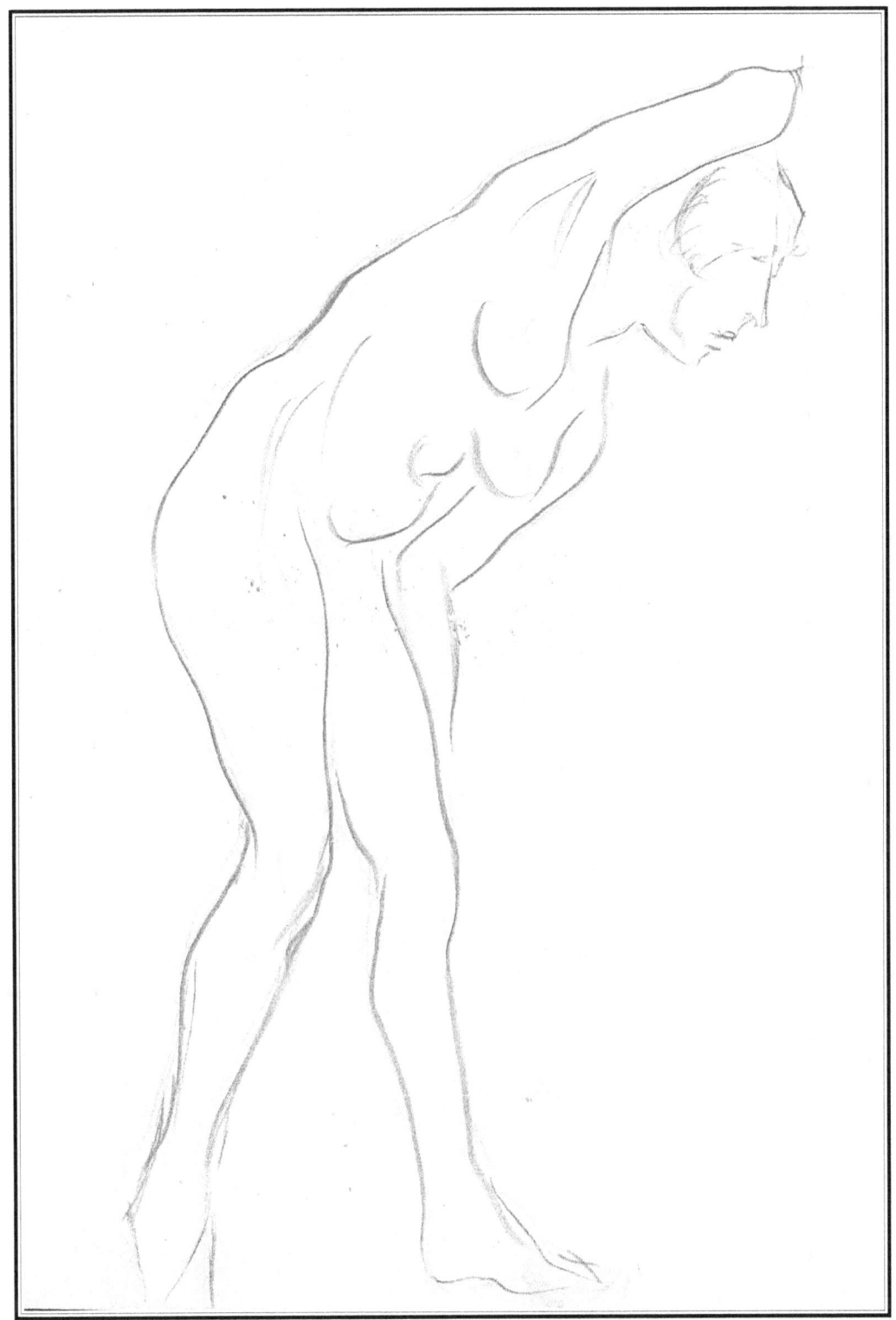

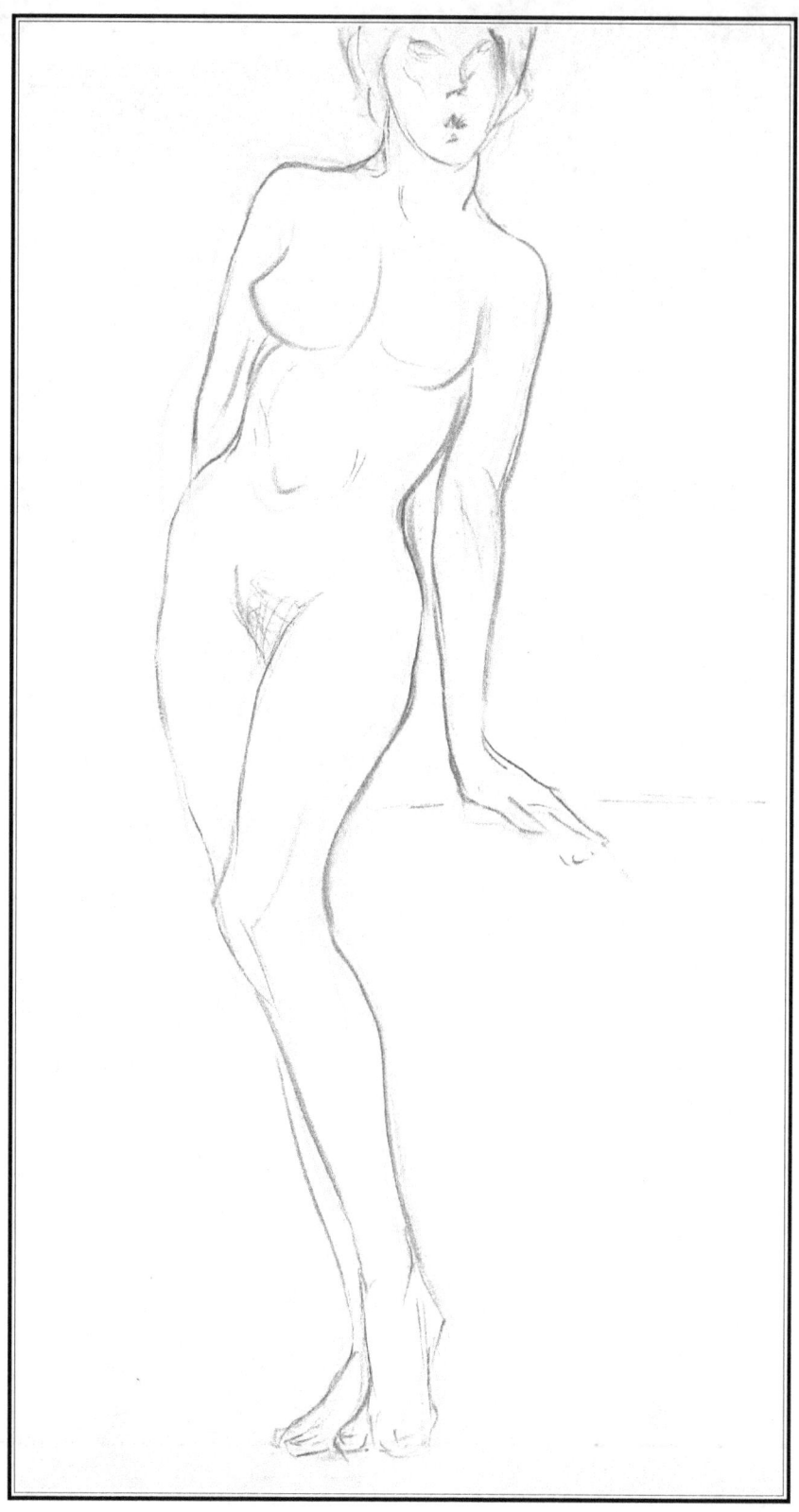

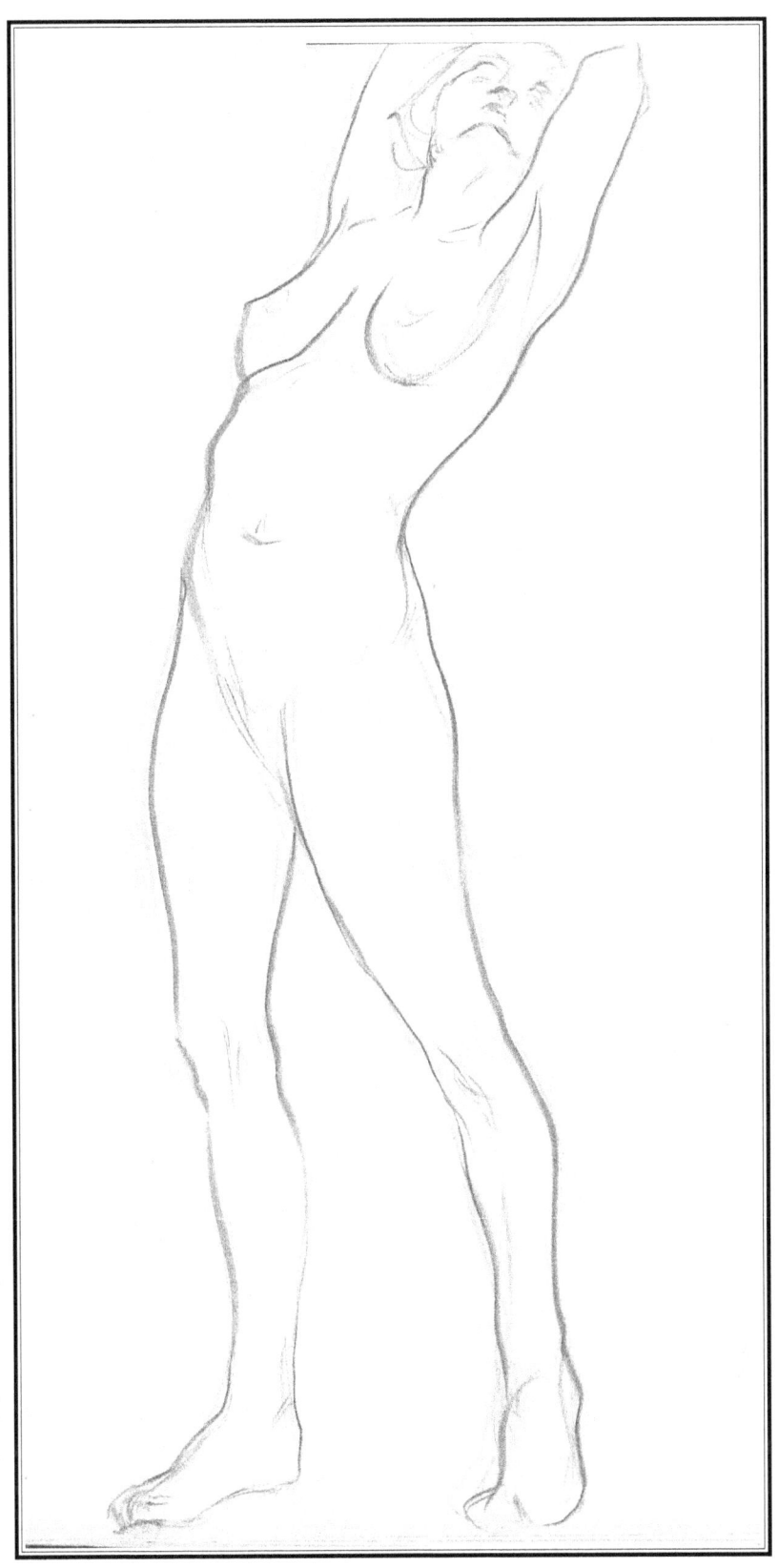

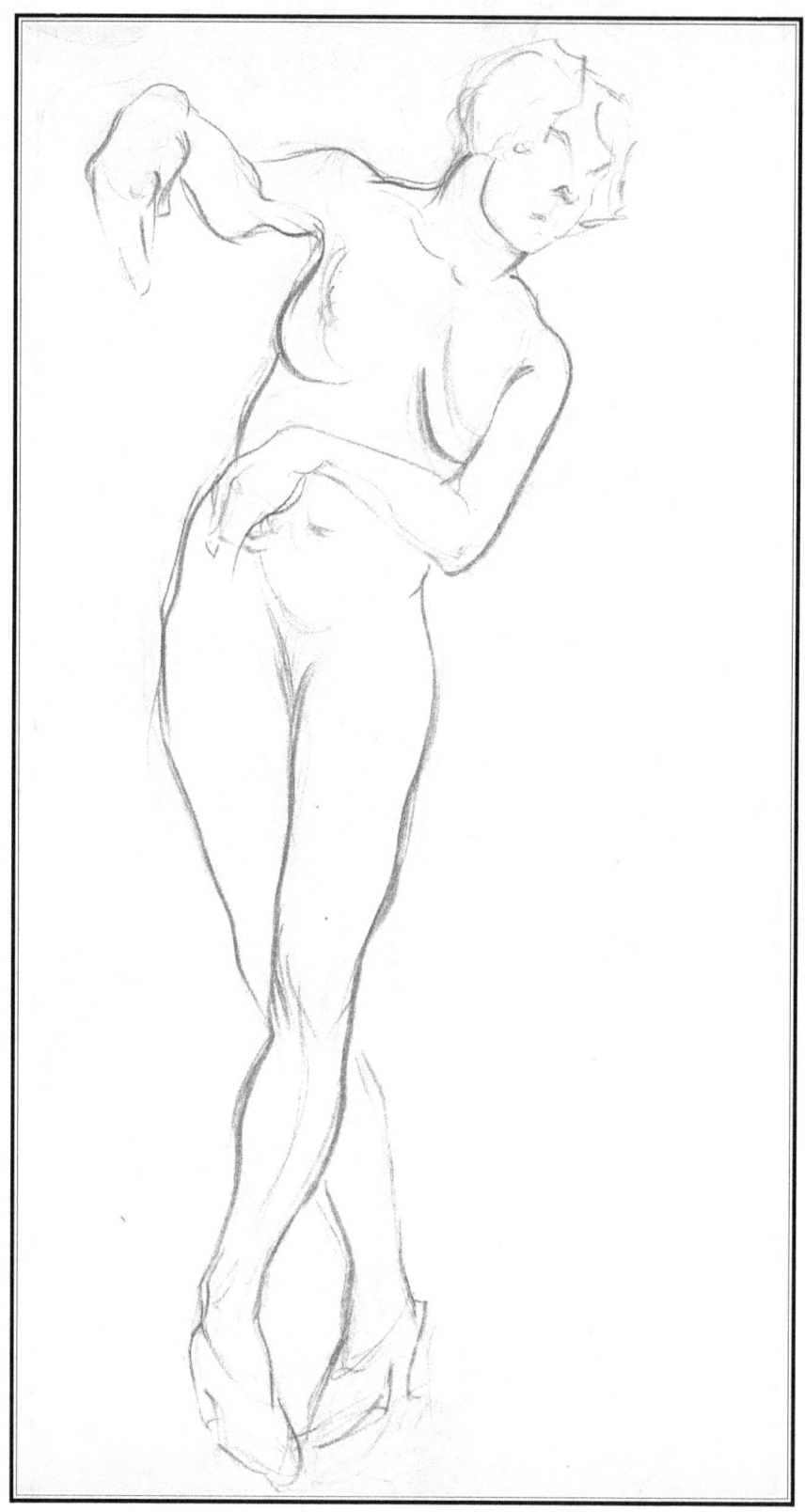

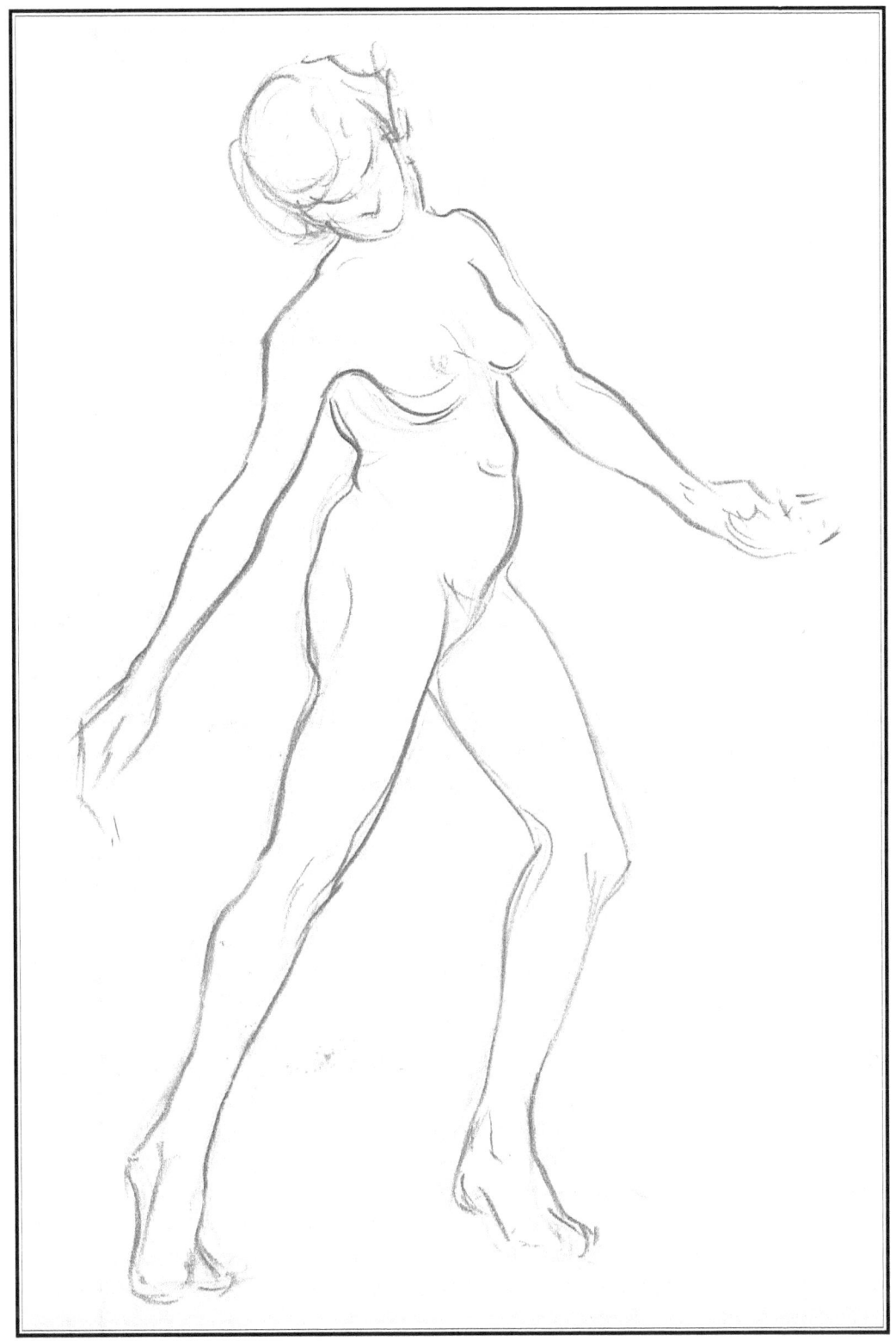

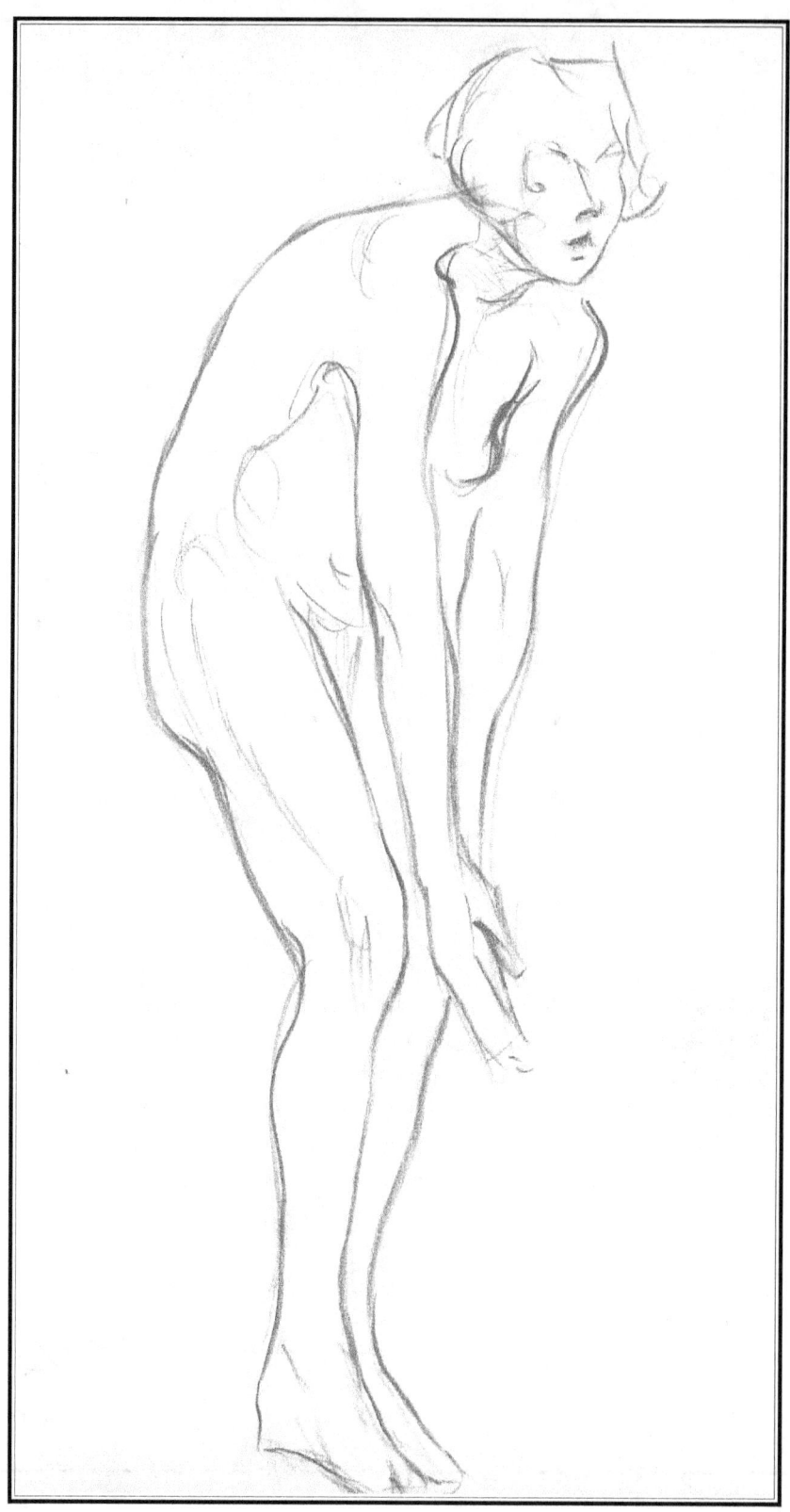

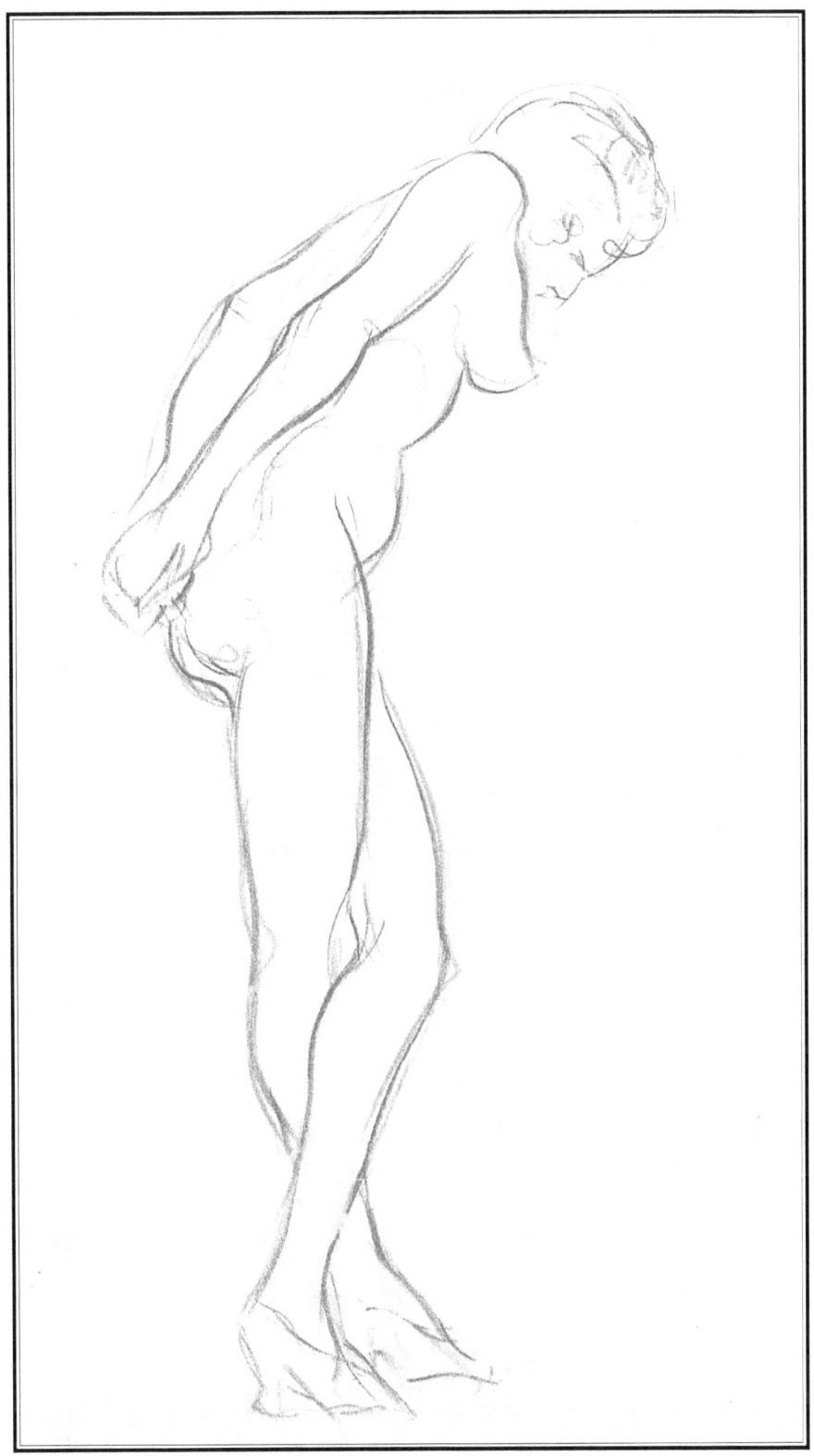

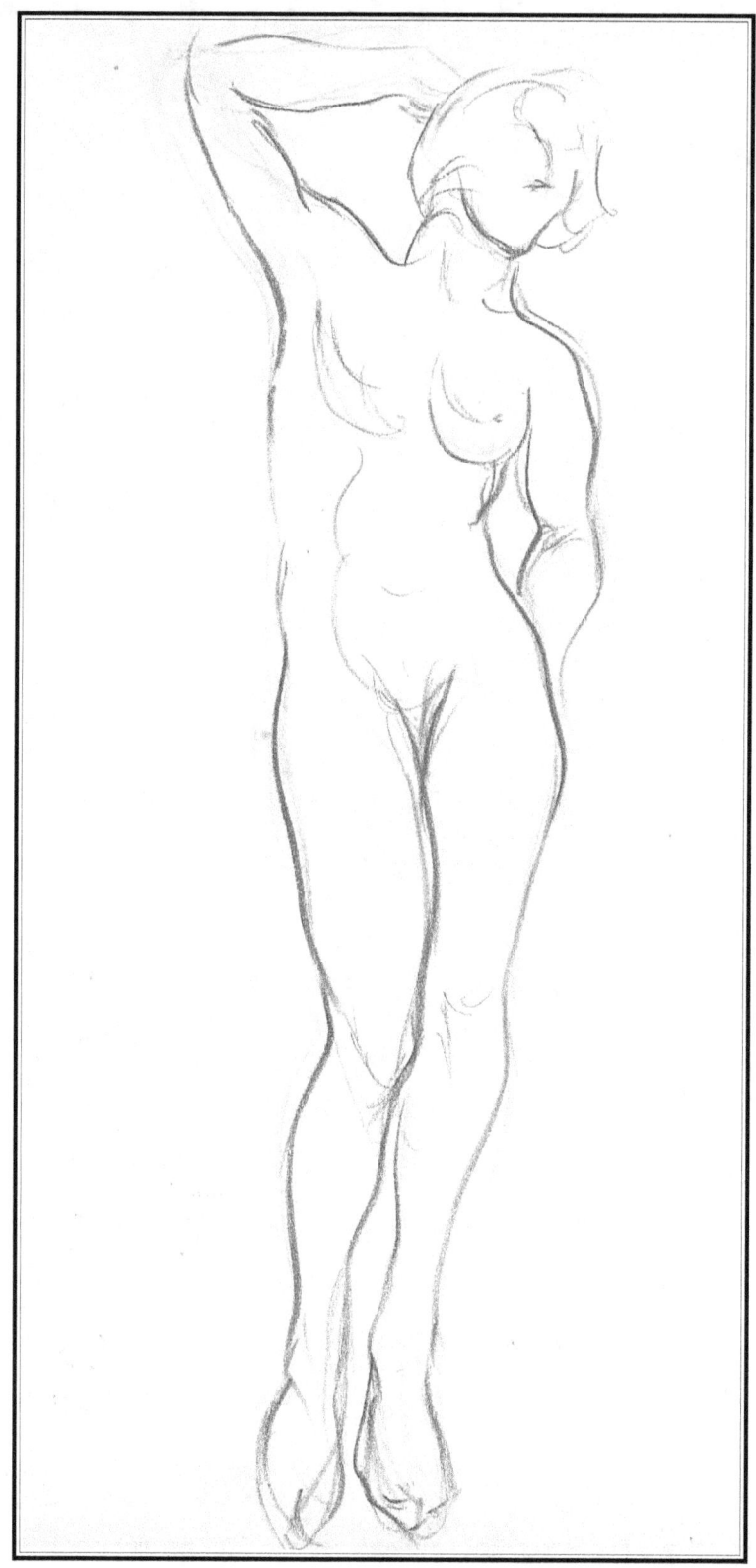

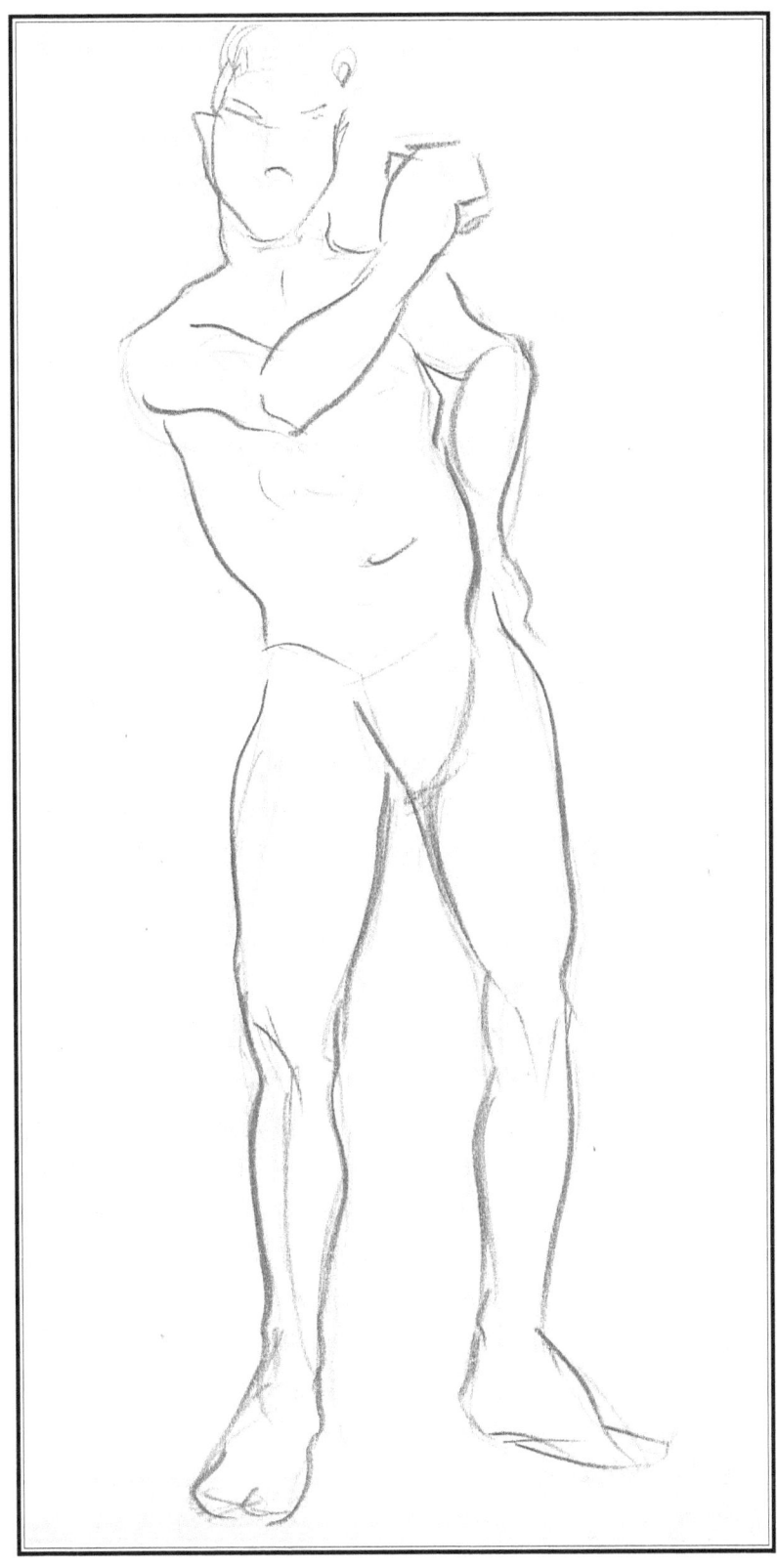

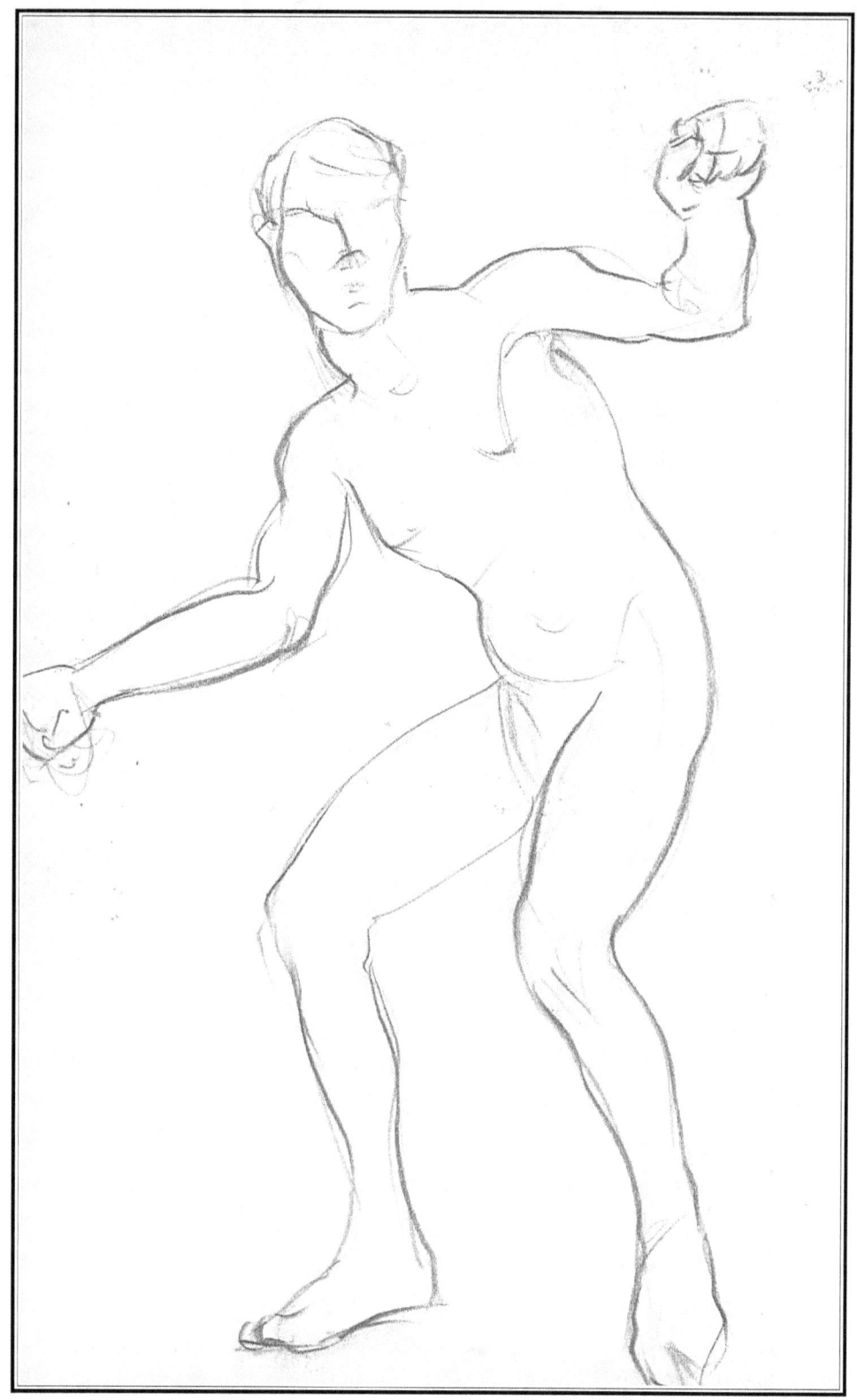

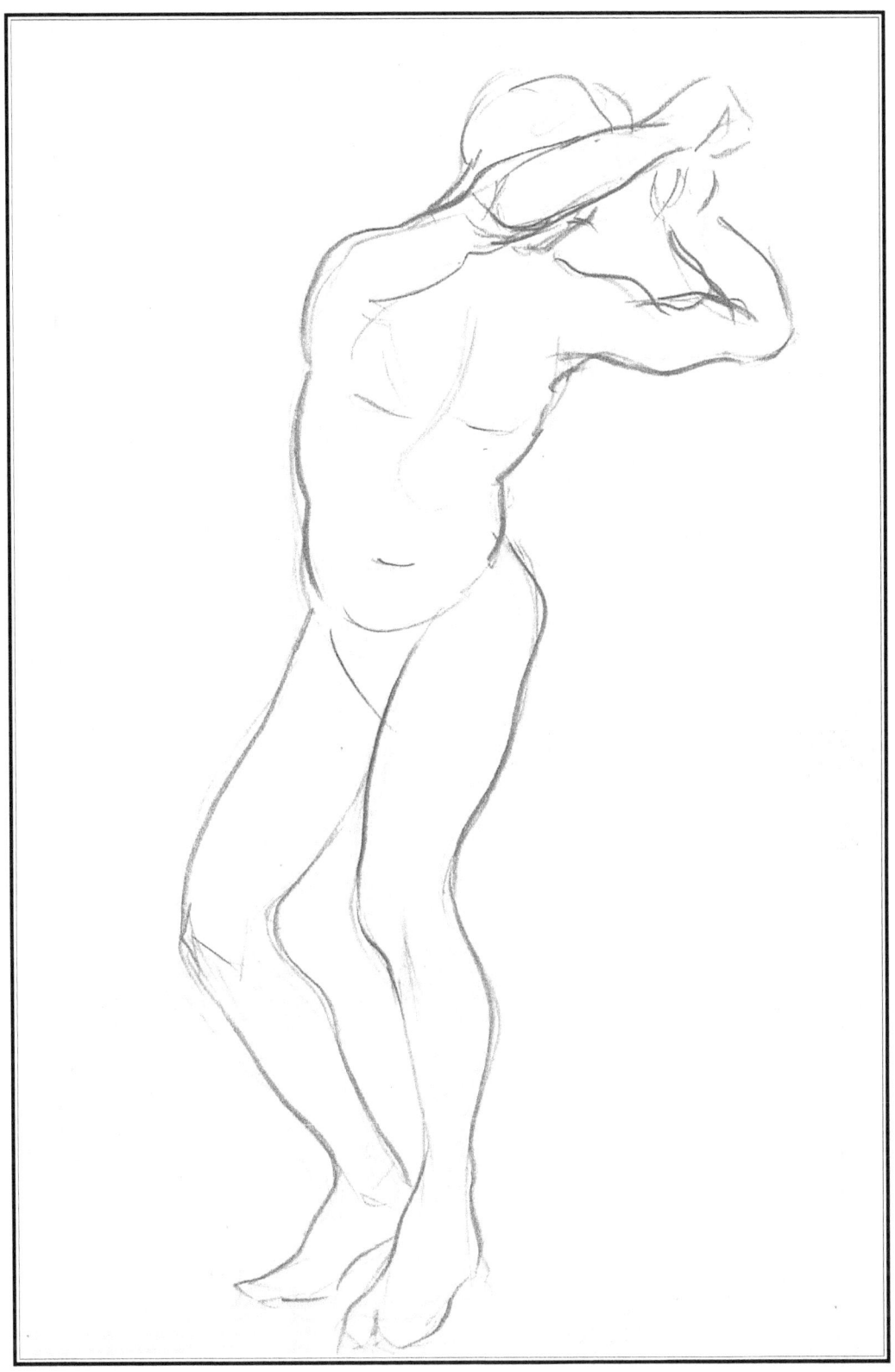

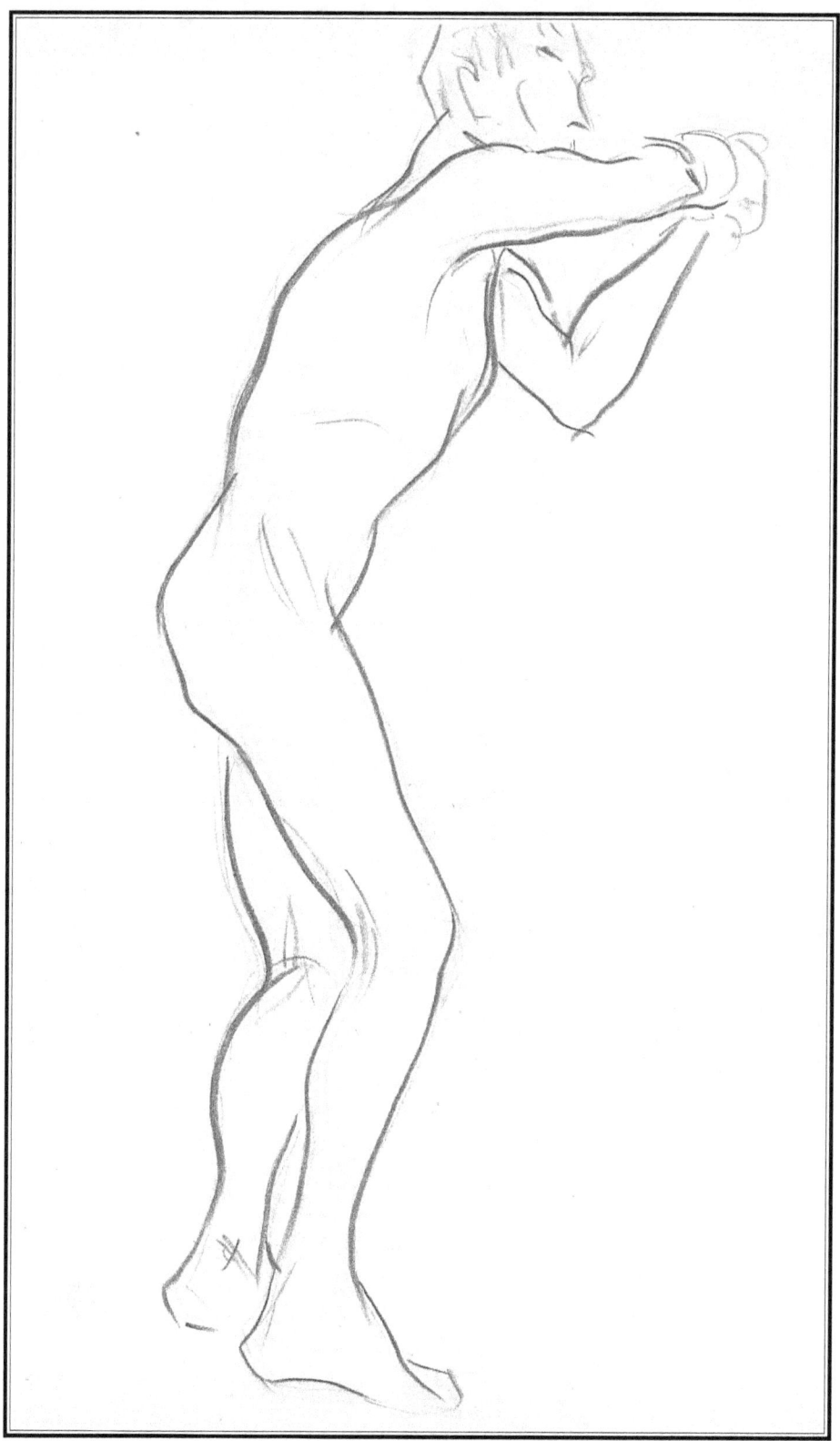

SOURCES

GRACE YOUNG, T.T.IV. Phila. School of Art, notebook, 1927-1928.

ANATOMY IN ART, A Practical Text Book, for the Art Students in the Study of the Human Form to which is Appended a Description and Analysis of the Art of Modelling and a chapter on the Laws of Proportion as Applied to the Human Figure, Jonathon Scott Hartley, New York, Press of Styles & Cash, 1891.

BUCHANAN'S INITIATORY DRAWING LESSONS for the Use of Writing Academies & Private Families Engraved Series to be Copied with the Pen, Edinburgh, Published by R. Buchanan, G. B. Whittaker and W. Curry, 1928.

FIGURE DRAWING AND COMPOSITION Being a Number of Hints for the Student and Designer Upon the Treatment of the Human Figure, Richard G. Hatton, London, Chapman and Hall, Ltd., 1902.

HANDATLAS DER ANATOMIE DES MENSCHEN, Werner Spalteholz, Leipzig, verlag van S. Hirzel, 1920.

DIE HANDZEICHNUNG Ihre Technik und Entwicklung, Wien, Kunstverlag Anton Schroll & Co., 1923.

HIEROGLYPHIC OR GREEK METHOD OF LIFE DRAWING, Adolphe Armand Braun, London, The Postal University, Paternoster House, B.T.Batsford, 1916.

THE HUMAN FORM AND ITS USE IN ART a Series of Studies for the Use of Art Students, Designers, Sculptors, Artists &, F. R. Yerbury and G. M. Ellwood, London, B. T. Bratsford, Ltd. 1924.

KING ALBERT'S BOOK a Tribute to the Belgian King and People from Representative Men and Women Throughout the World, The Daily Telegraph in conjunction with The Daily Sketch, The Glasgow Herald, and Hodder and Stoughton, London, 1914.

DIE RASSENSHÖNHEIT DES WEIBES, Prof. Dr. C. H. Stratz, Stuttgart, verlag van Ferdinand Enke, 1921.

STUDIES OF THE HUMAN FIGURE with Some Notes on Drawing and Anatomy, G. M. Ellwood and F. R. Yerbury, London, B. T. Bratsford, Ltd. 1918.

www.ingramcontent.com/pod-product-compliance
Lightning Source LLC
Chambersburg PA
CBHW080908170526
45158CB00008B/2032